EYE　YONEYAMA MAI

EYE　YONEYAMA MAI

Author: YONEYAMA MAI

Designer: Kusano Tsuyoshi (Tsuyoshi Kusano Design)
Editor: Oba Yoshiyuki

Printed and Bound in Japan by Shinano Co.,Ltd.

PIE International Inc.

2-32-4 Minami-Otsuka, Toshima-ku, Tokyo 170-0005 JAPAN
international@pie.co.jp
www.pie.co.jp/english

ISBN978-4-7562-5782-6 (Outside Japan)
Printed in Japan

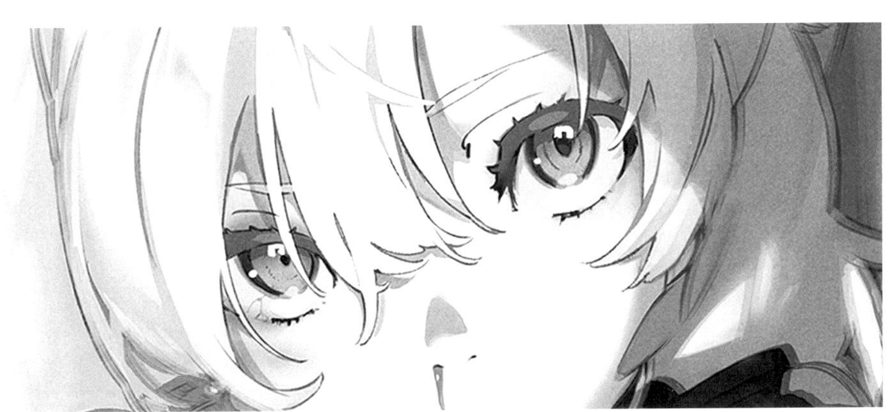

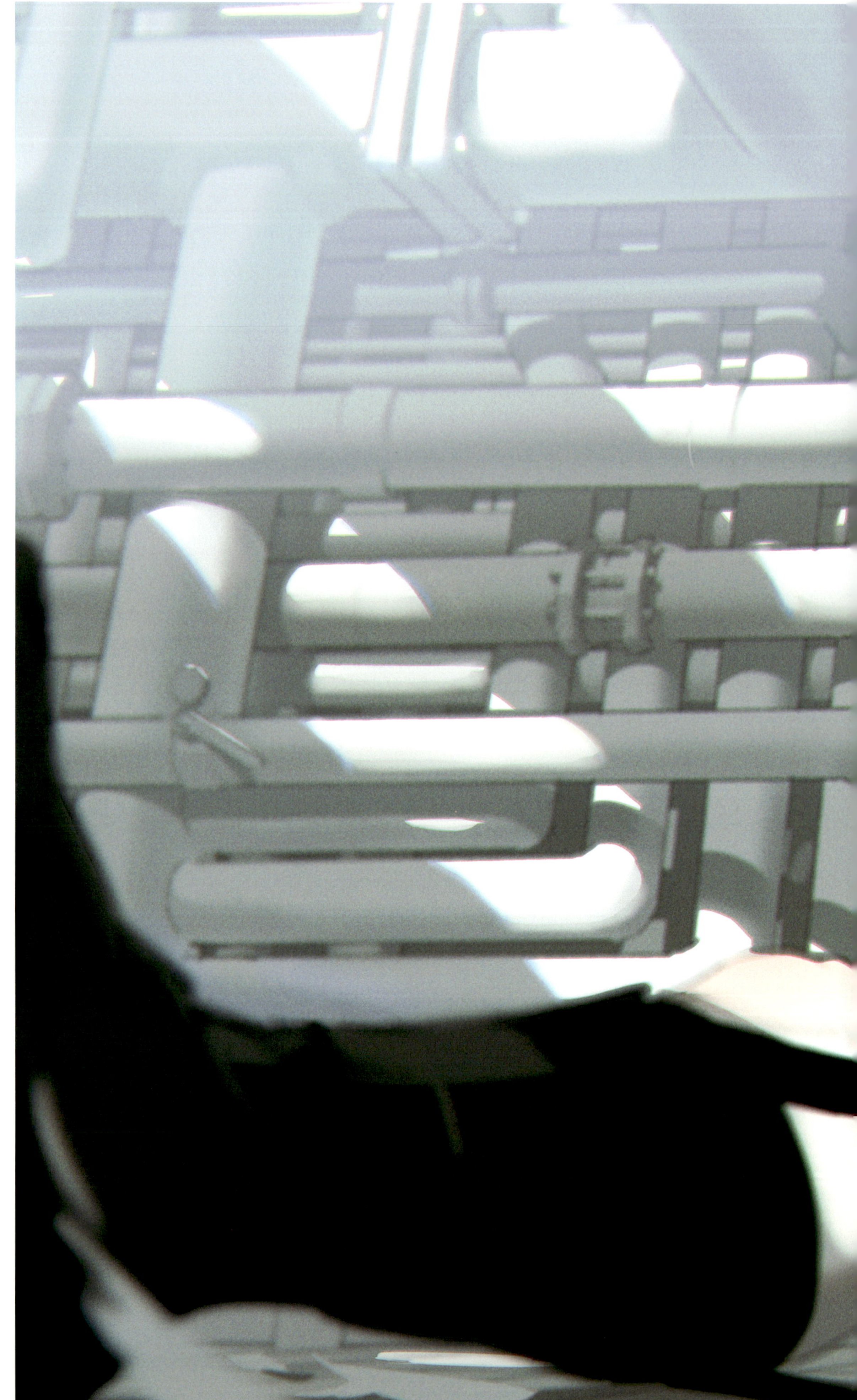

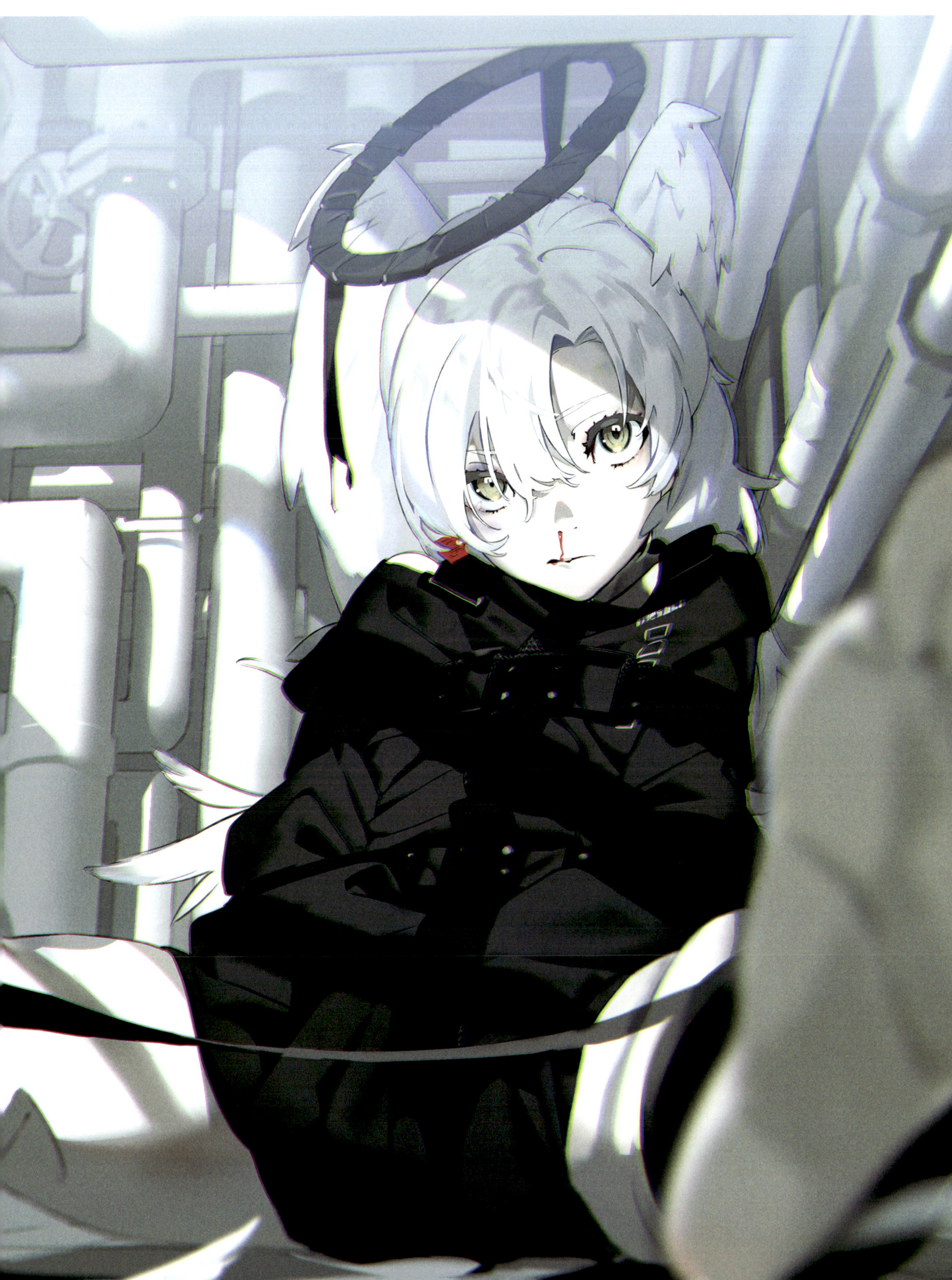

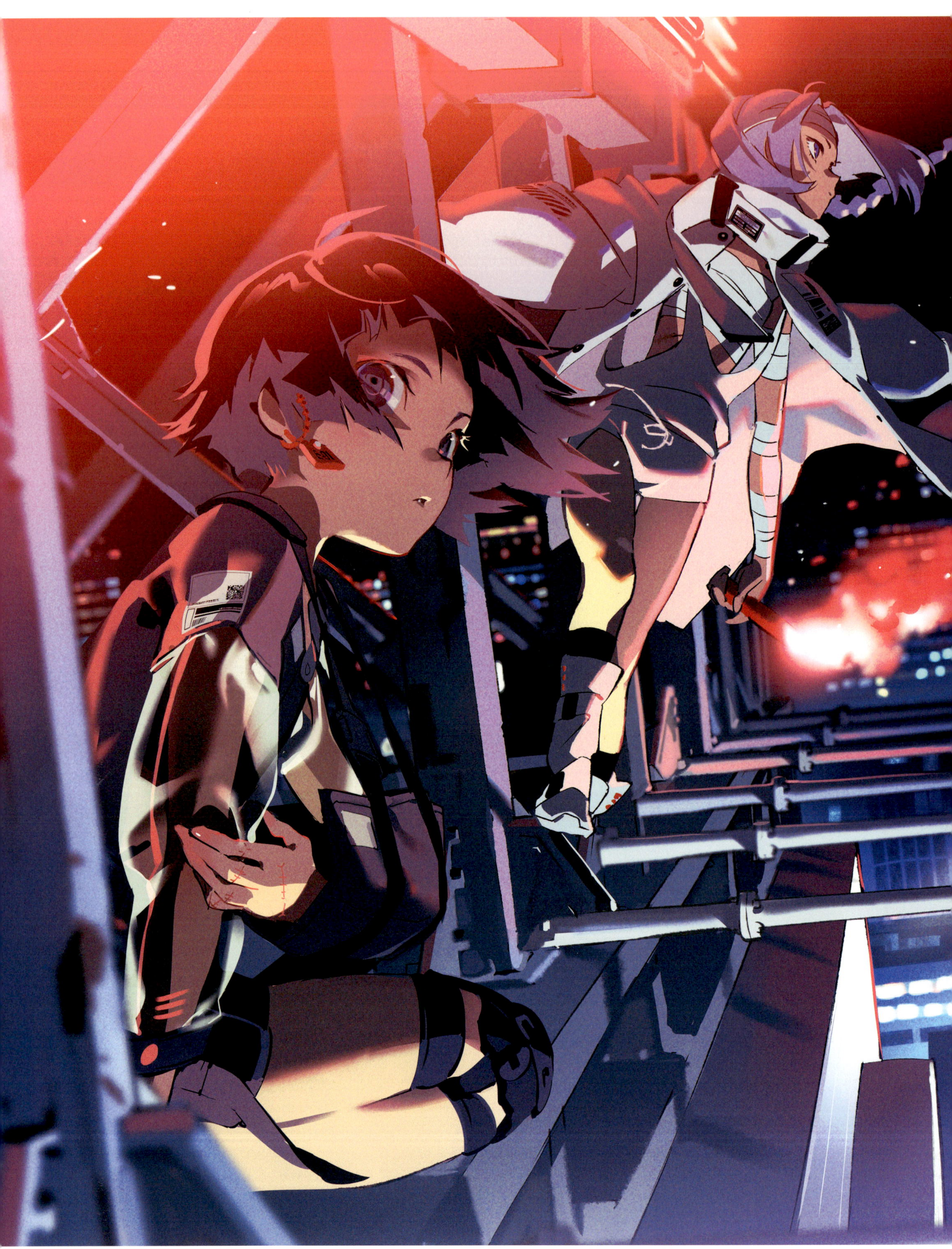

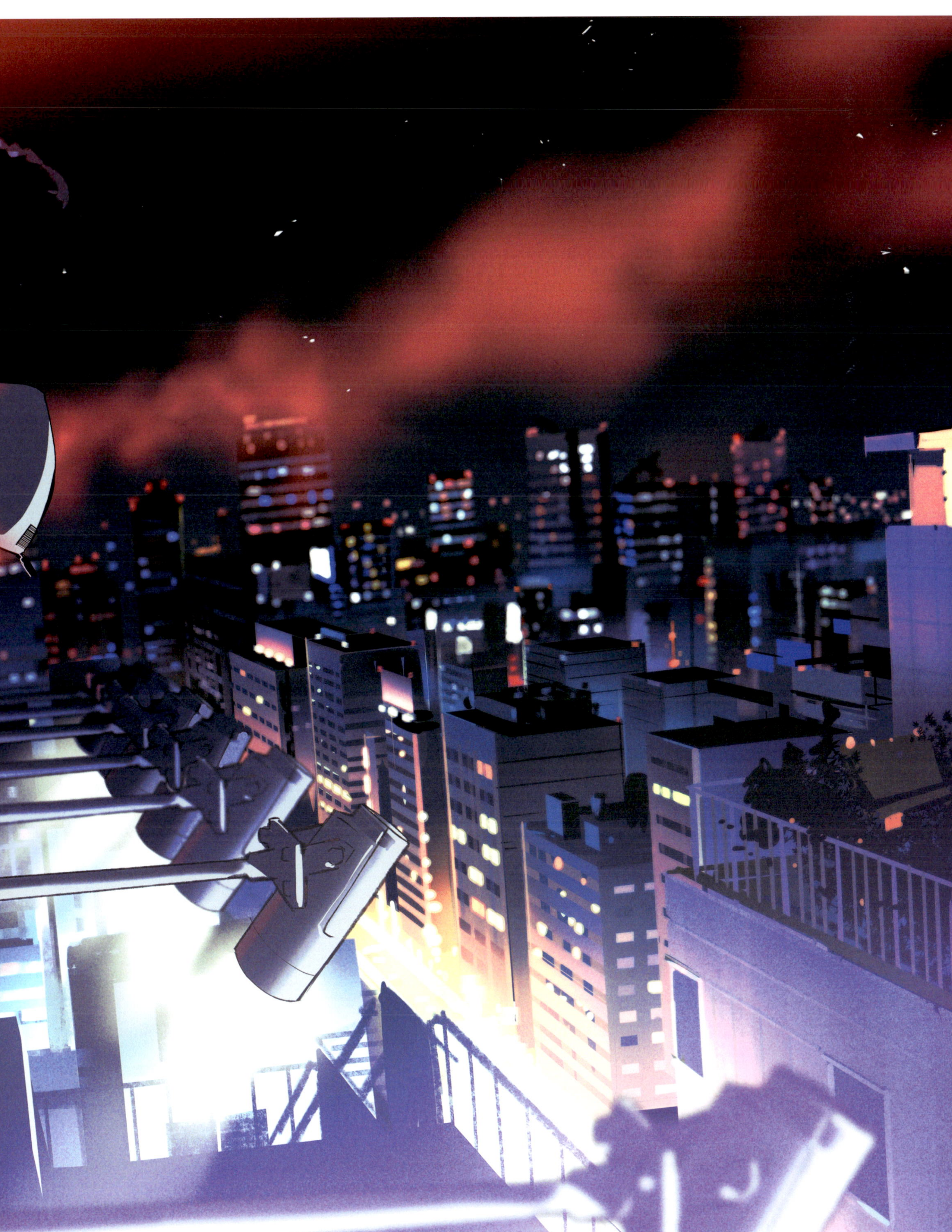

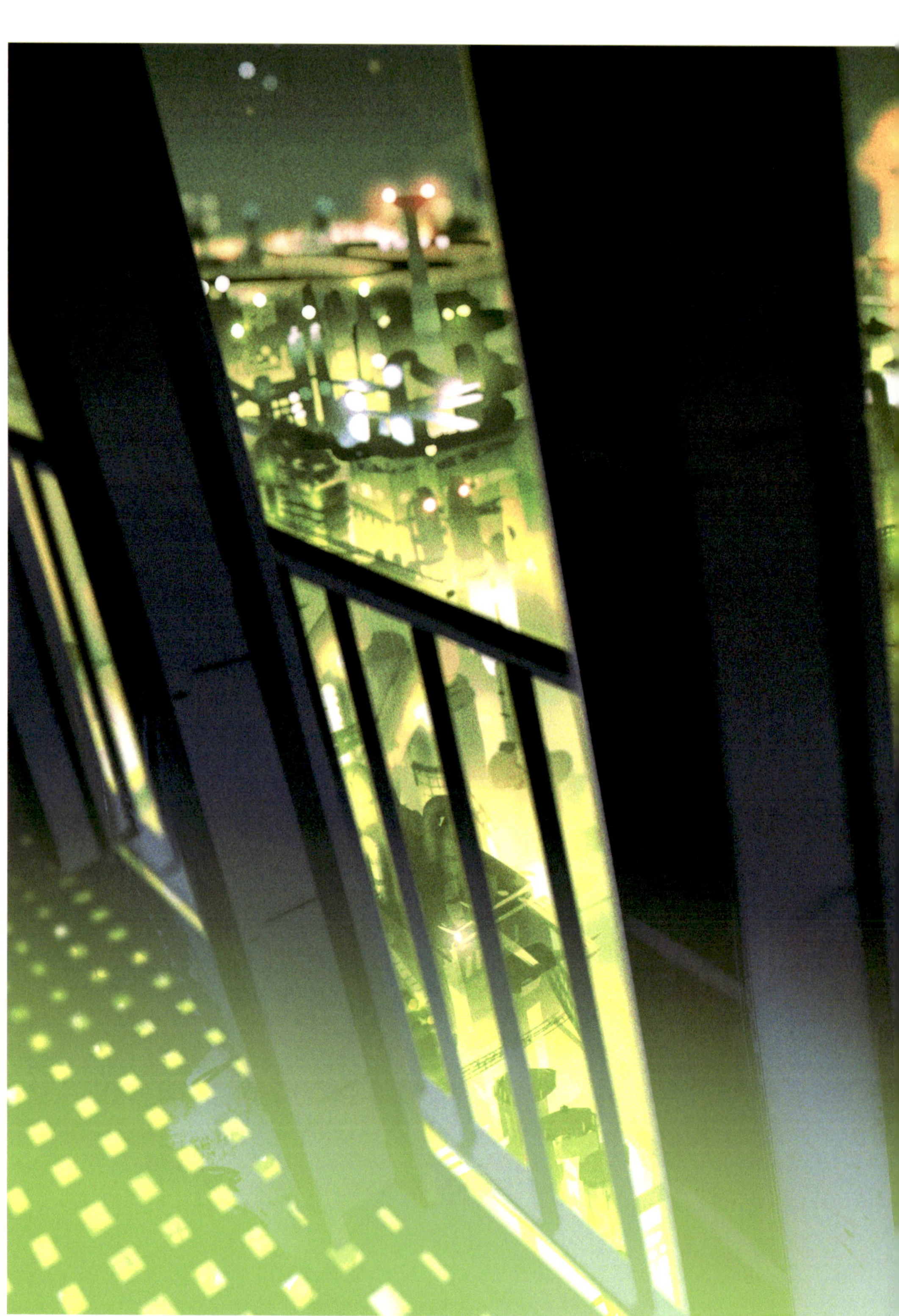

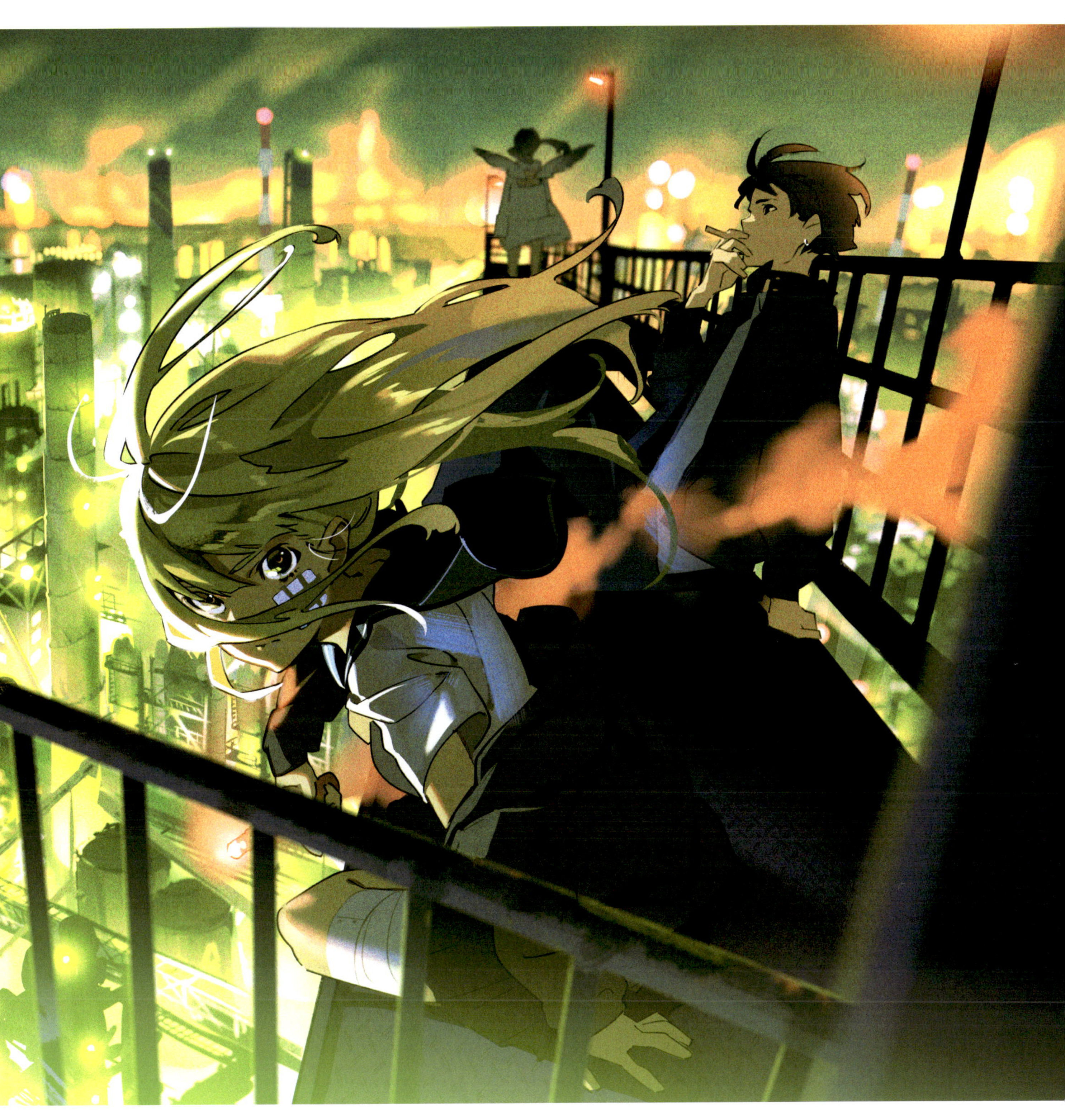

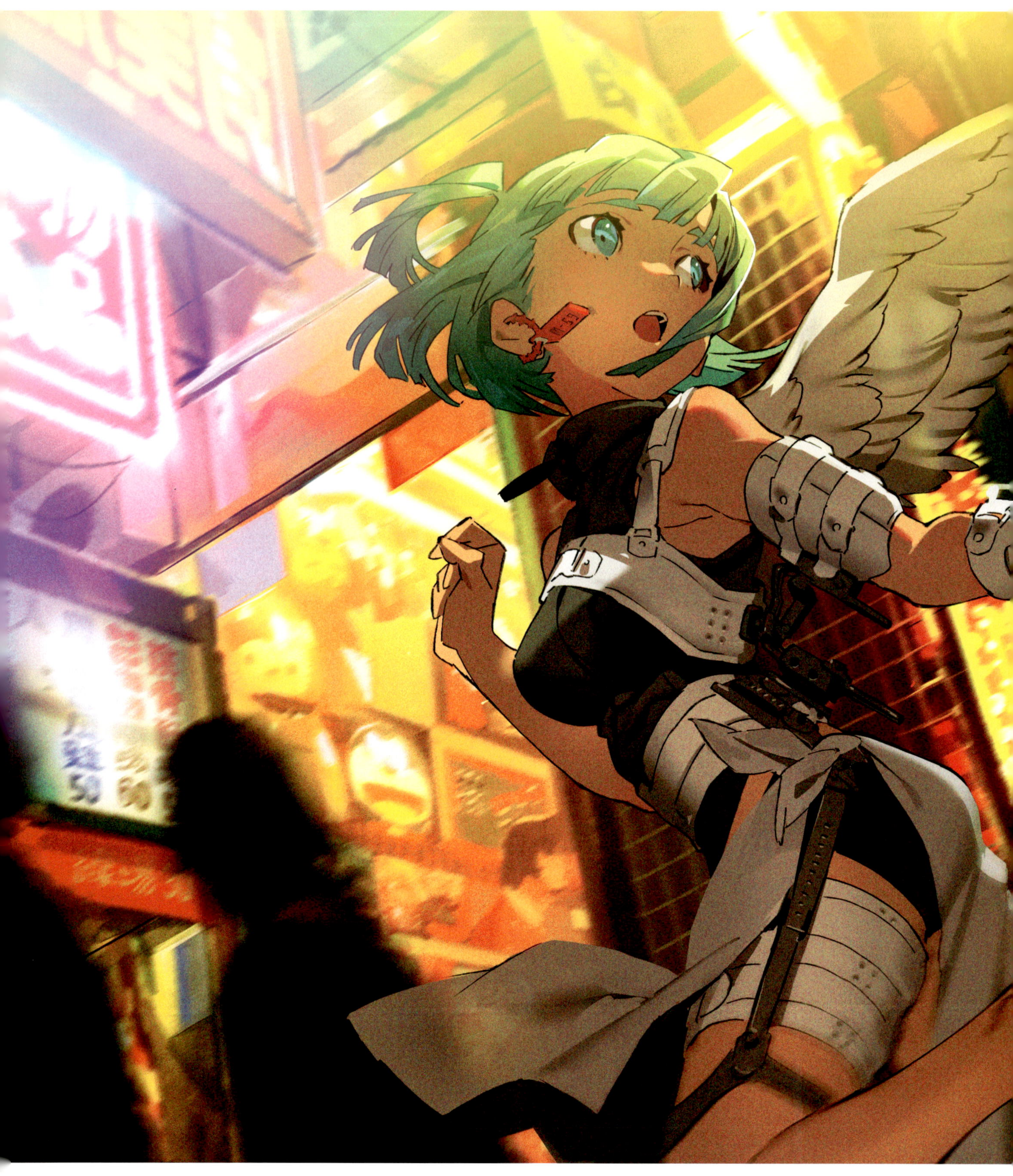

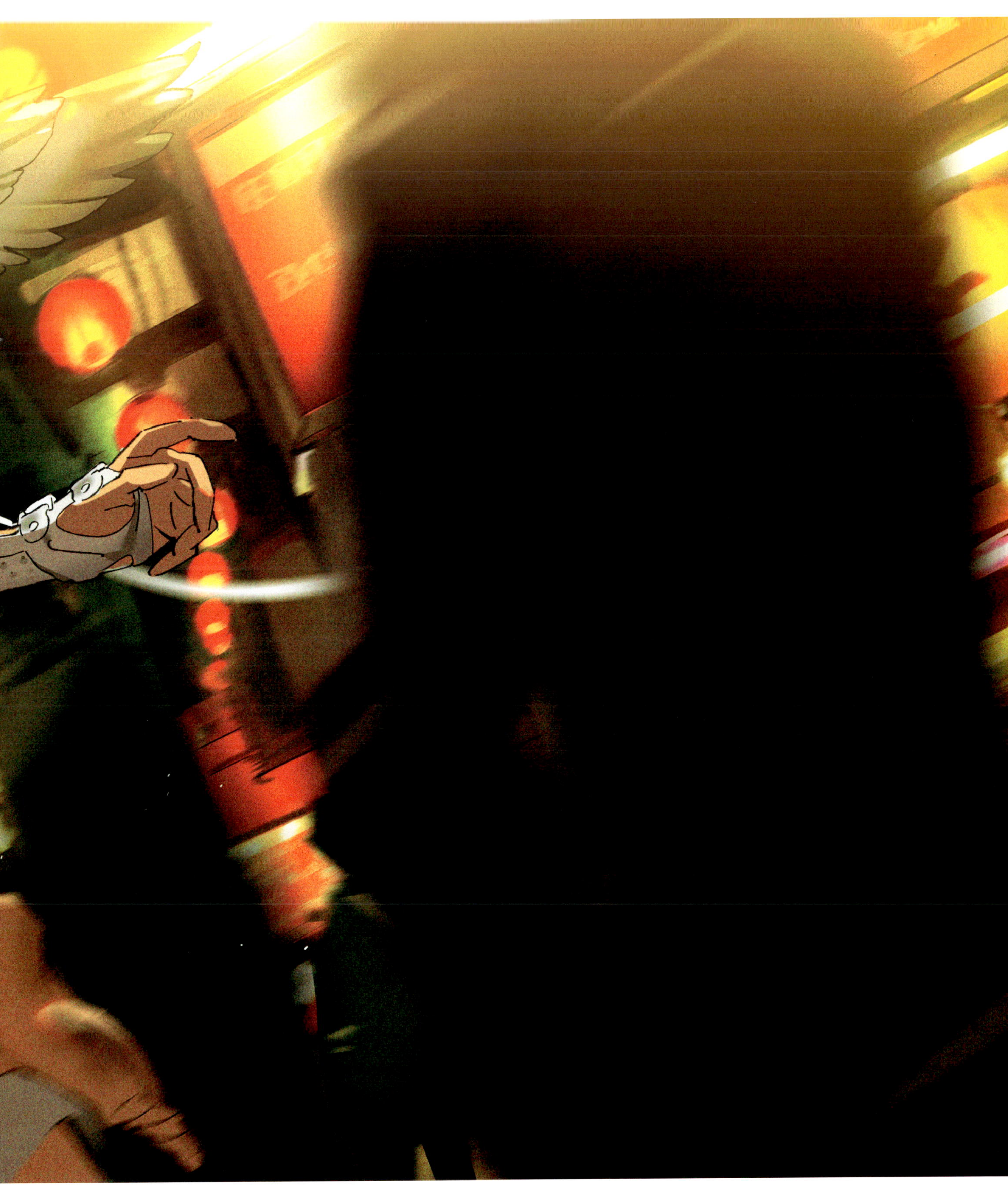

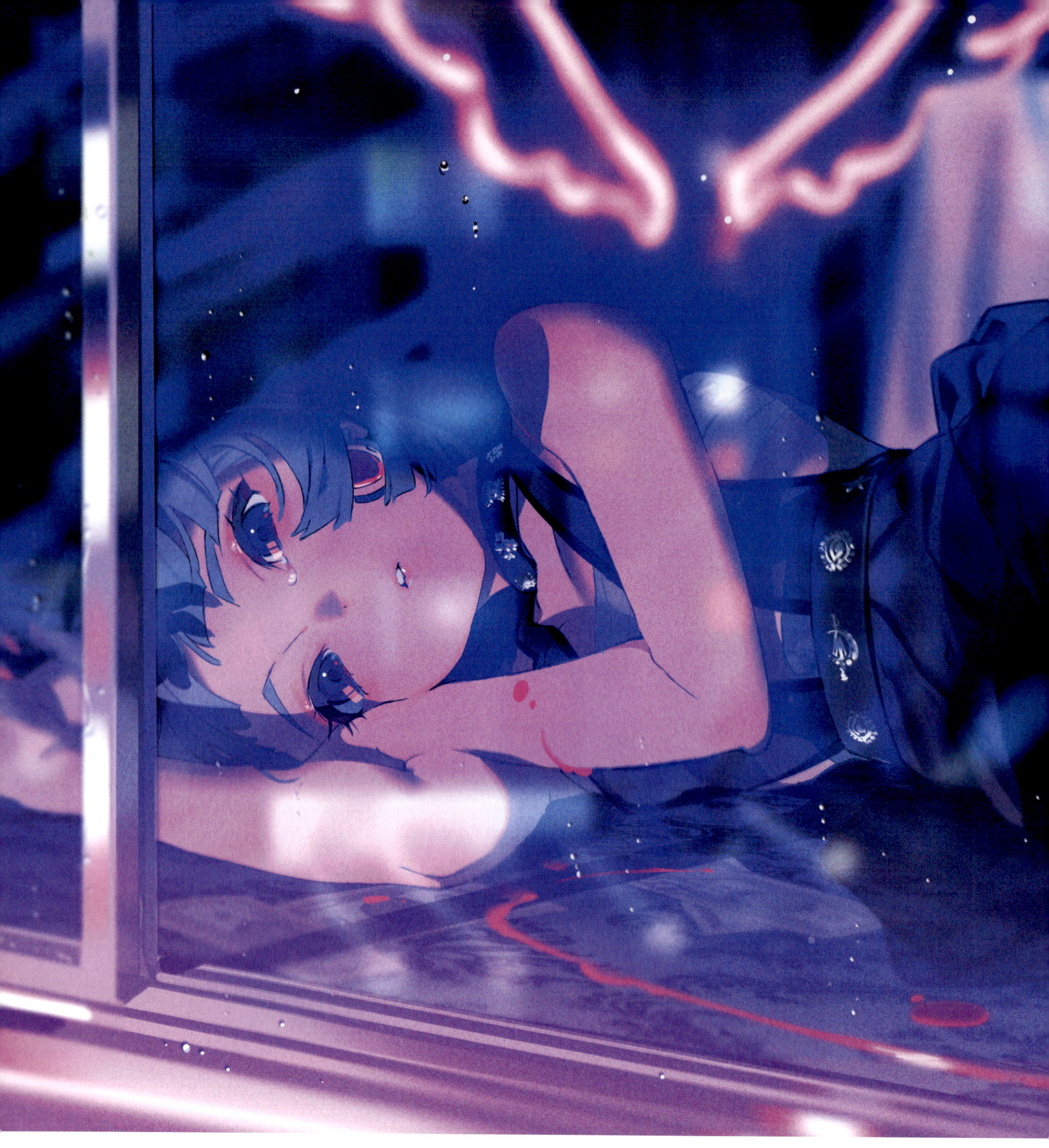

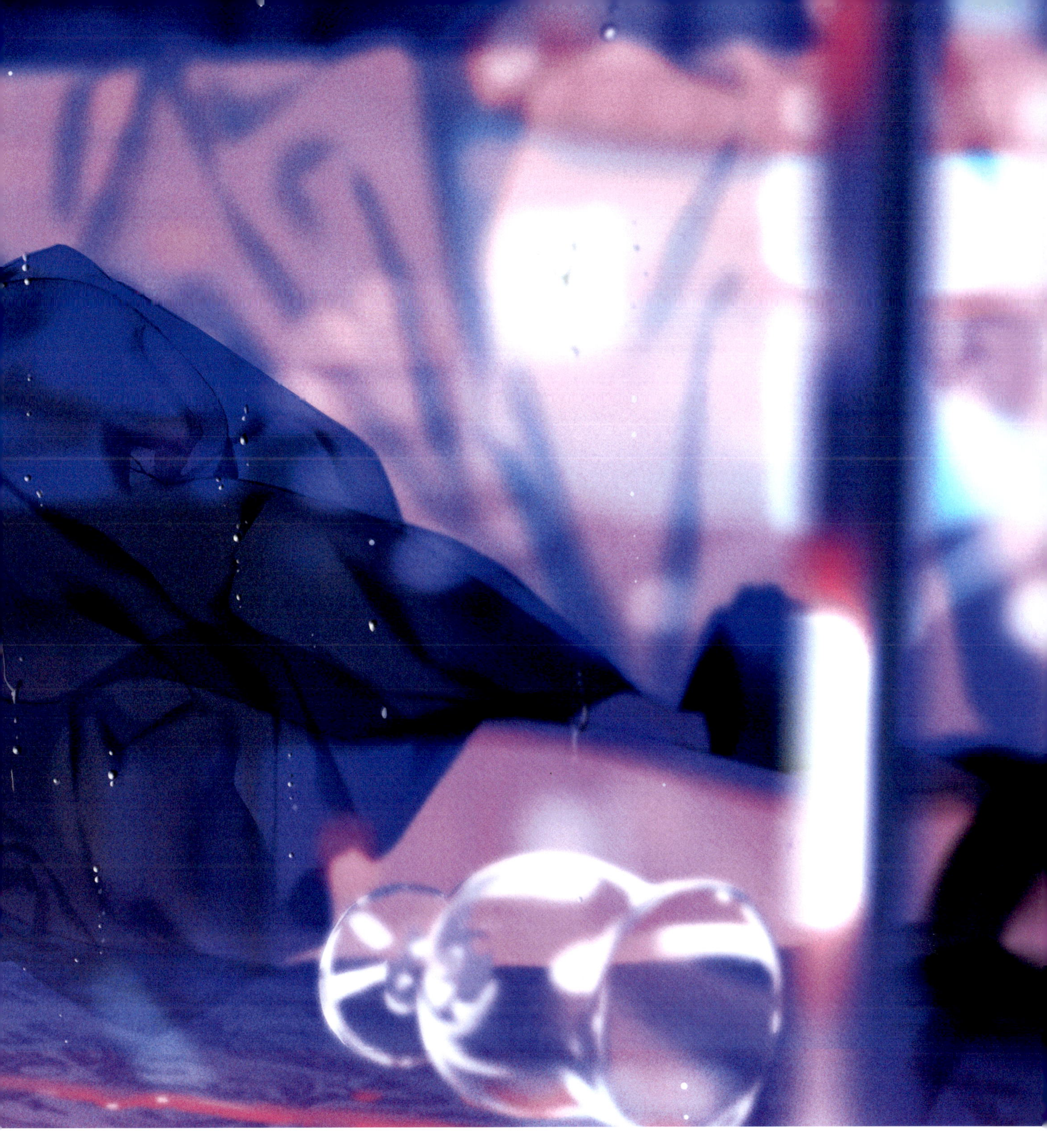

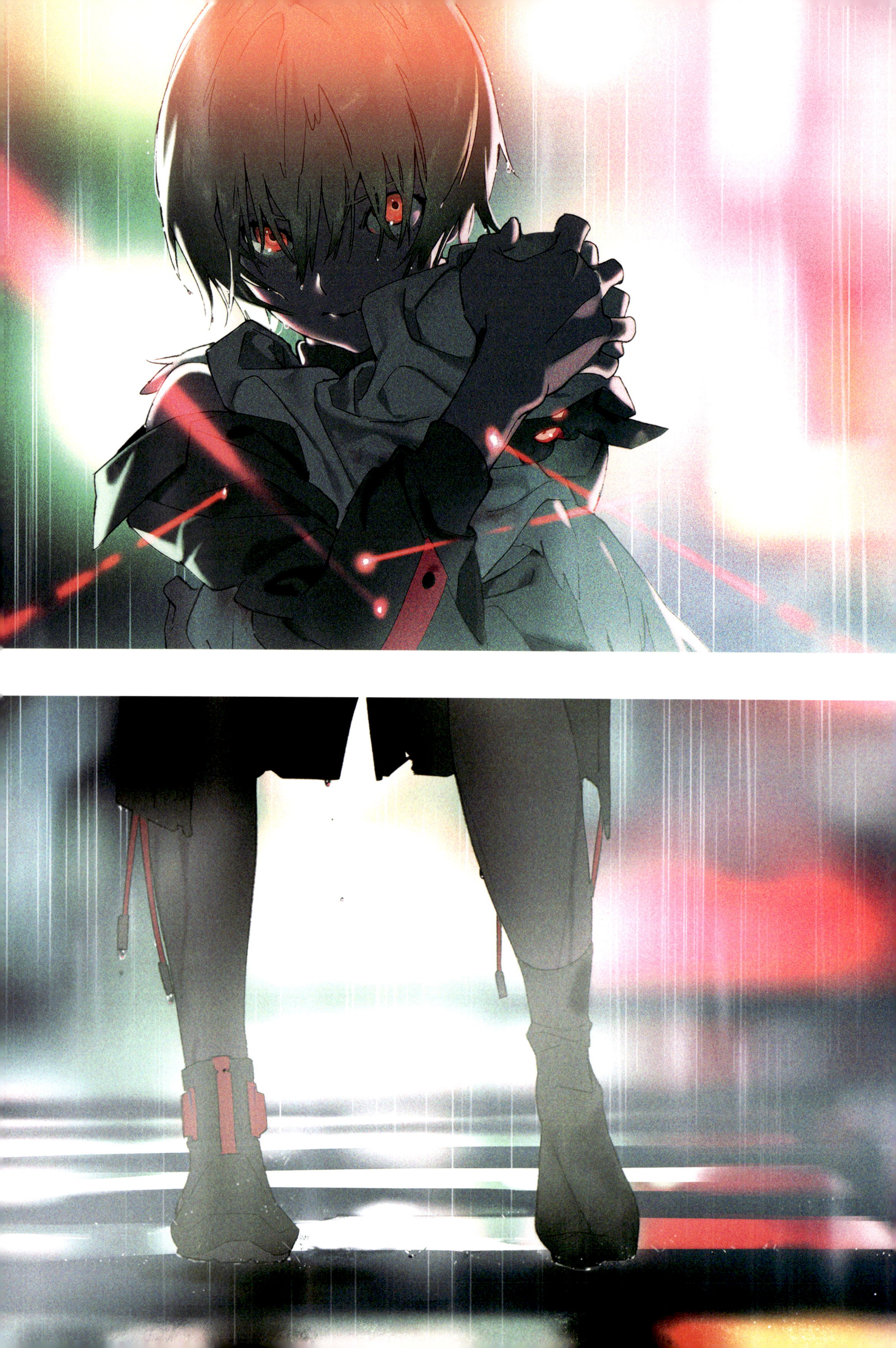

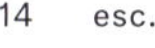

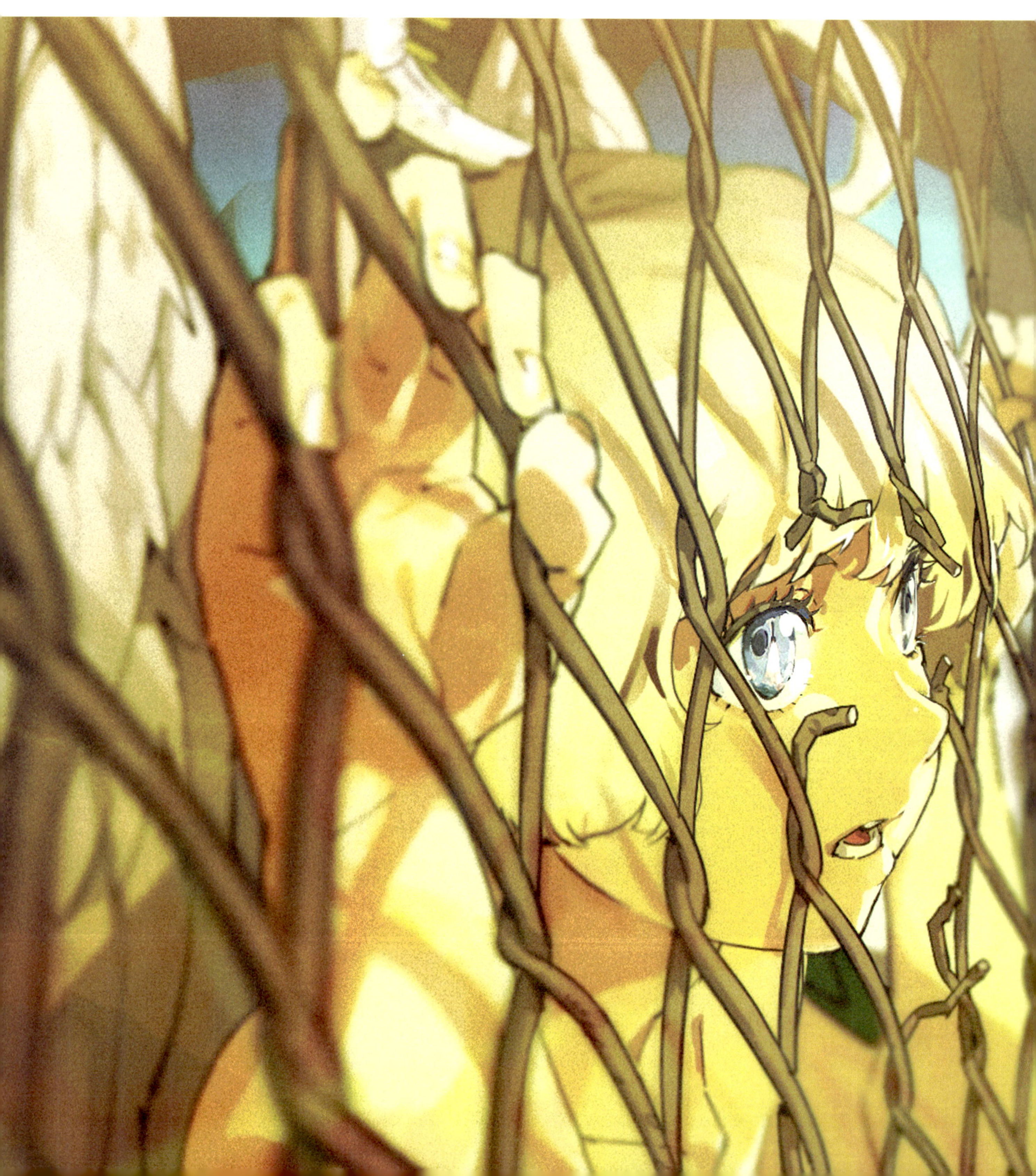

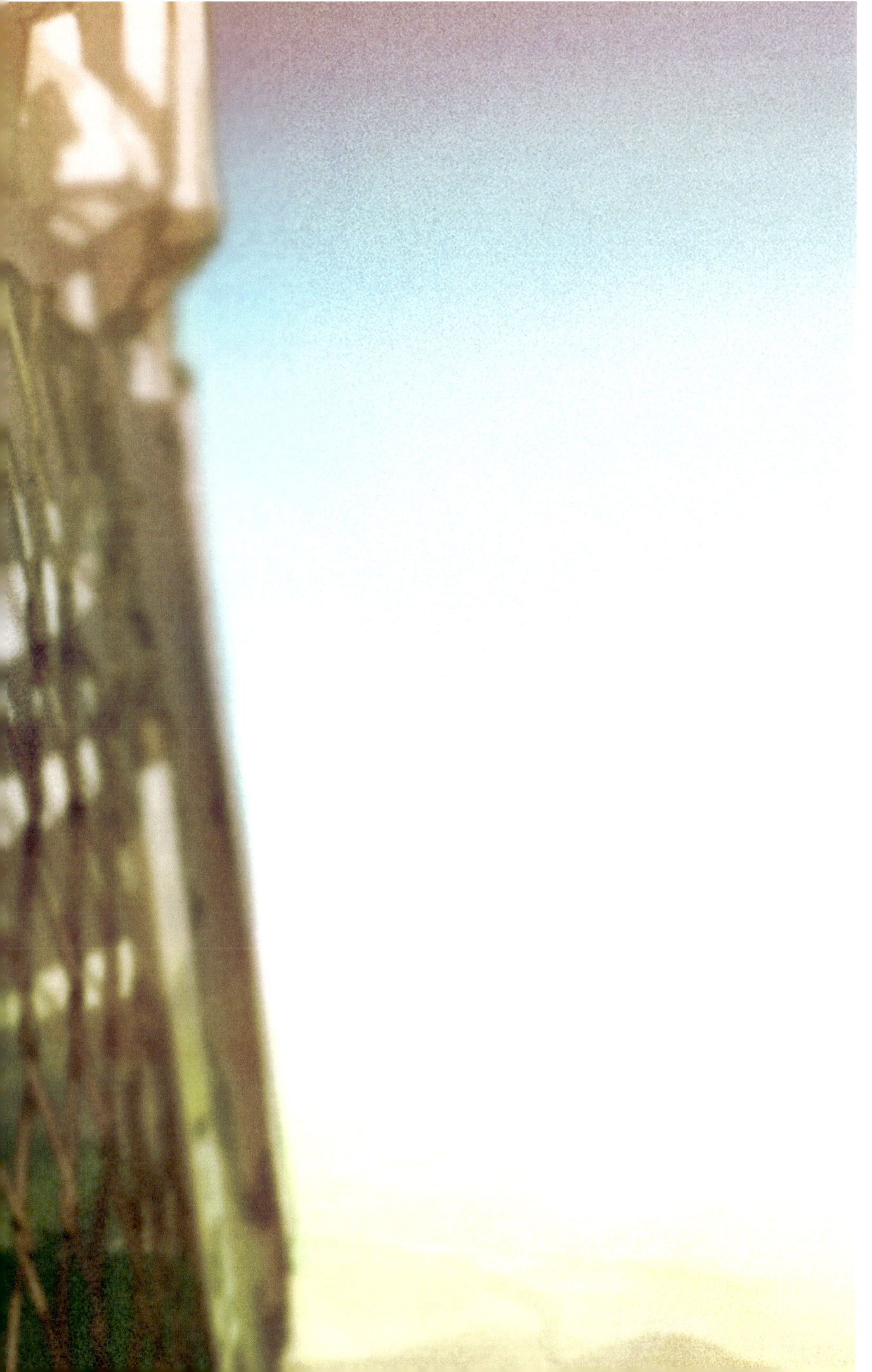

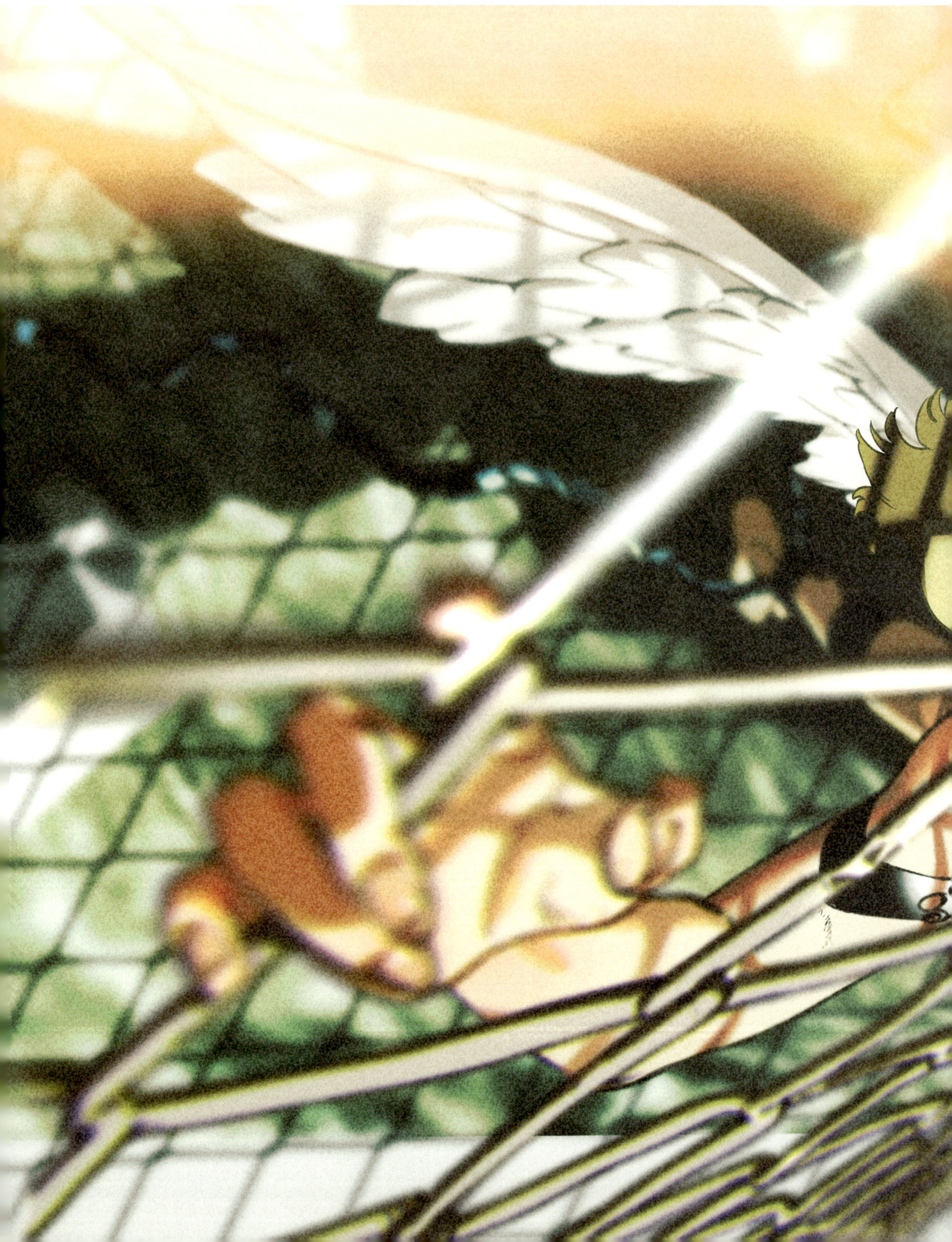

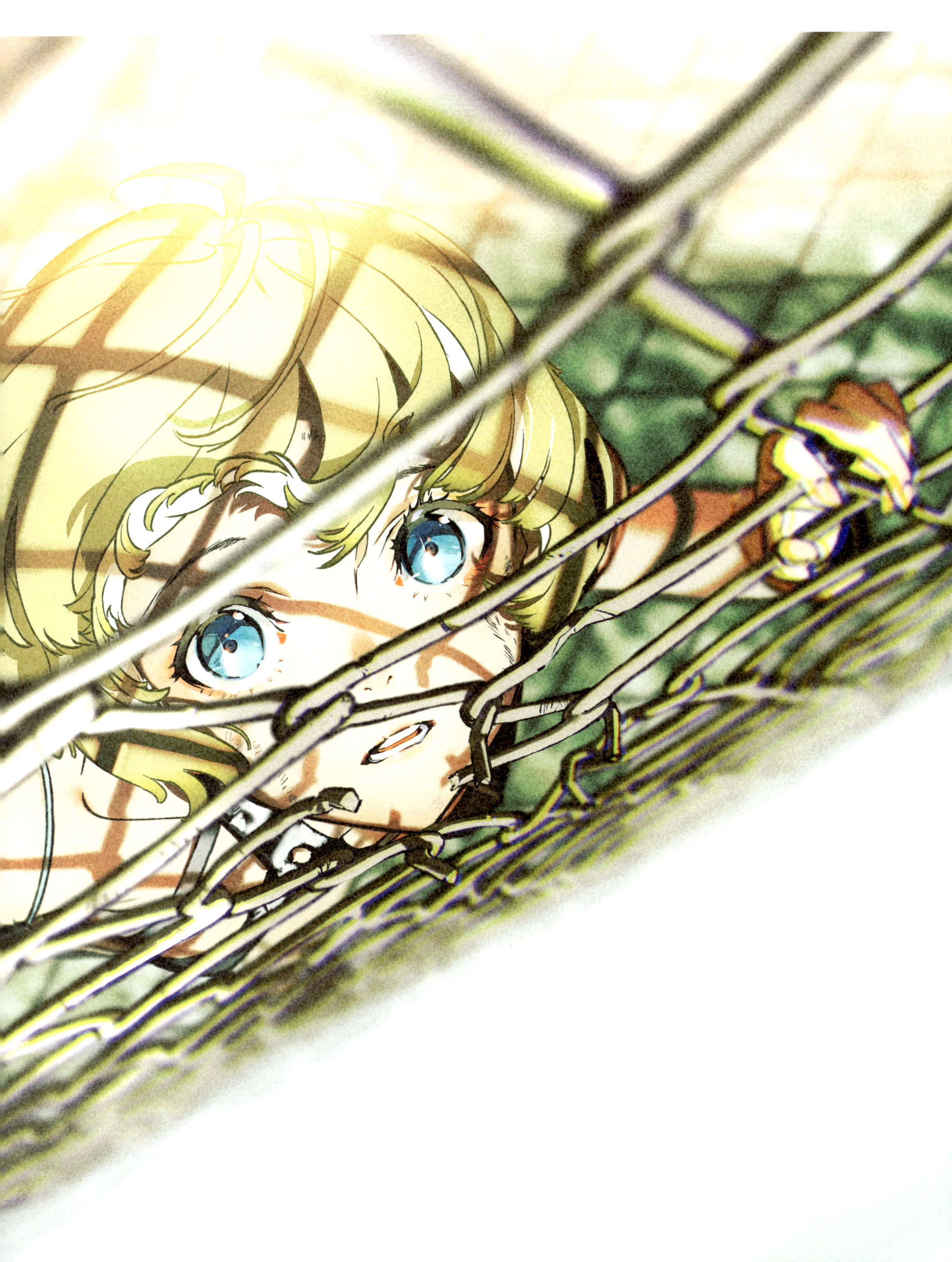

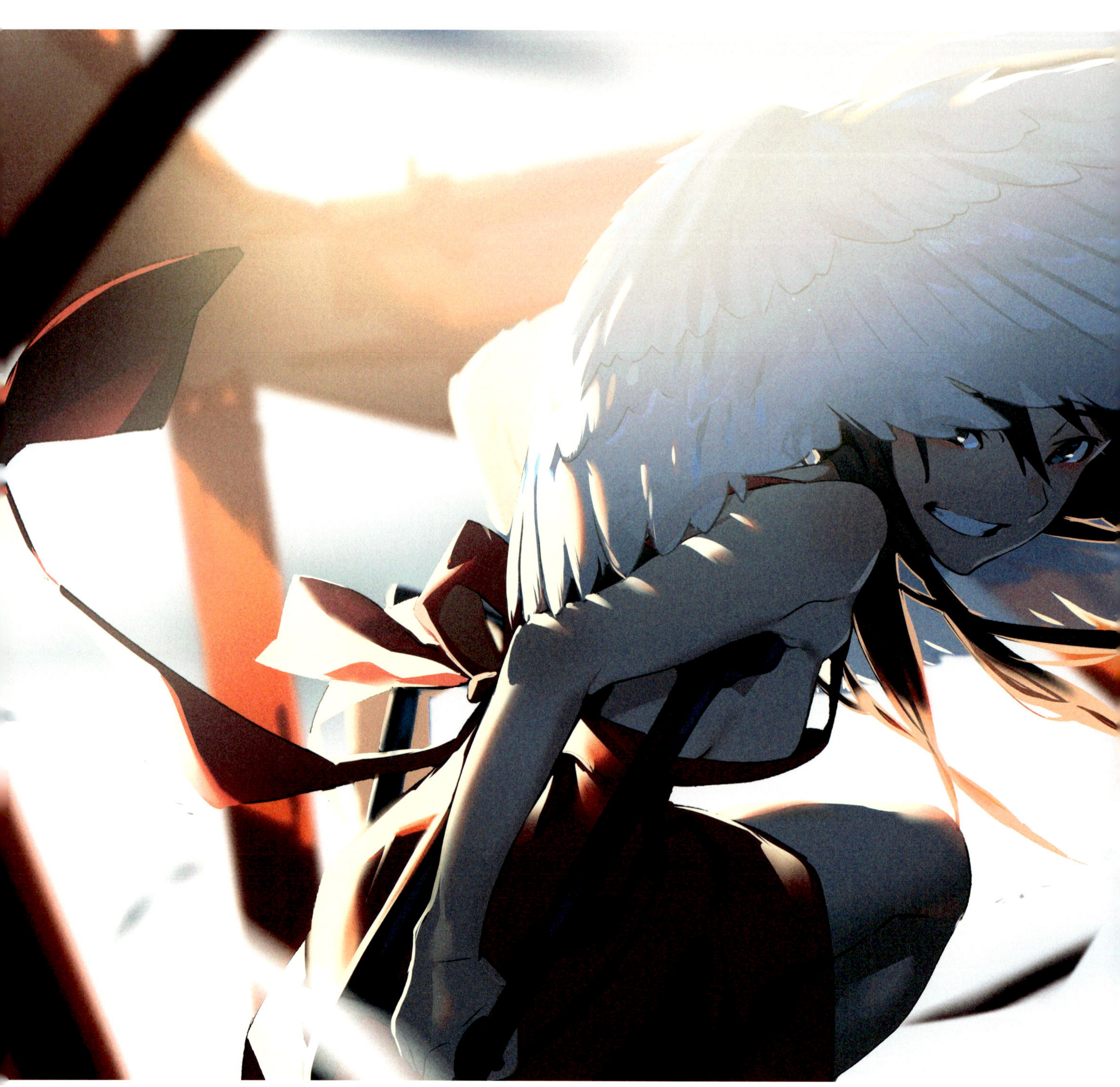

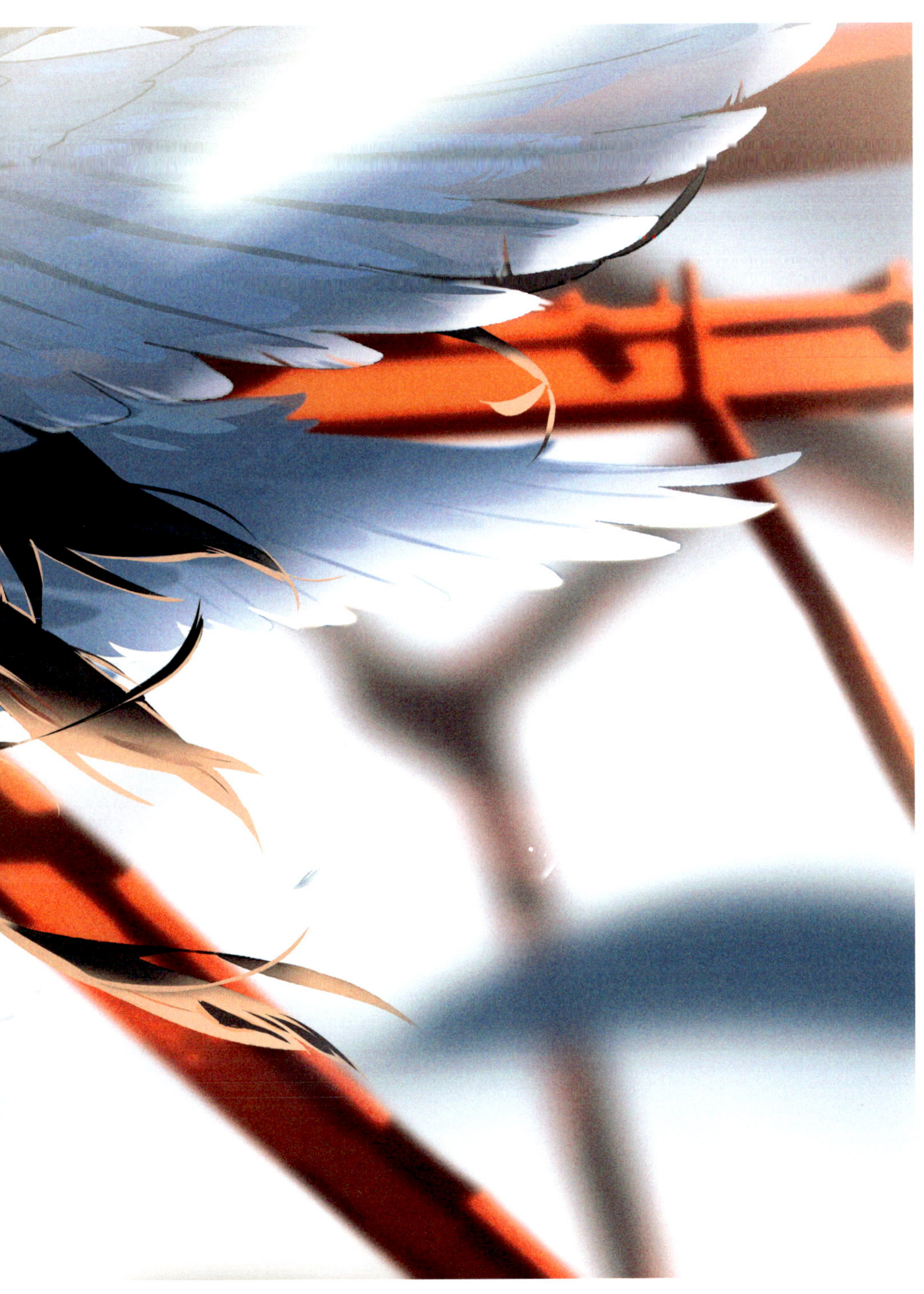

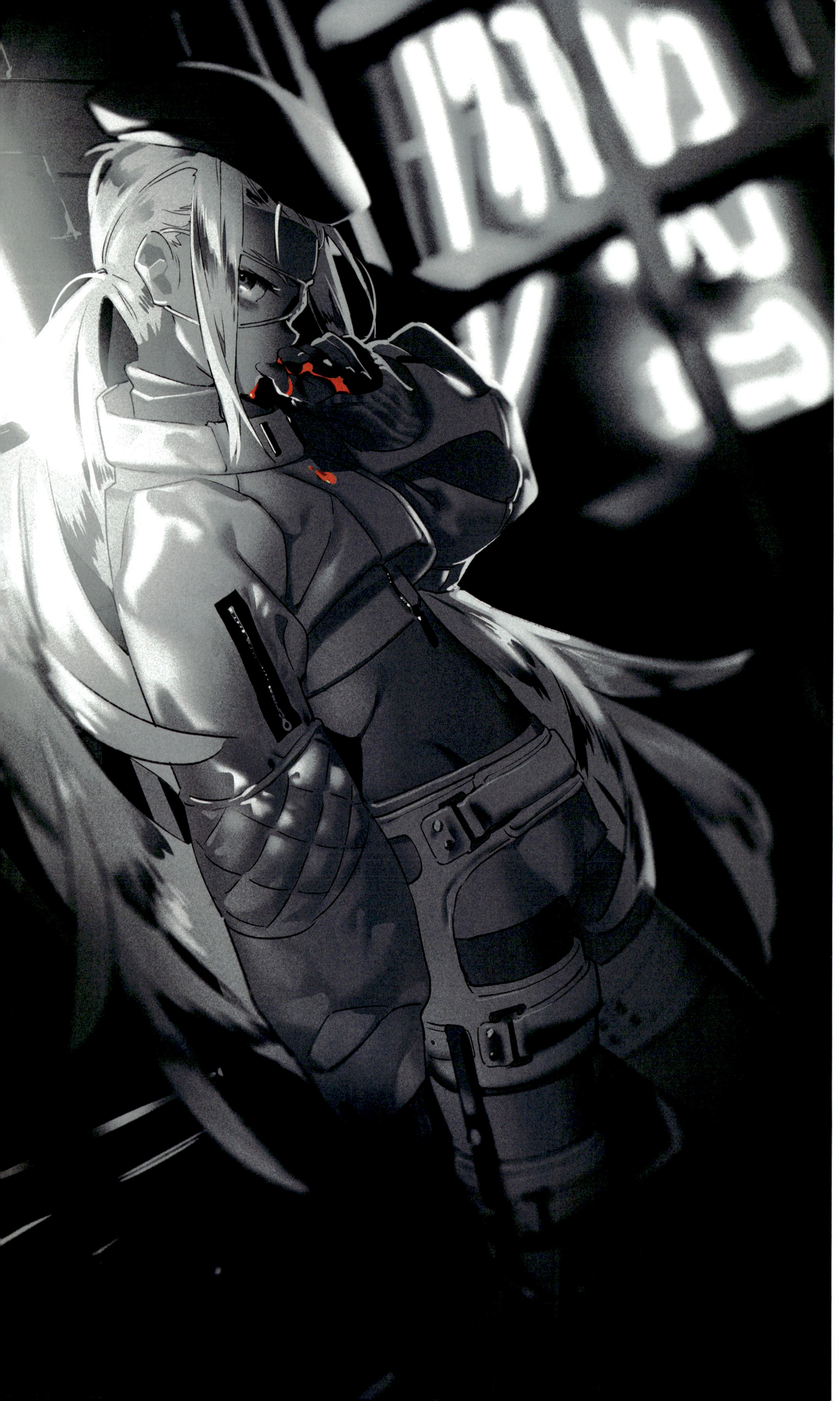

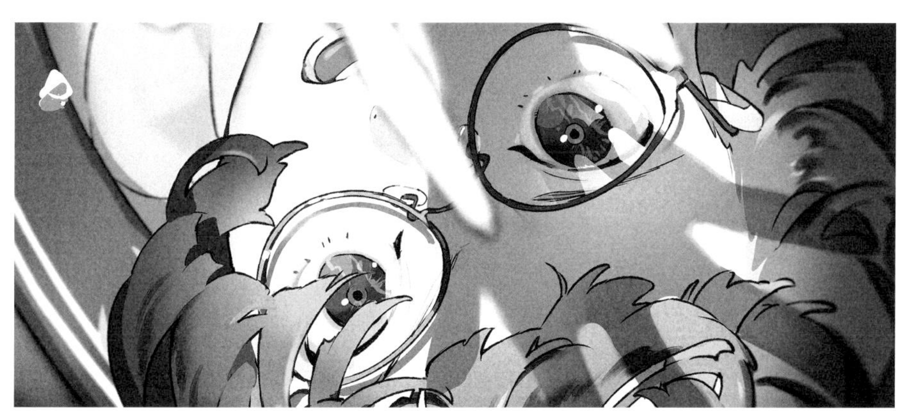

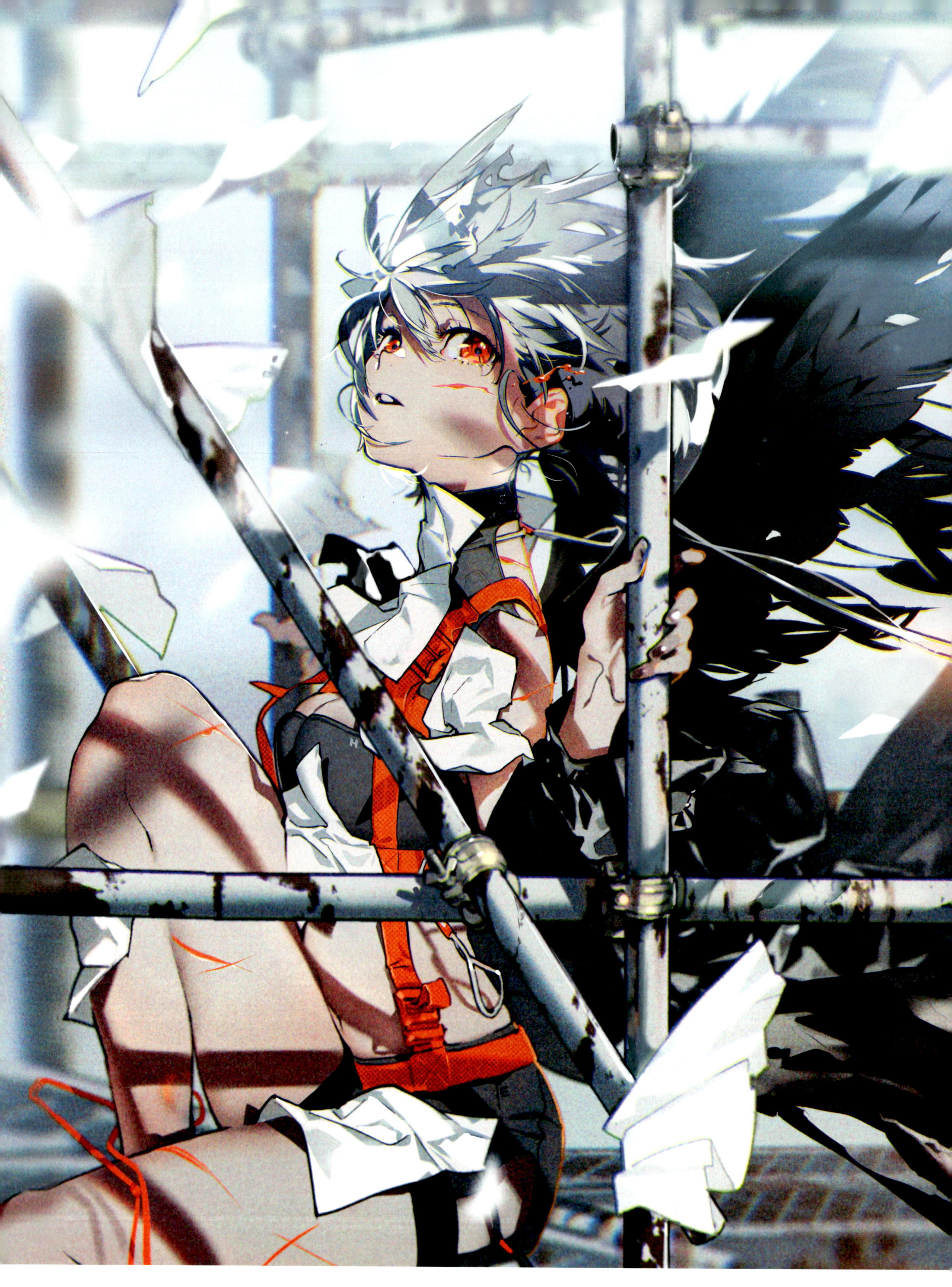

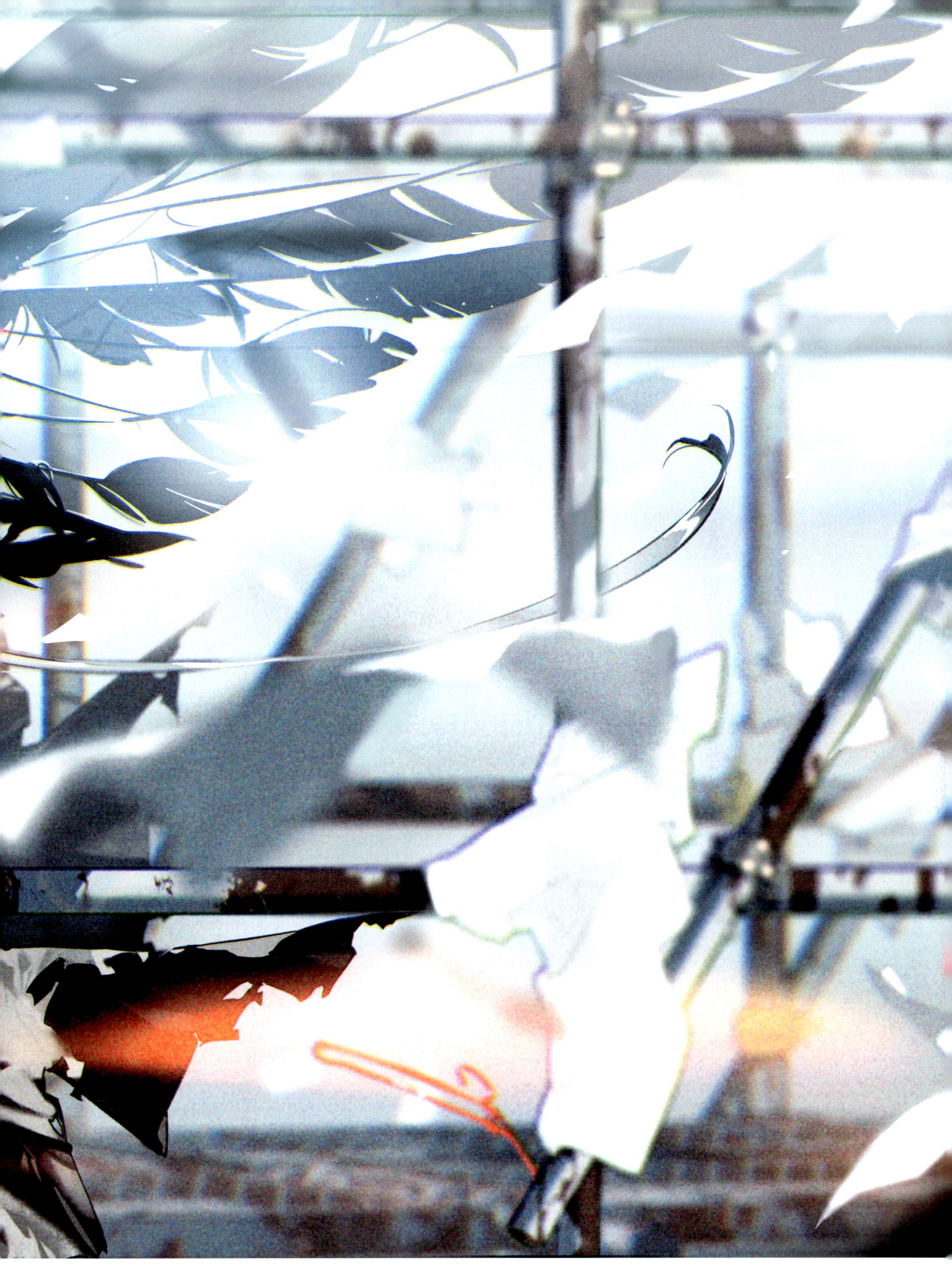

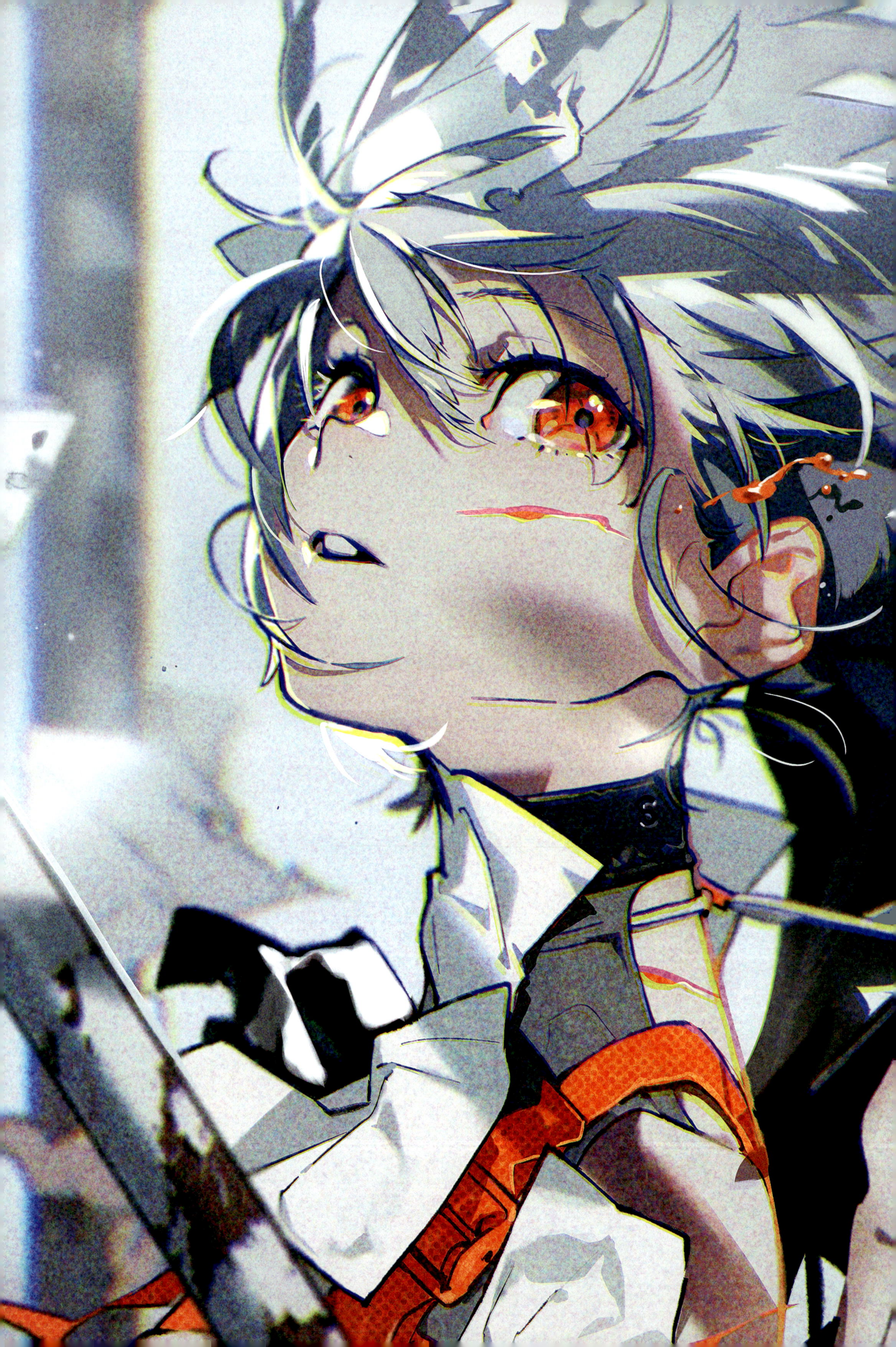

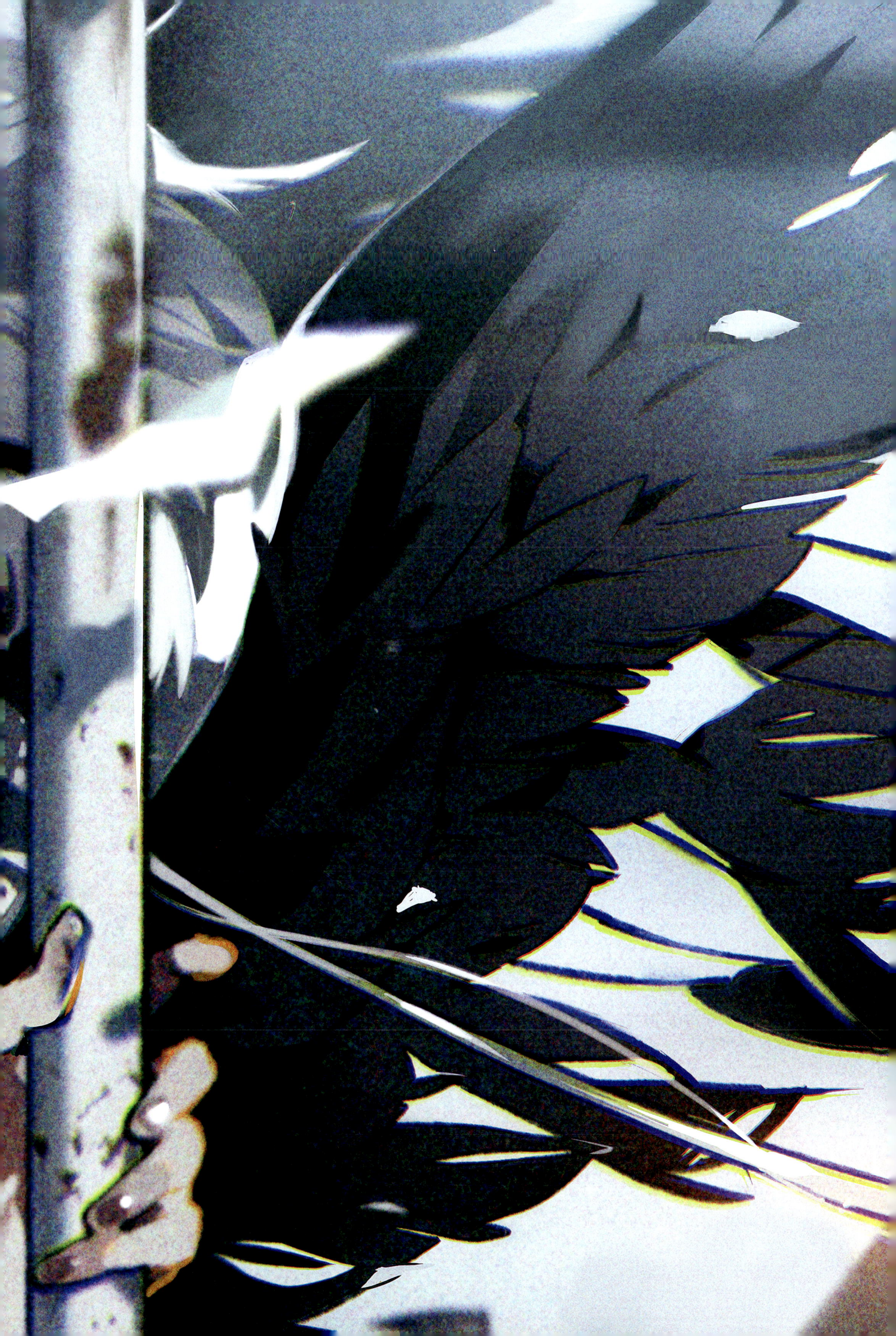

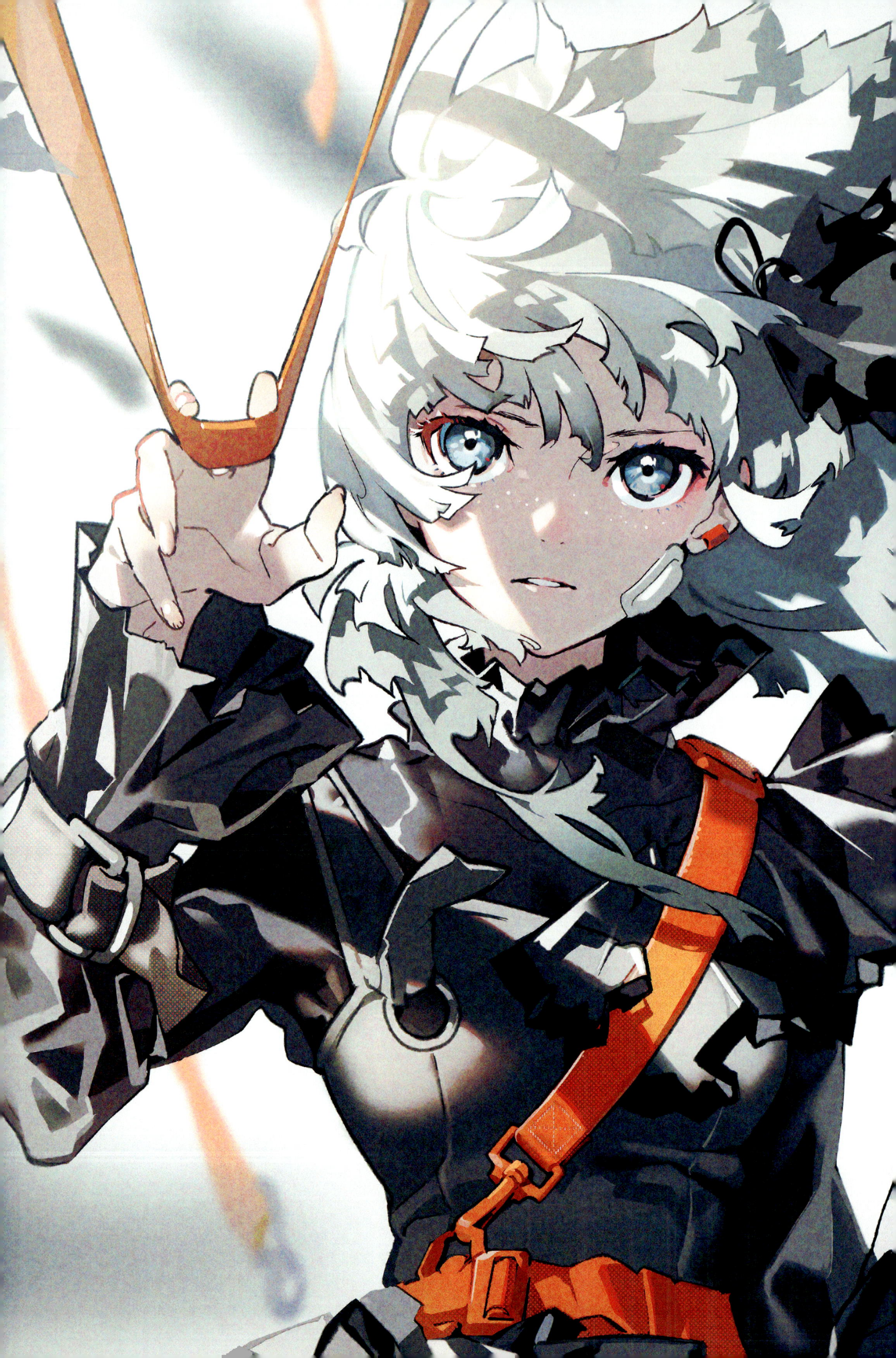

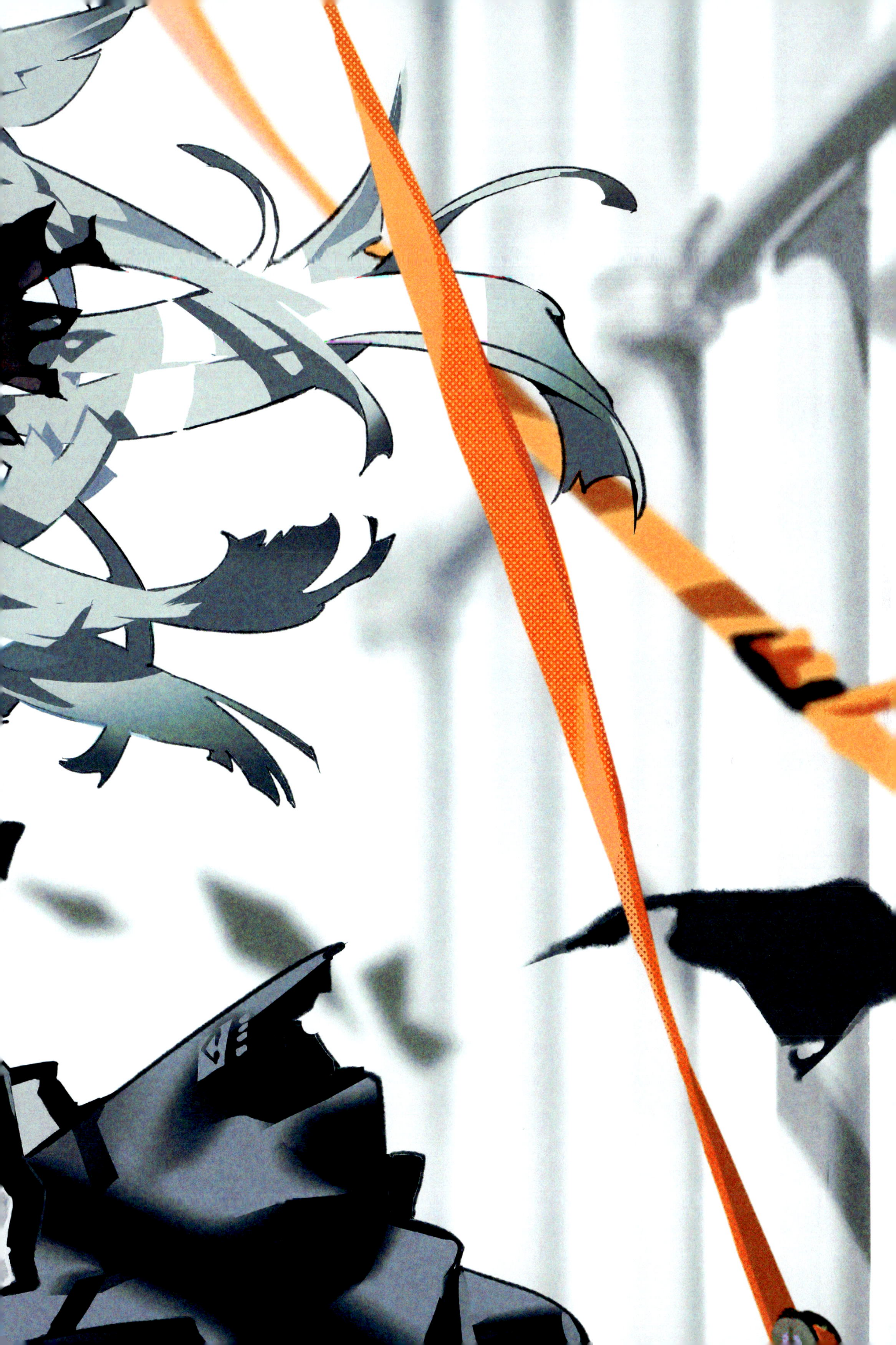

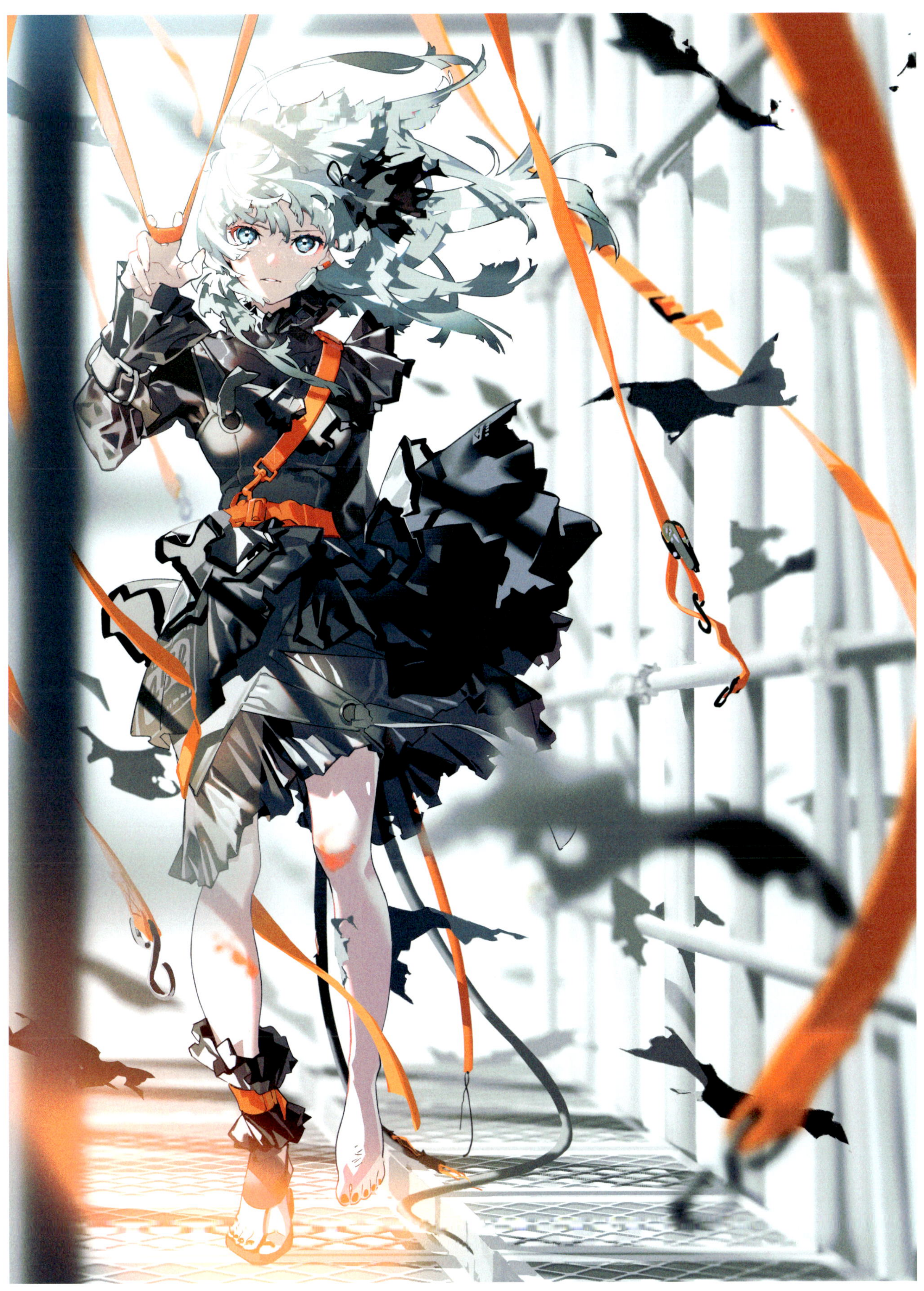

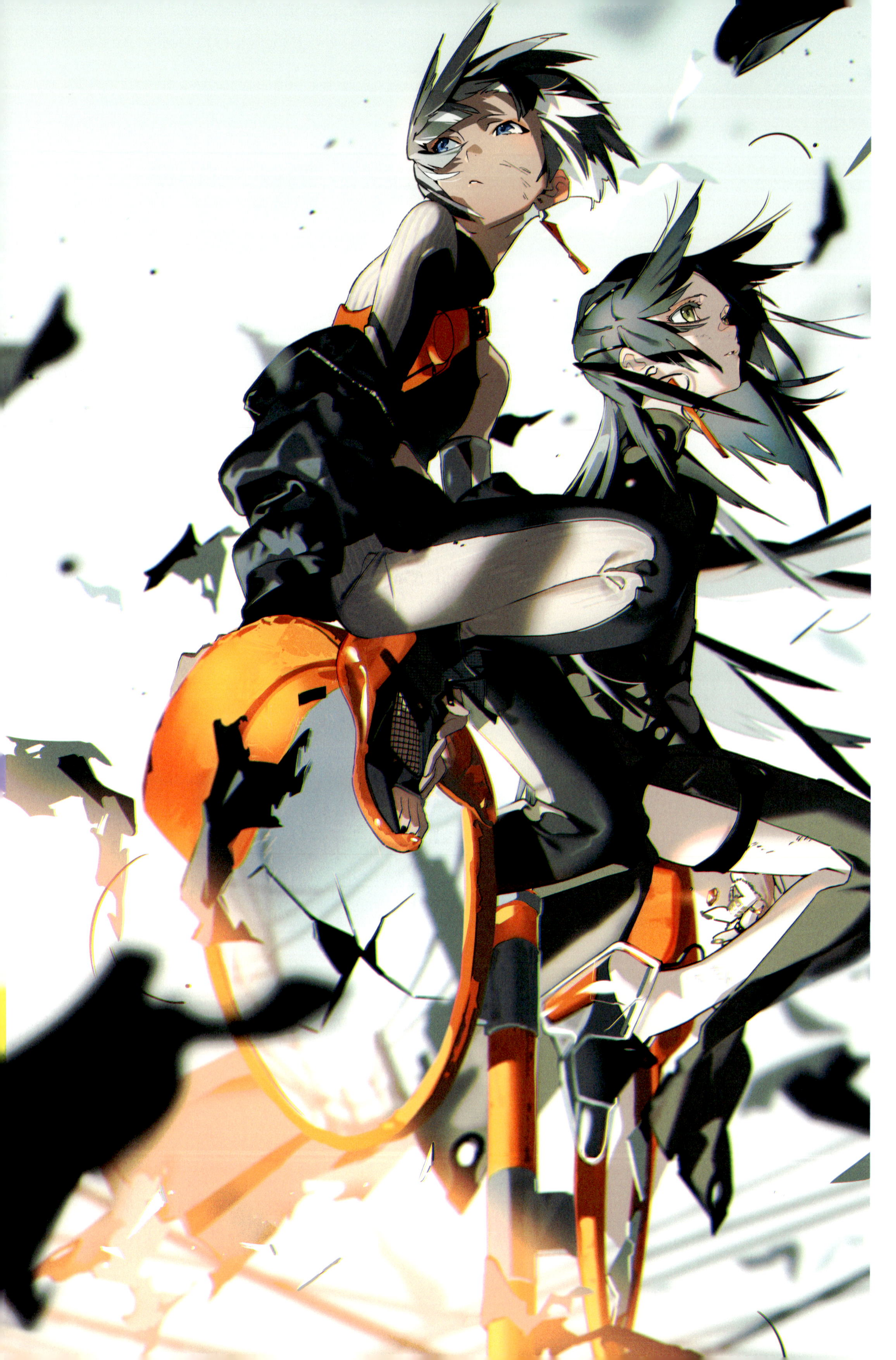

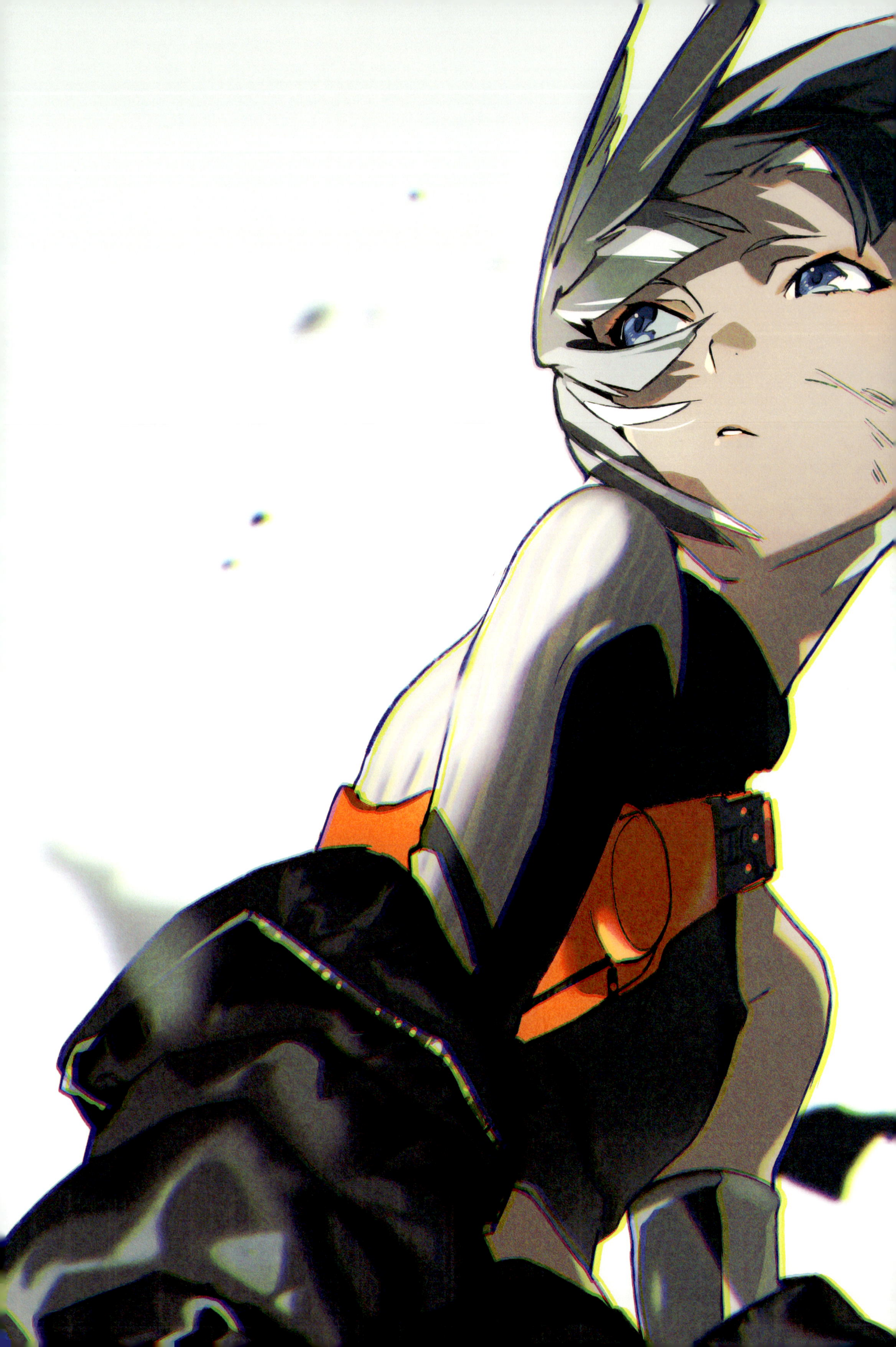

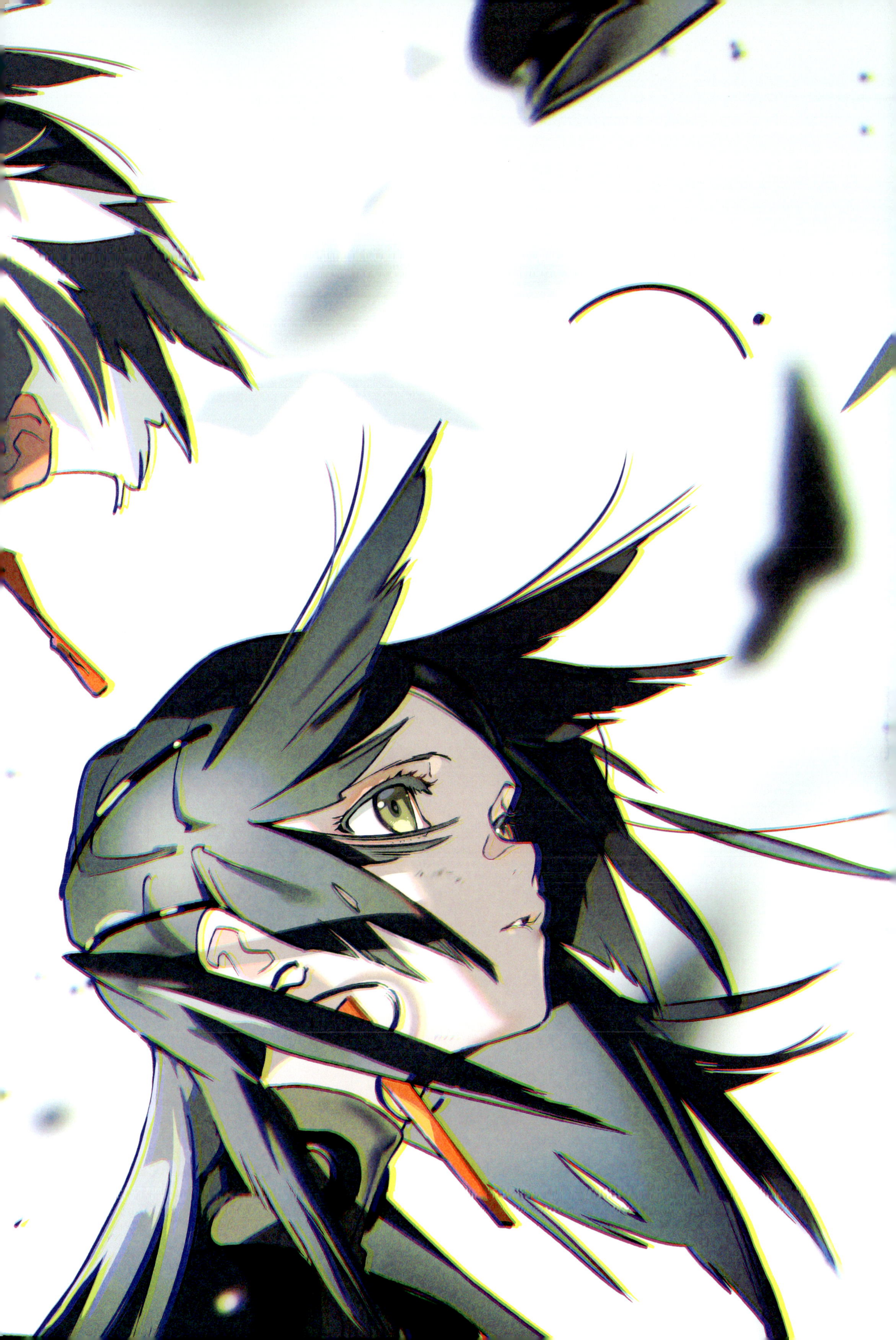

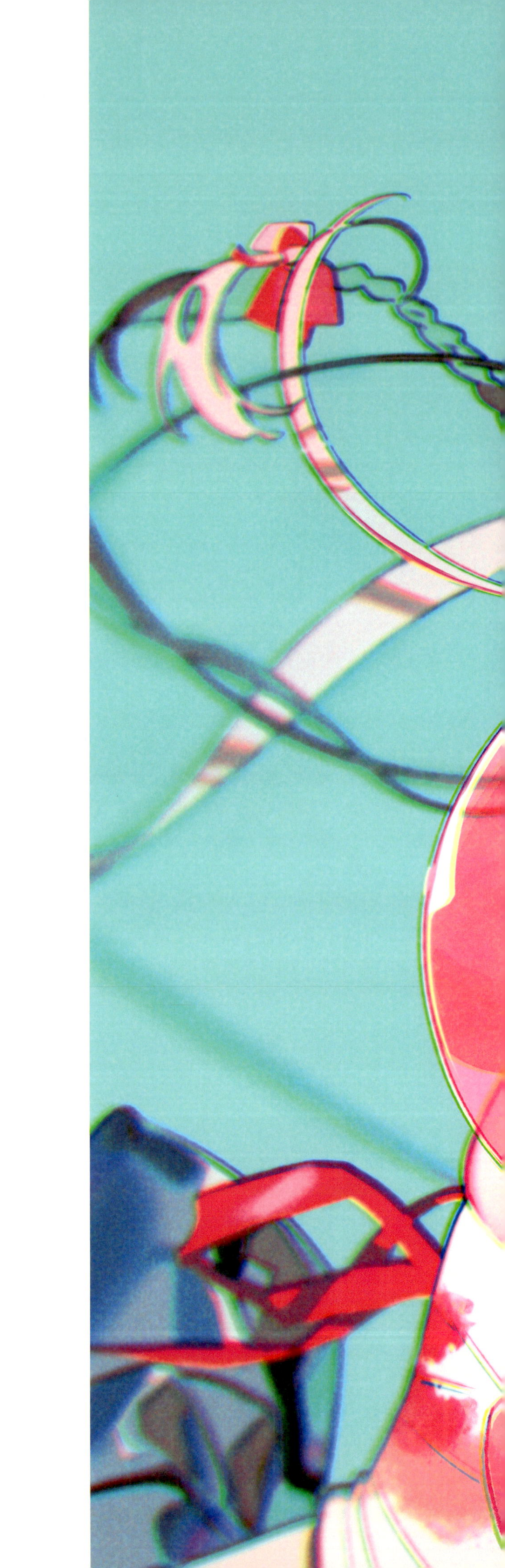

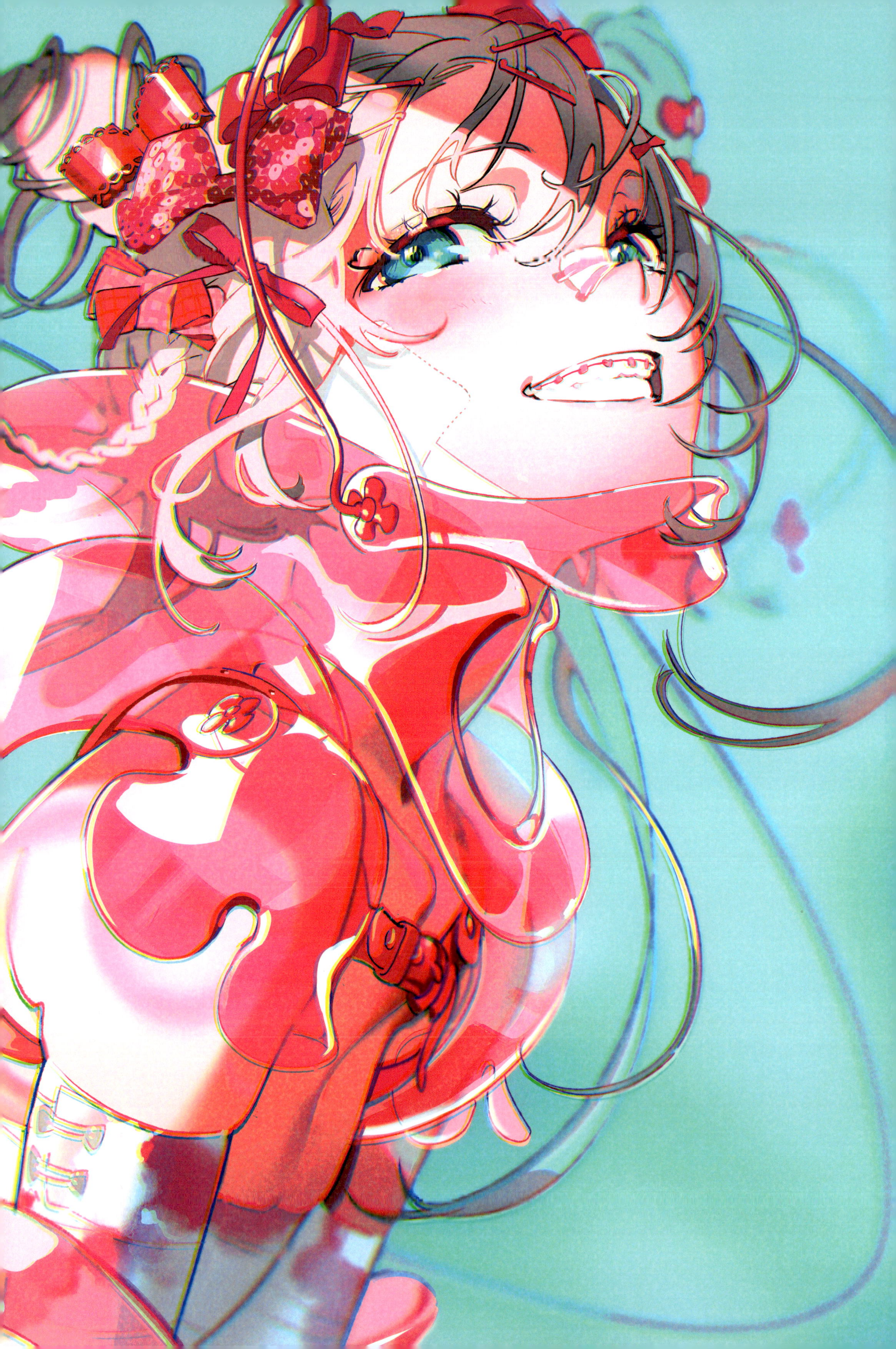

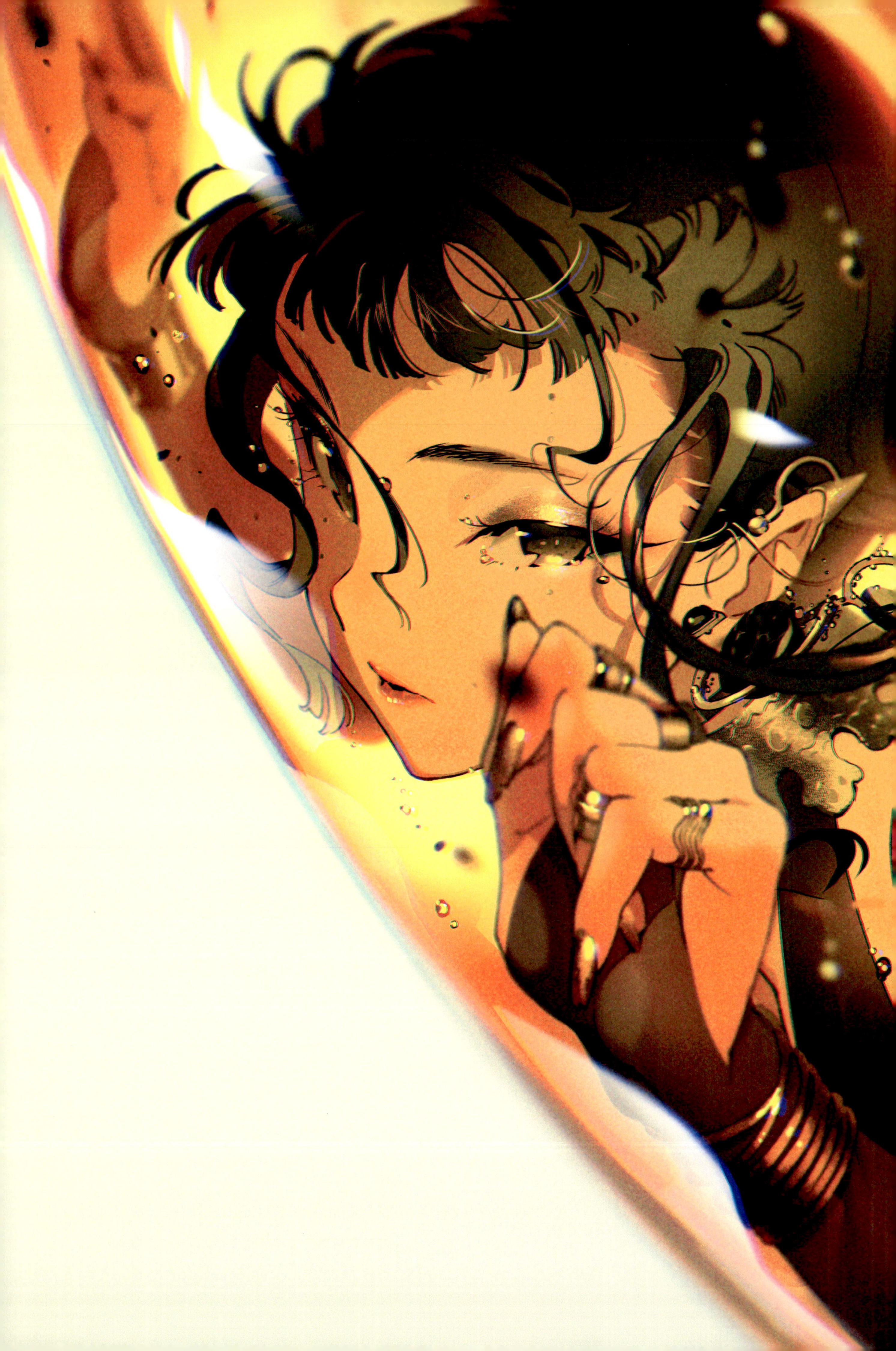

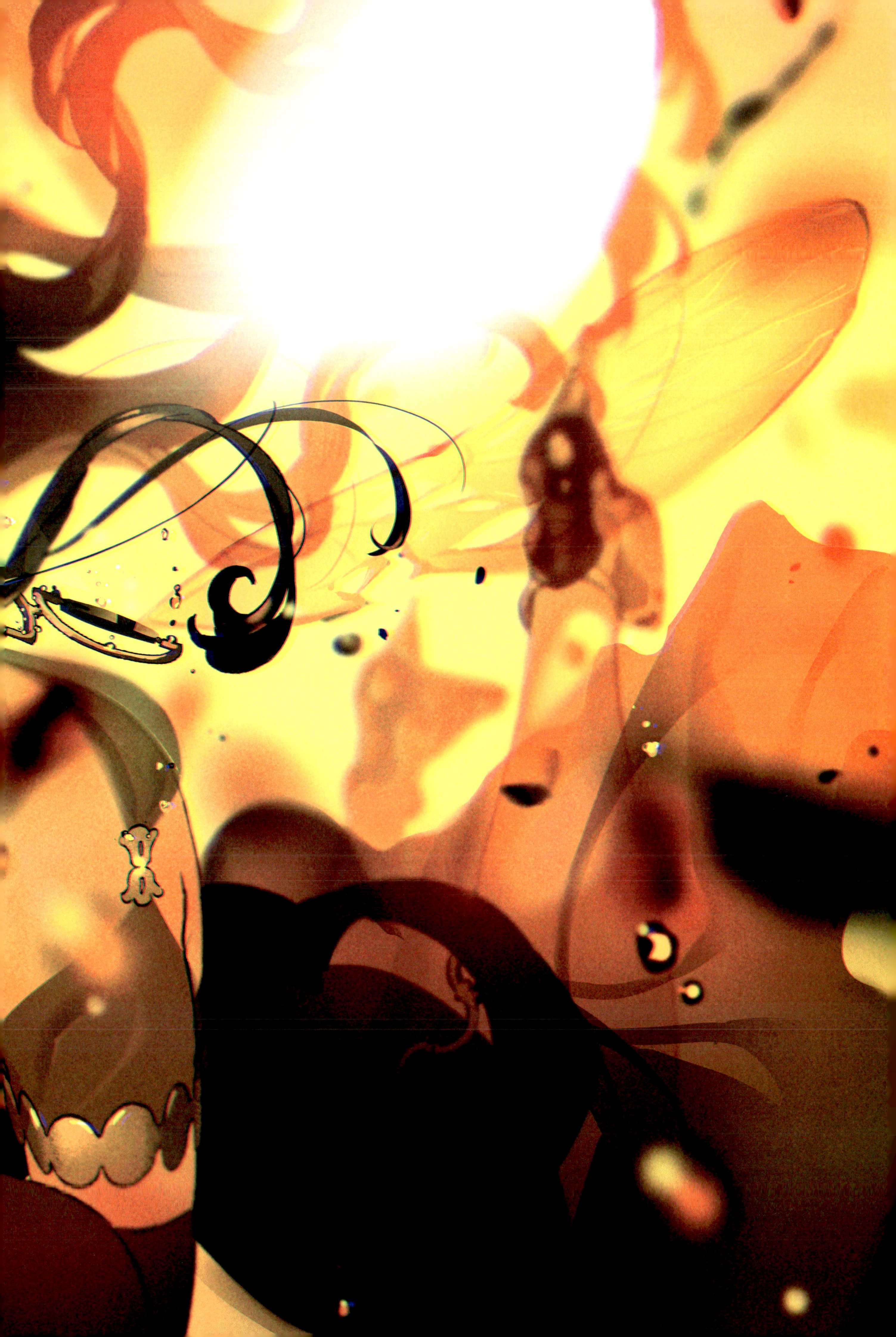

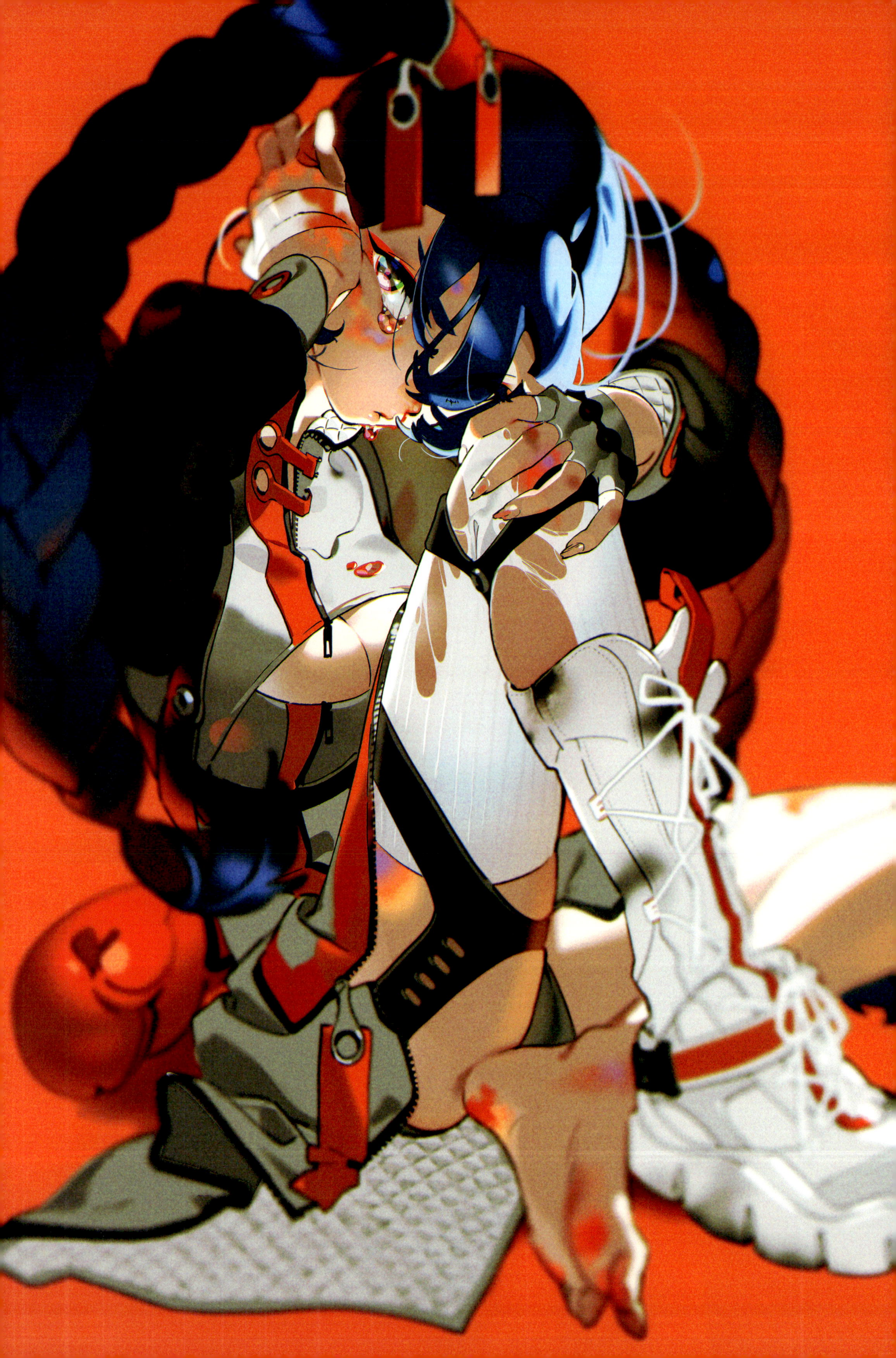

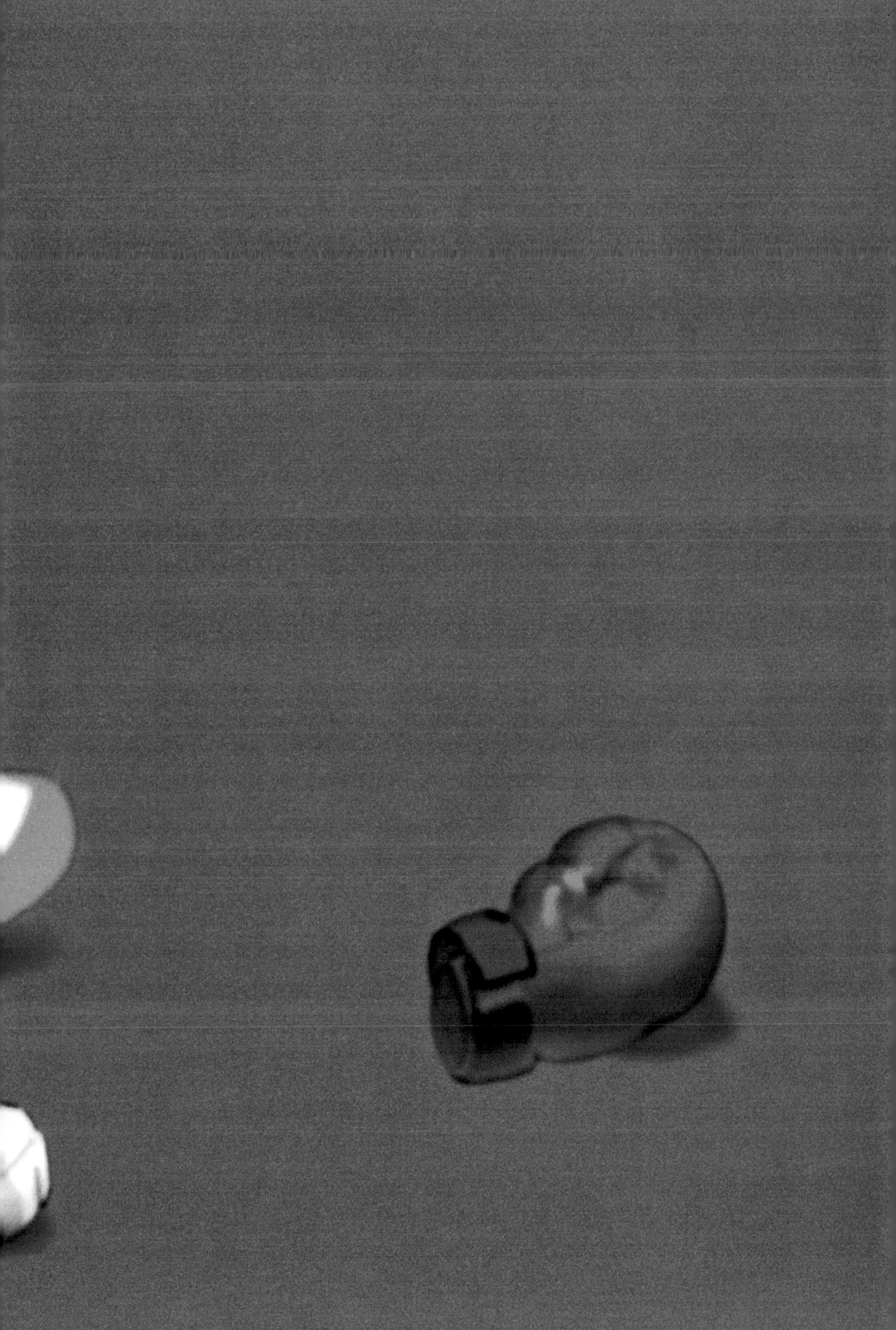

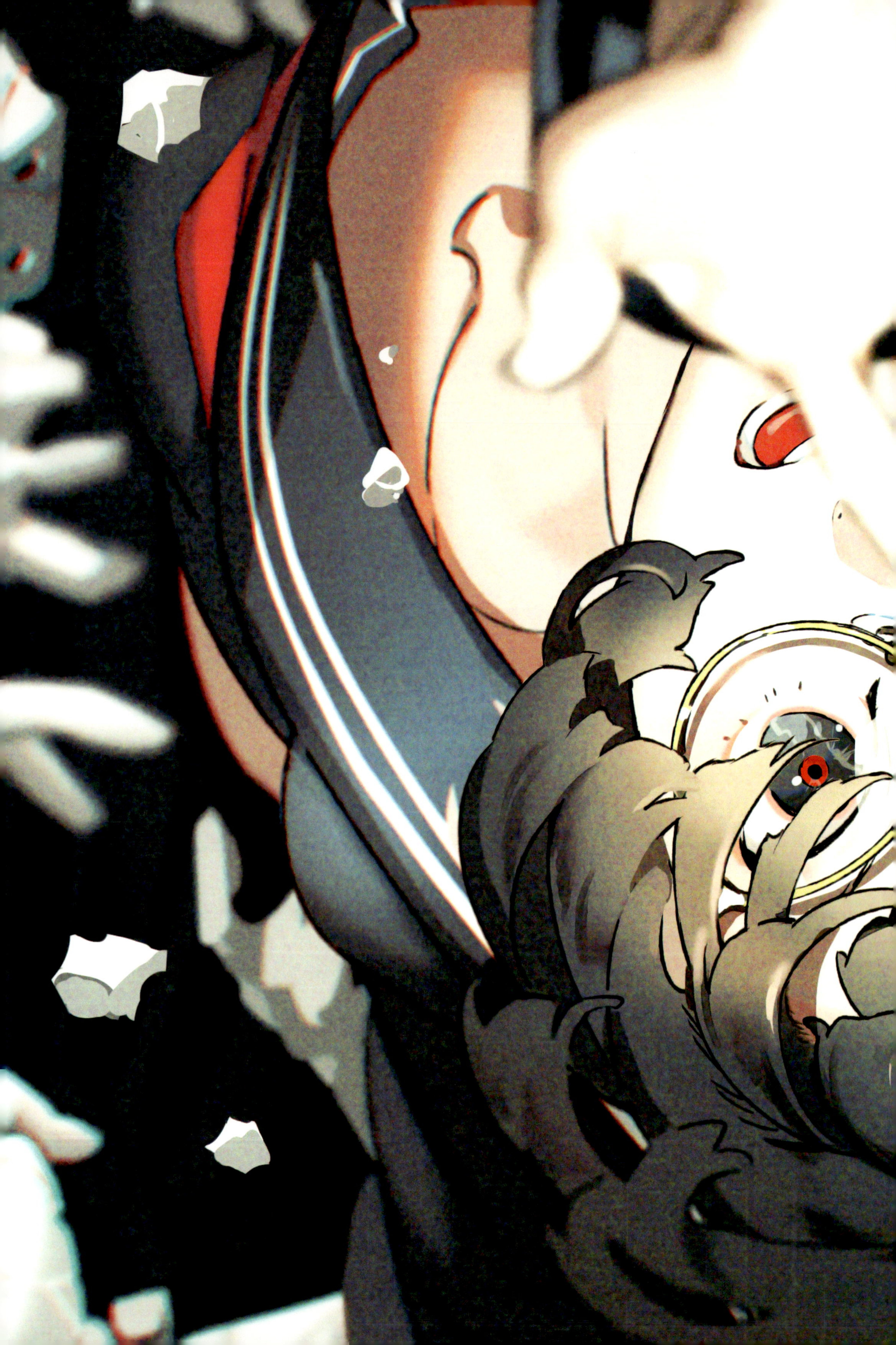

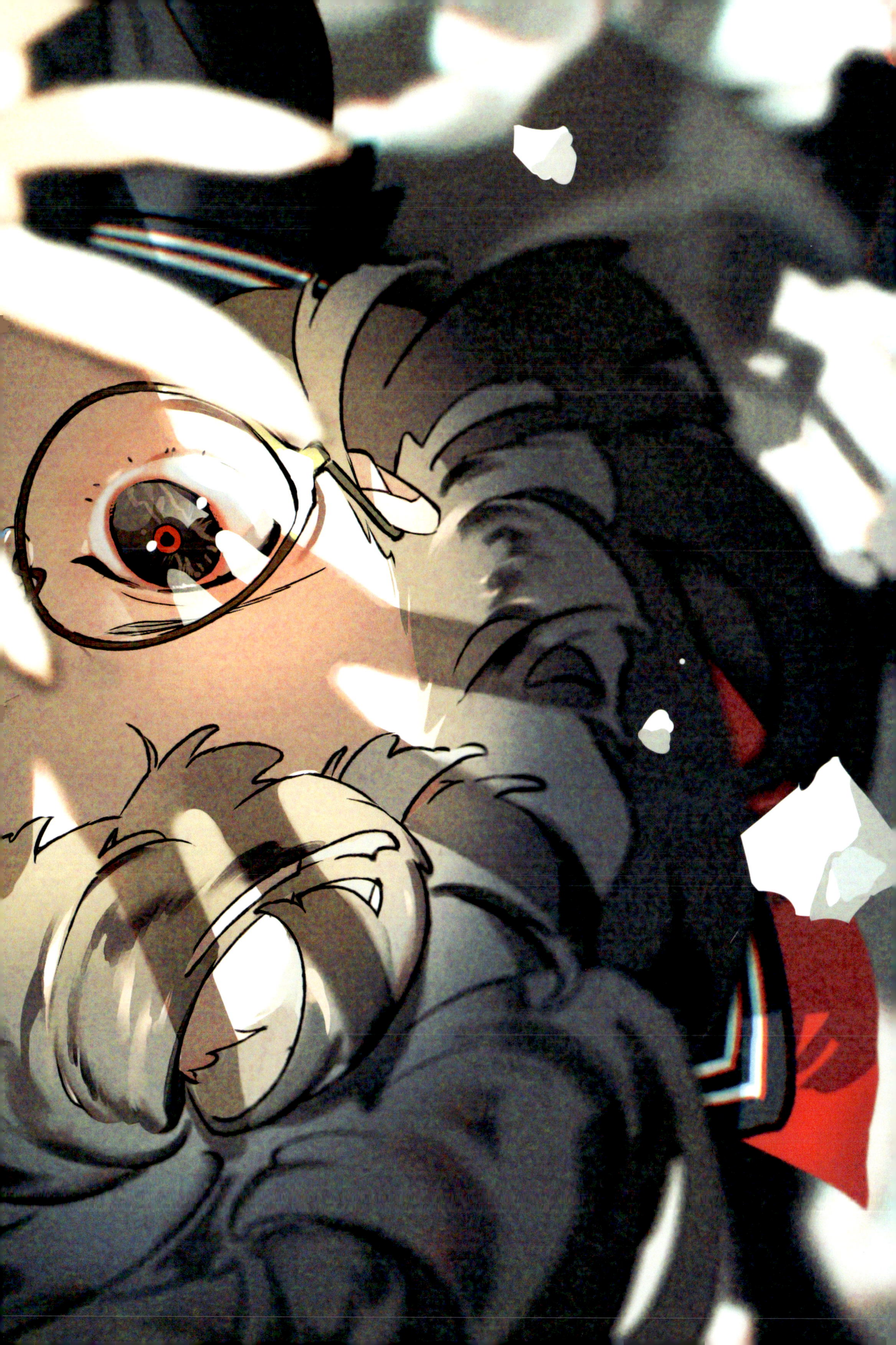

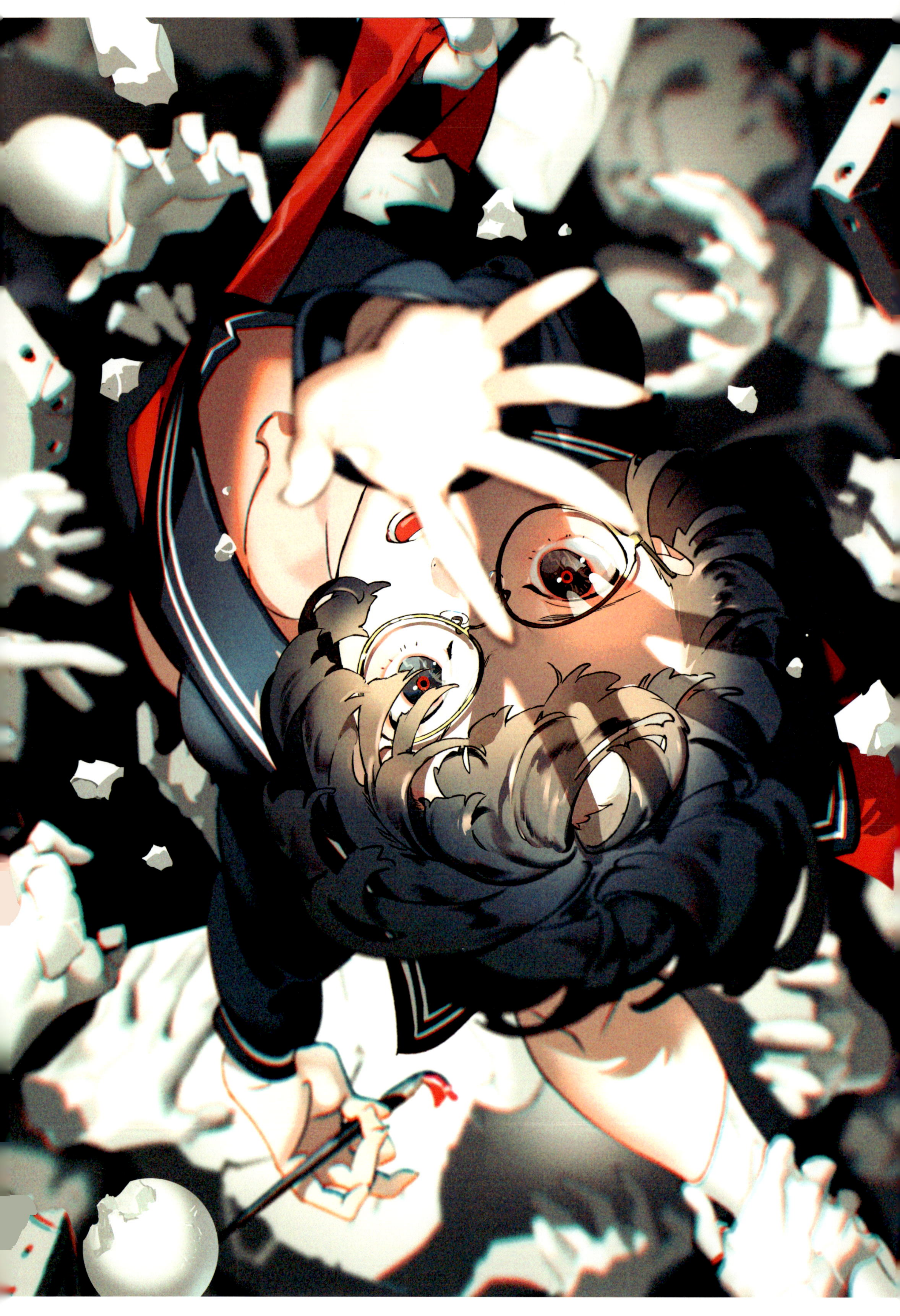

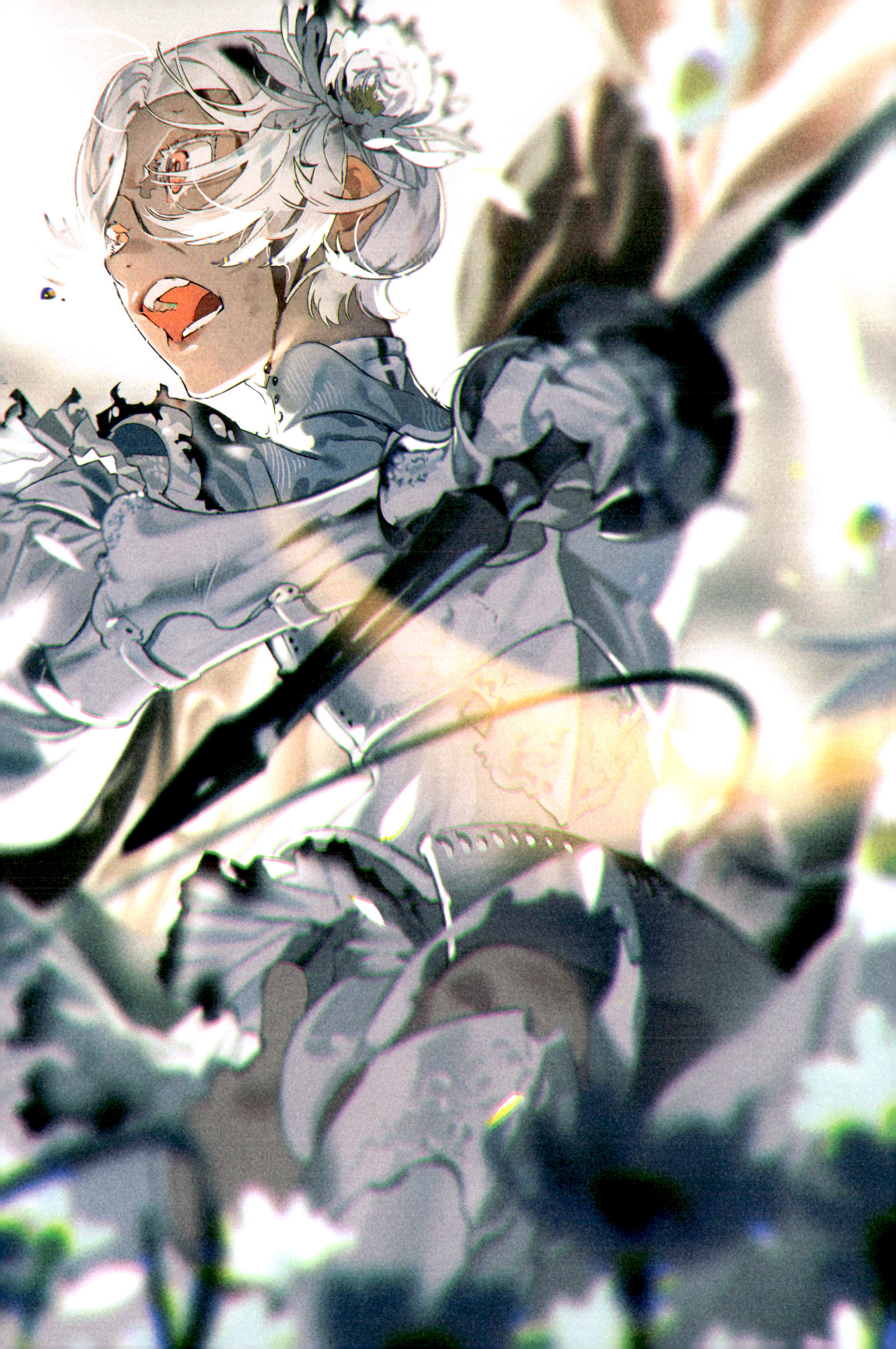

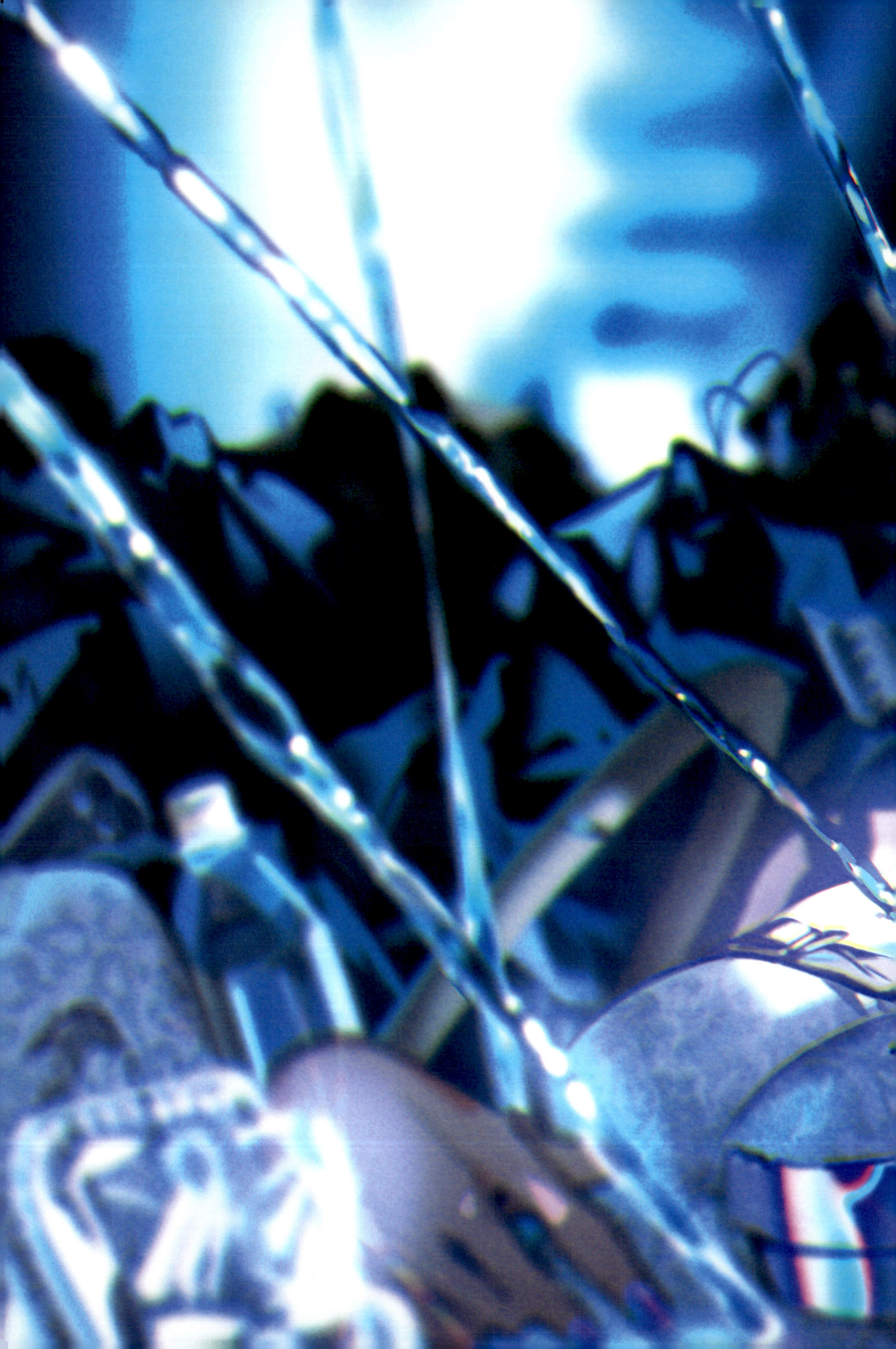

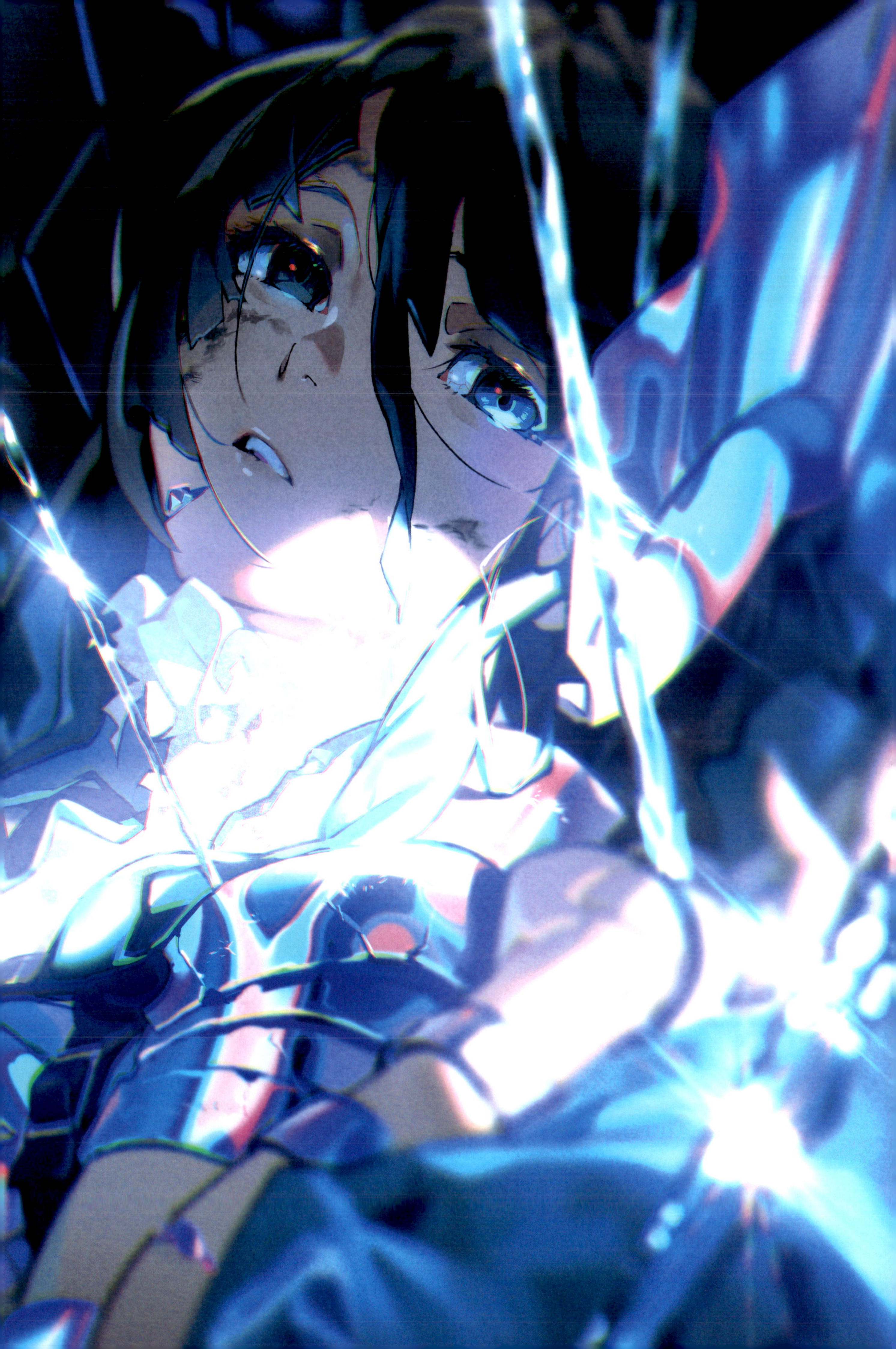

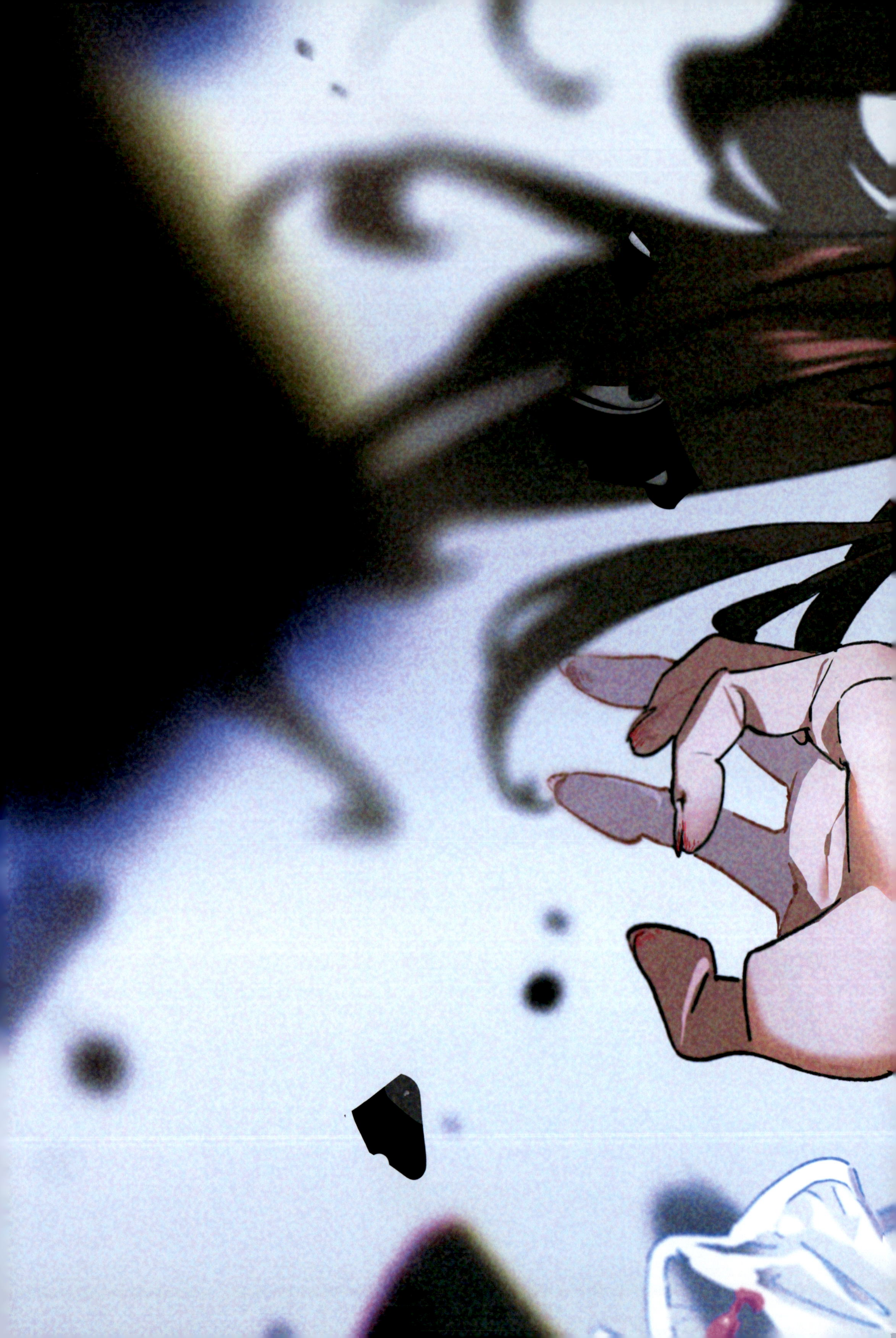

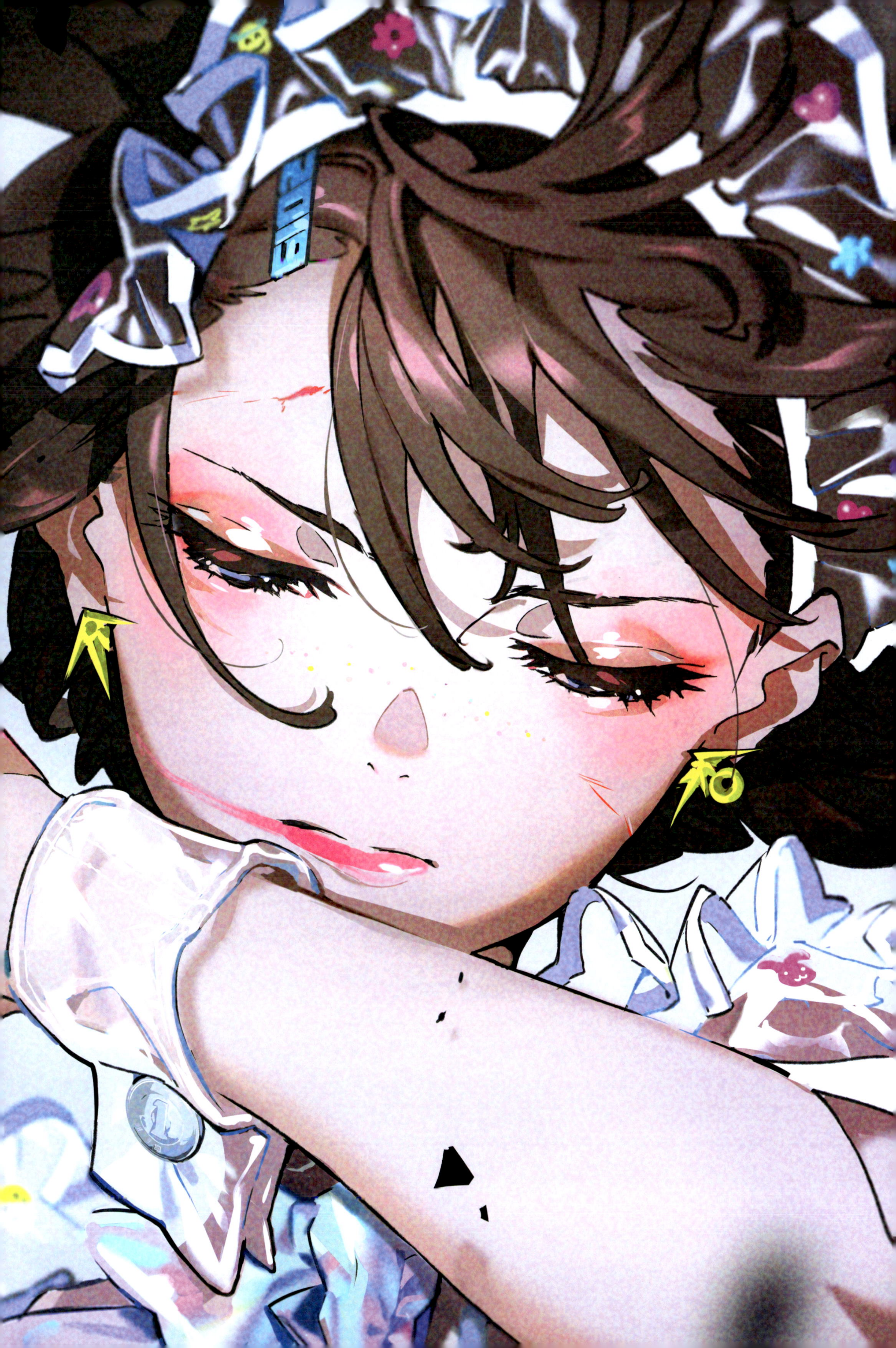

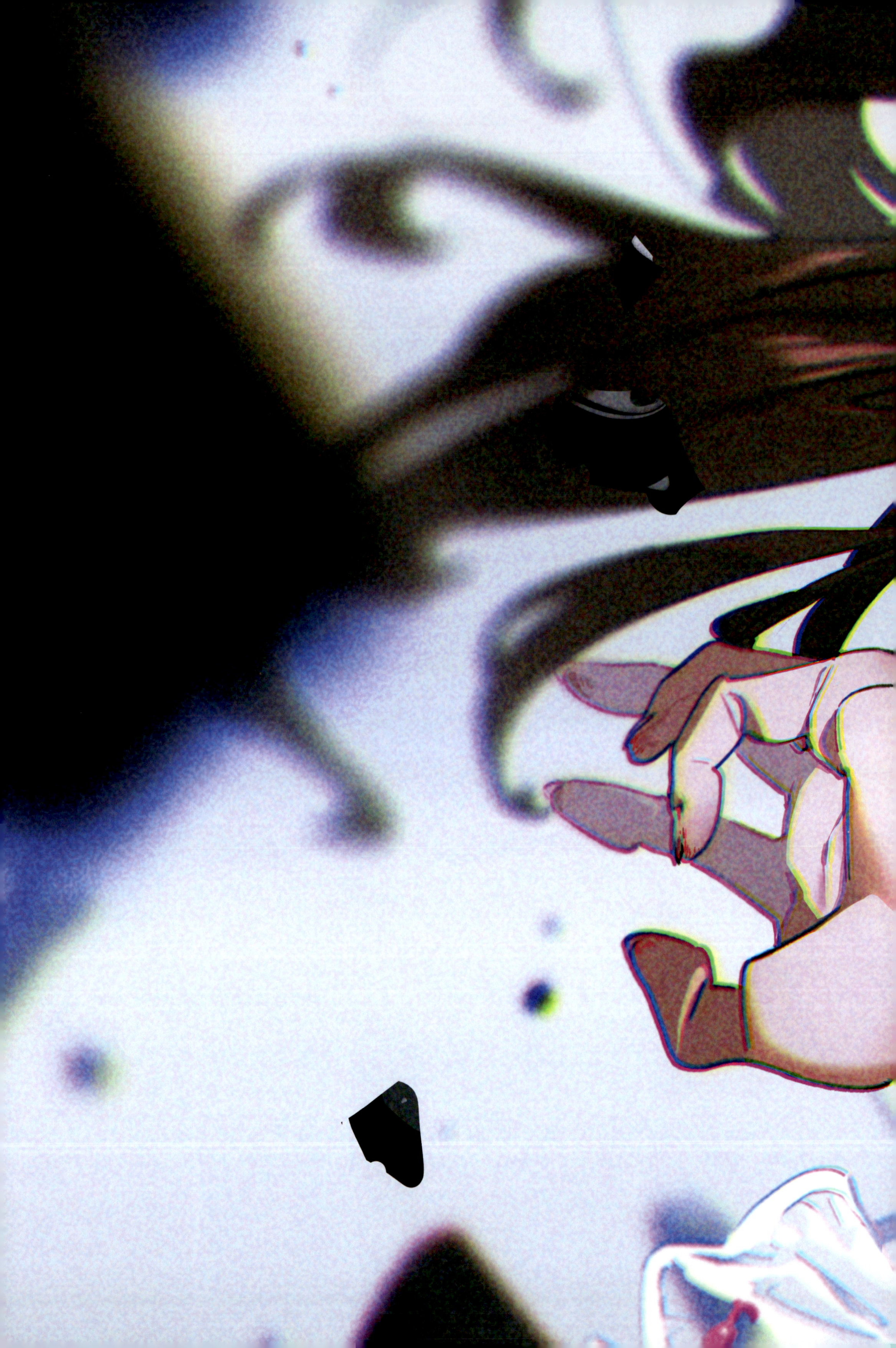

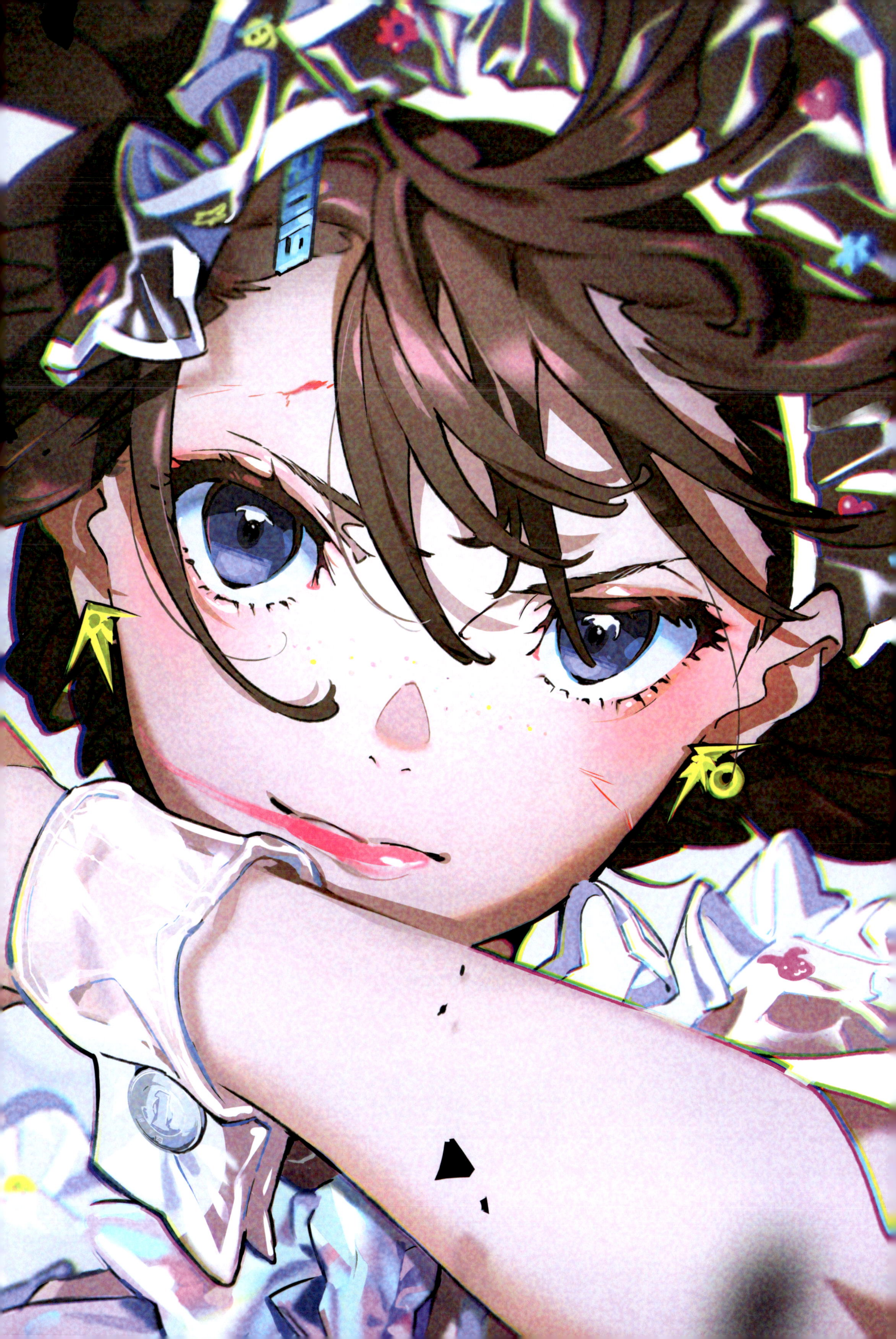

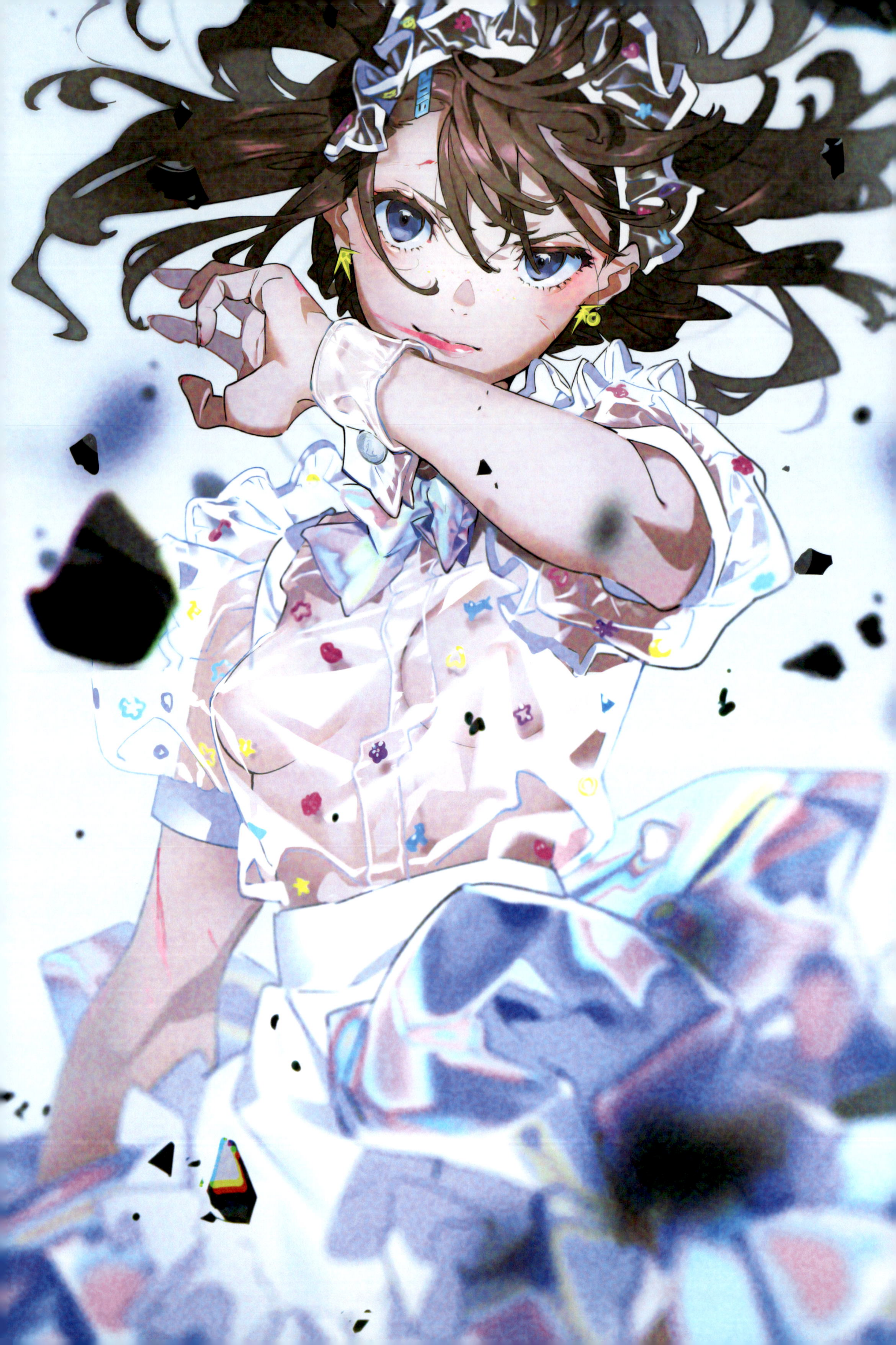

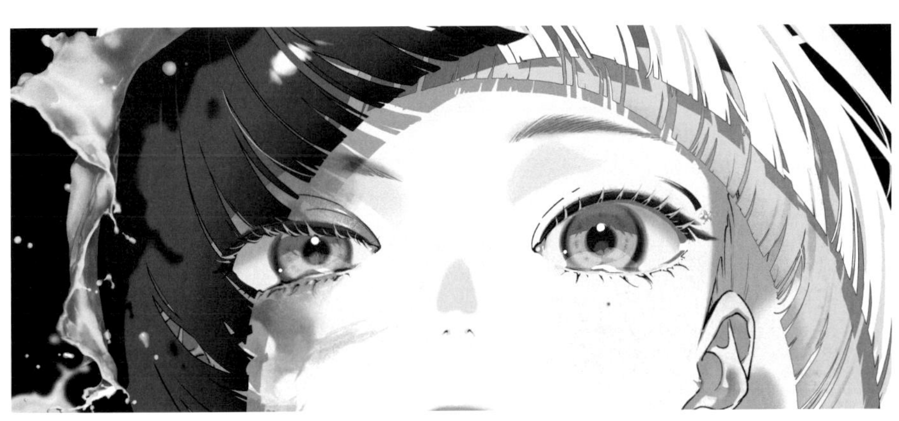

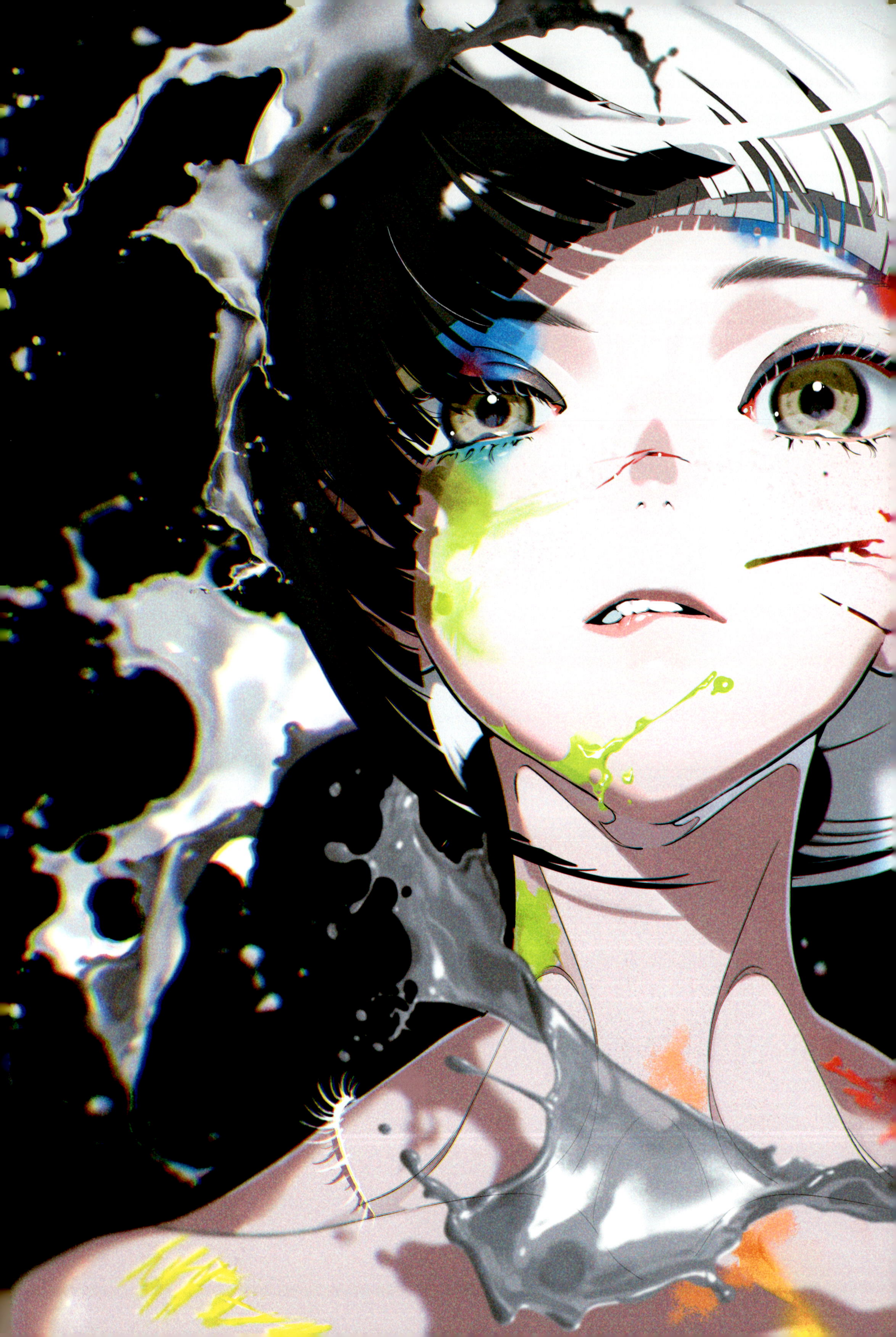

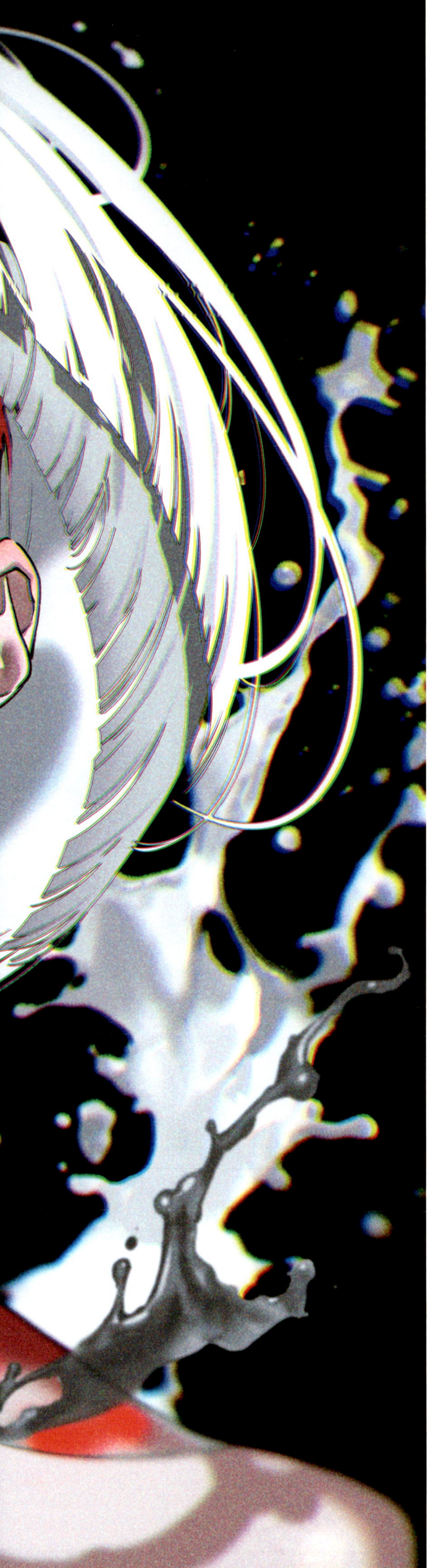

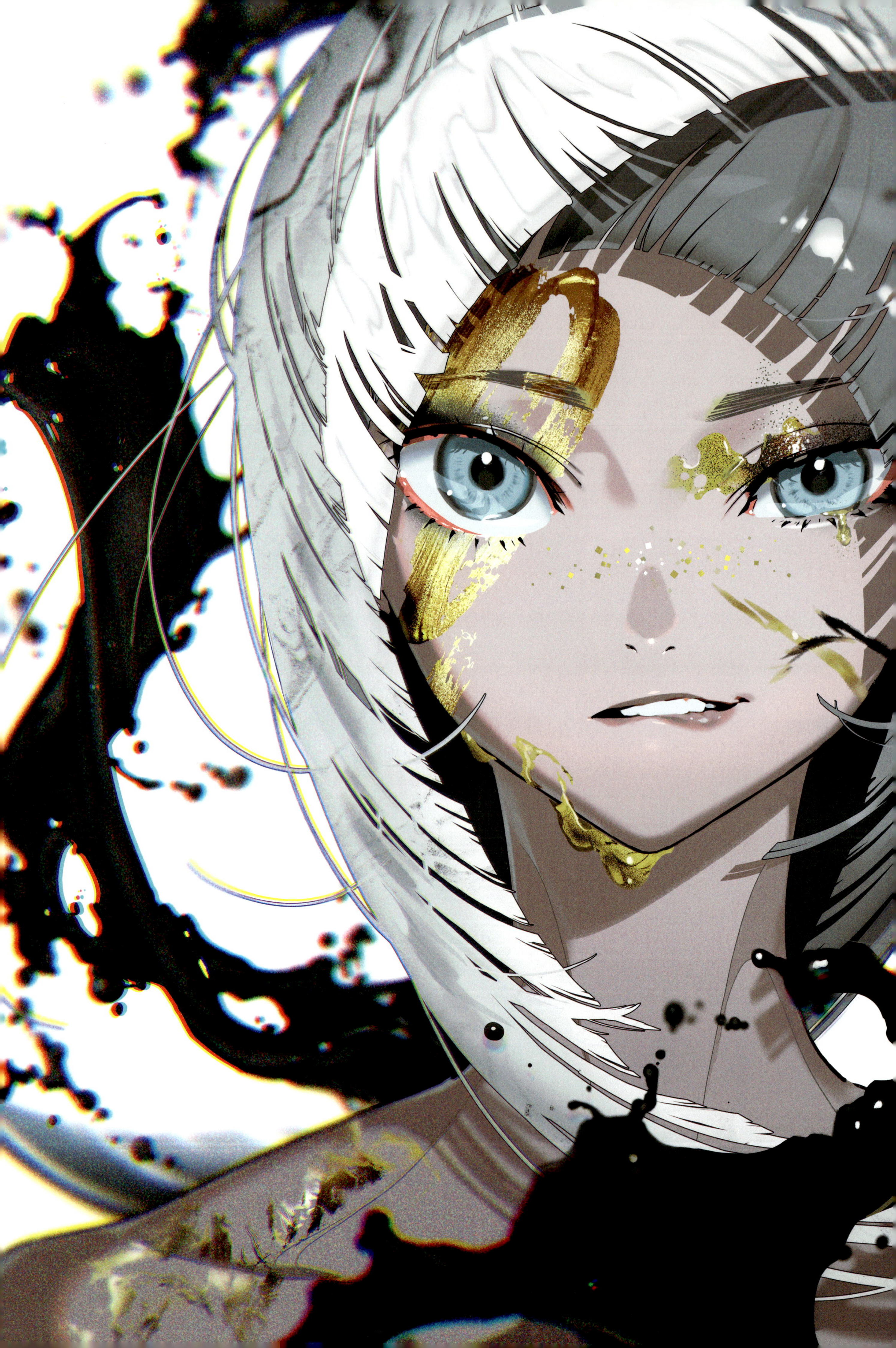

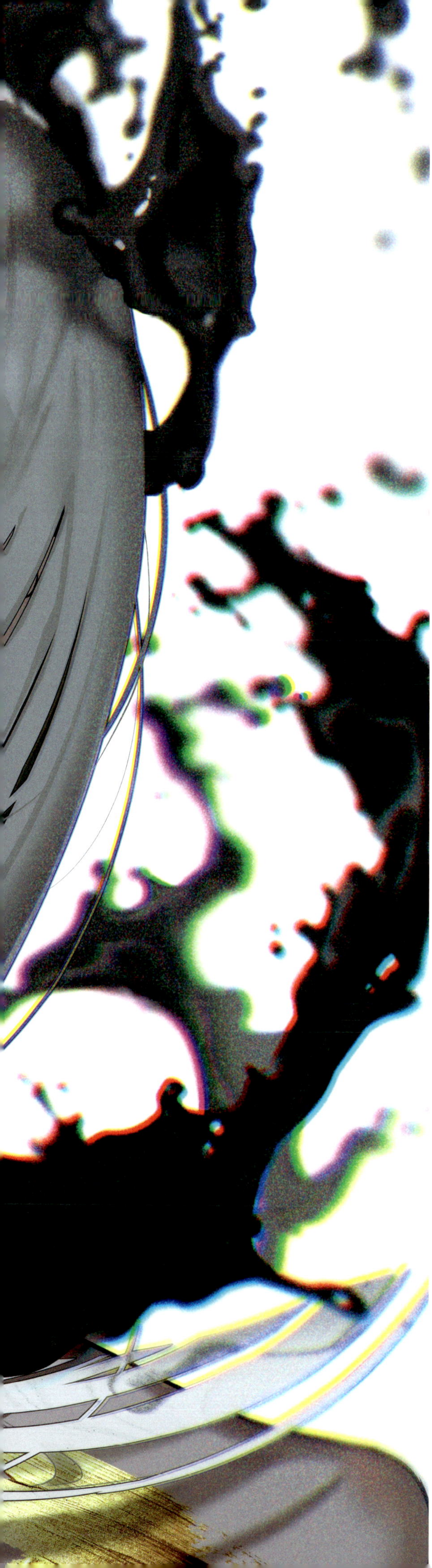

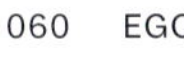

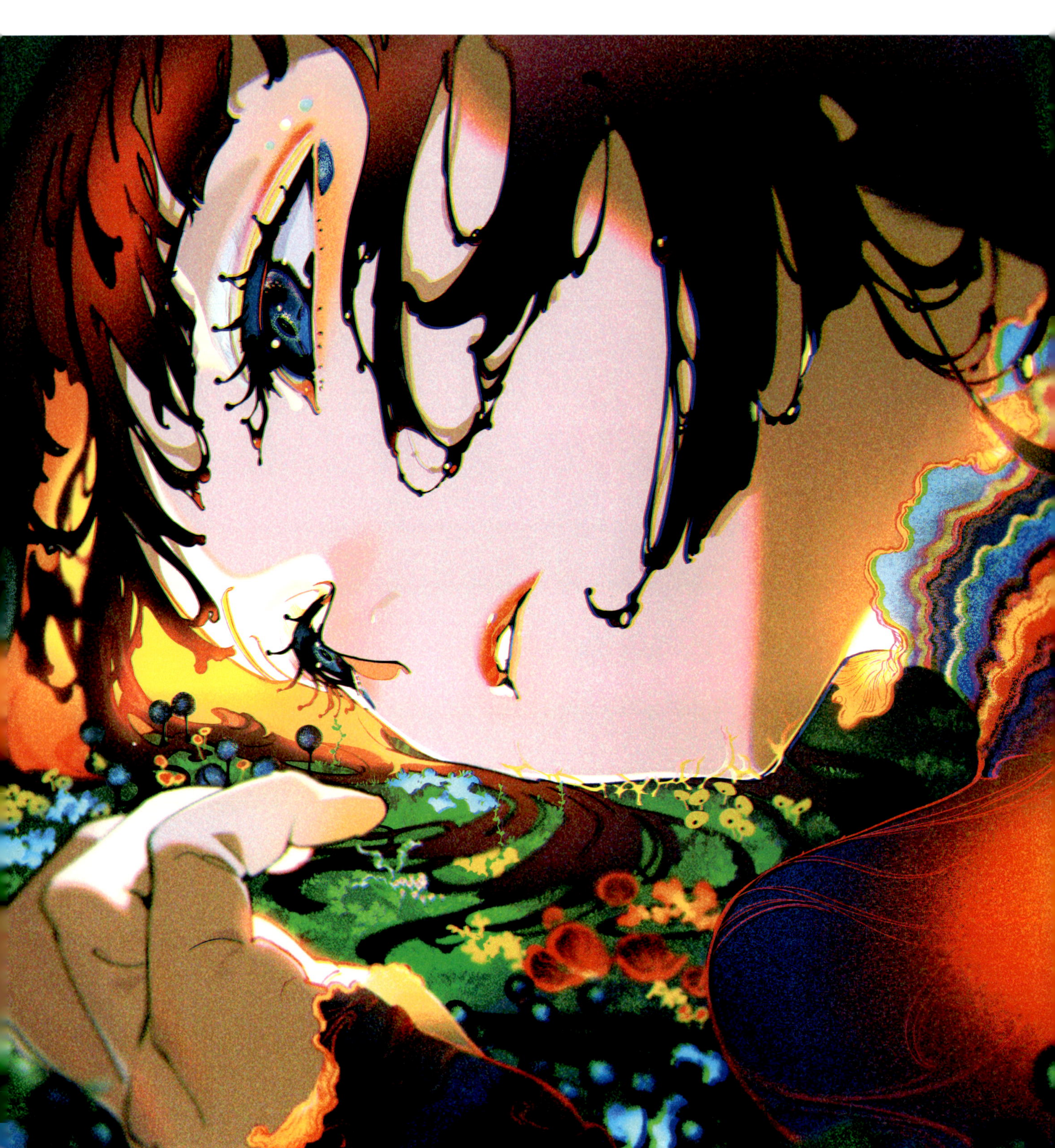

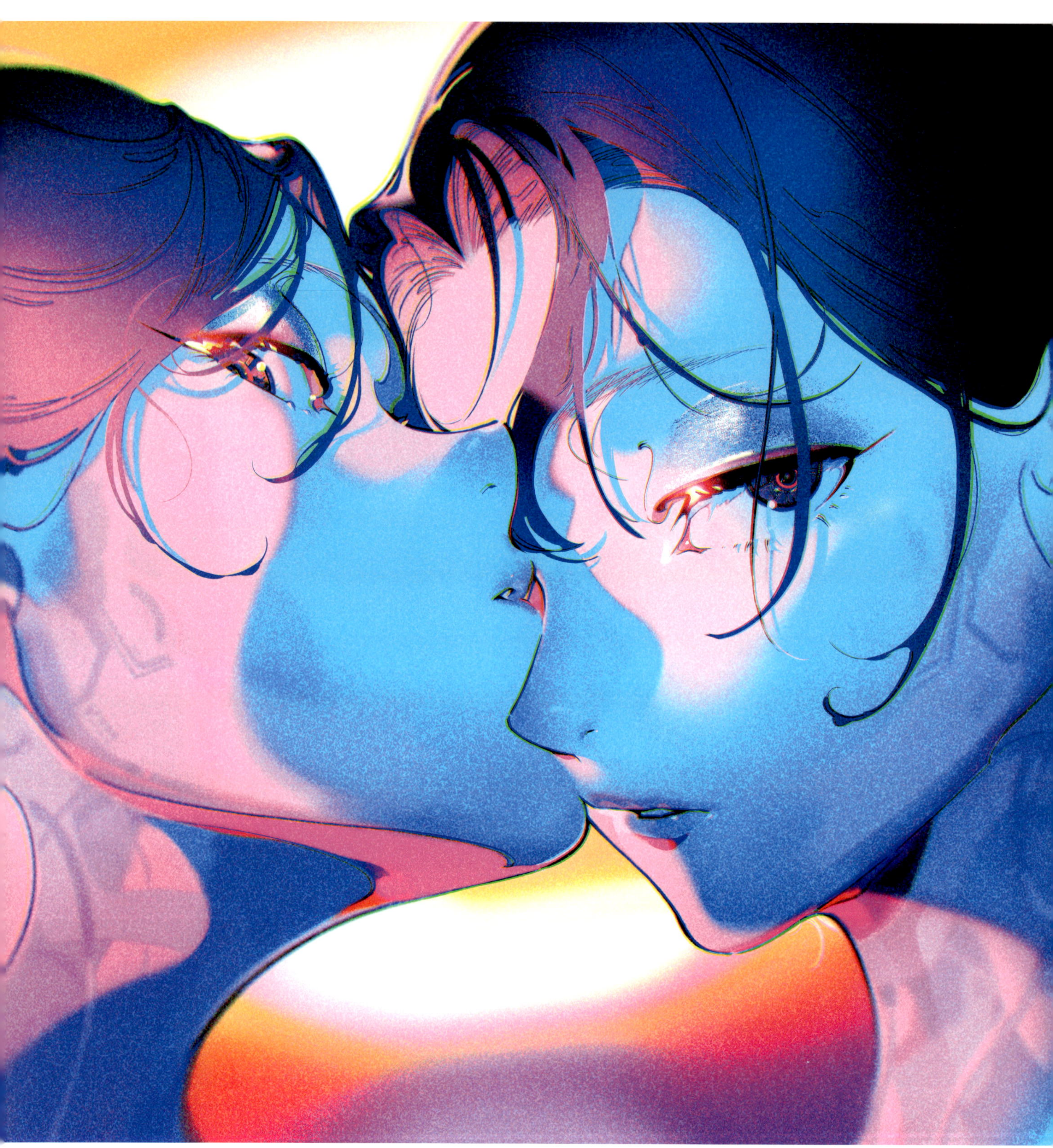

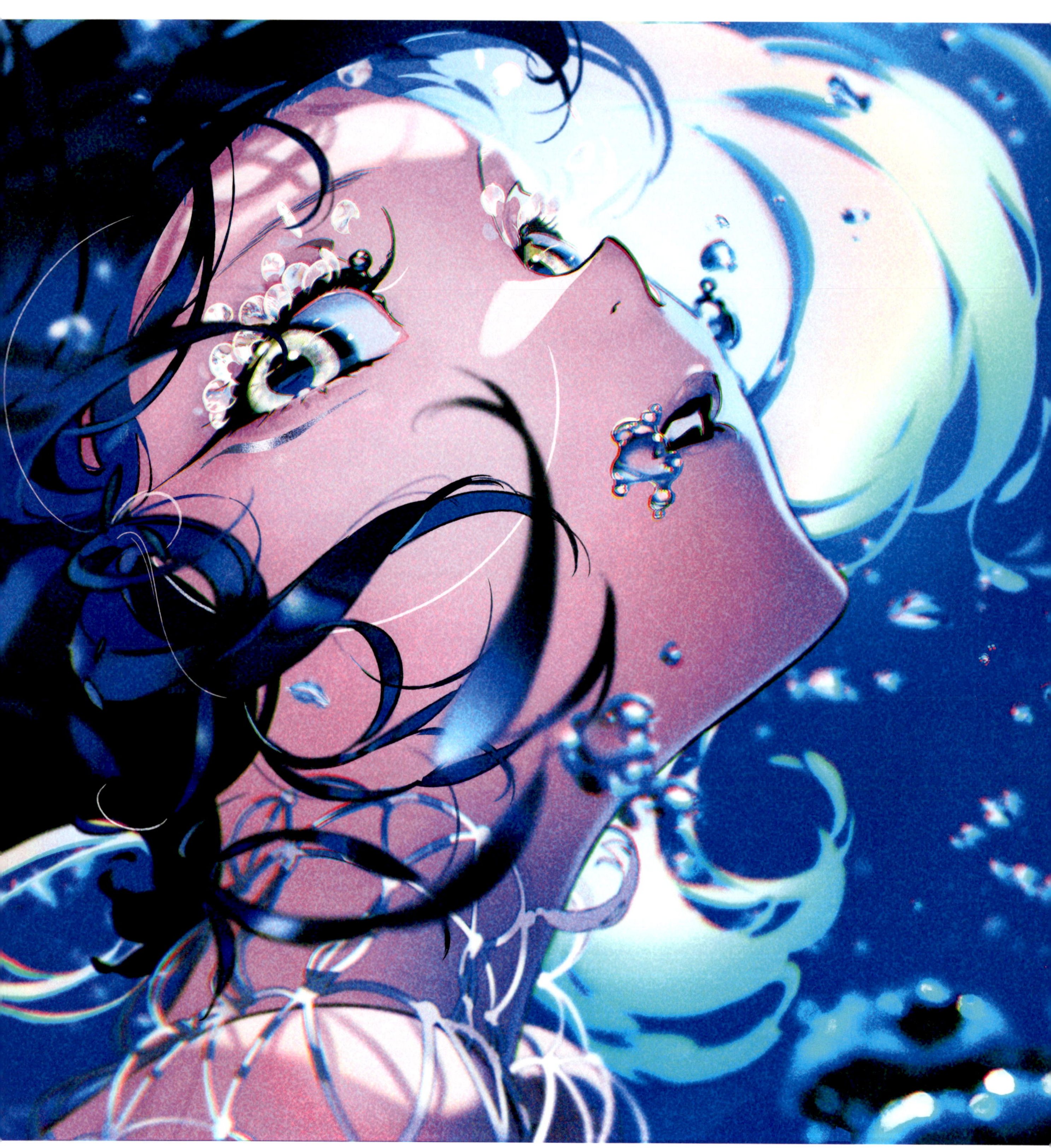

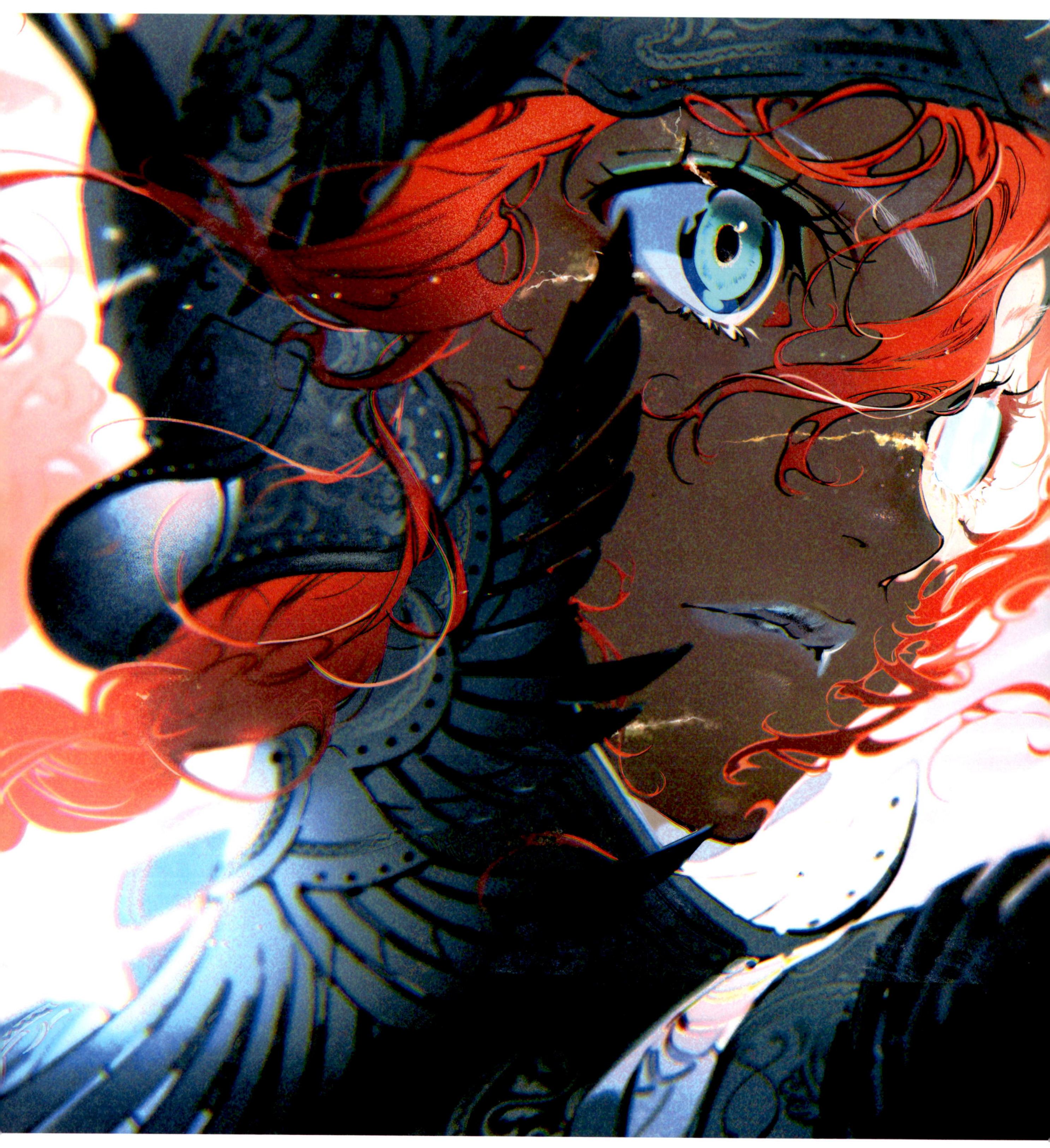

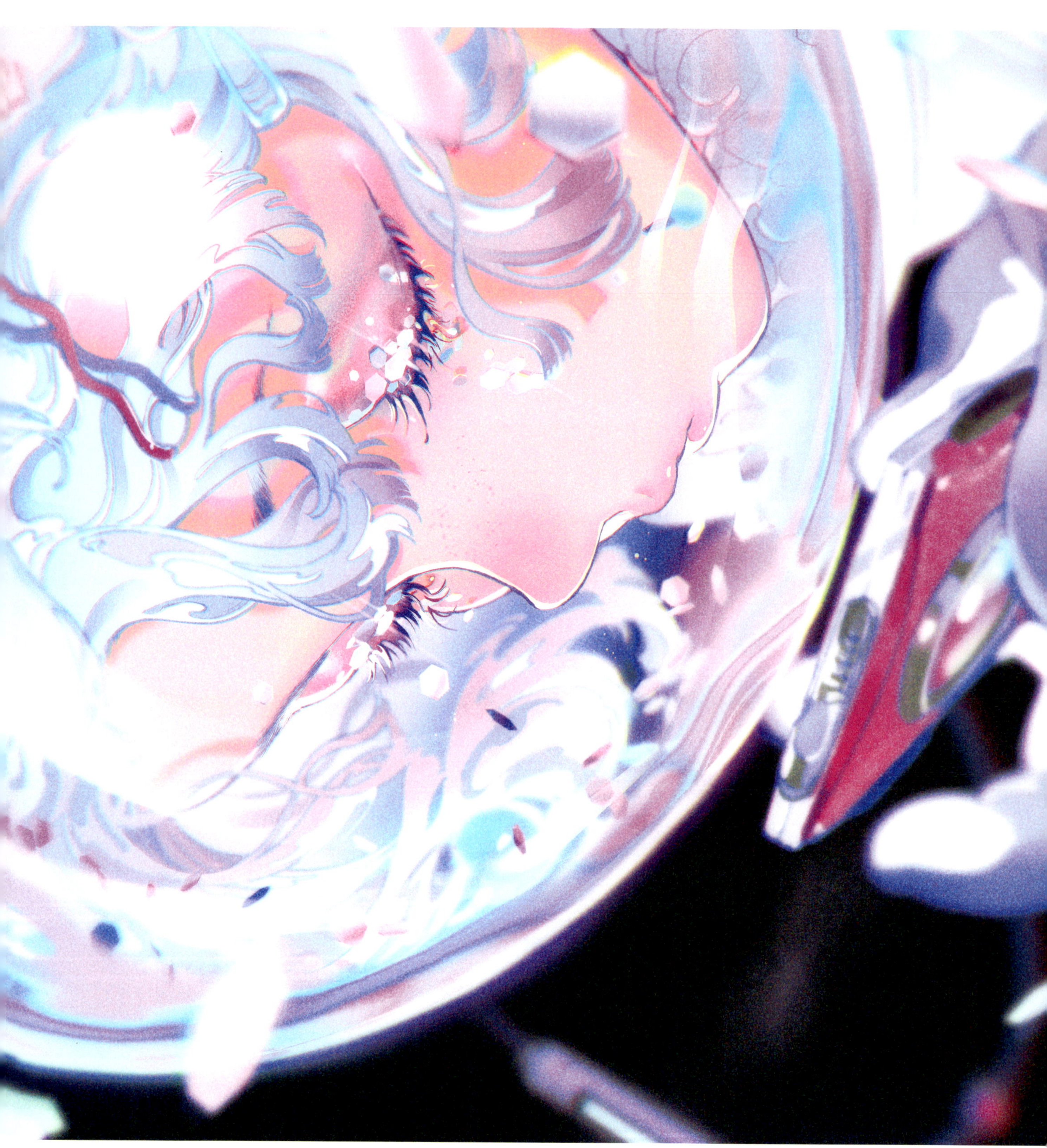

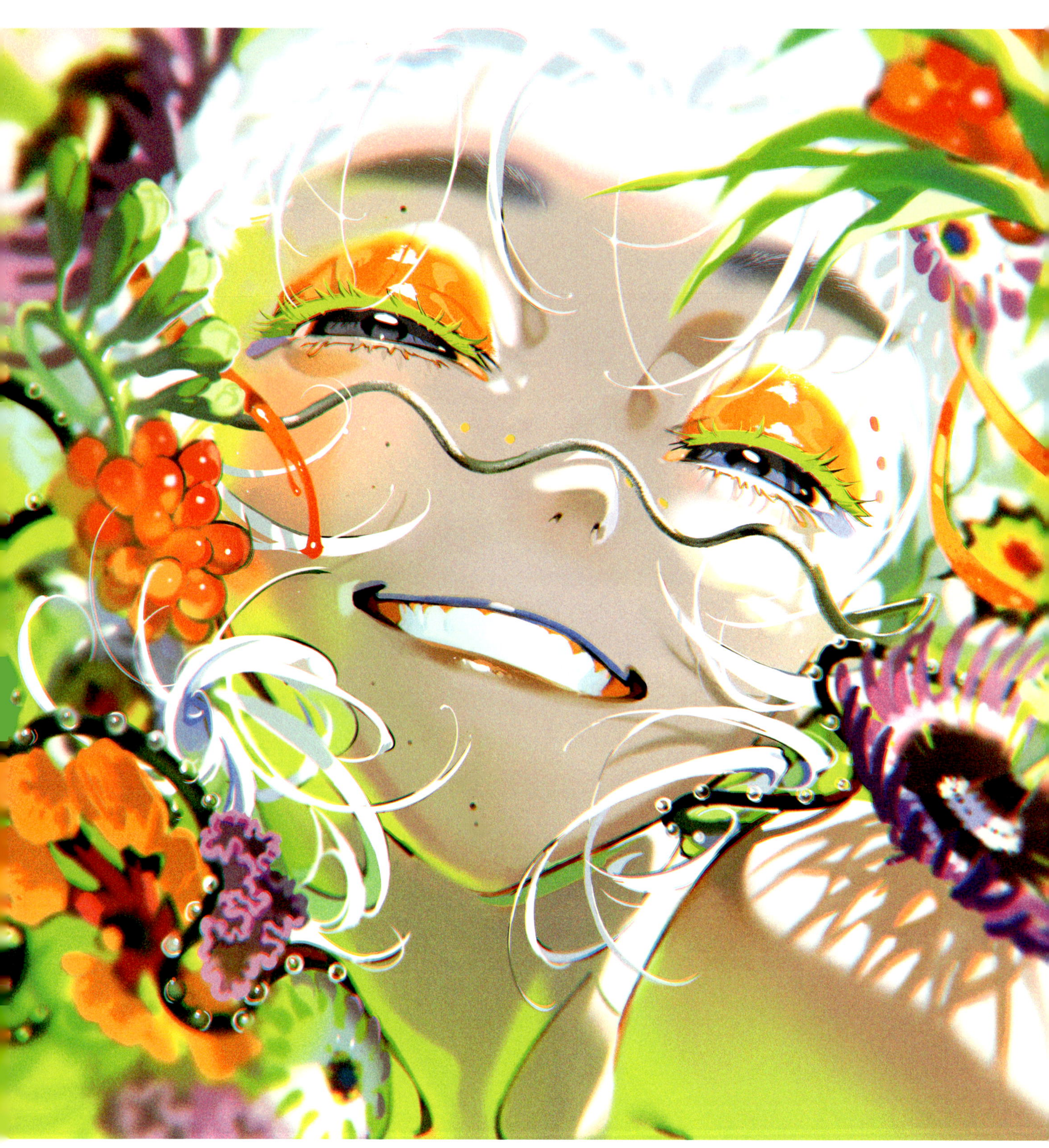

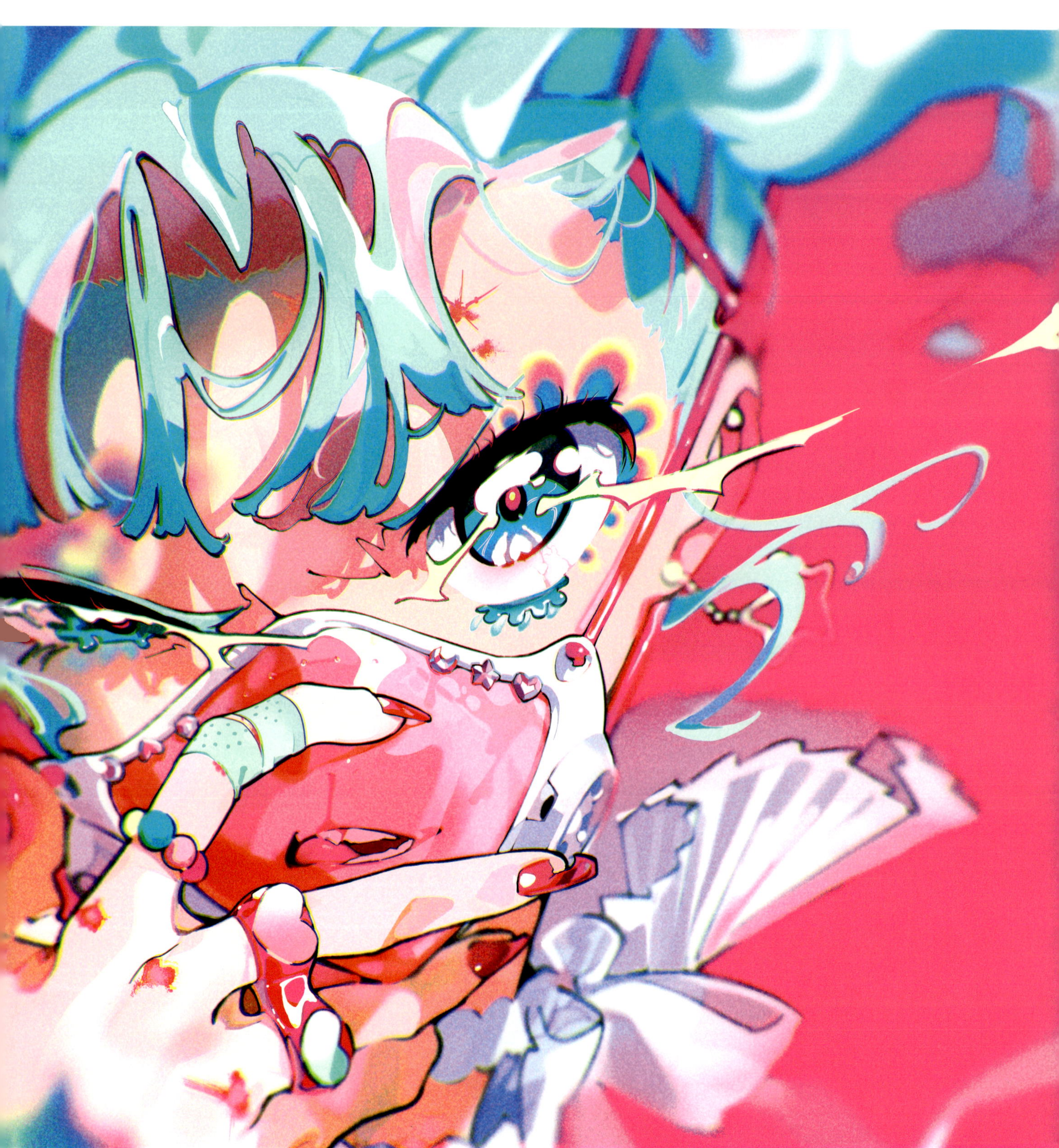

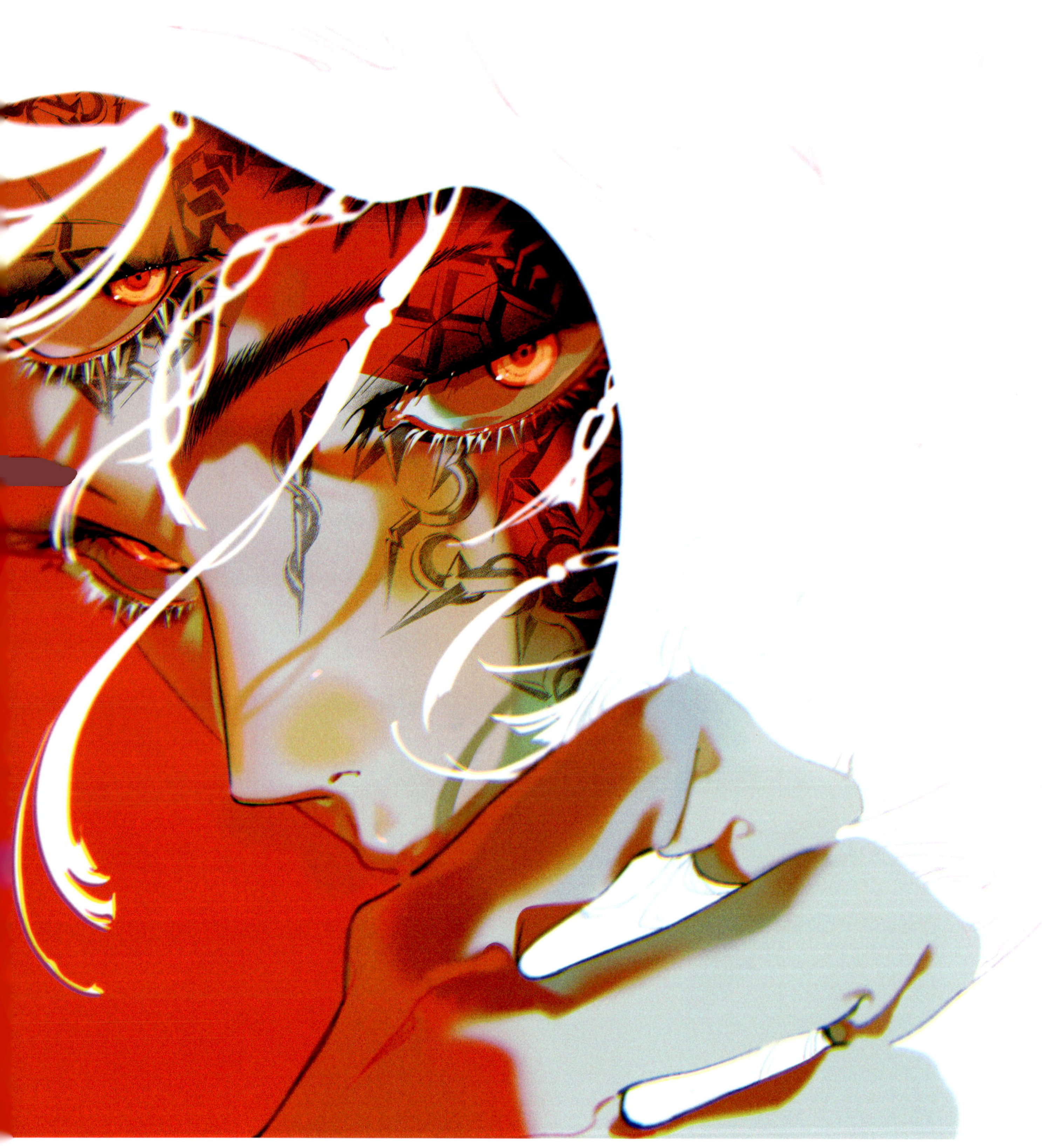

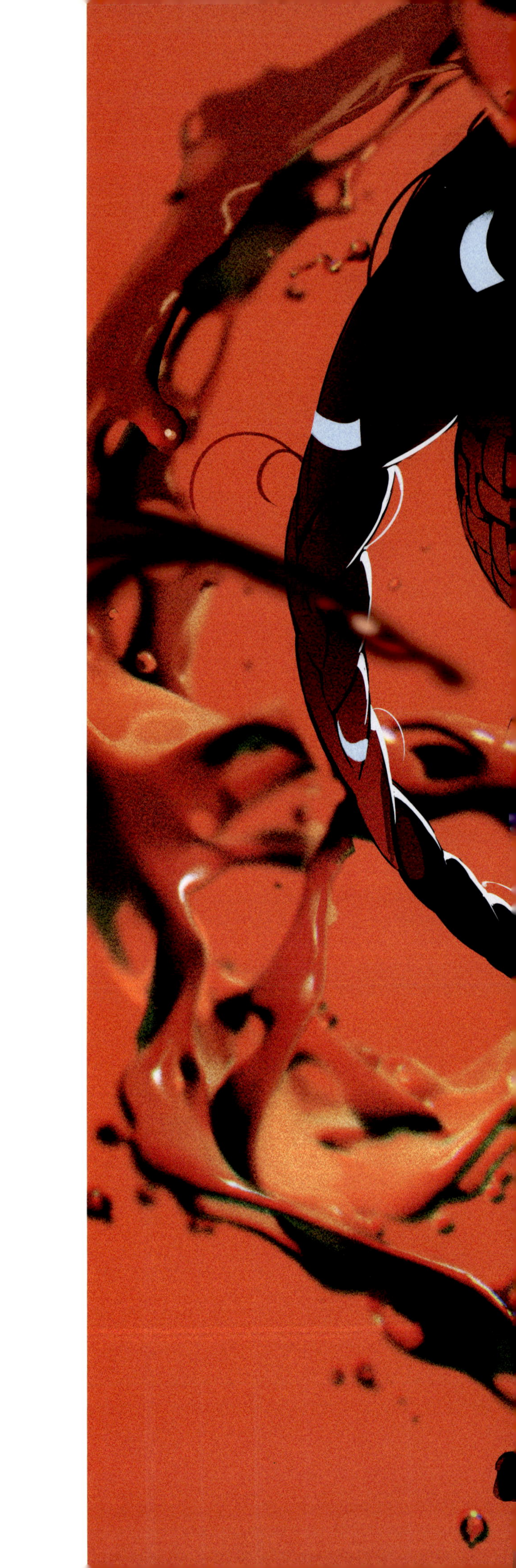

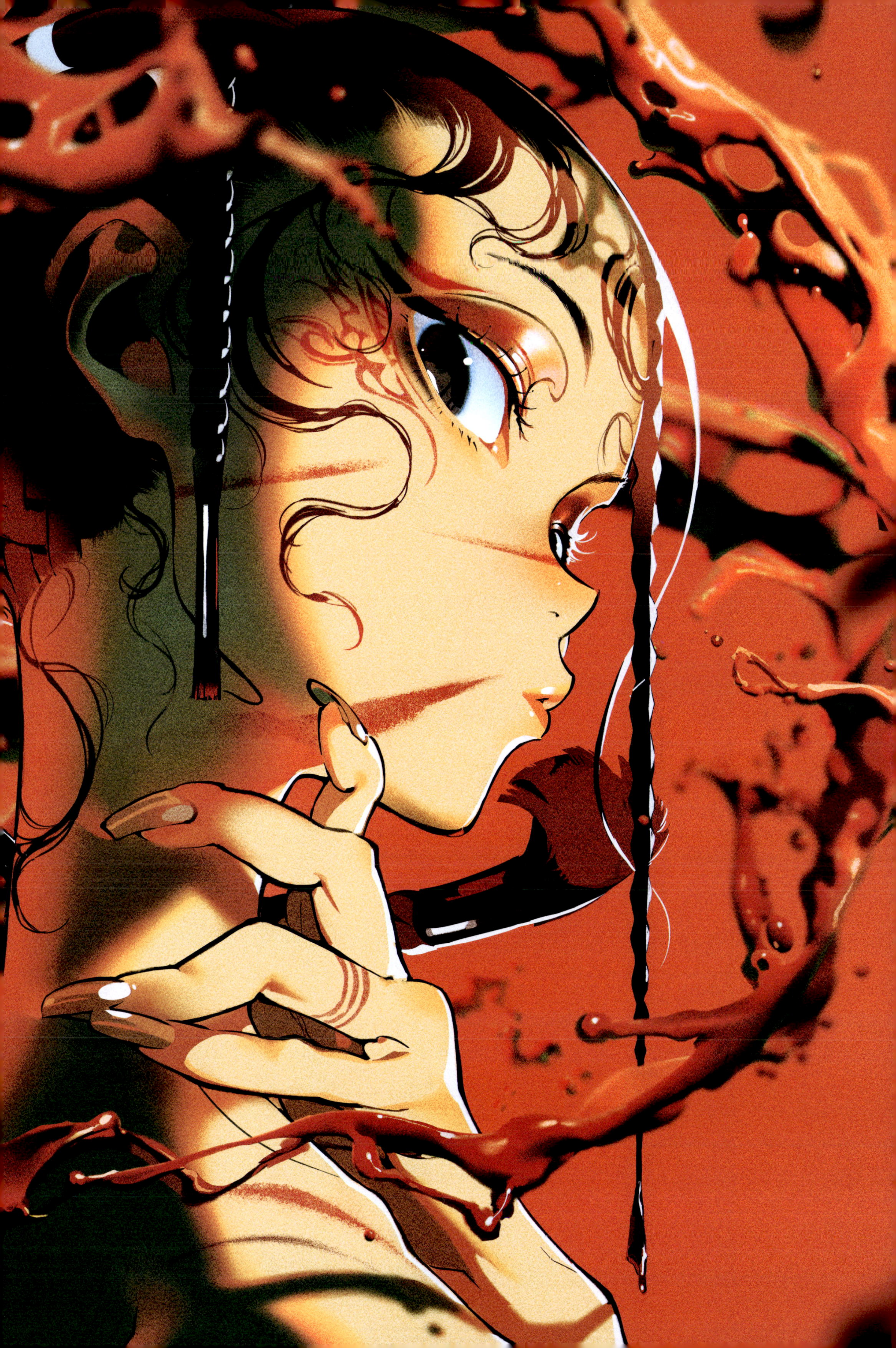

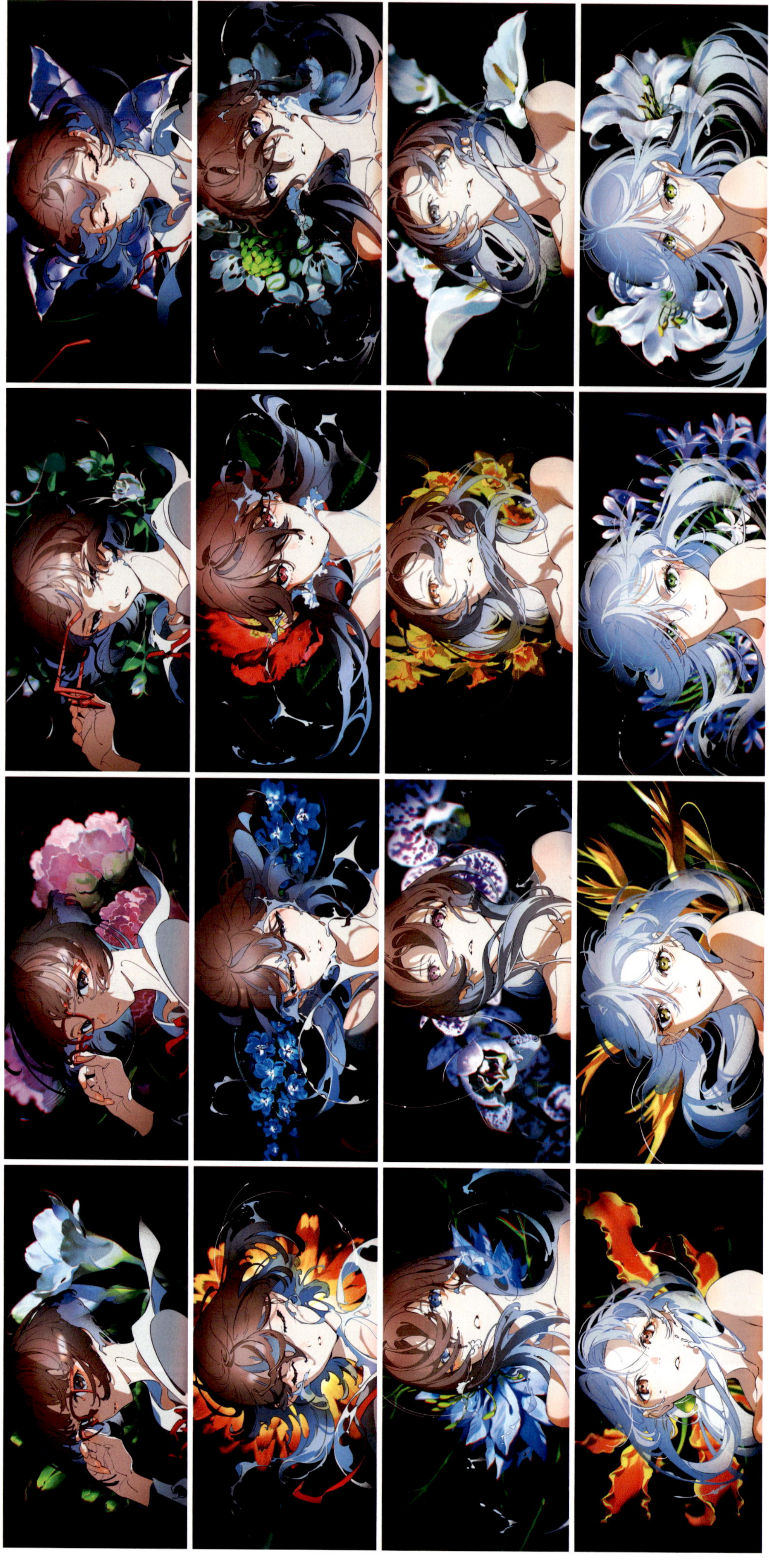

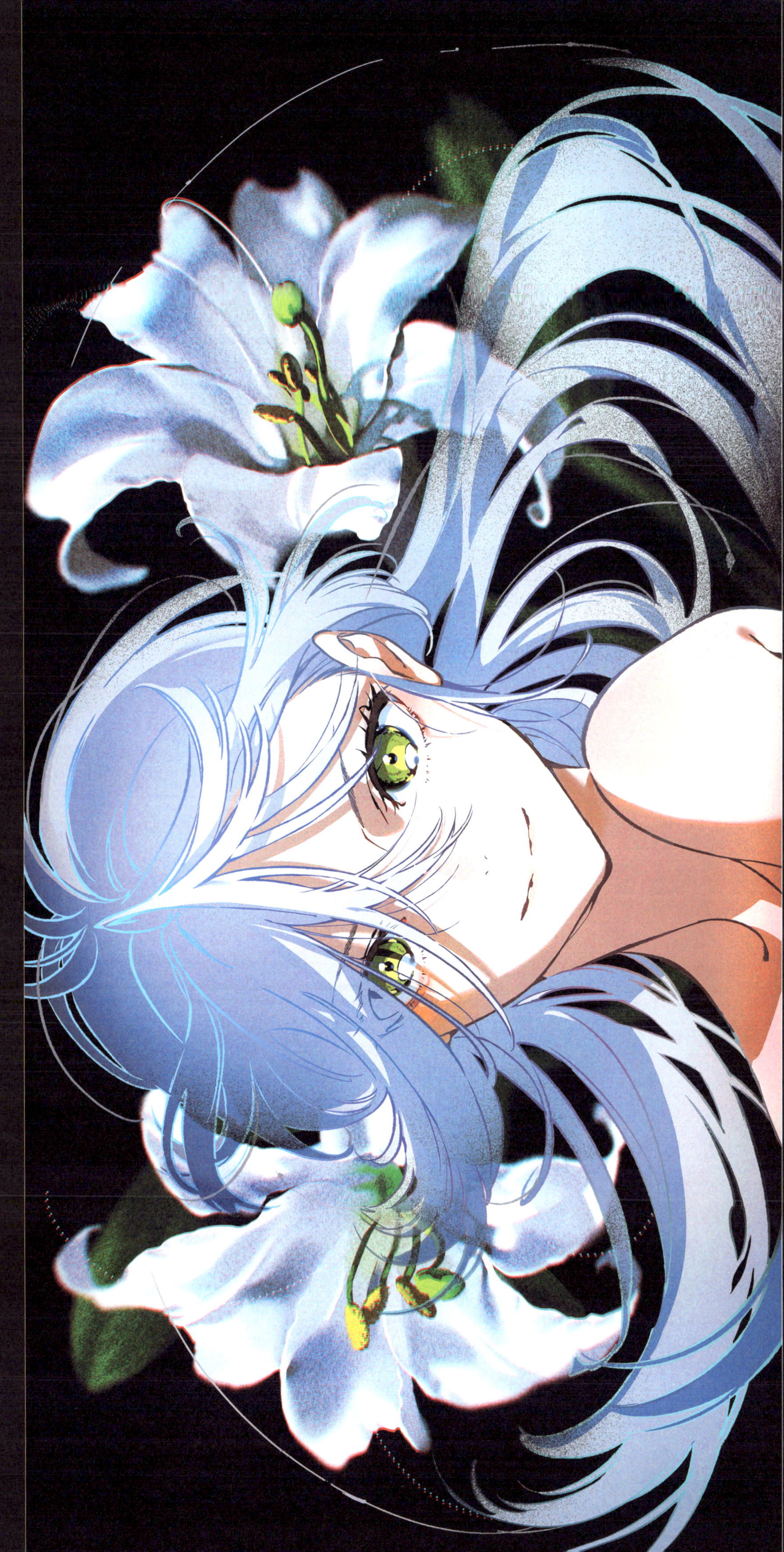

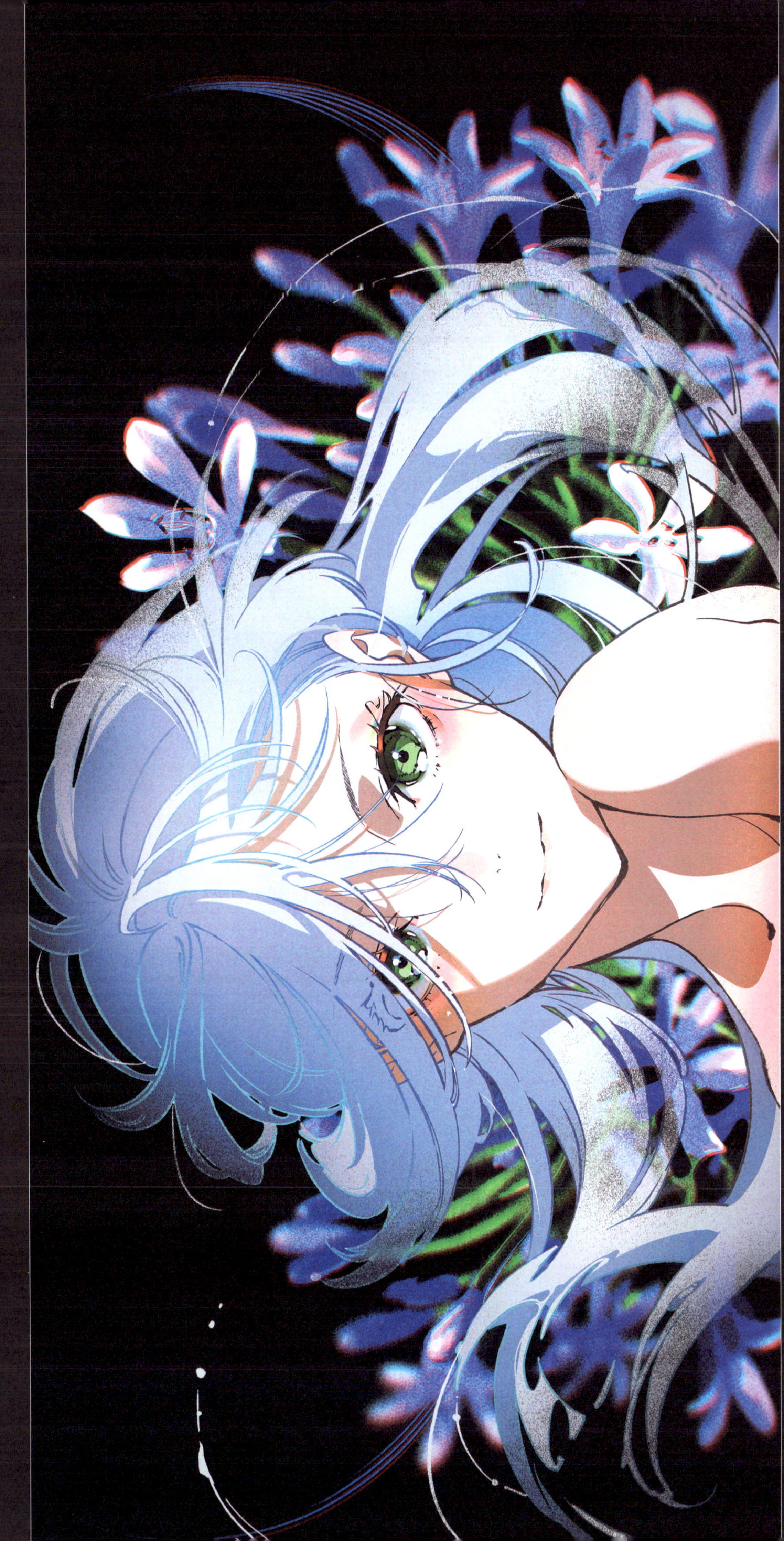

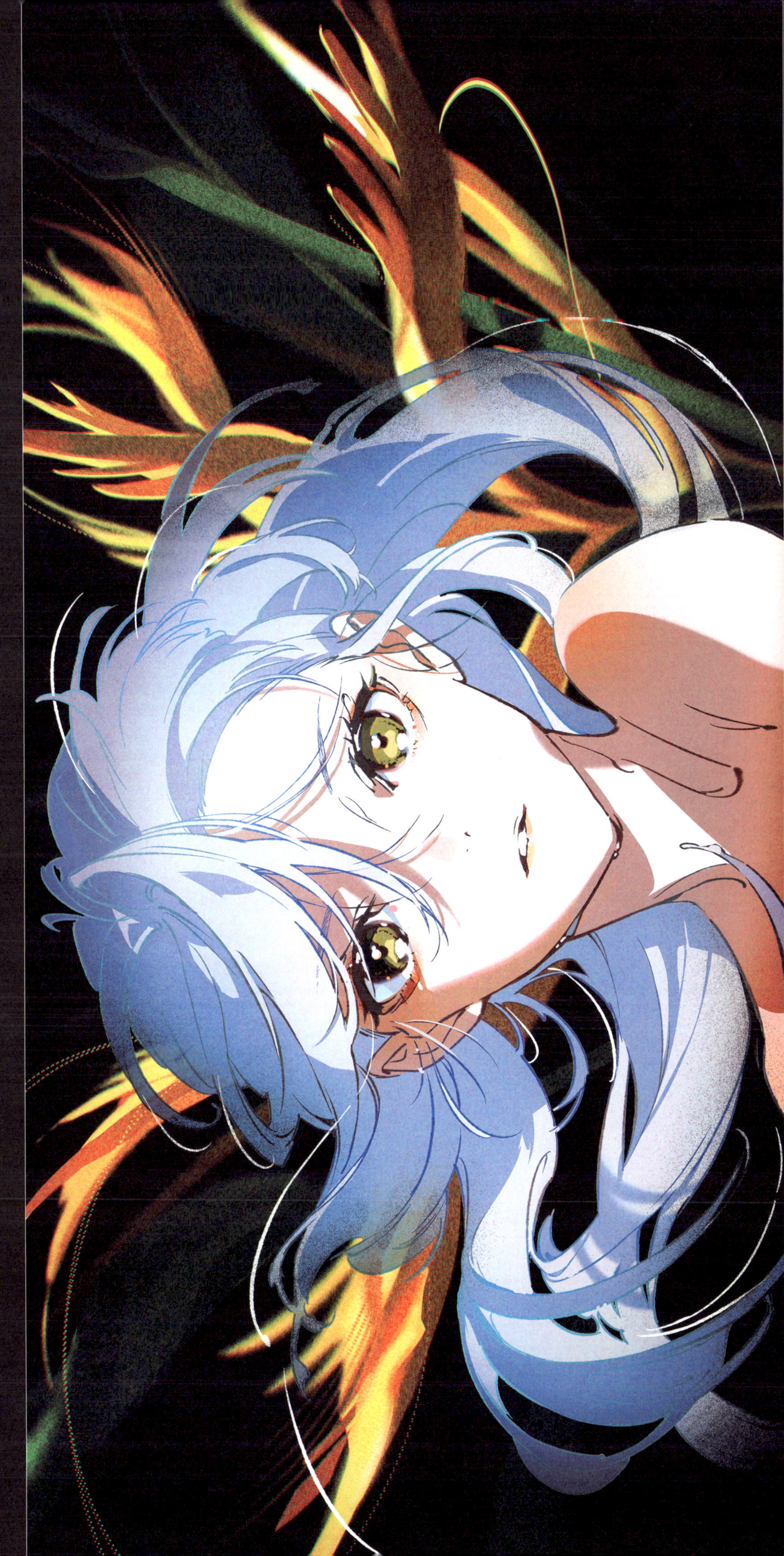

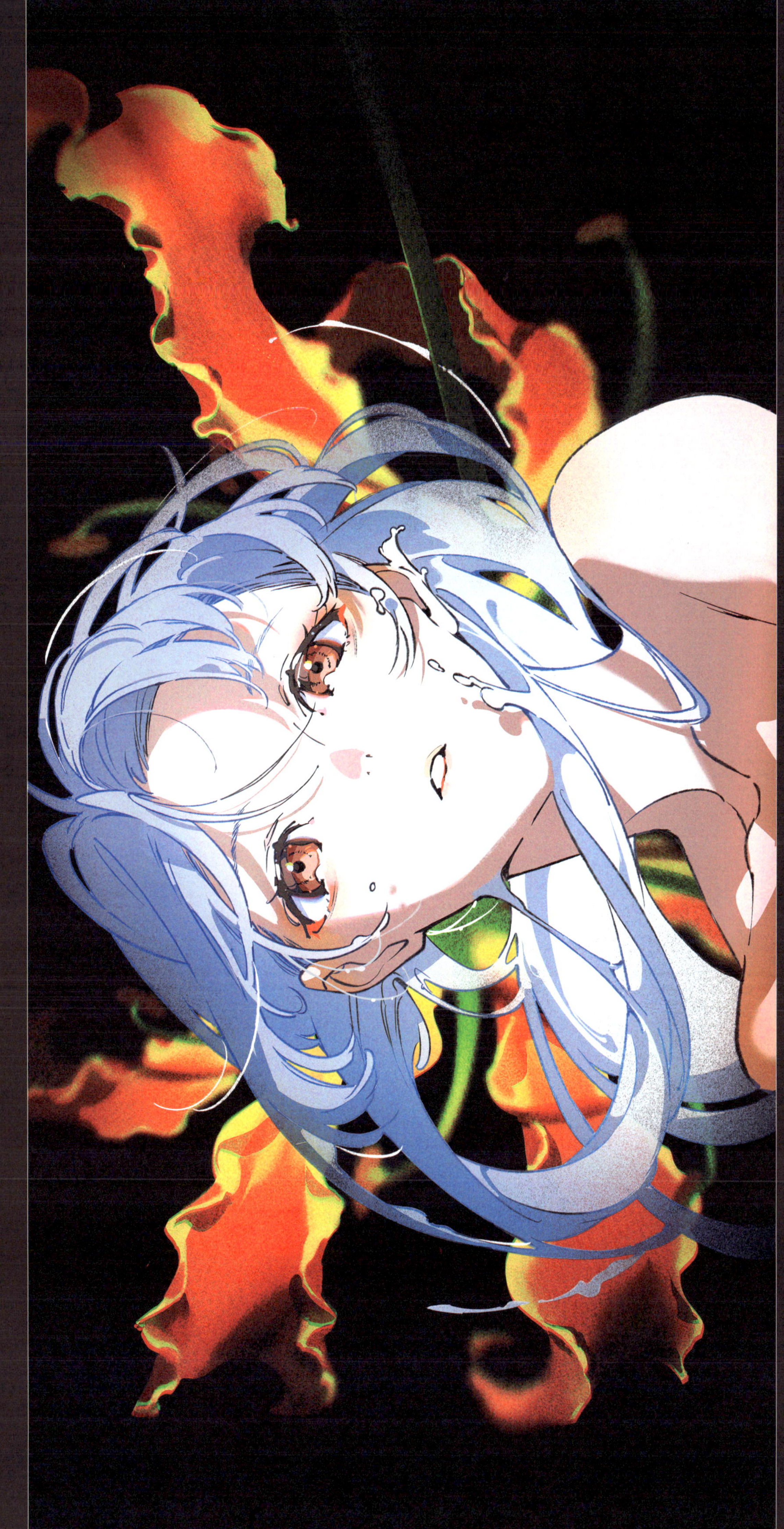

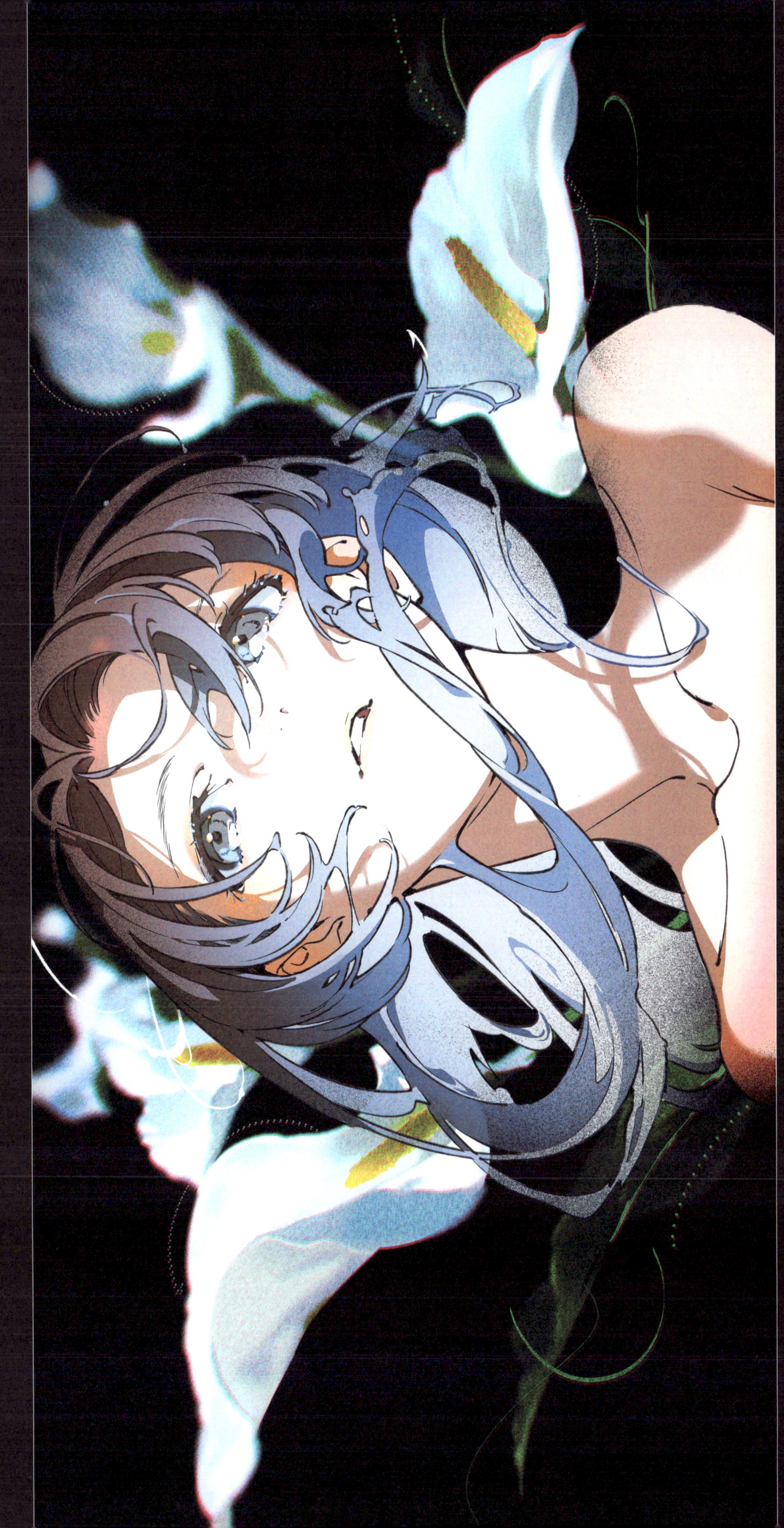

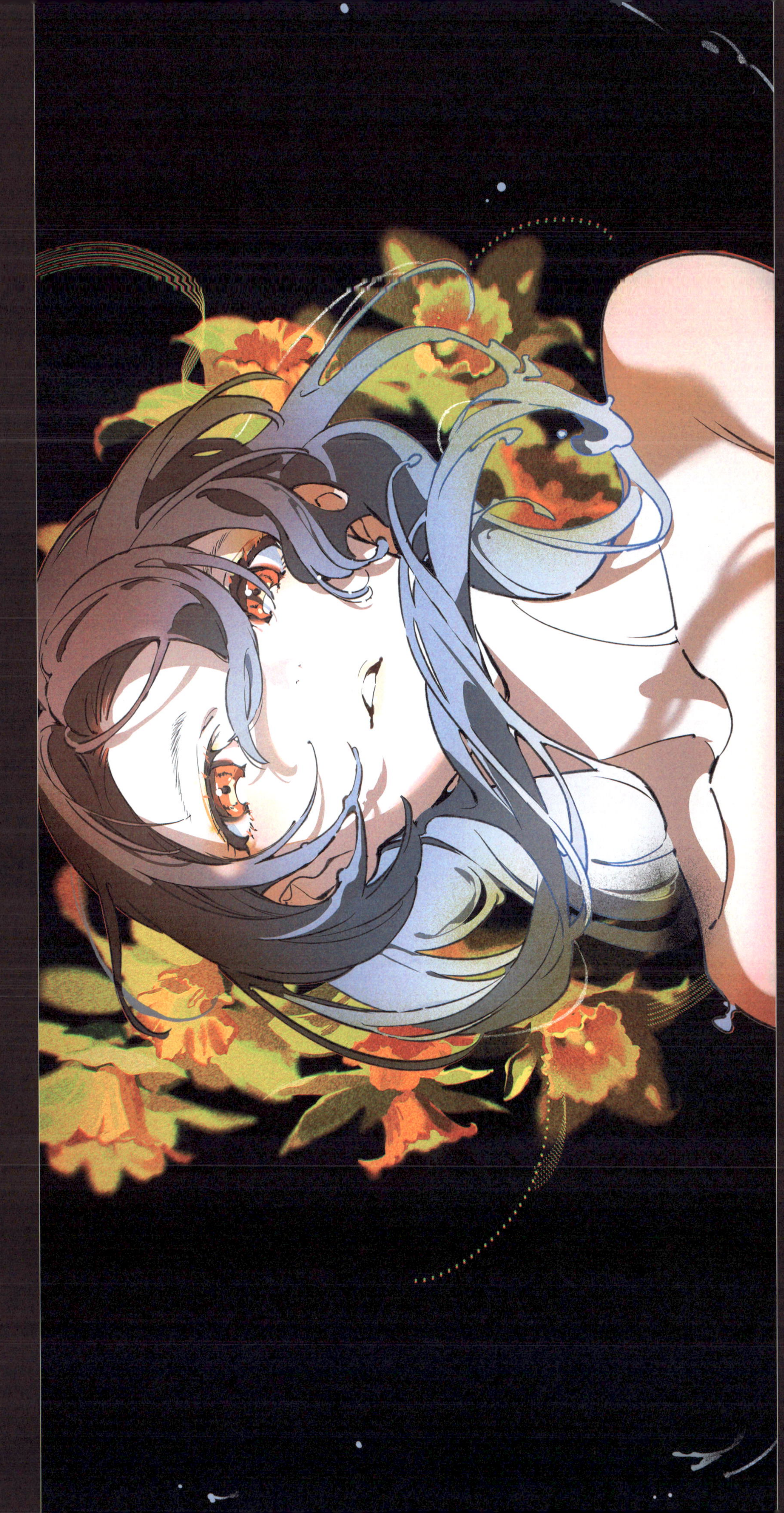

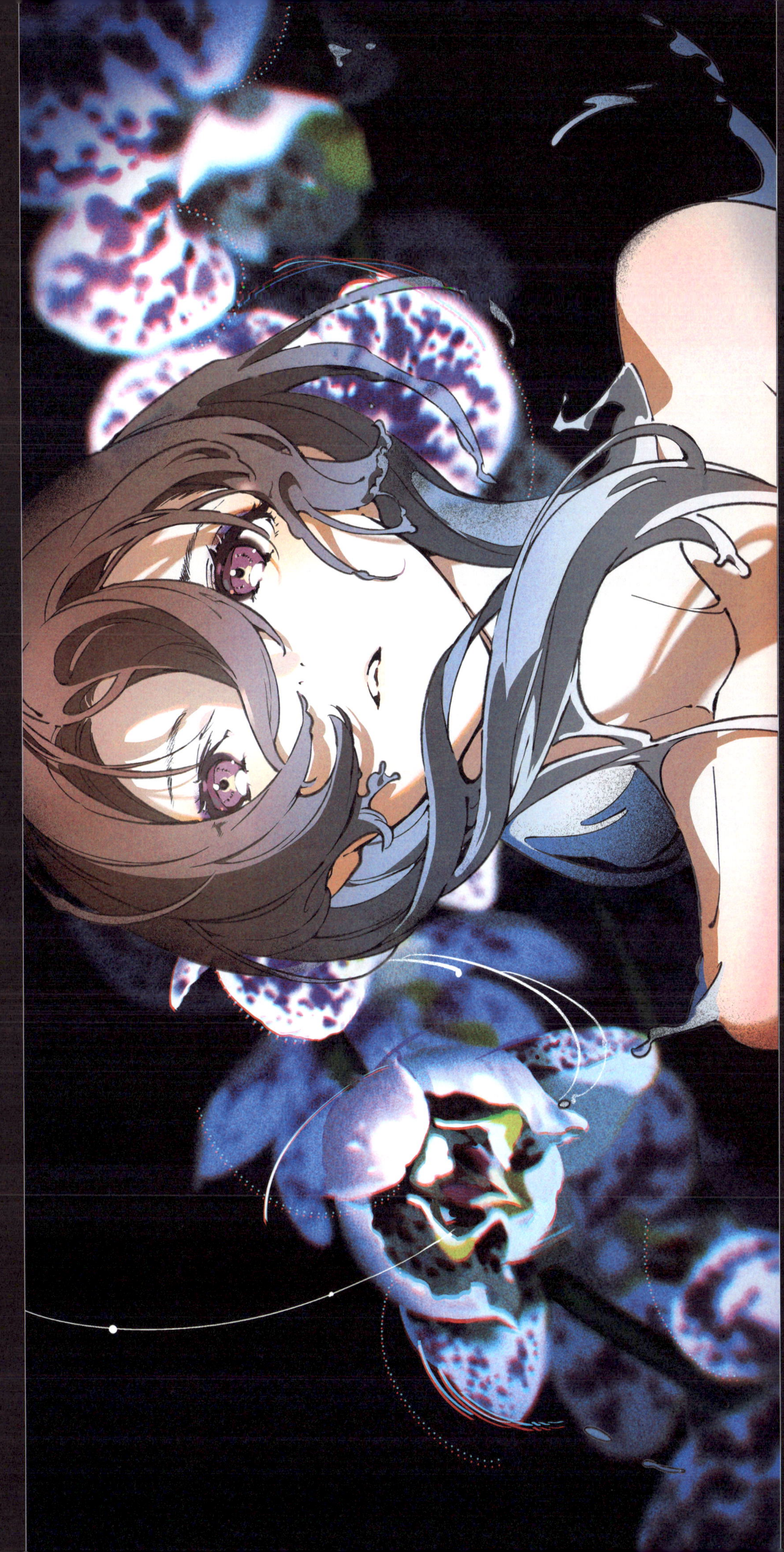

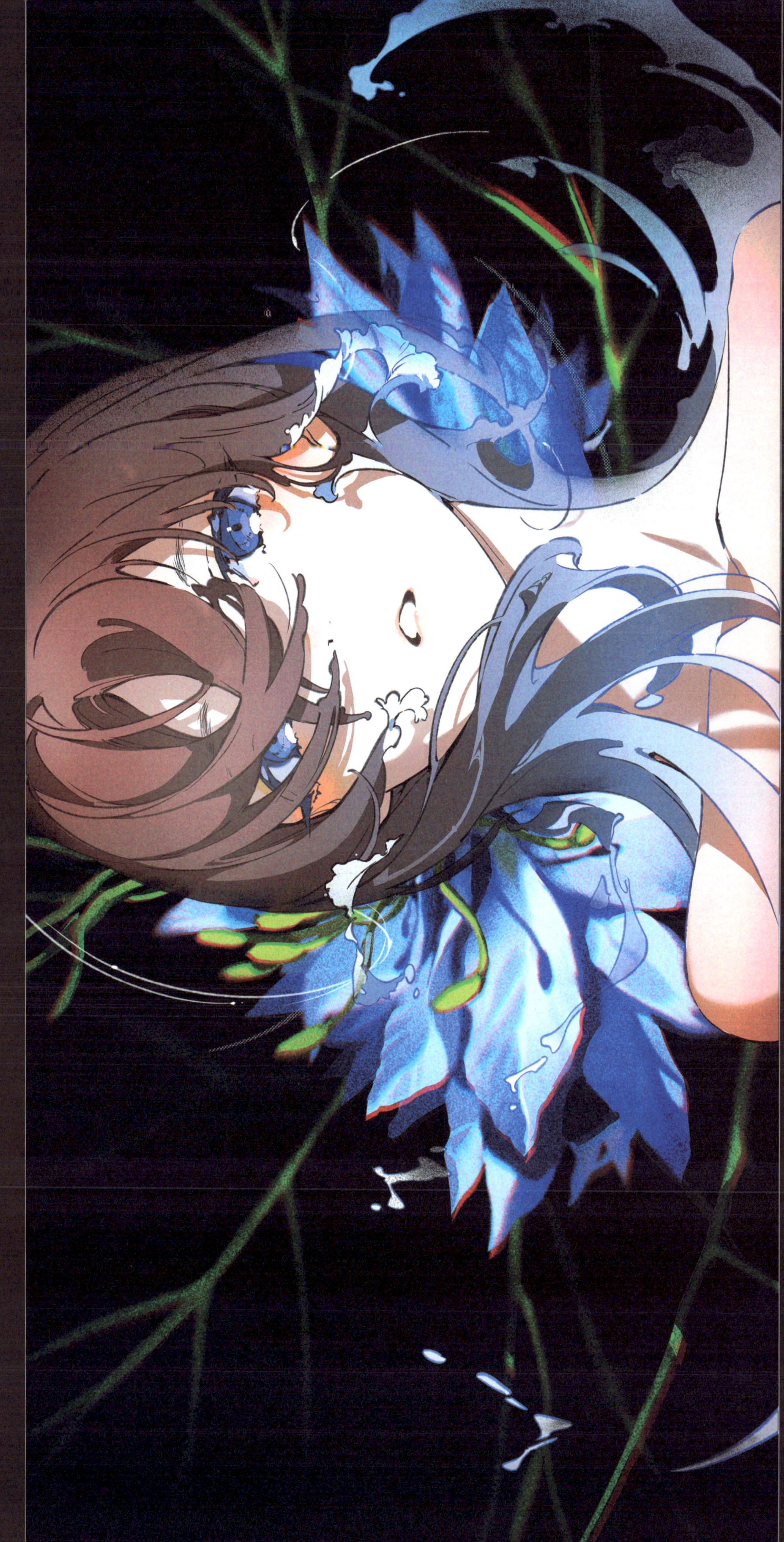

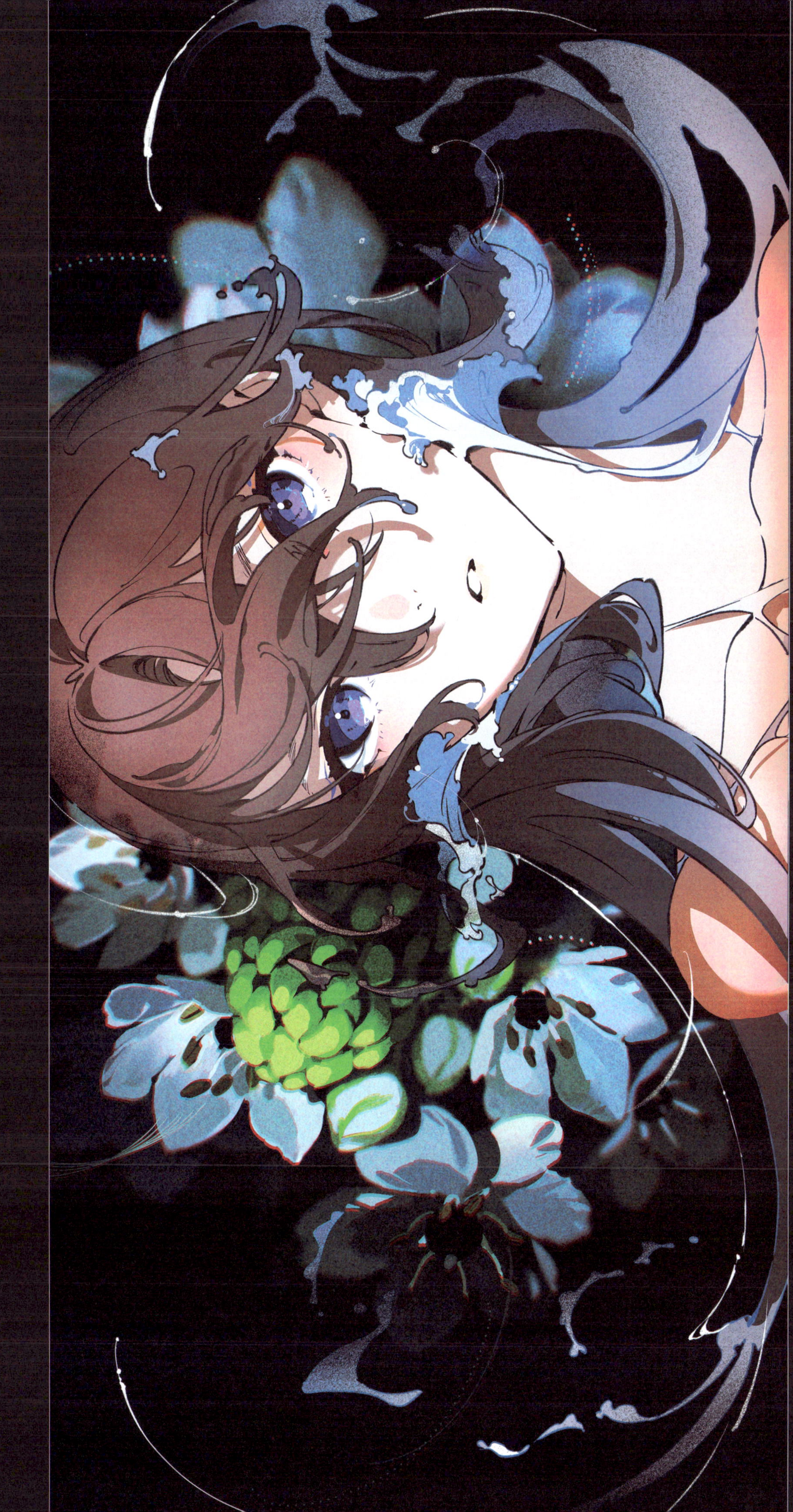

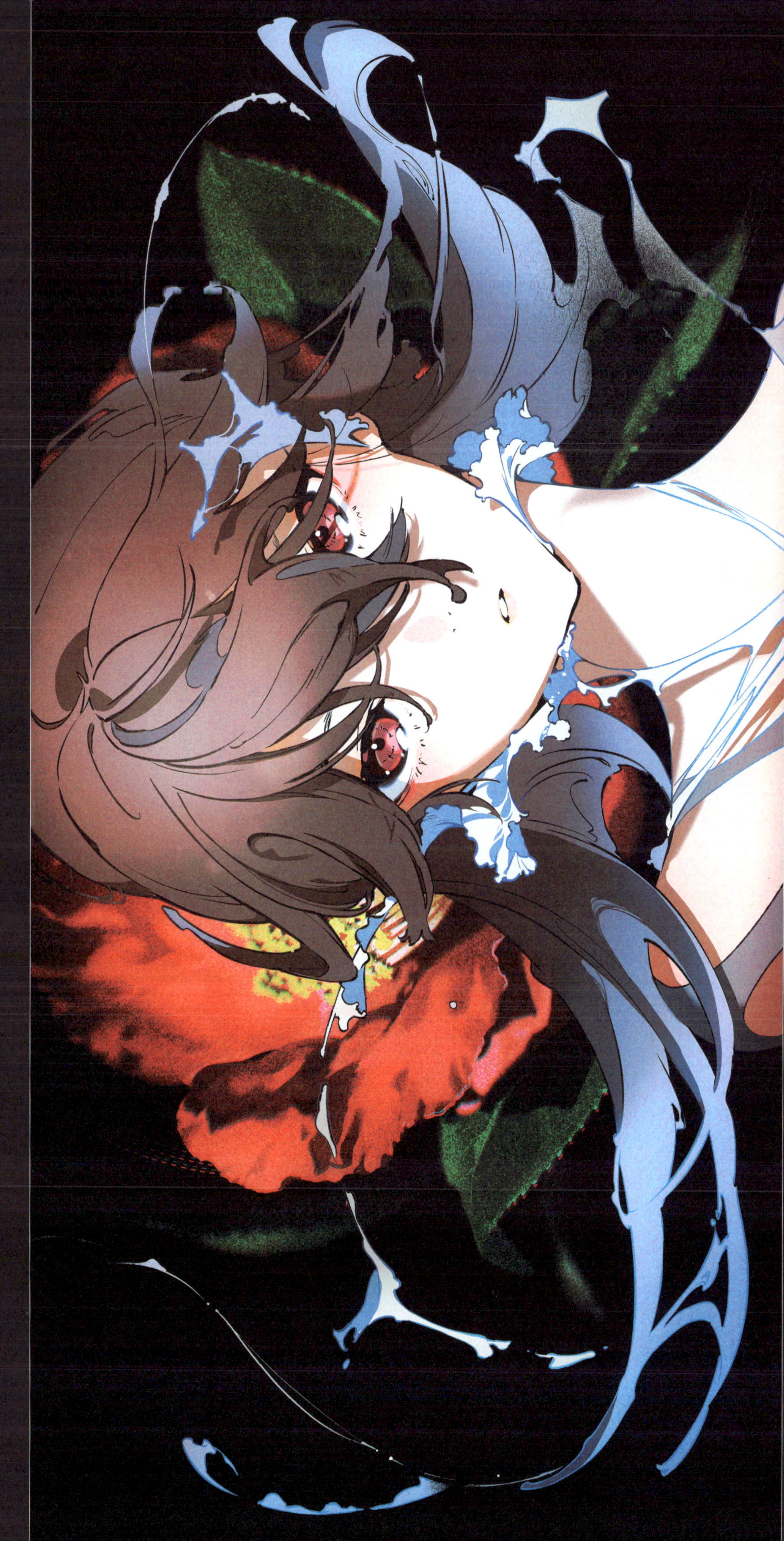

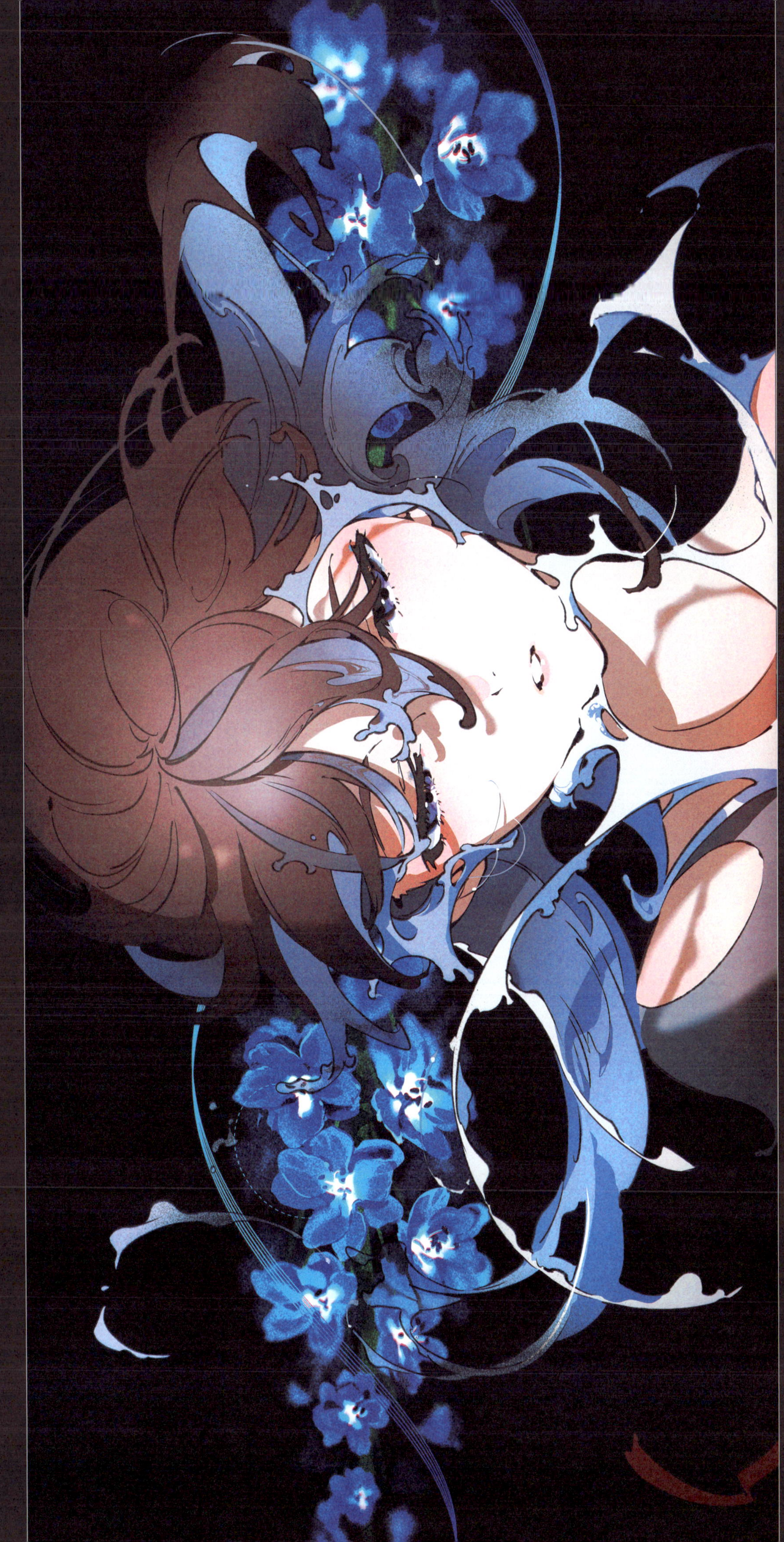

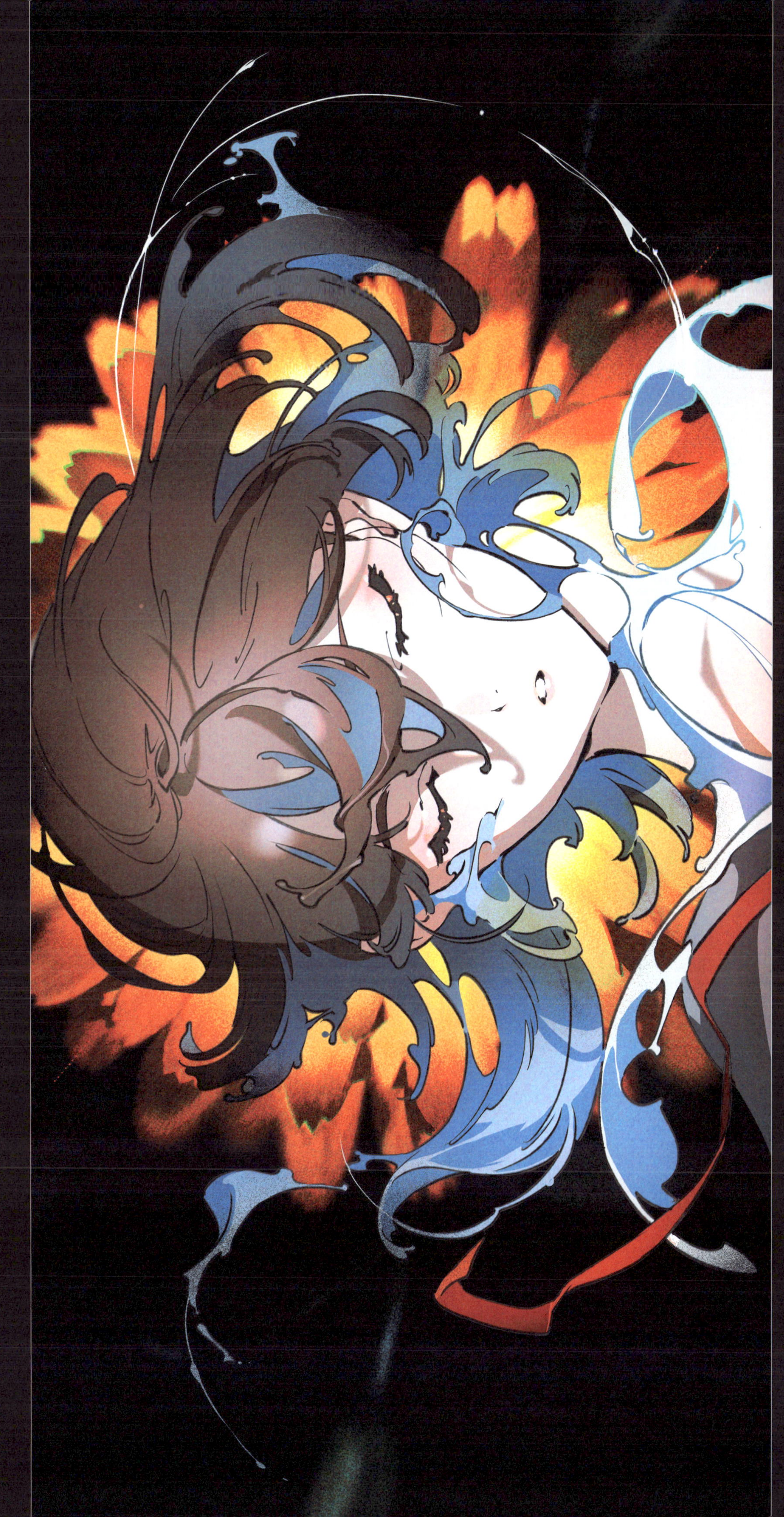

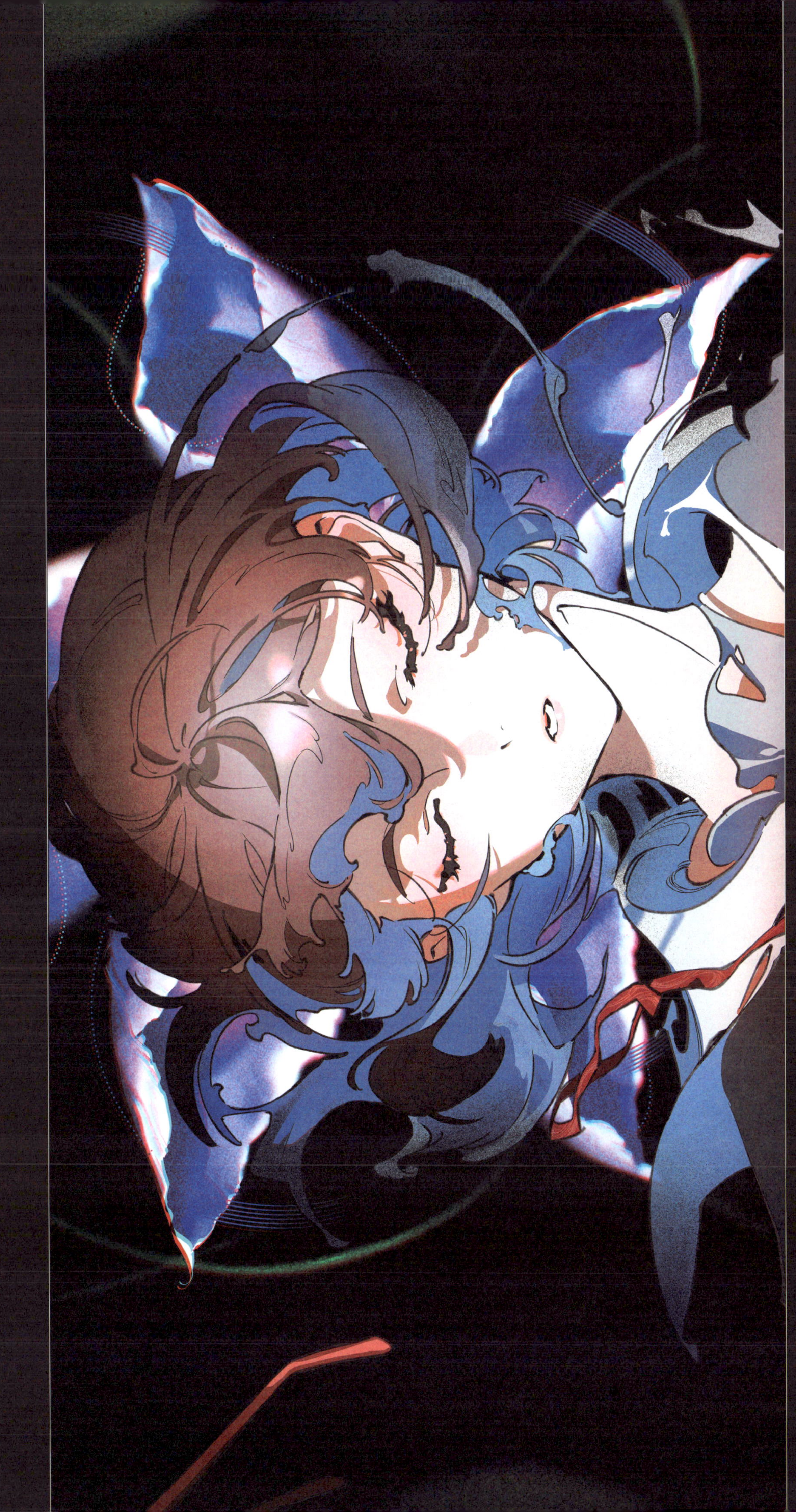

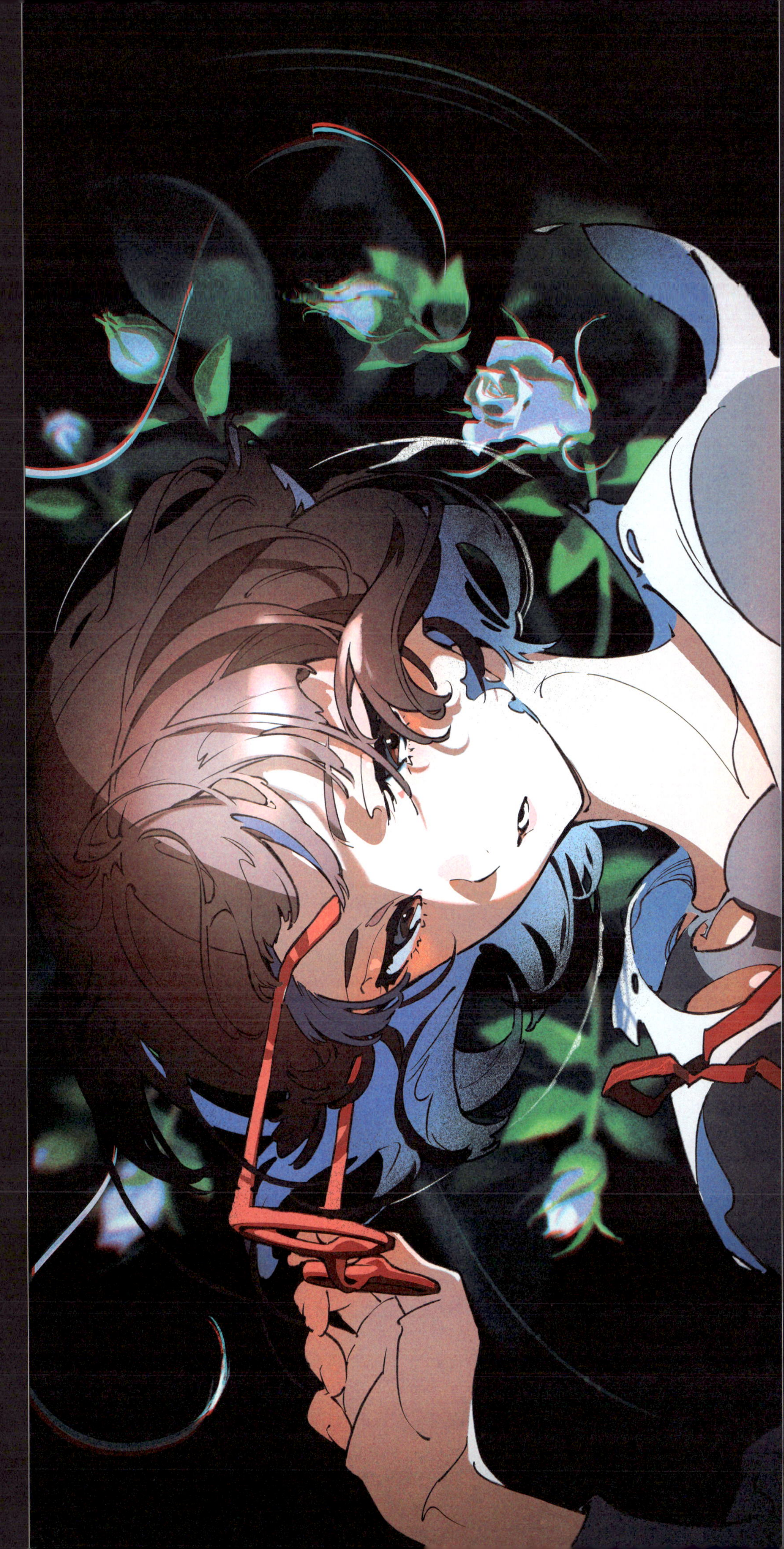

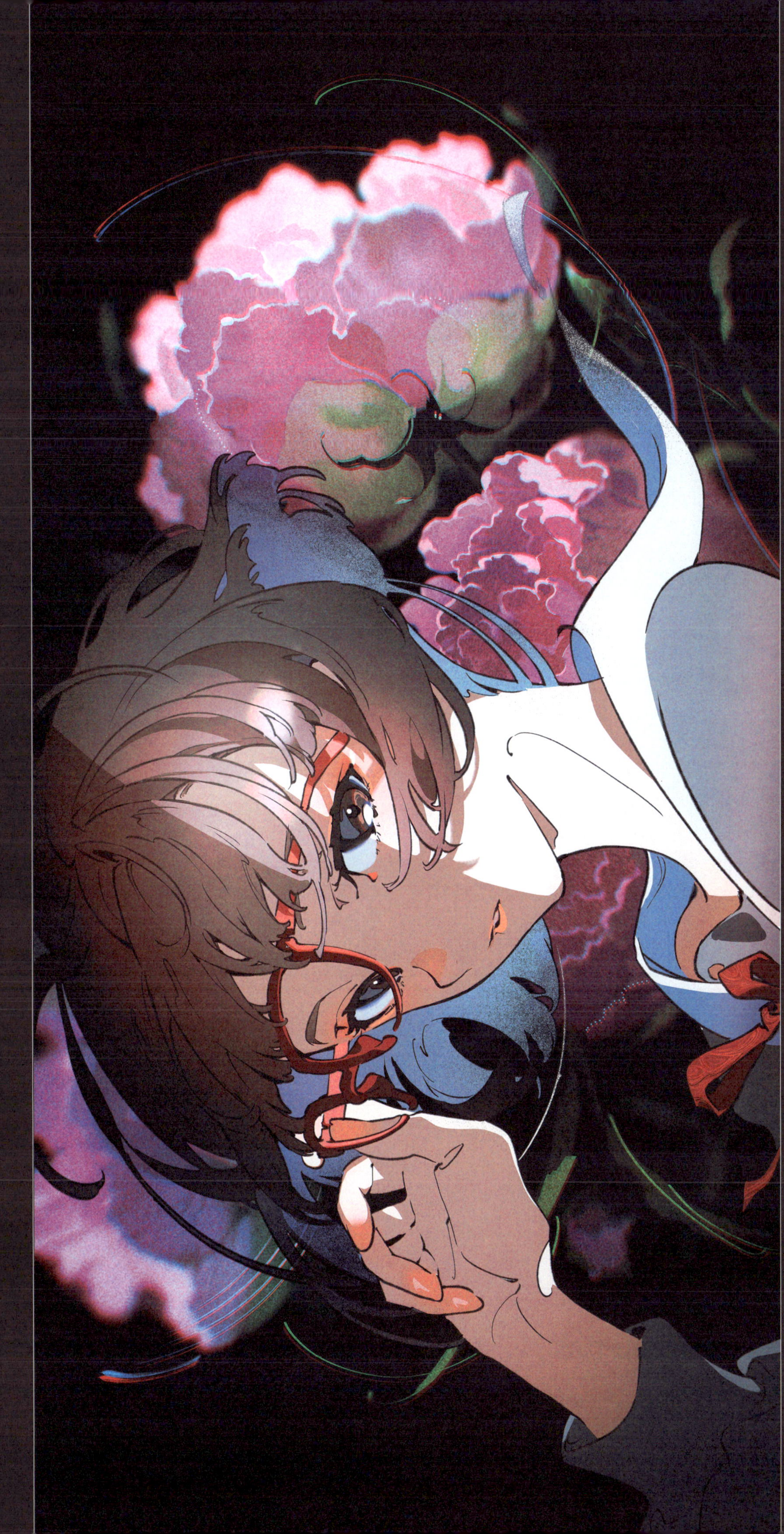

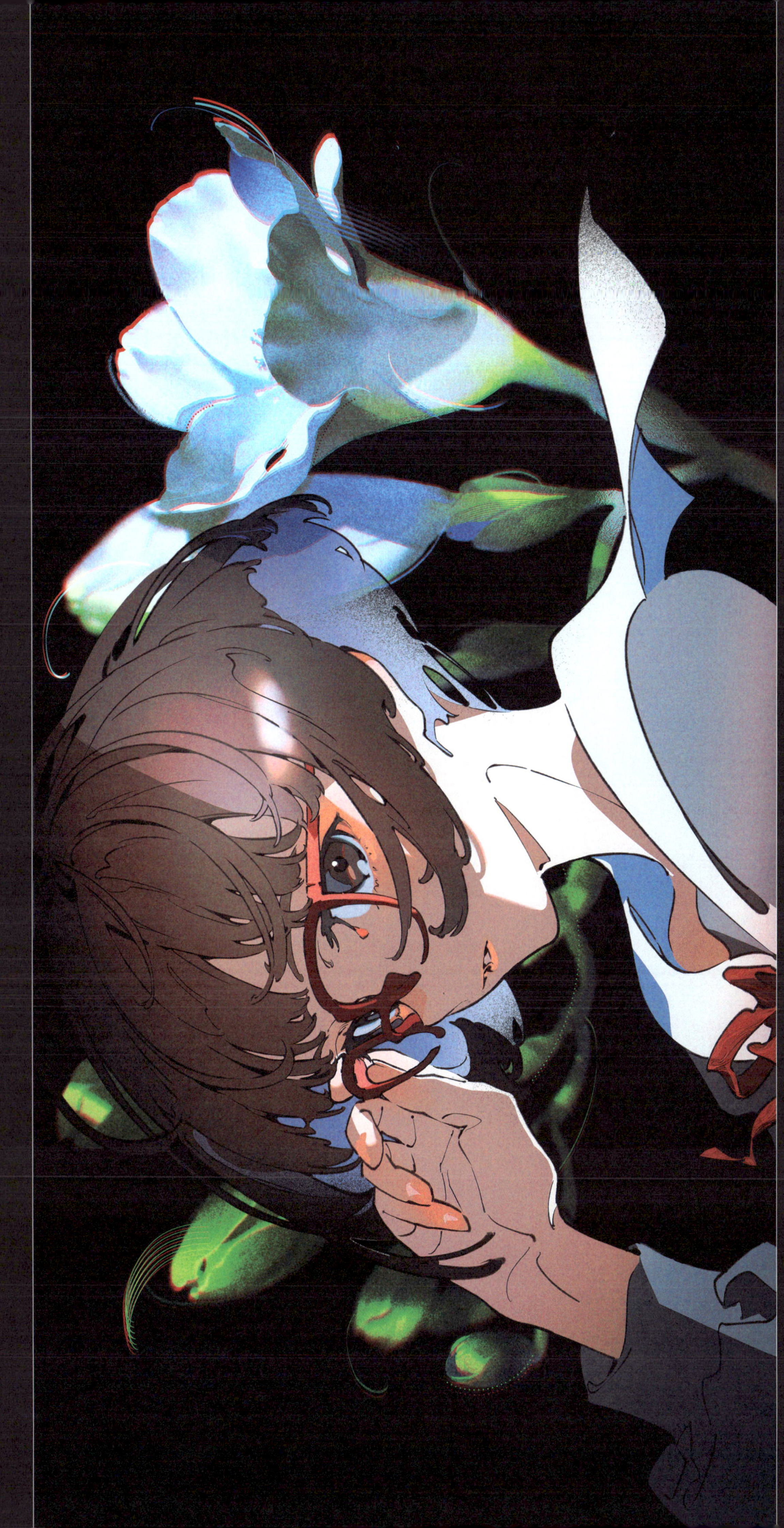

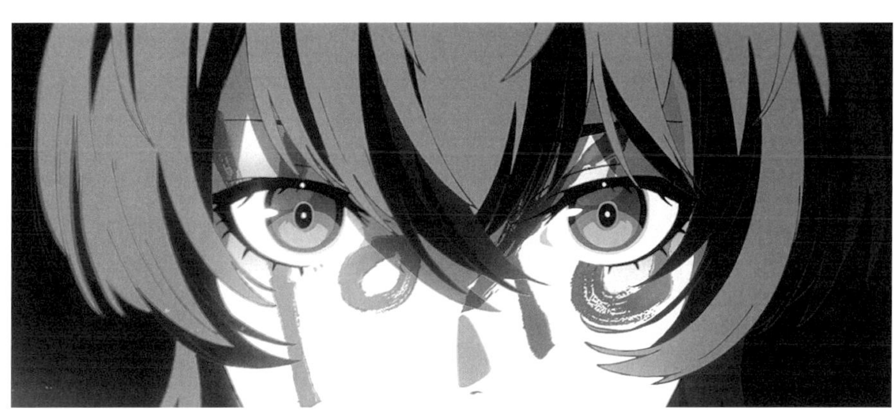

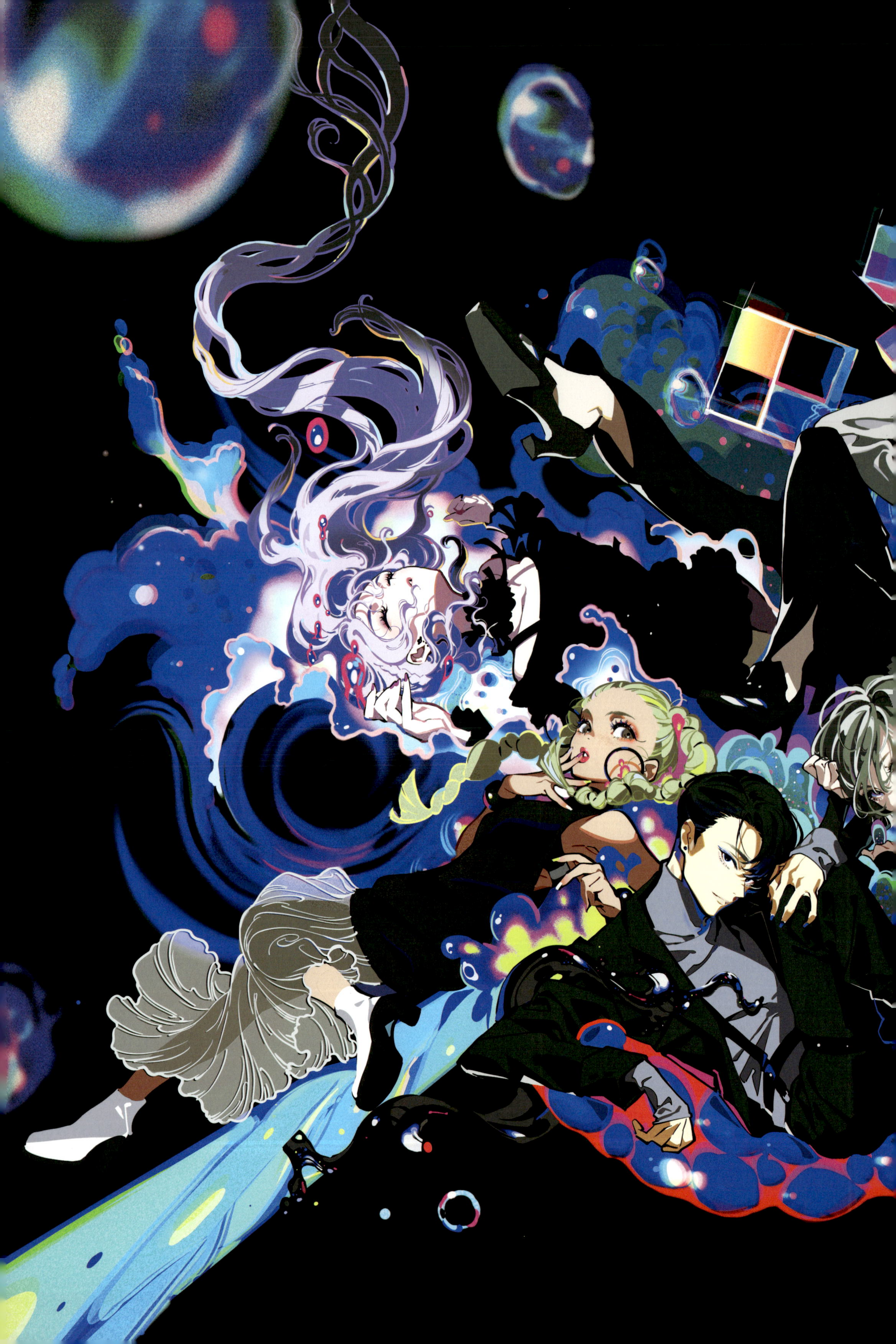

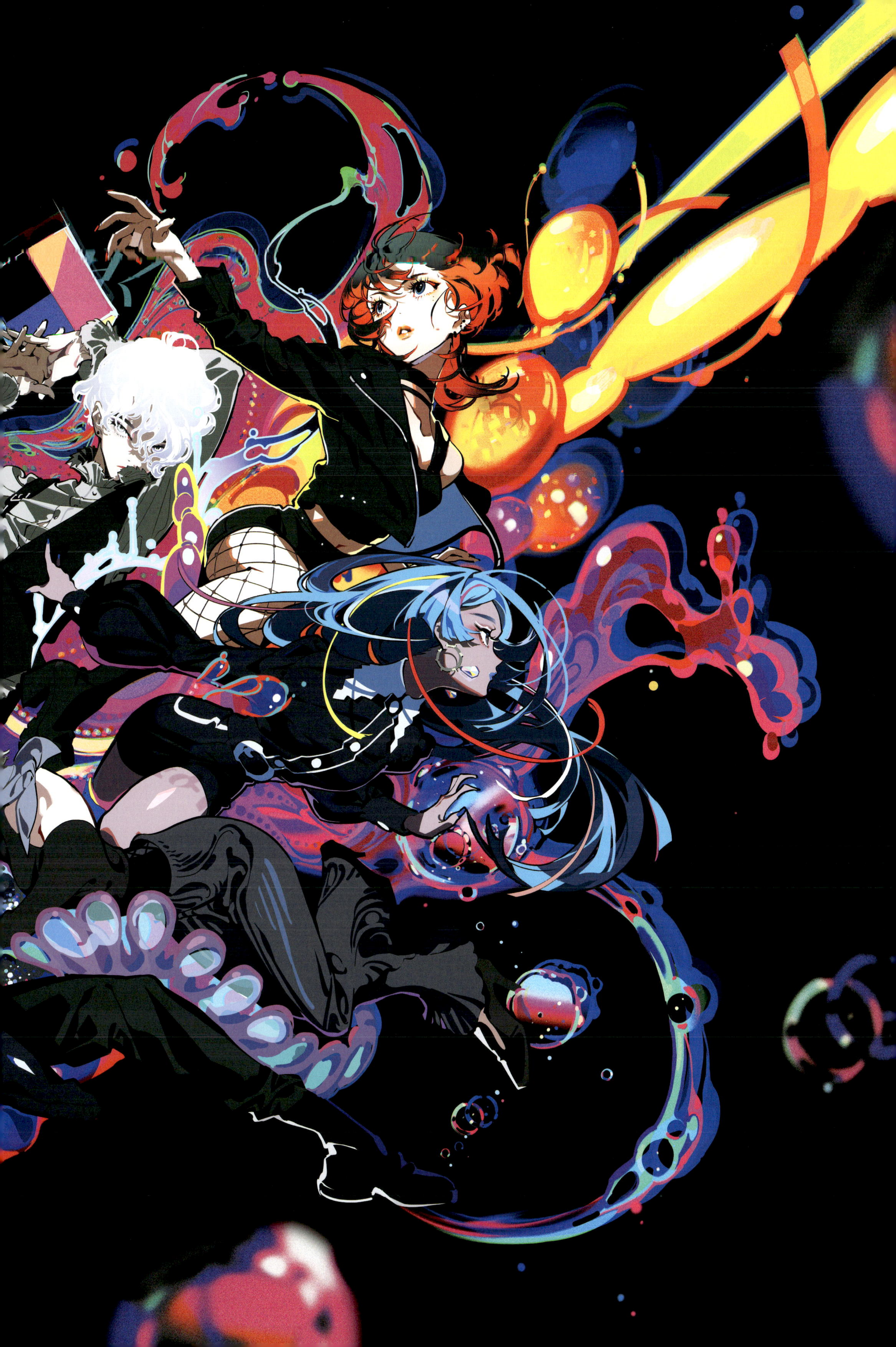

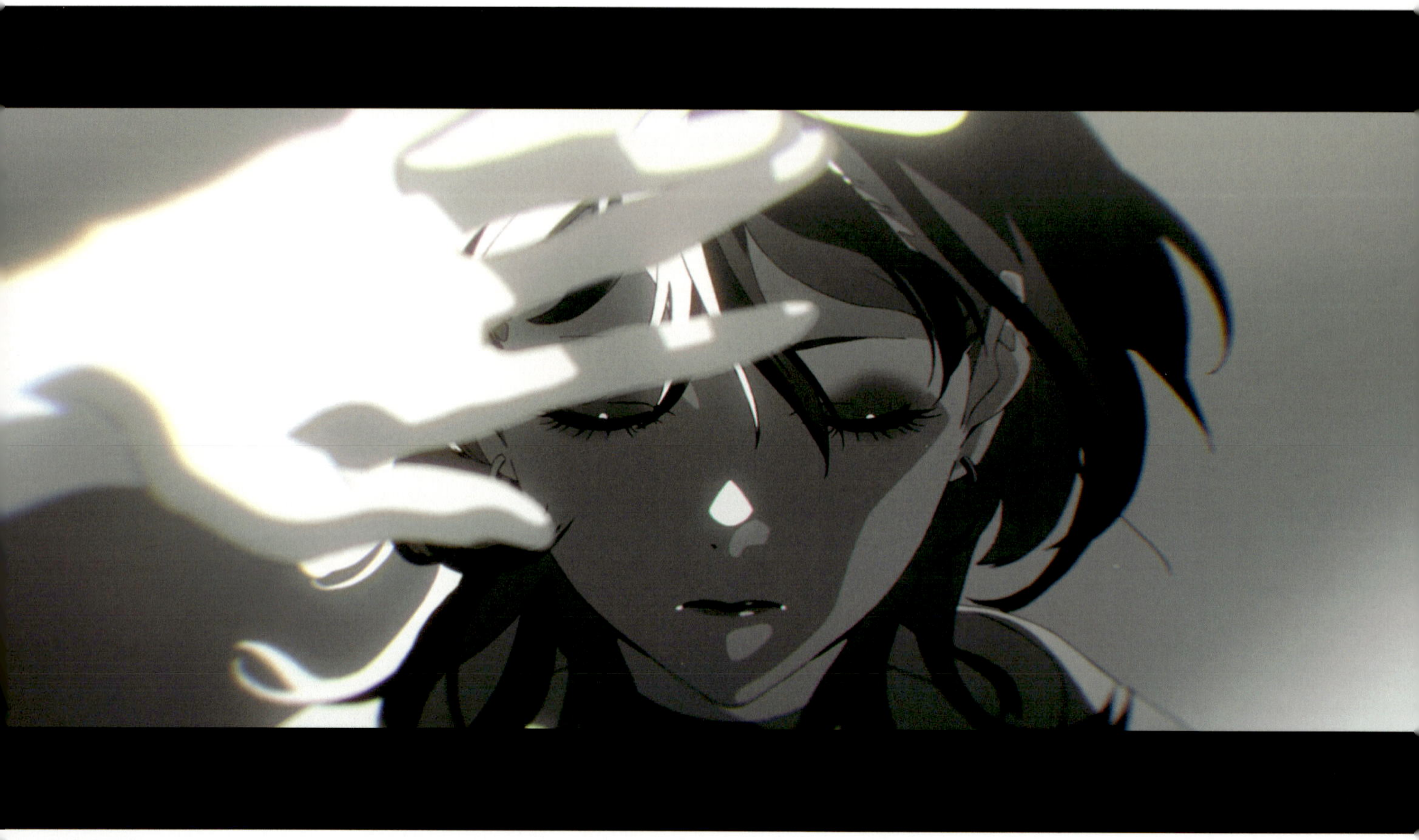

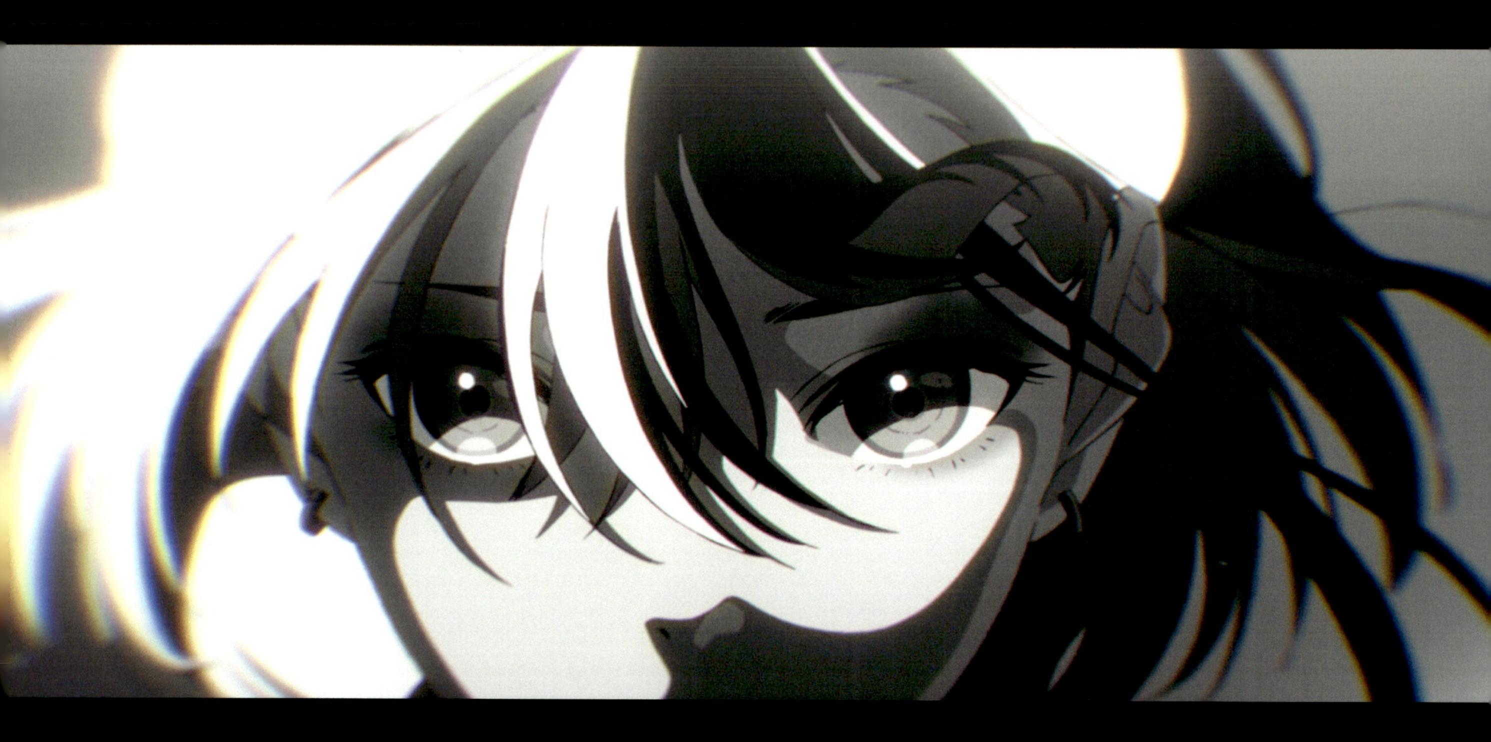

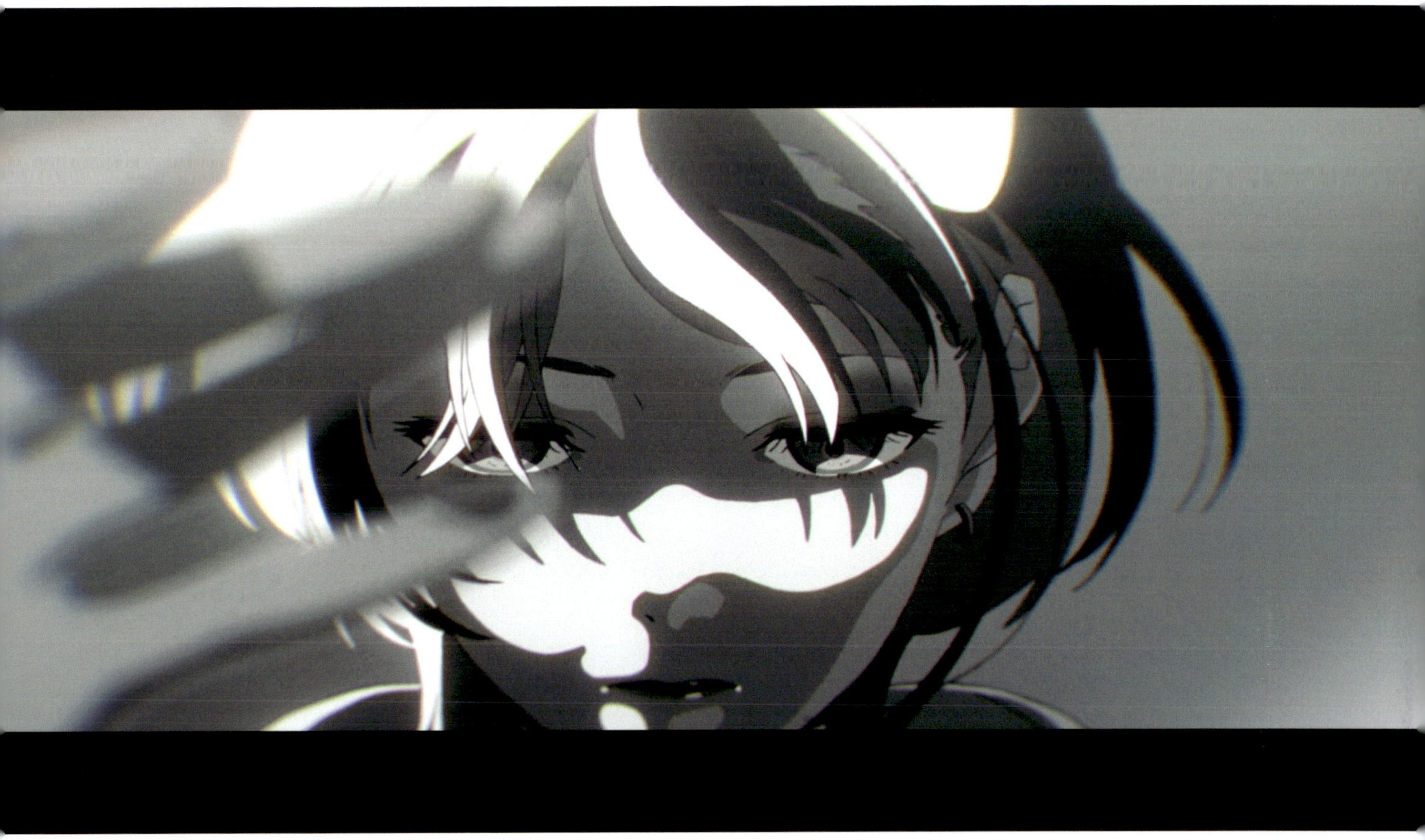

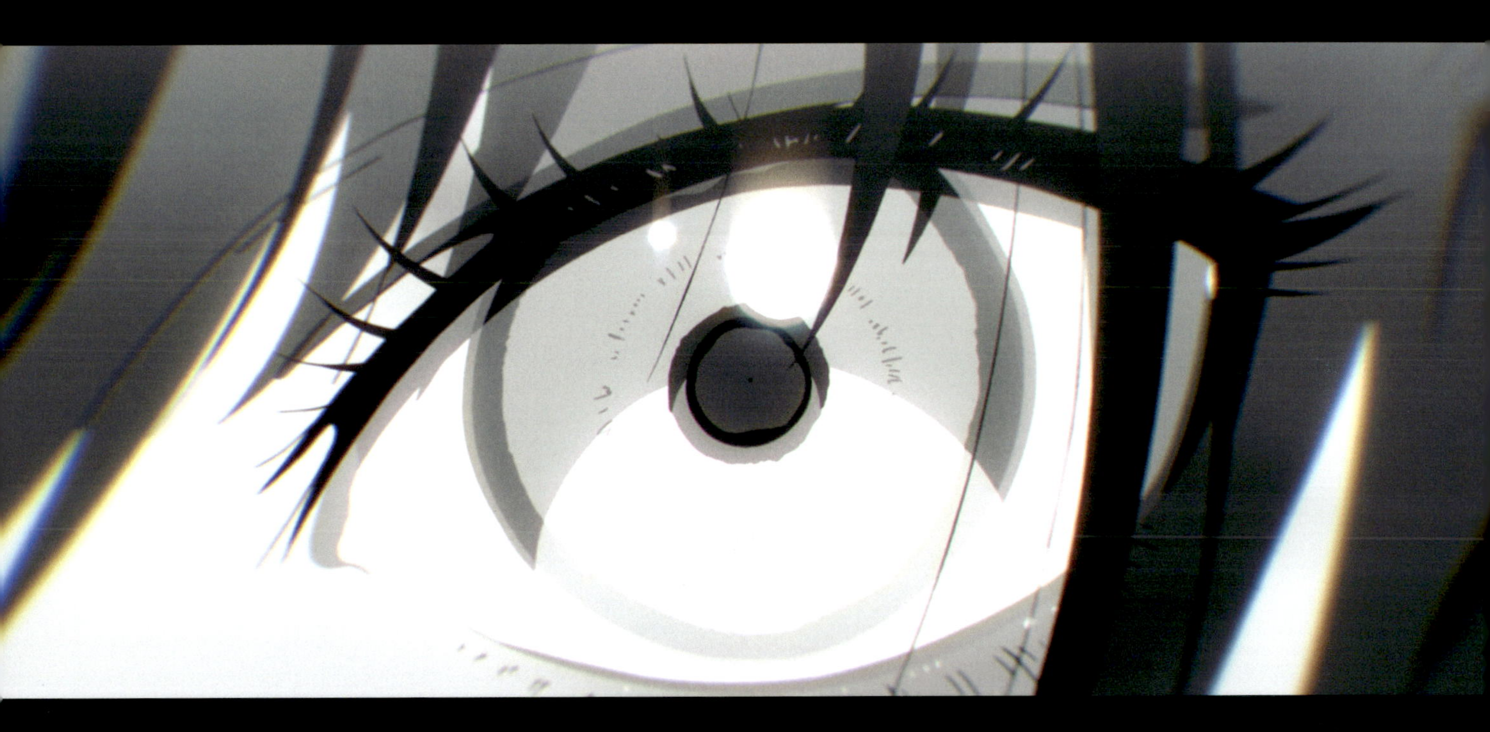

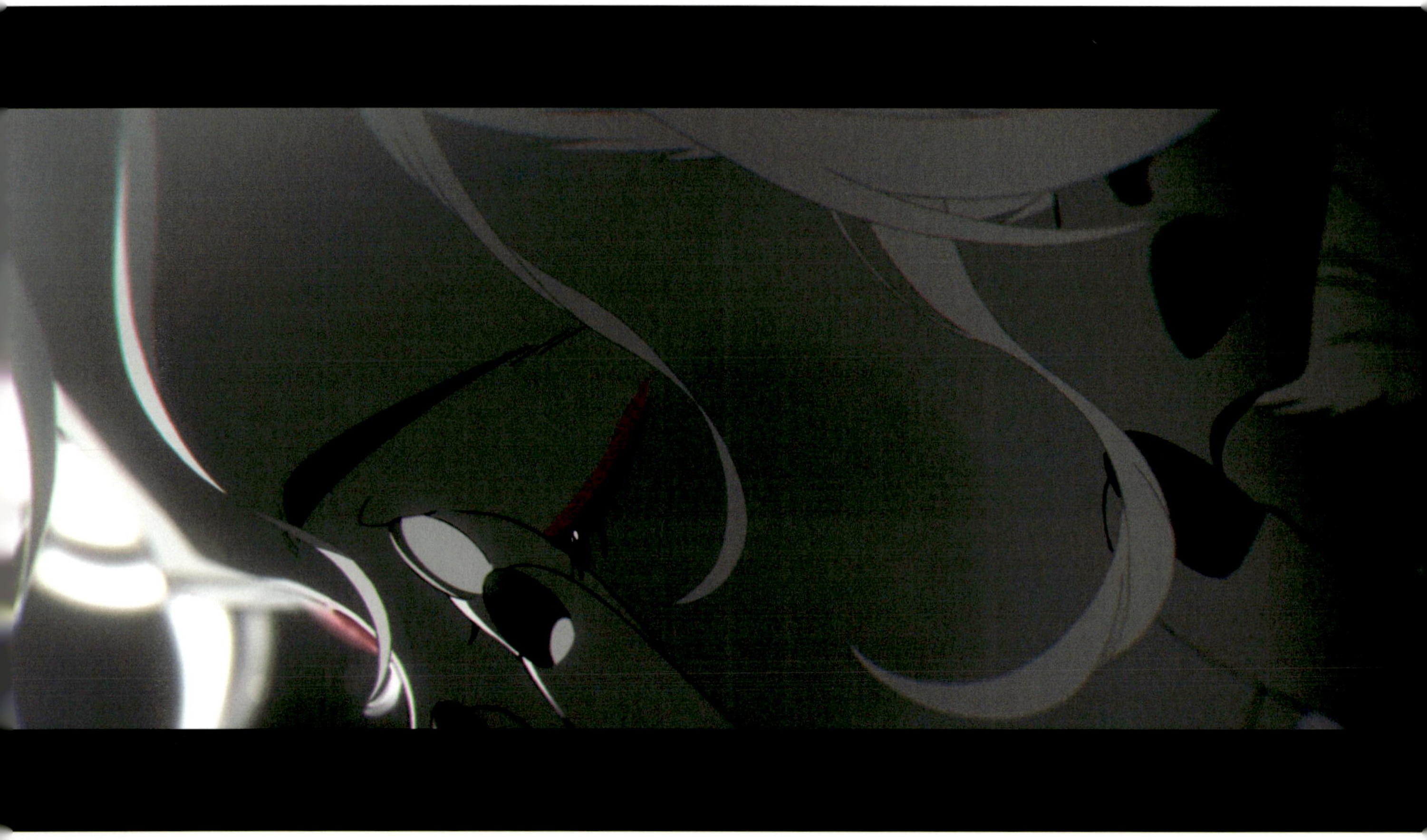

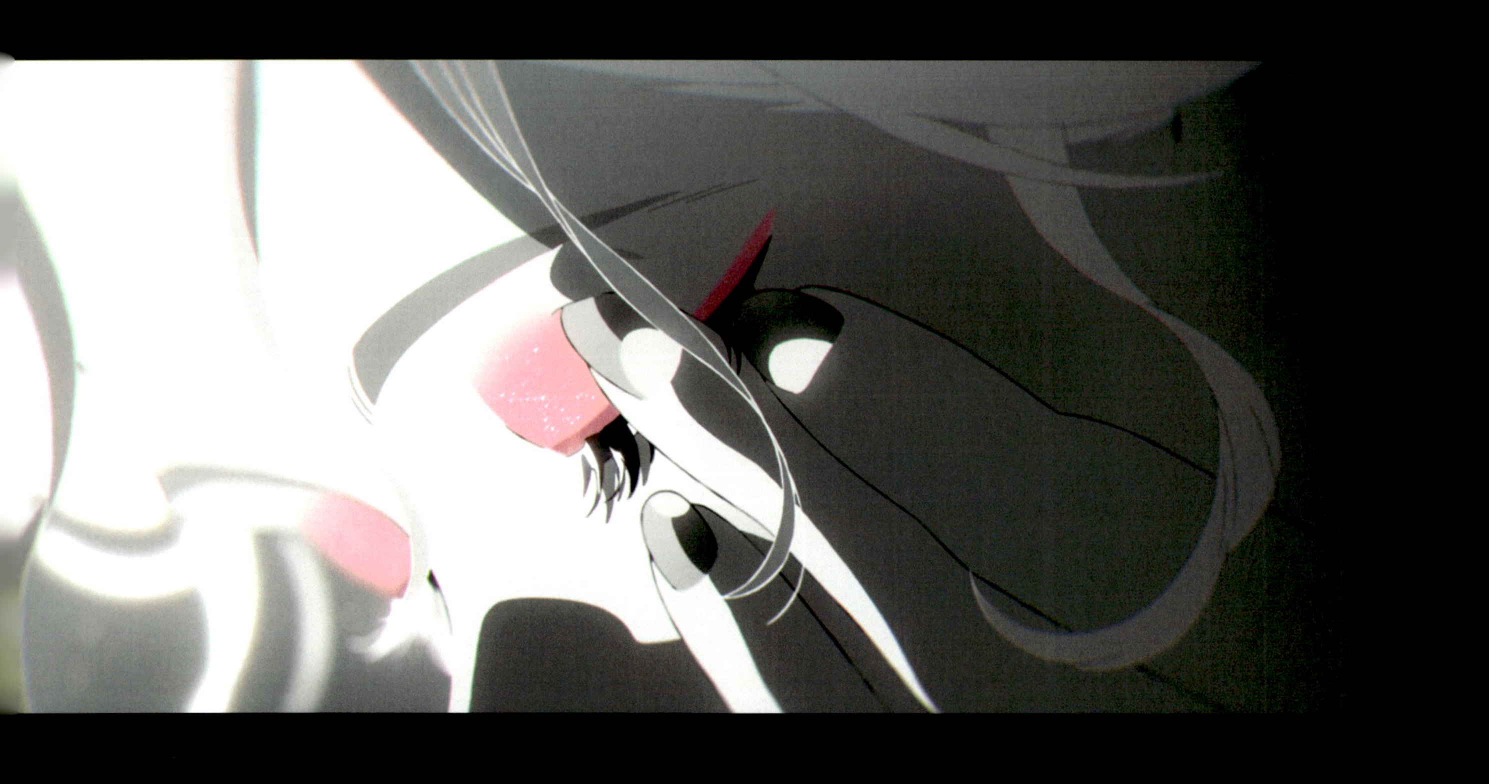

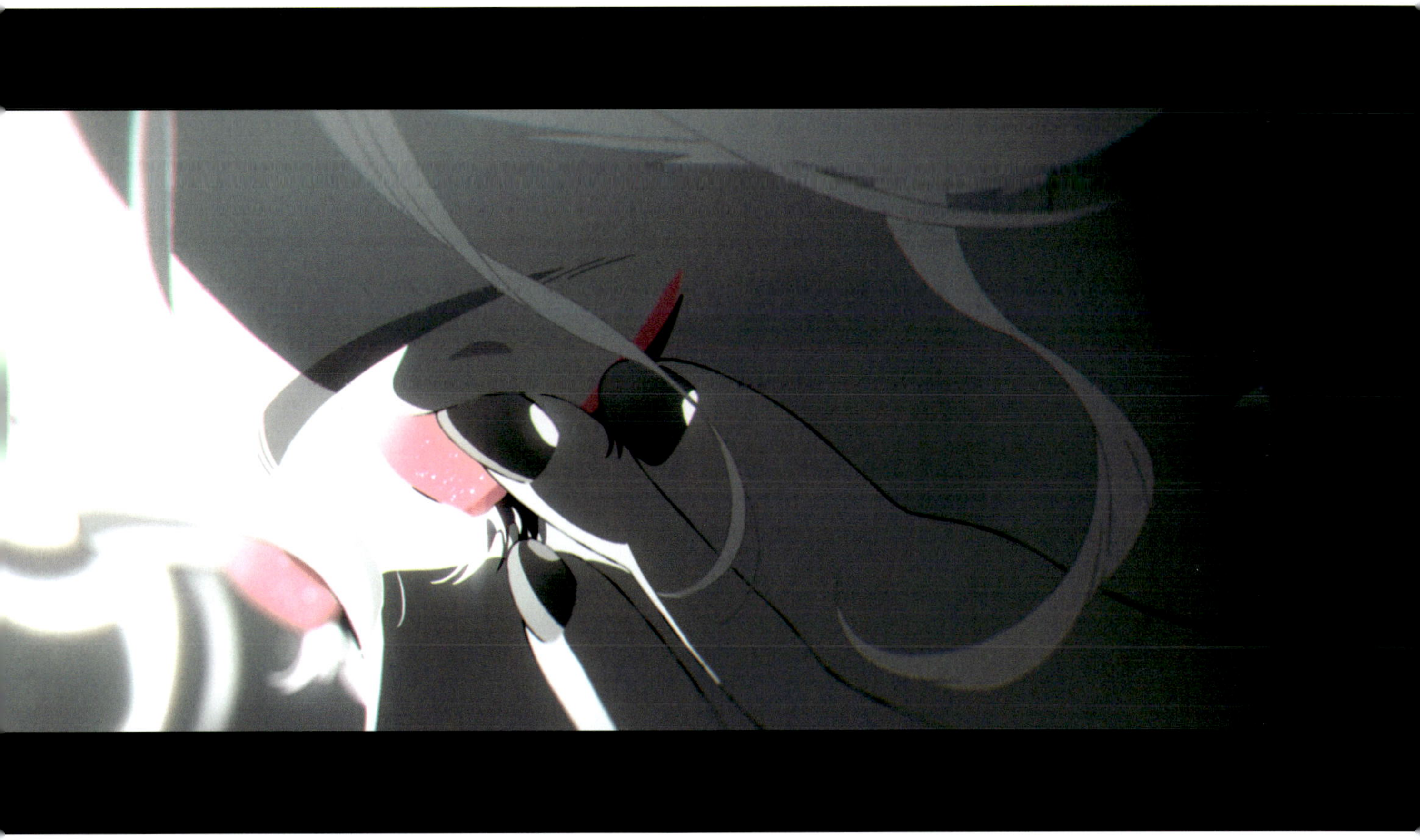

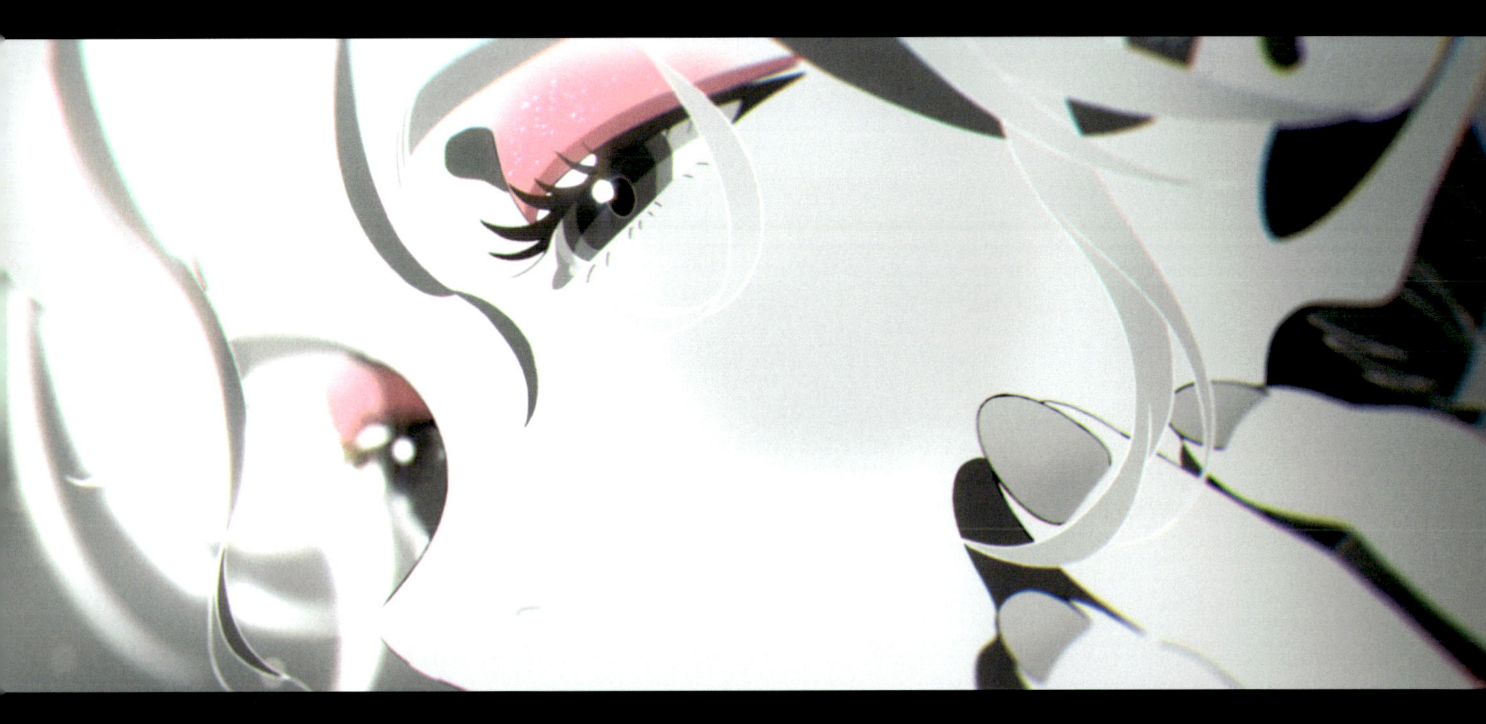

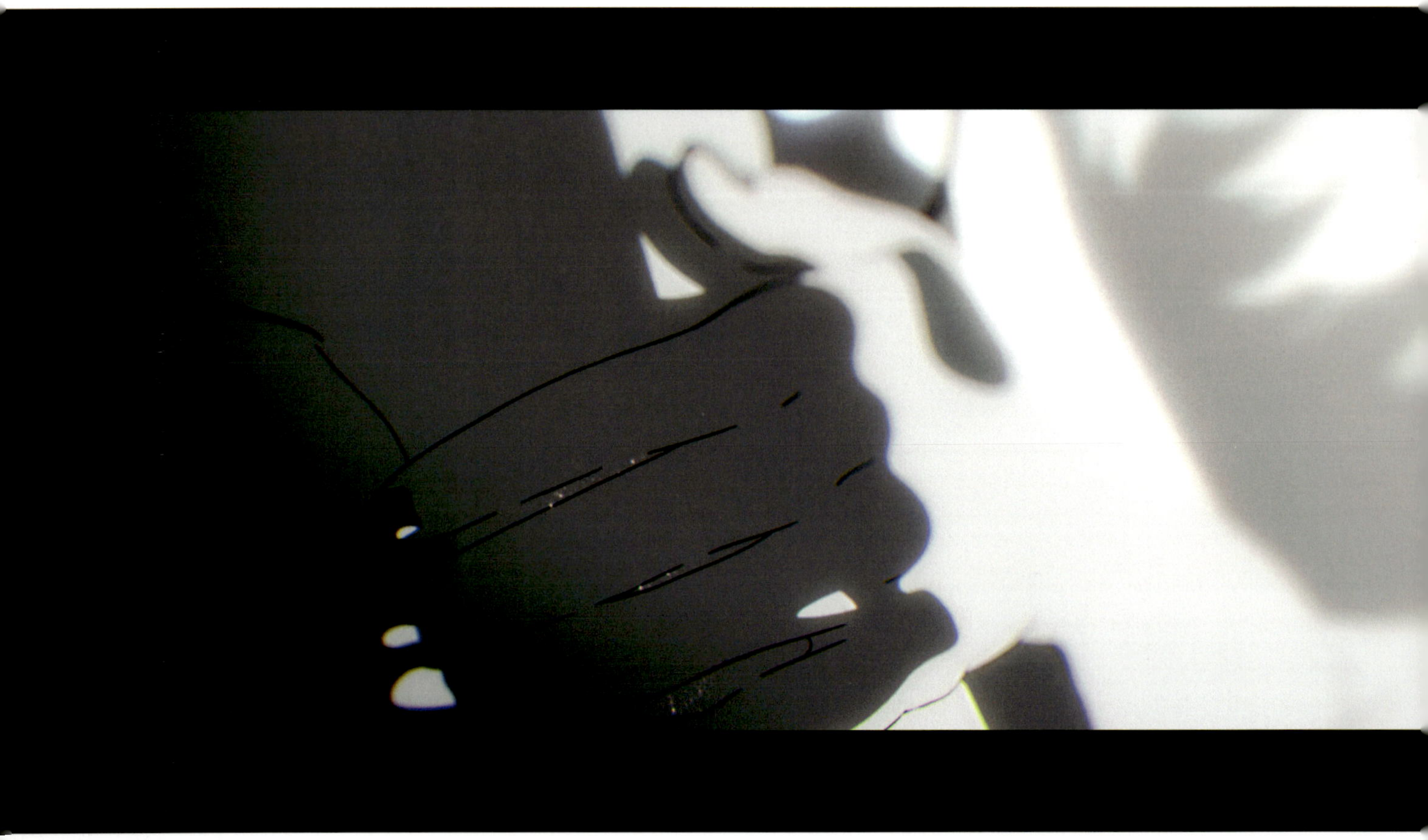

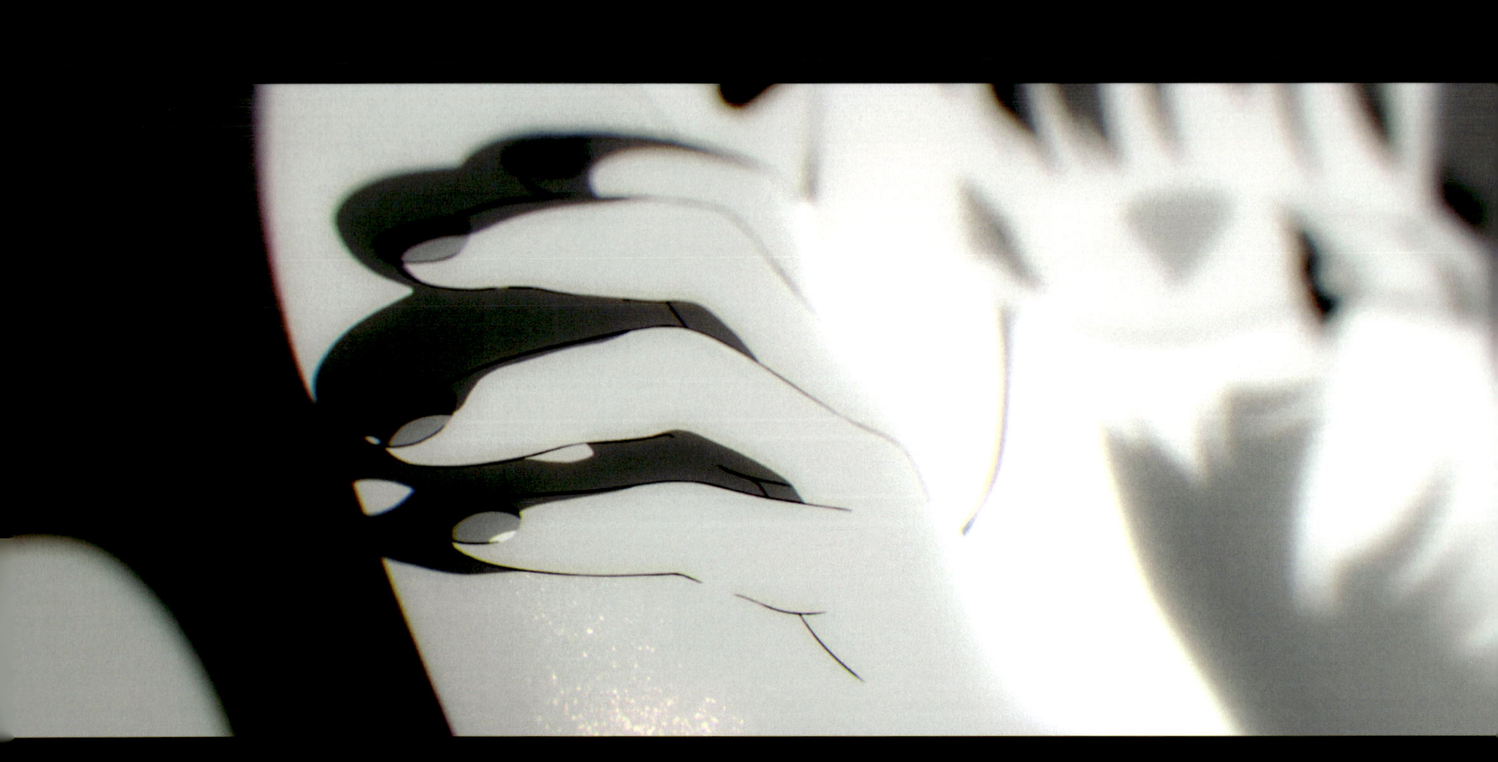

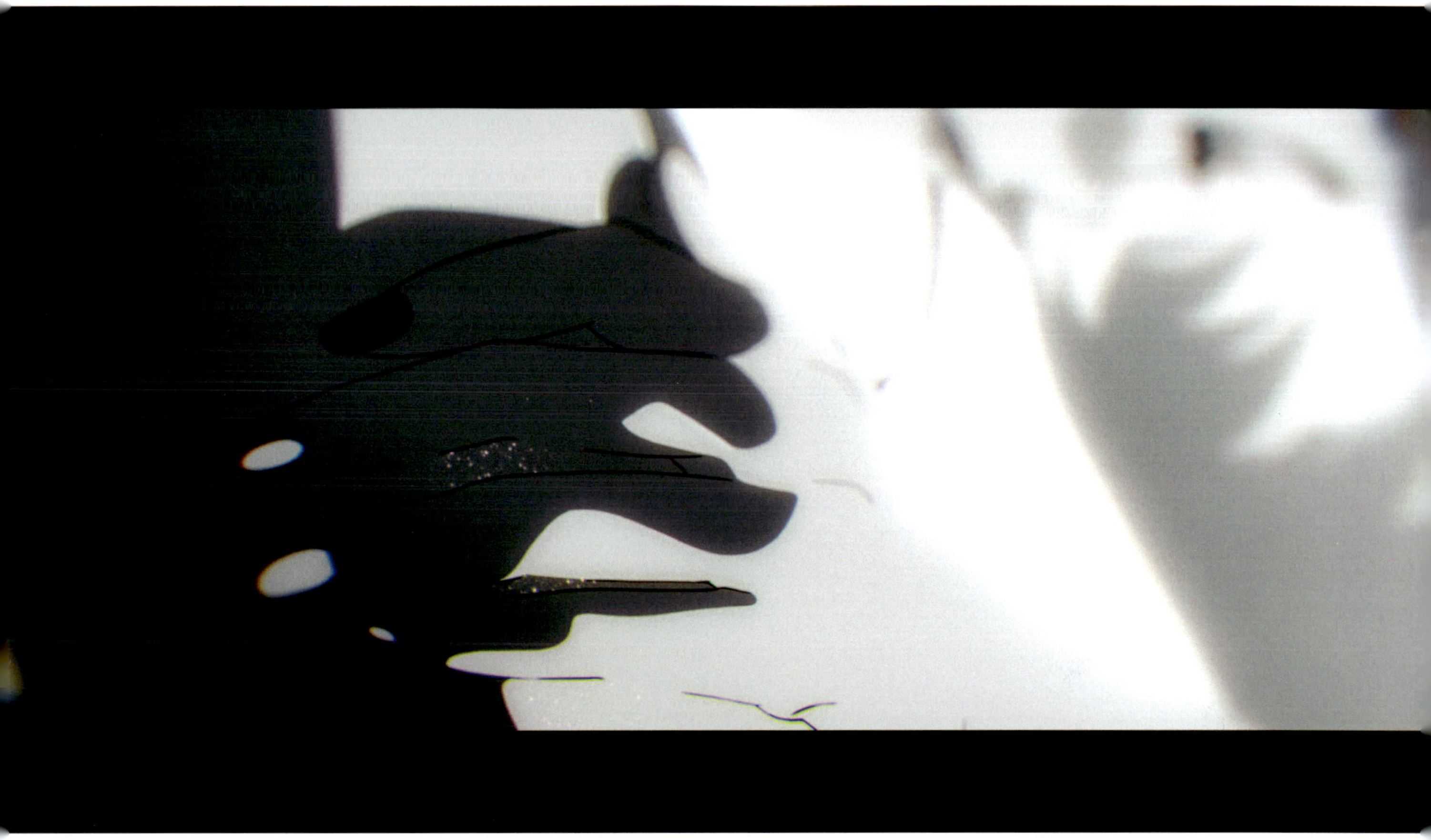

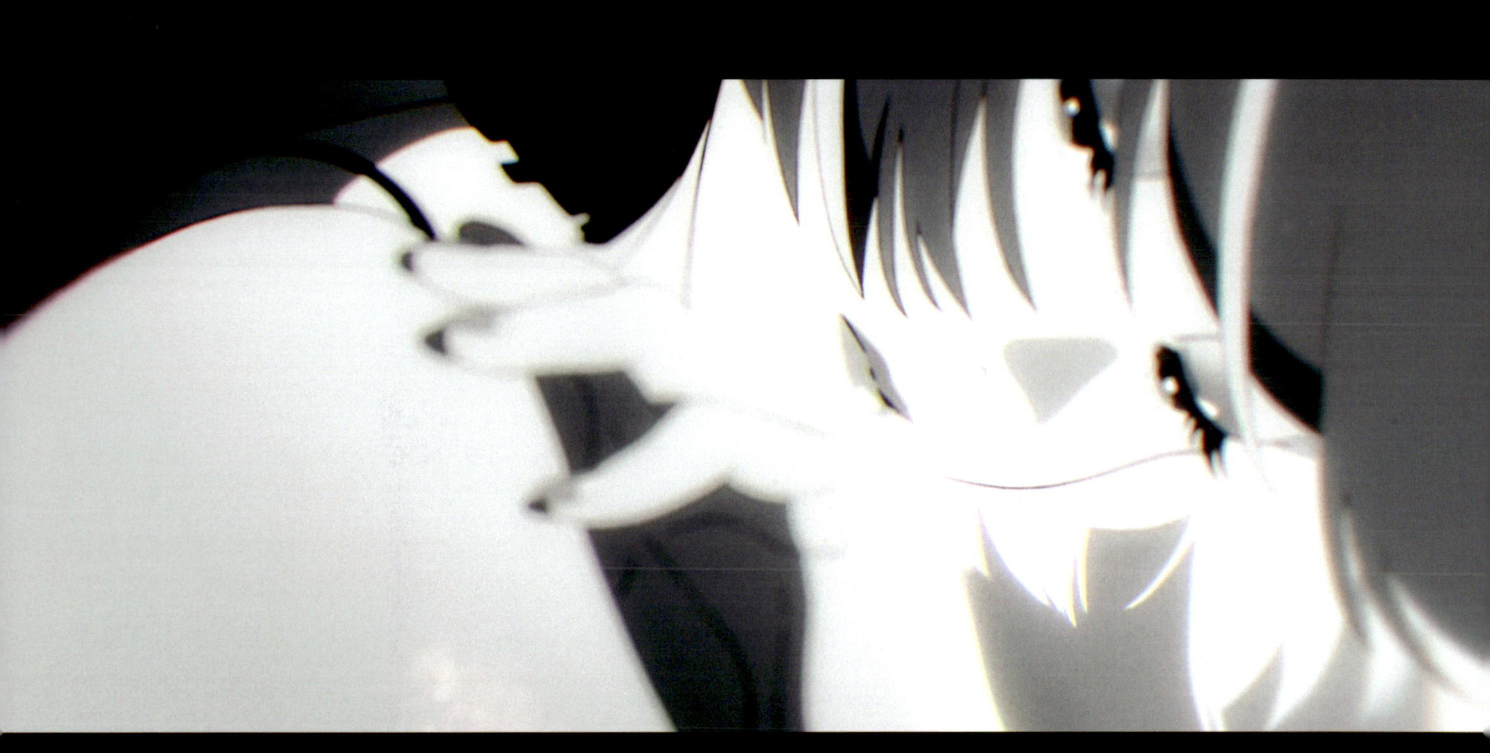

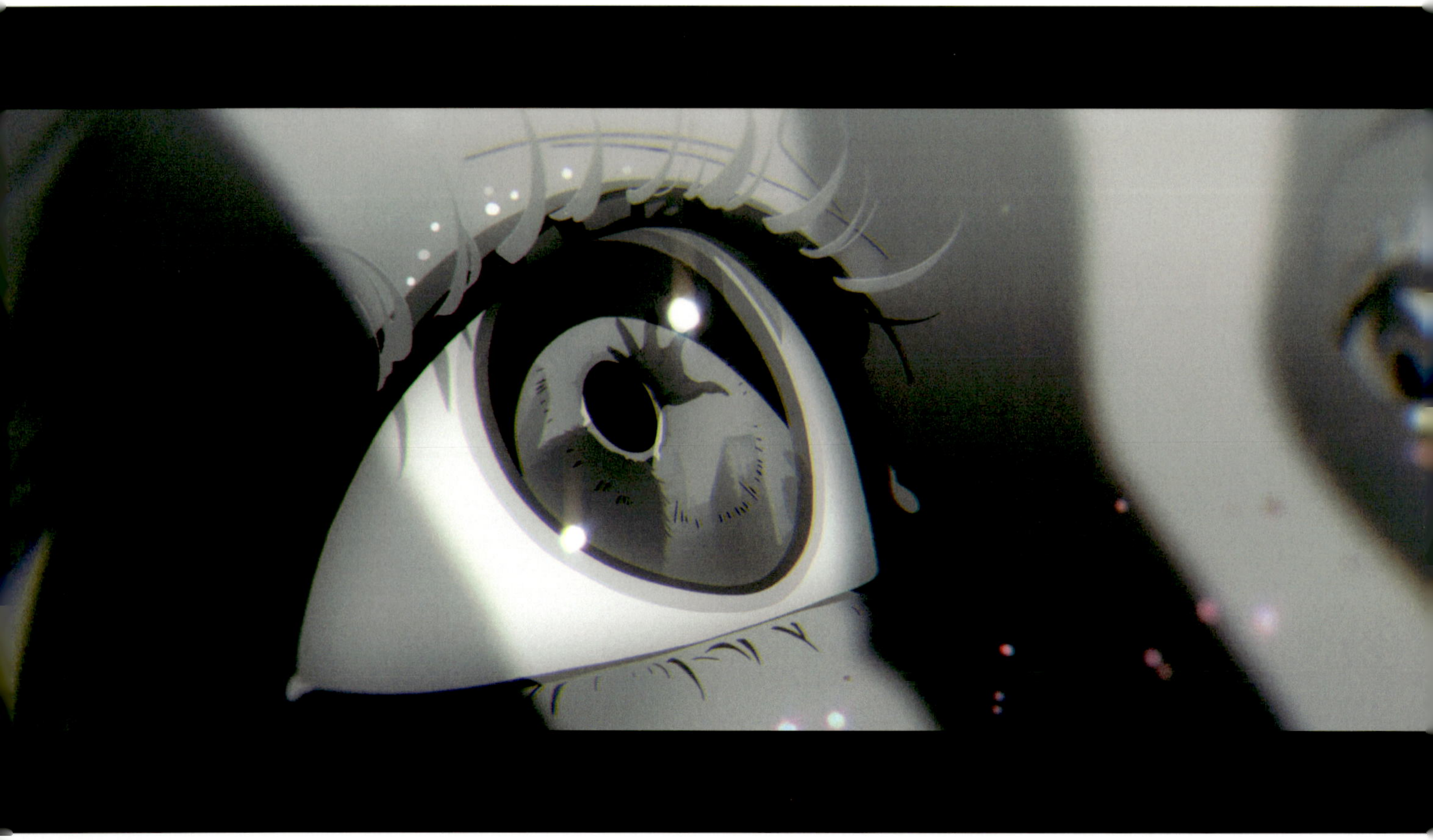

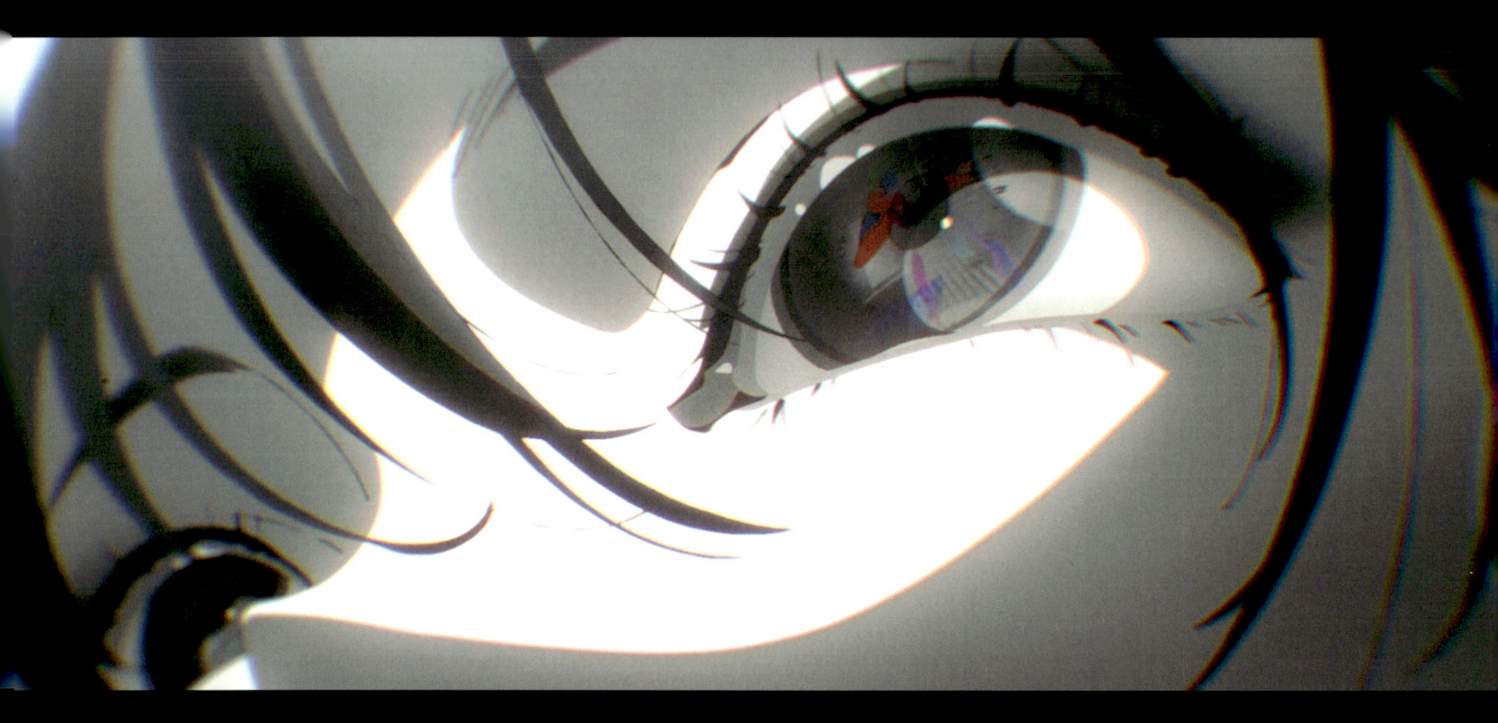

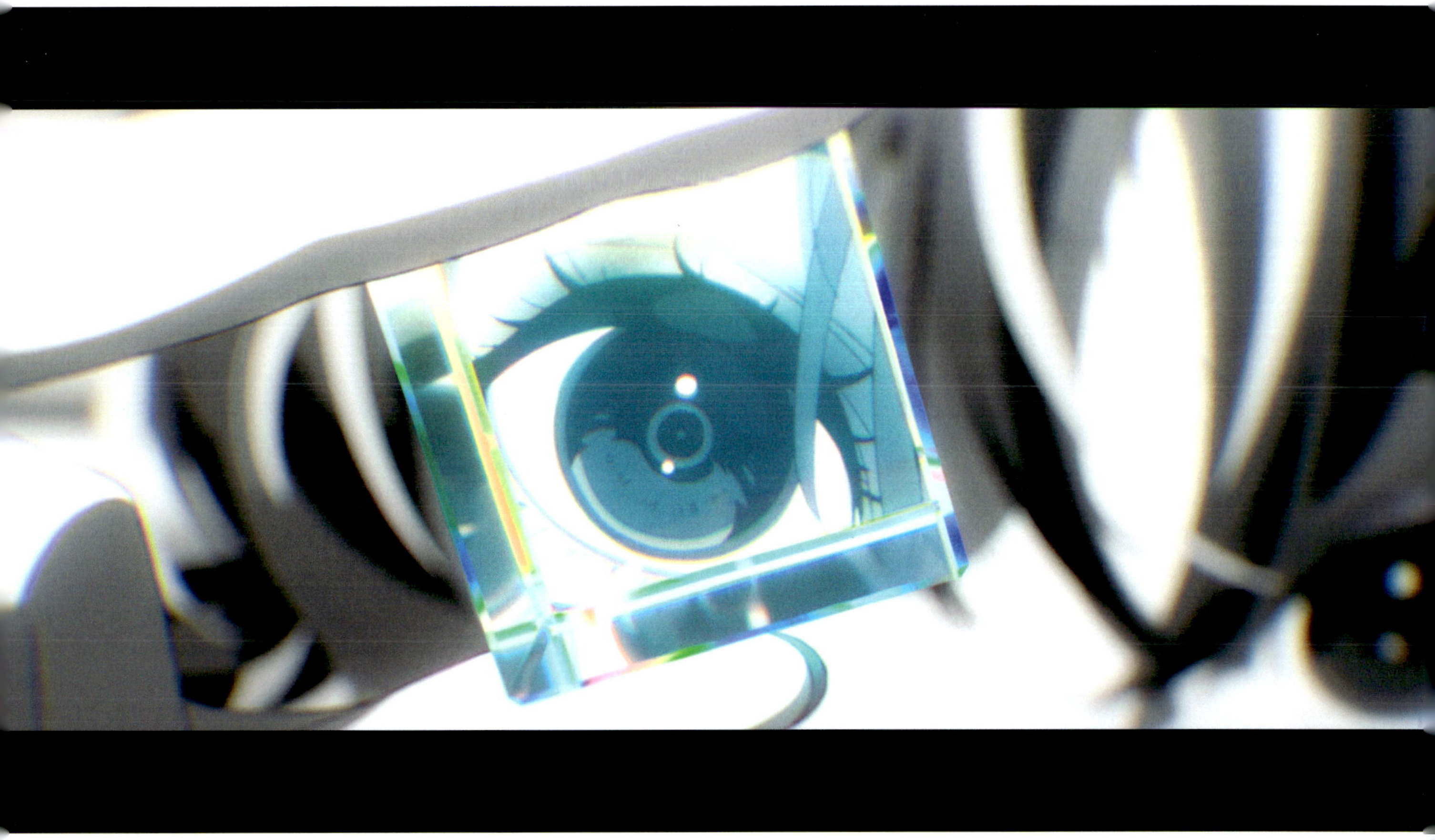

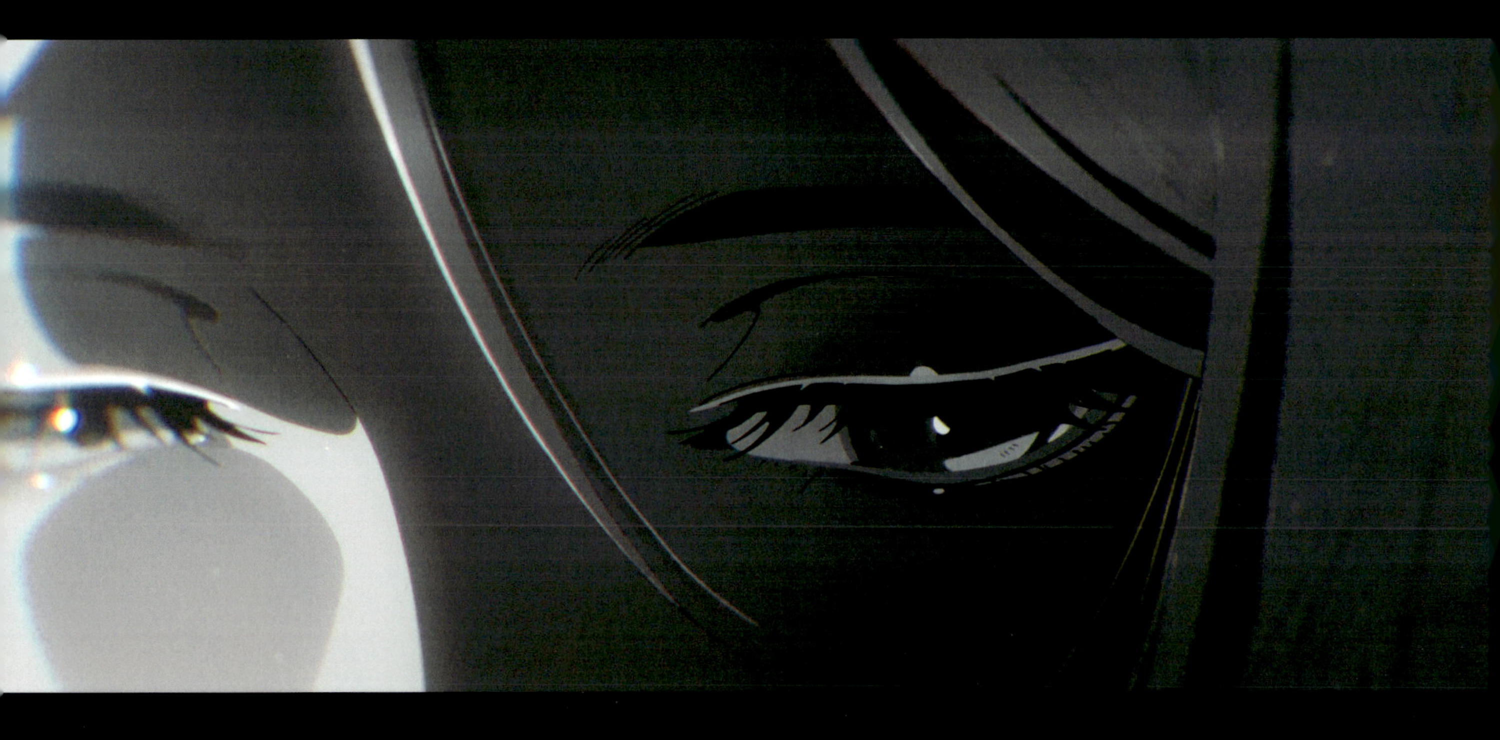

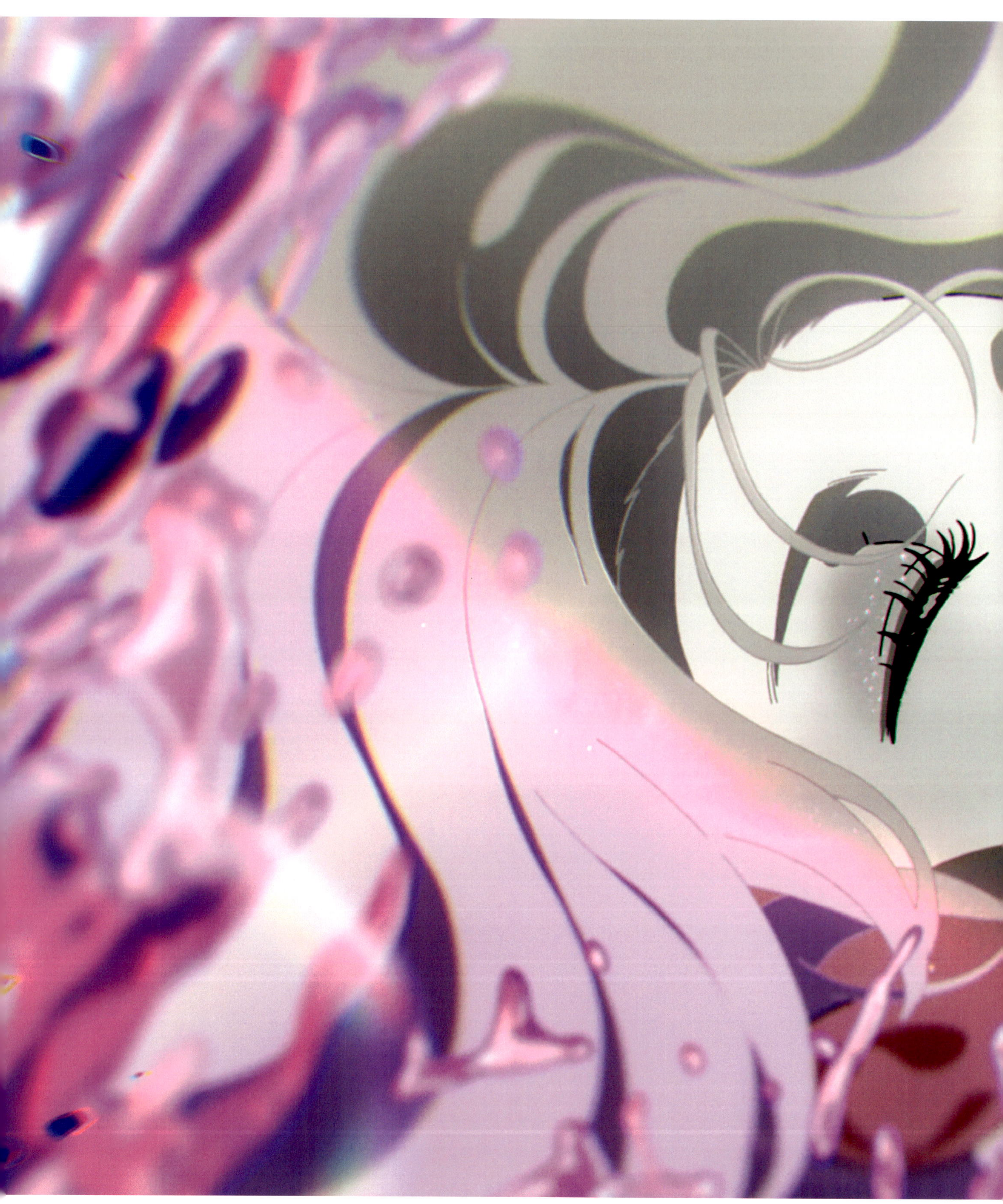

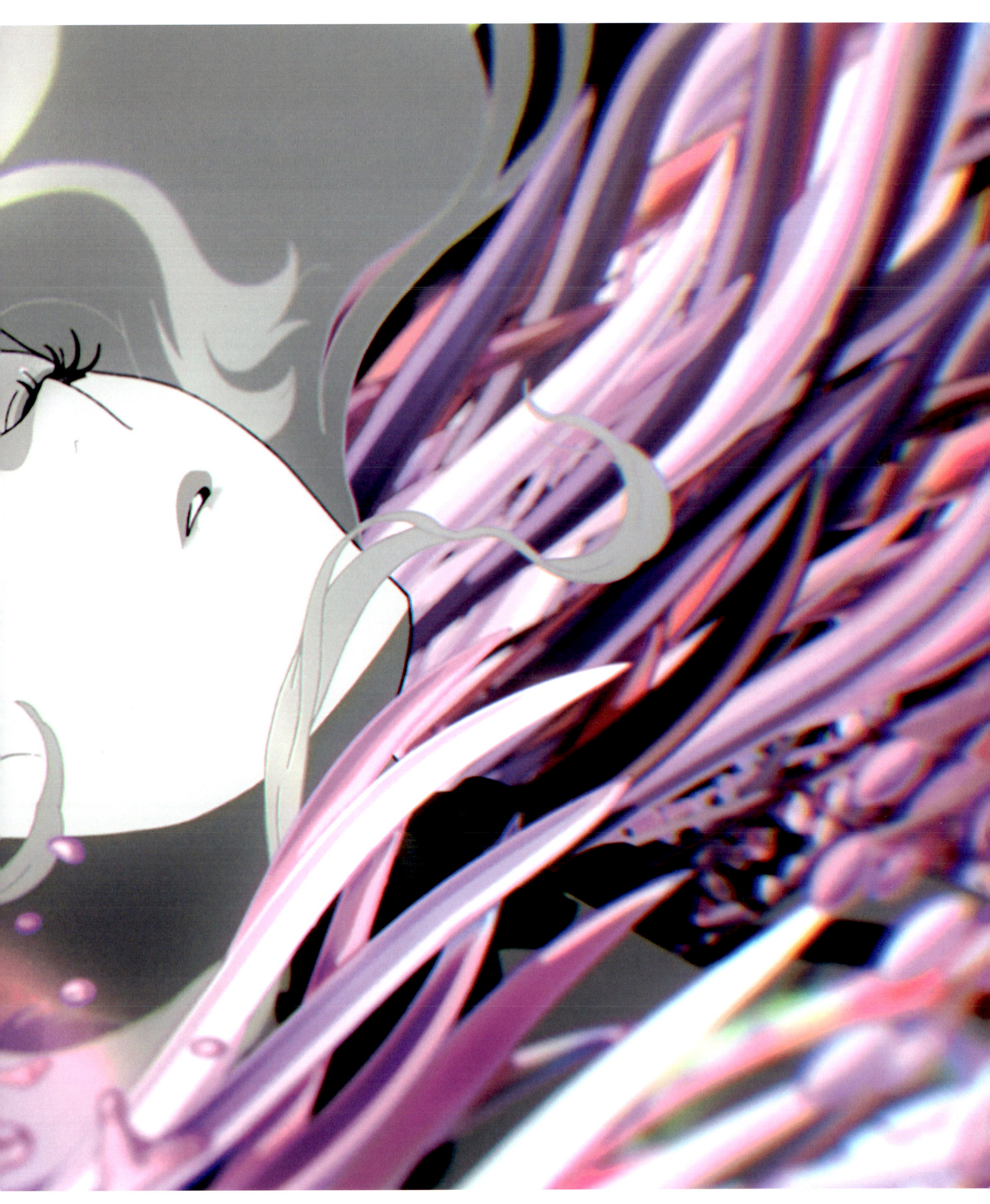

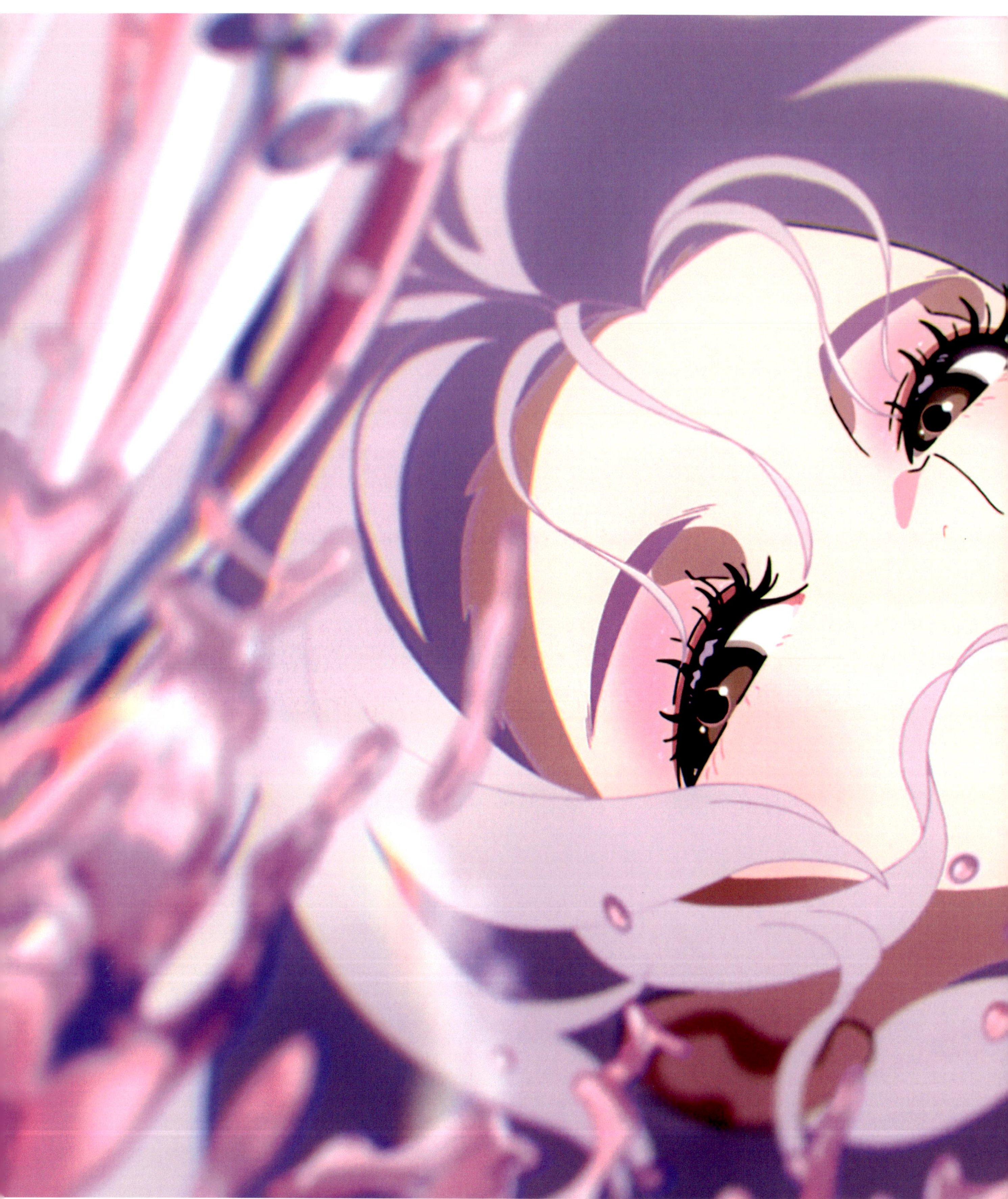

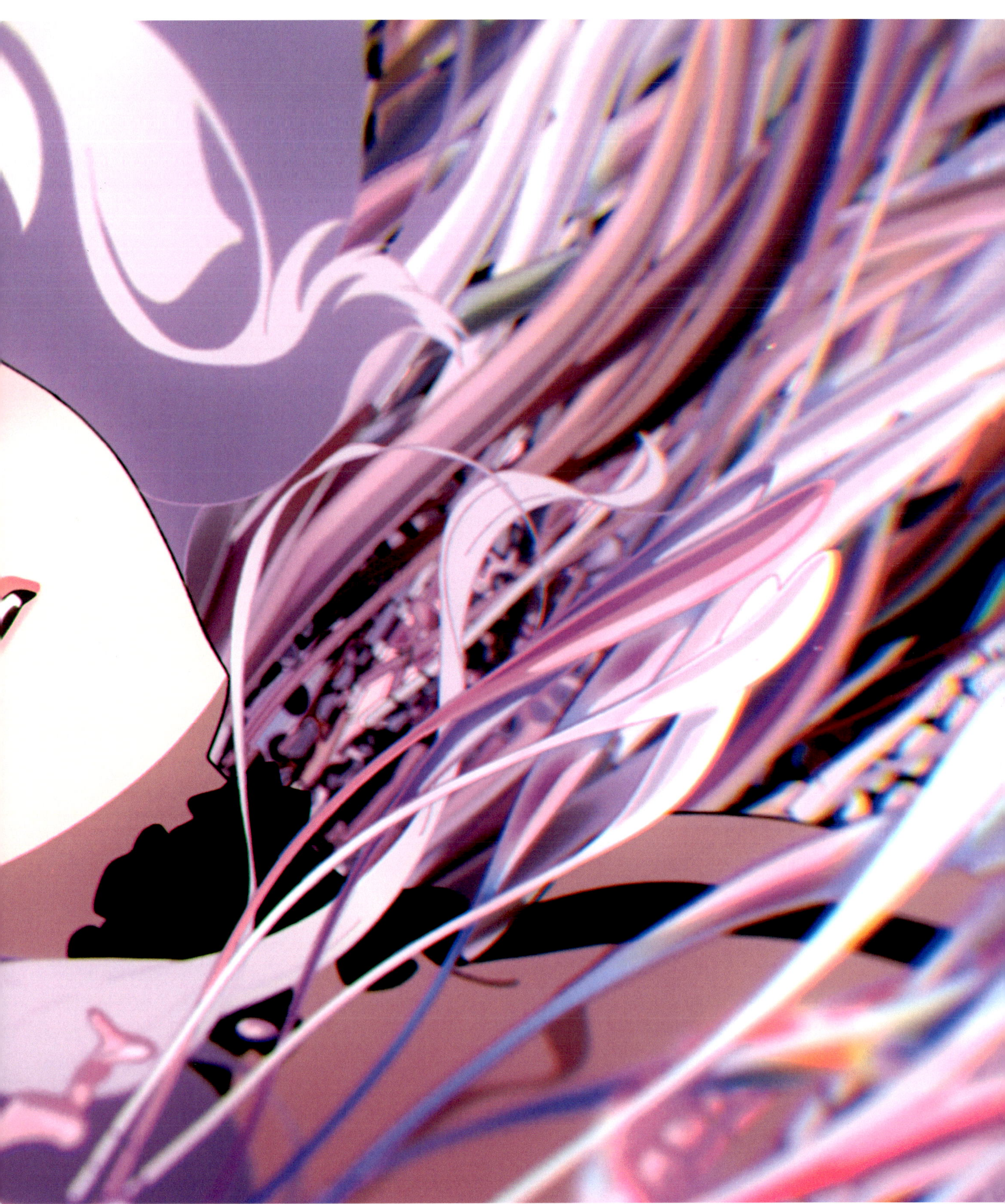

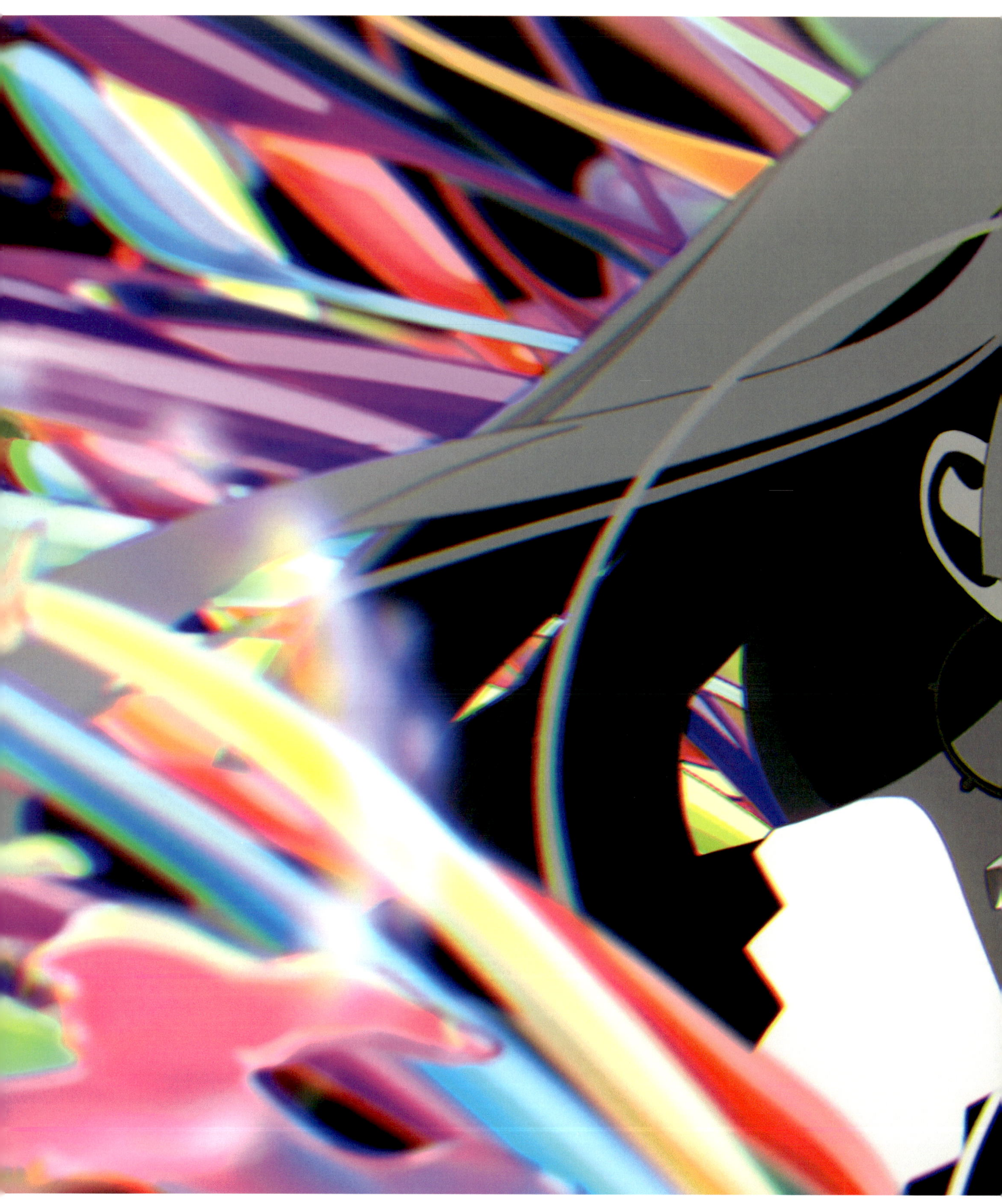

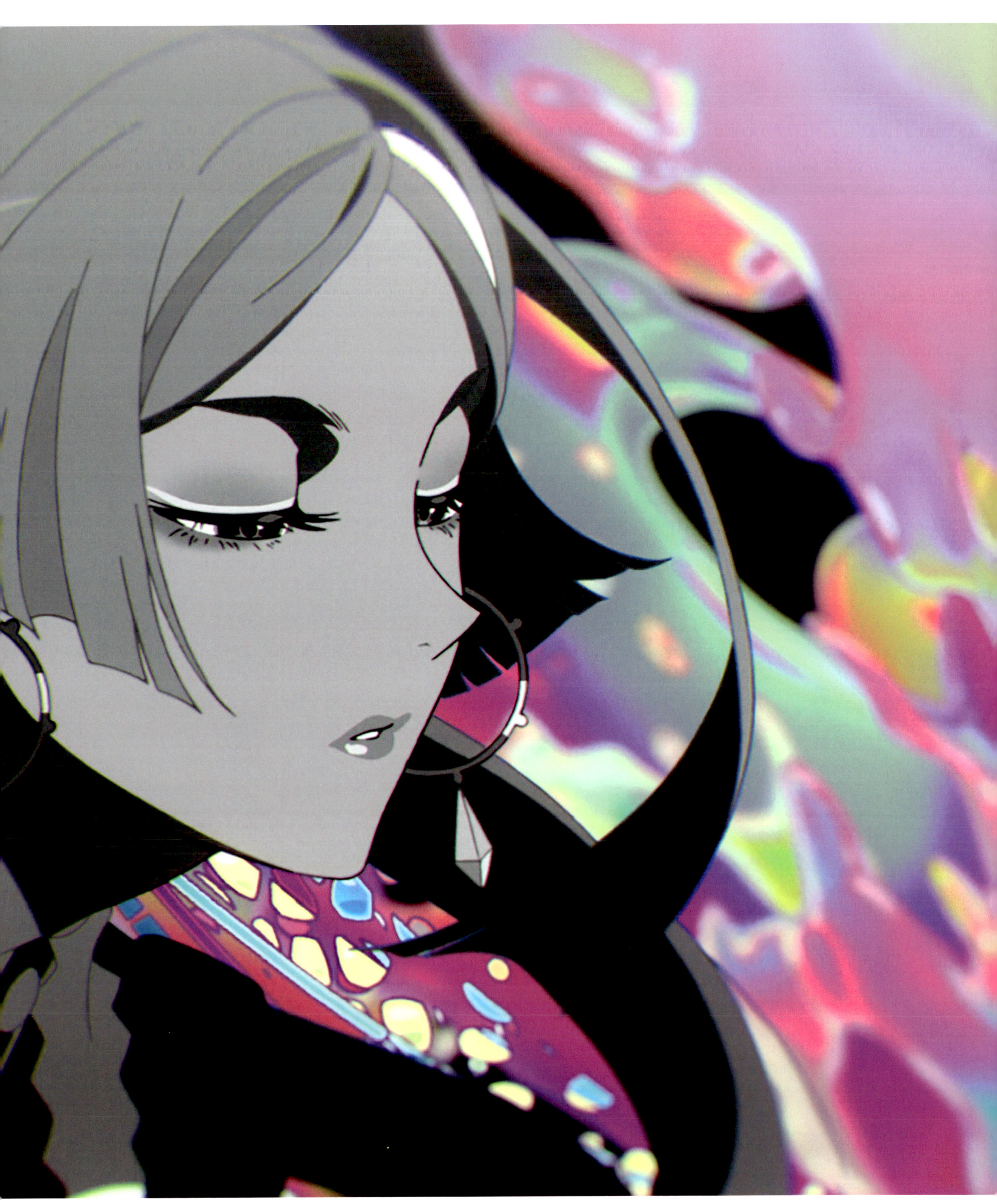

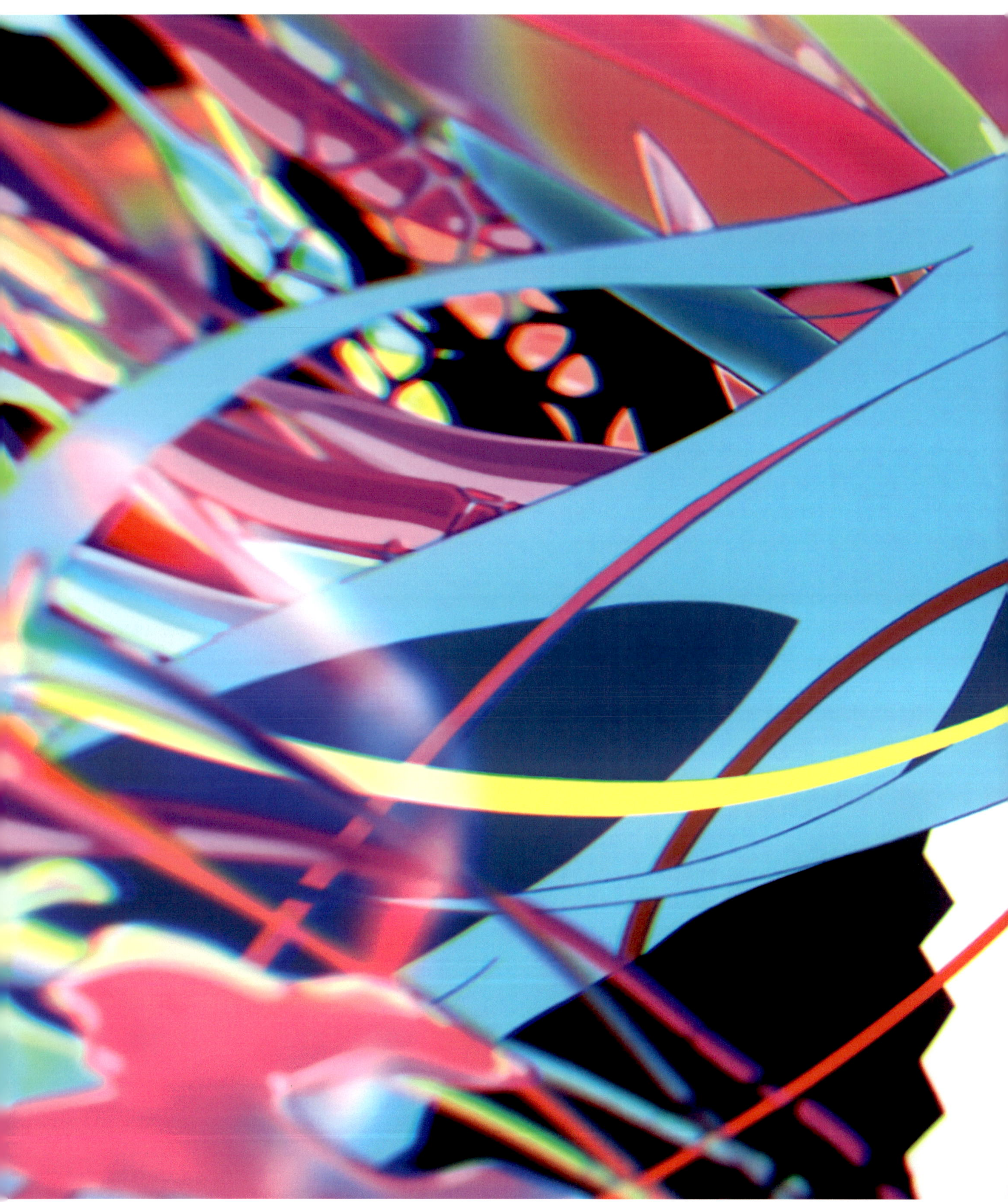

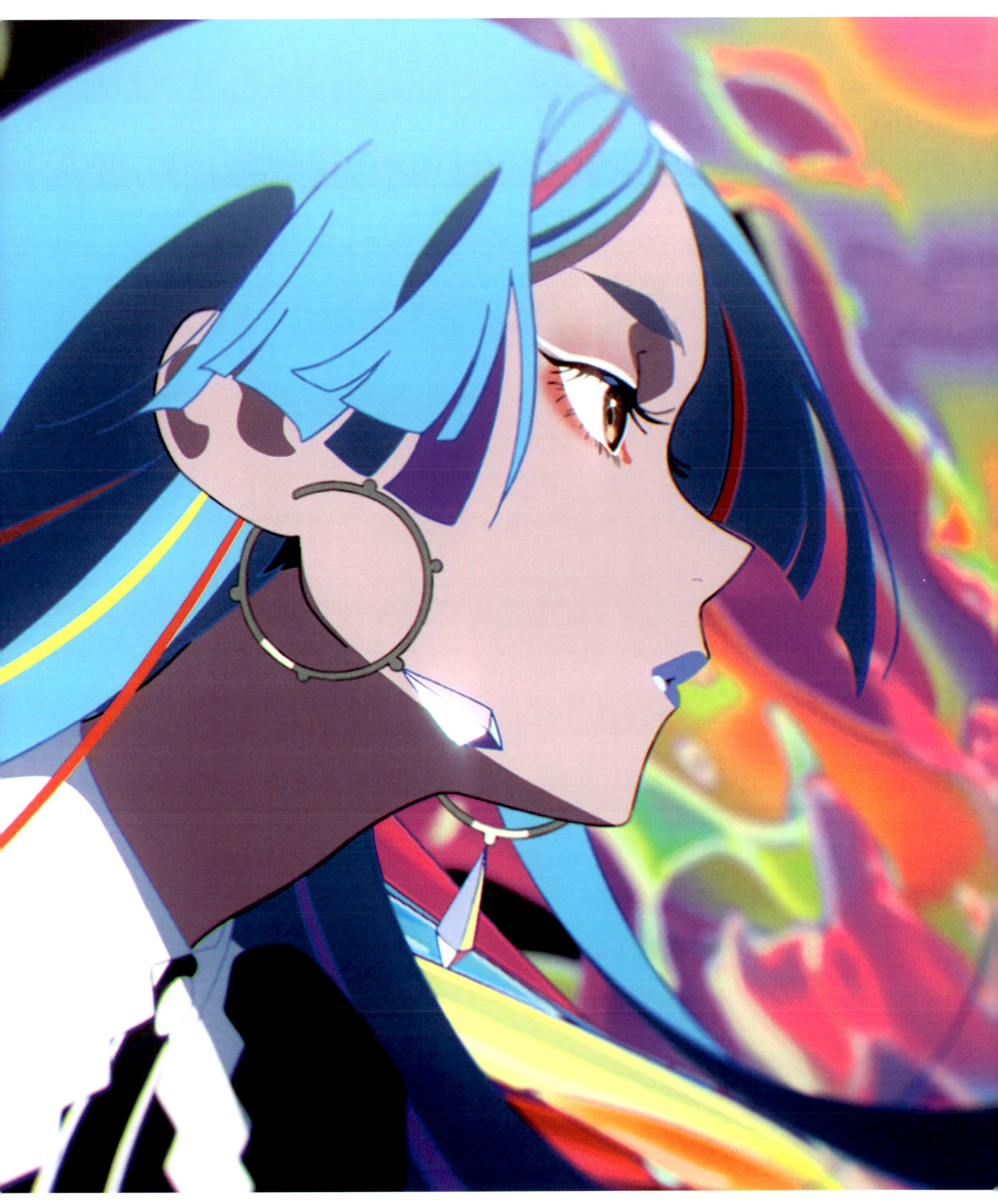

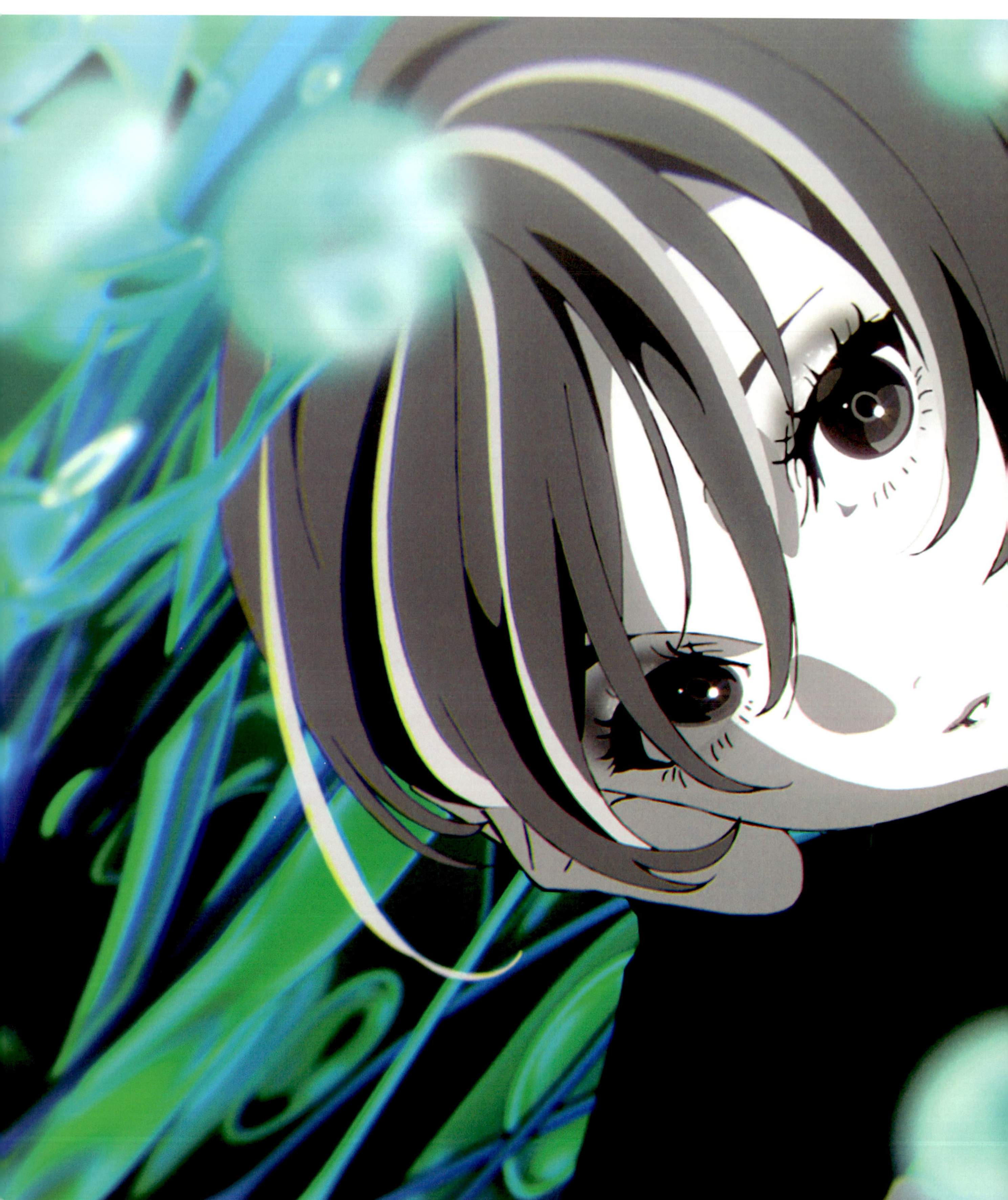

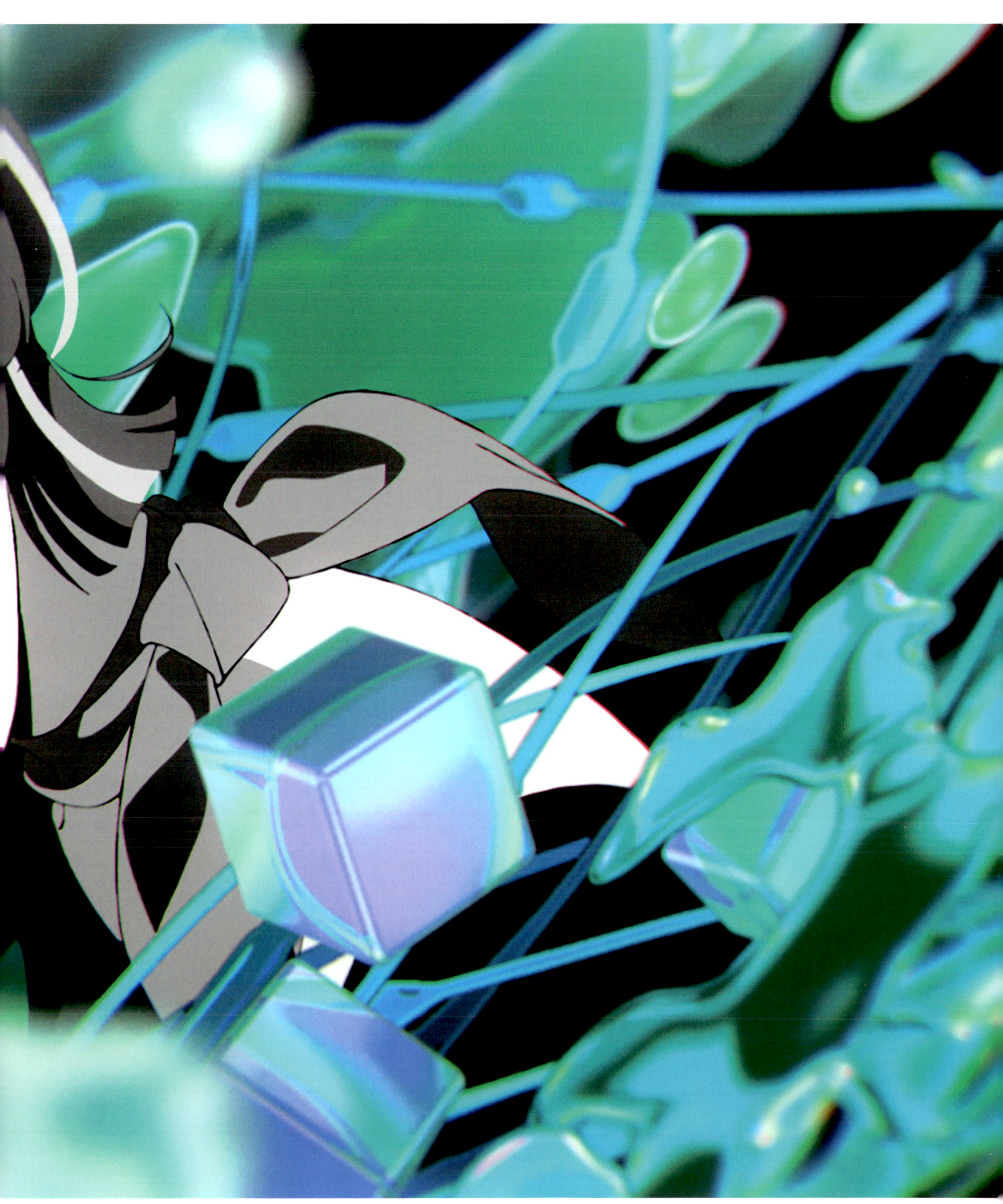

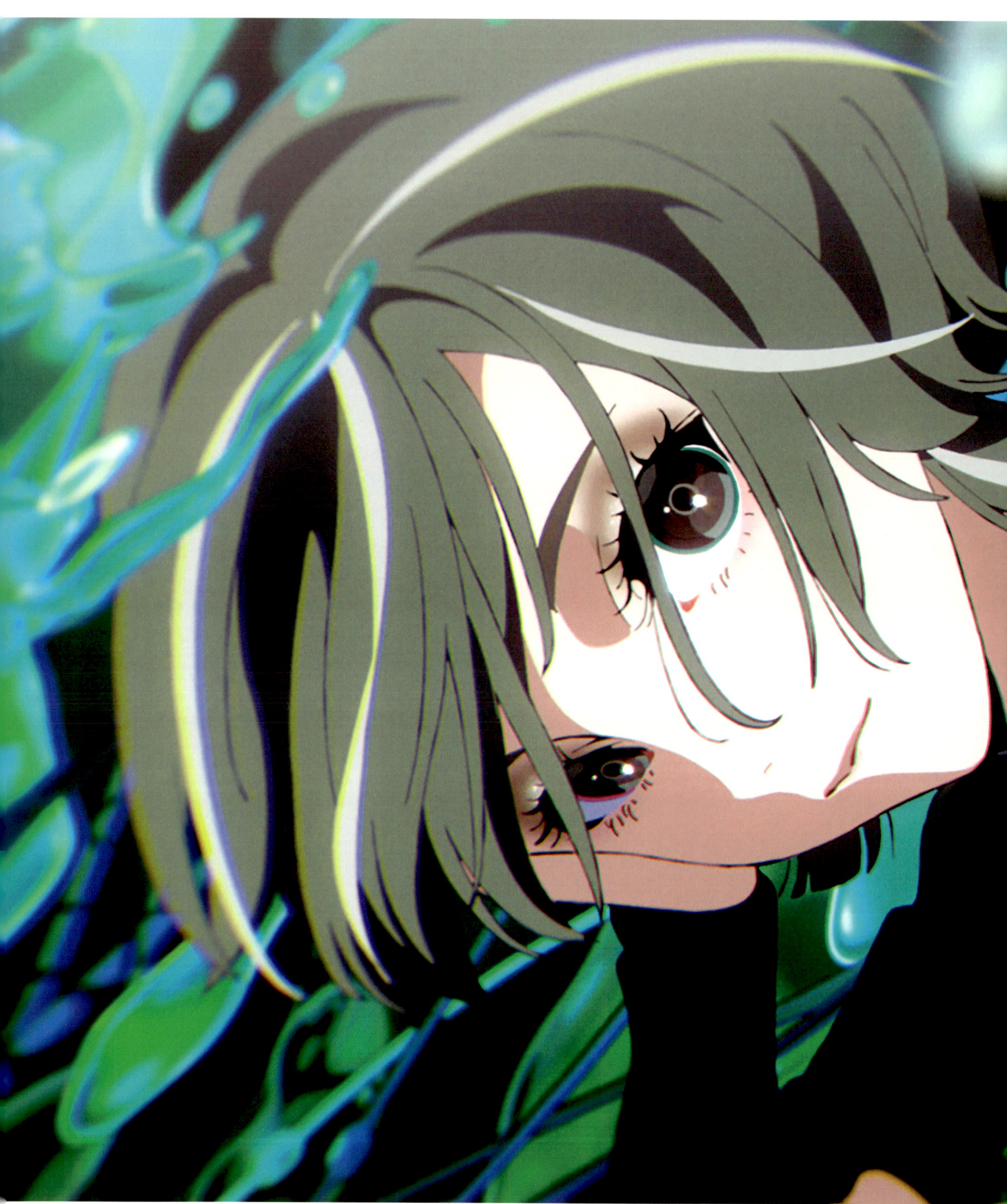

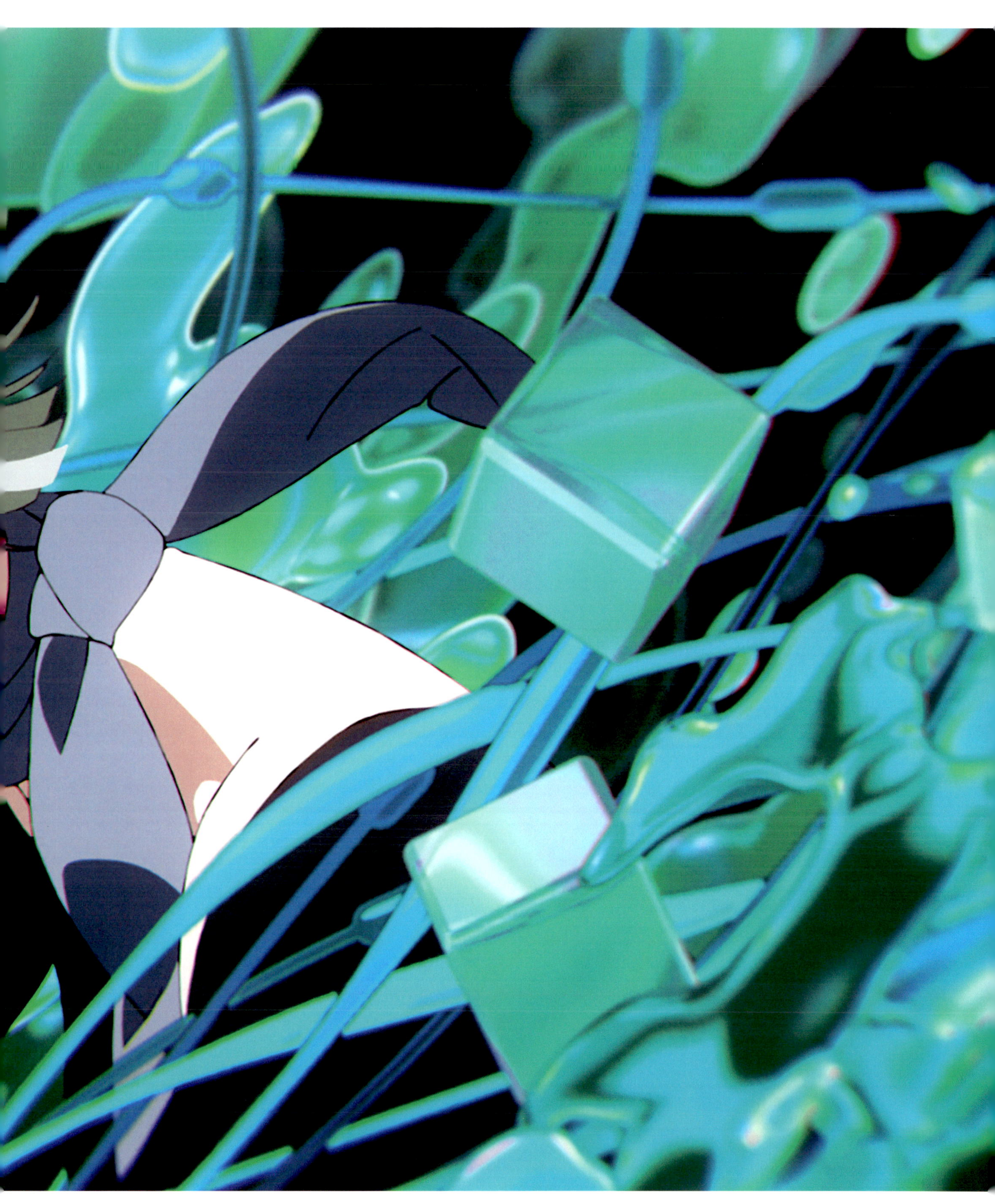

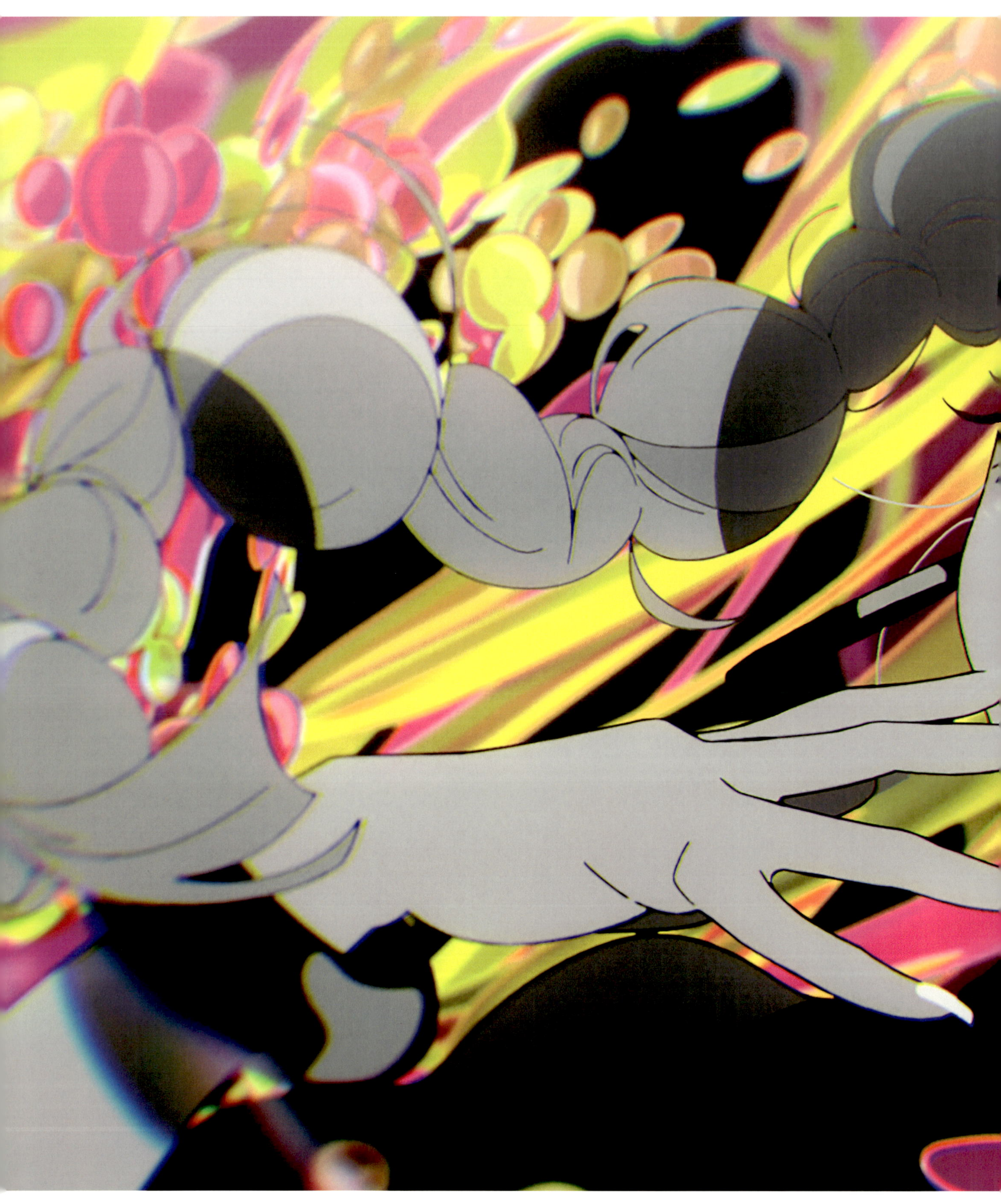

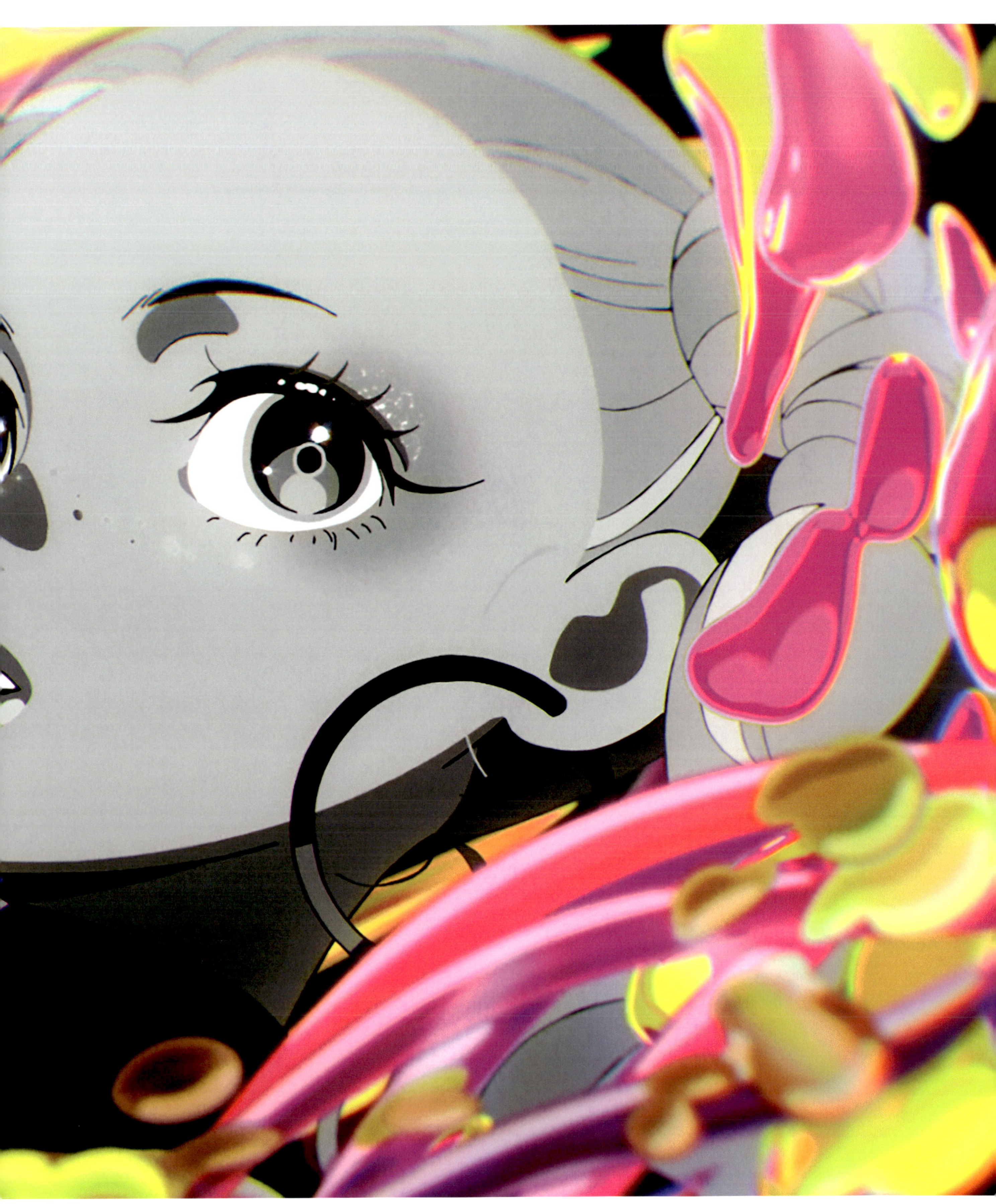

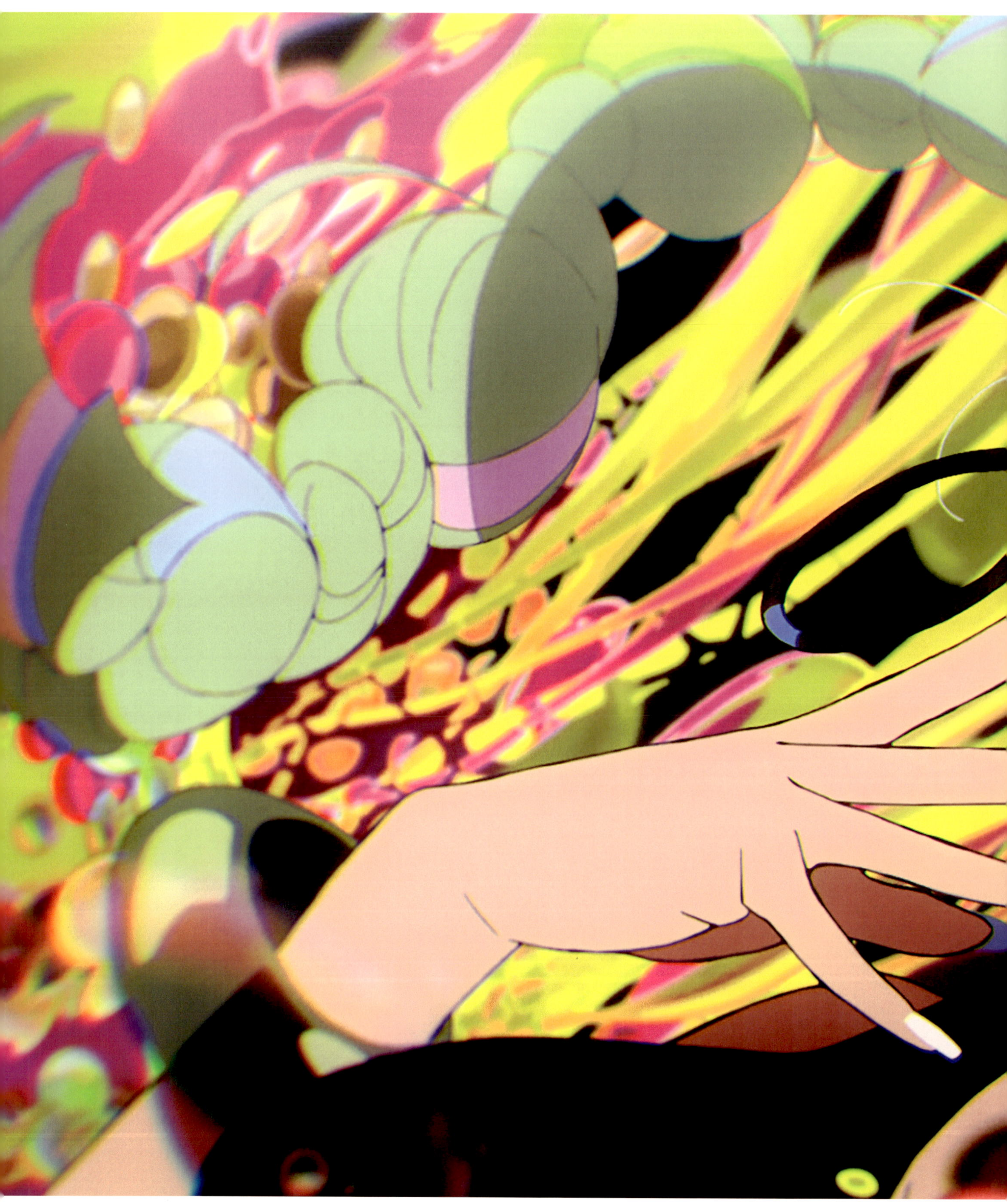

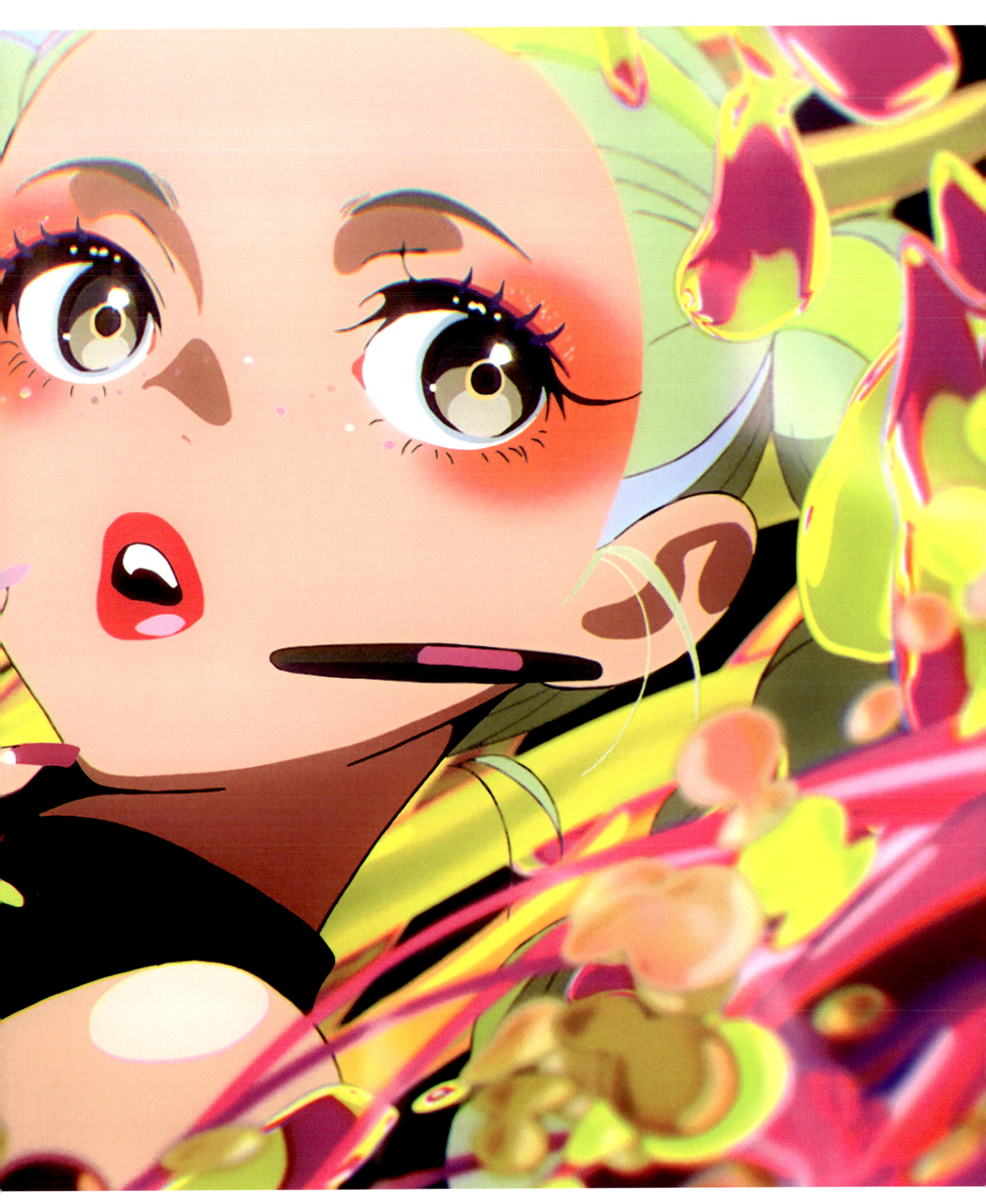

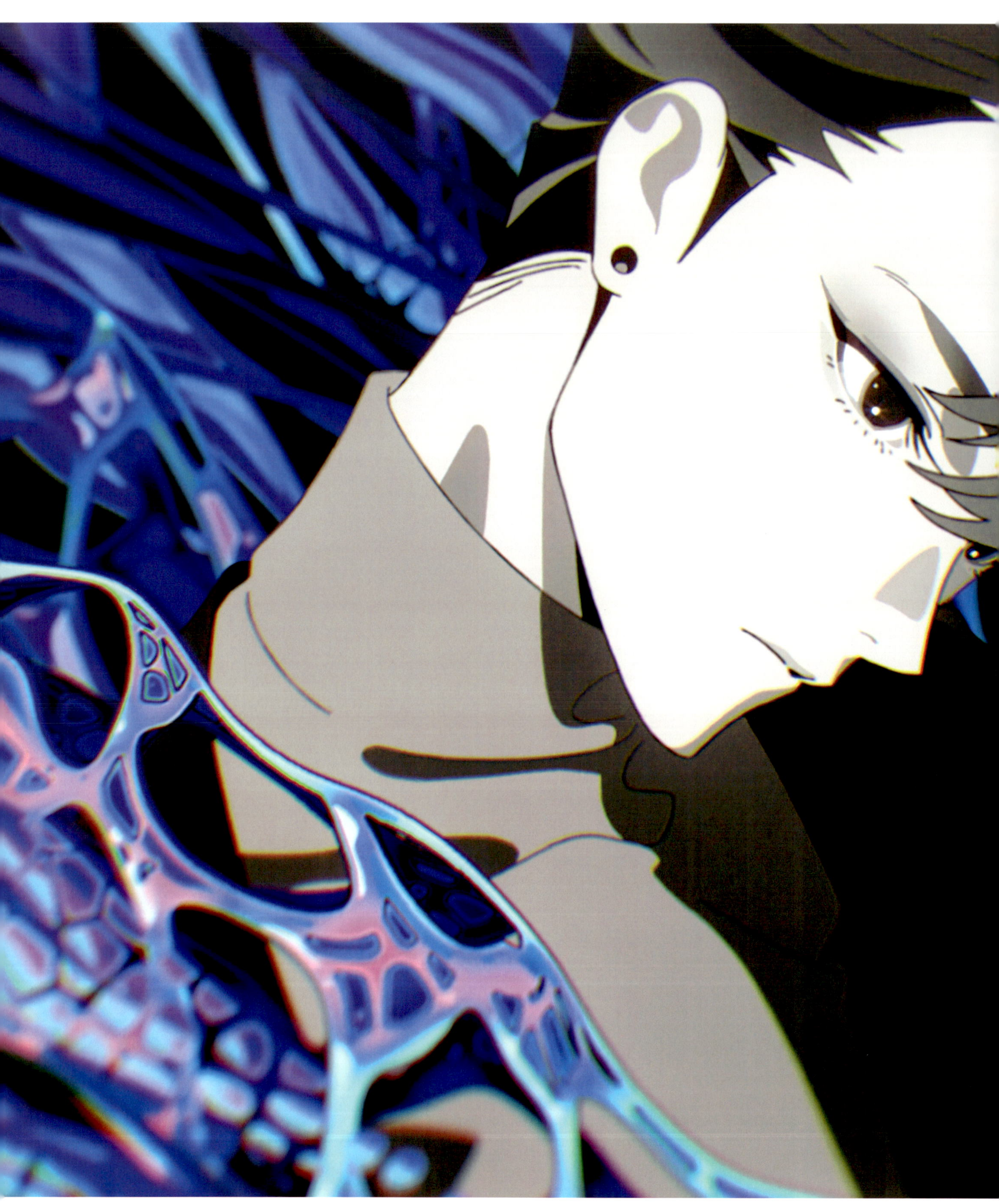

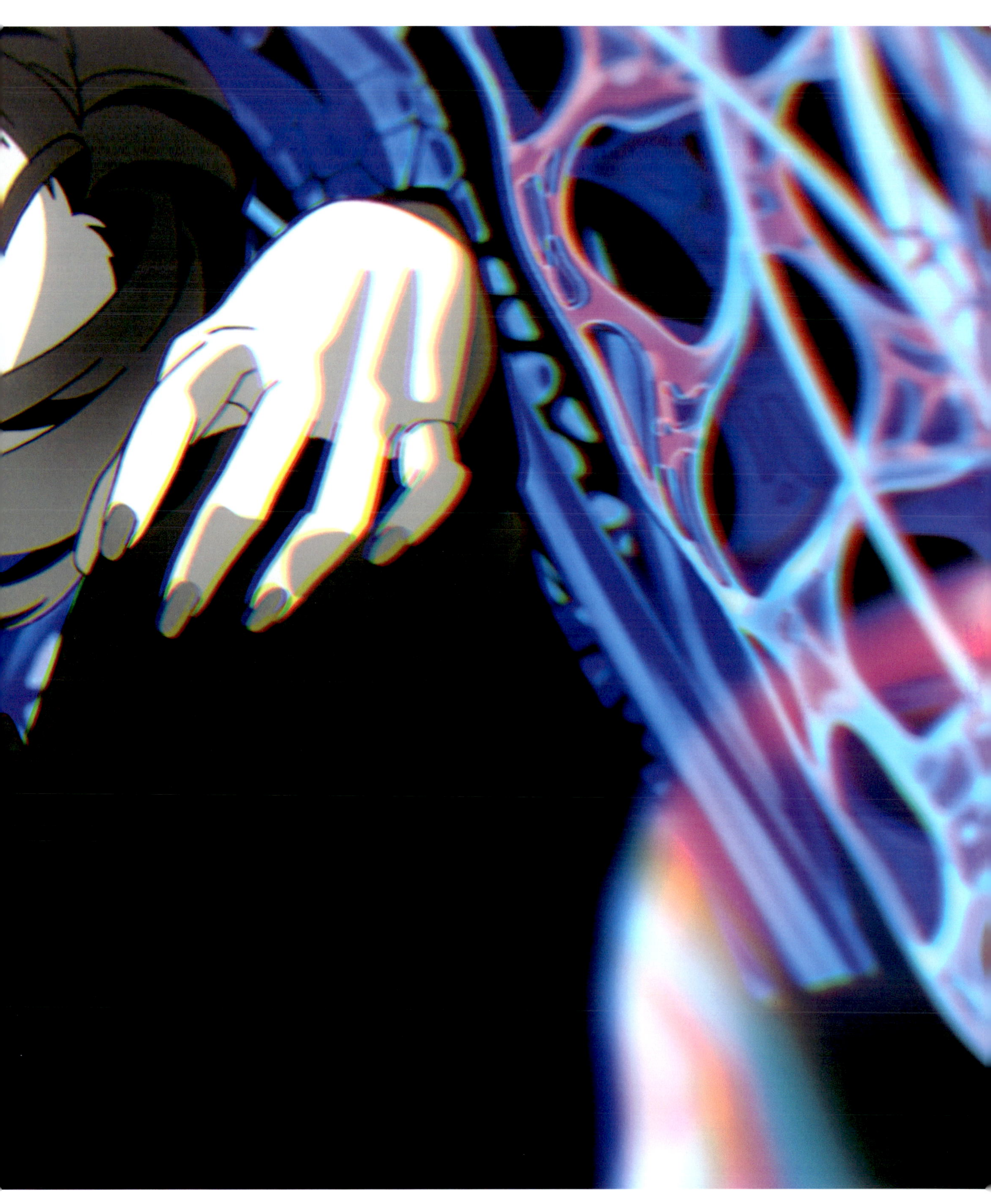

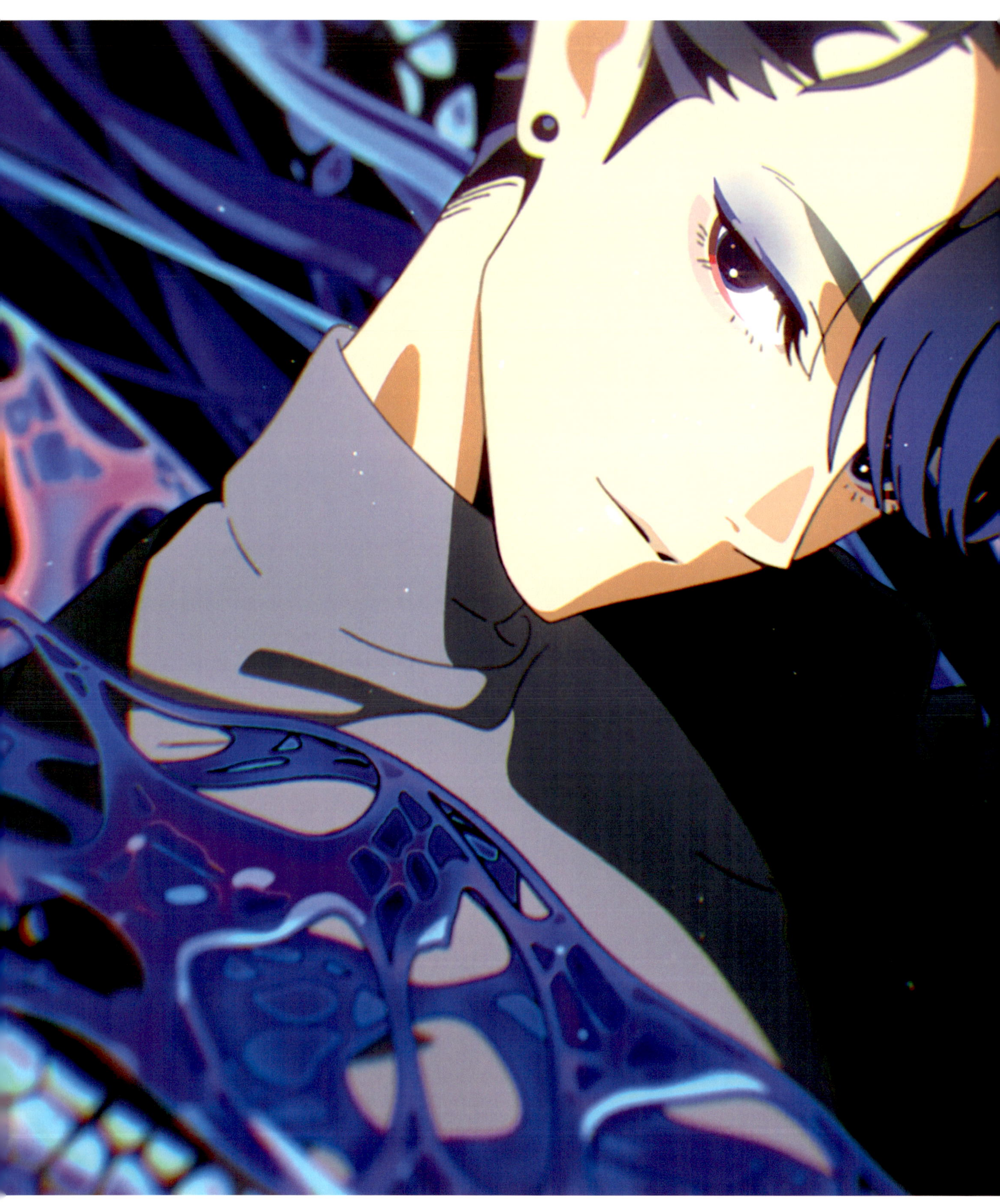

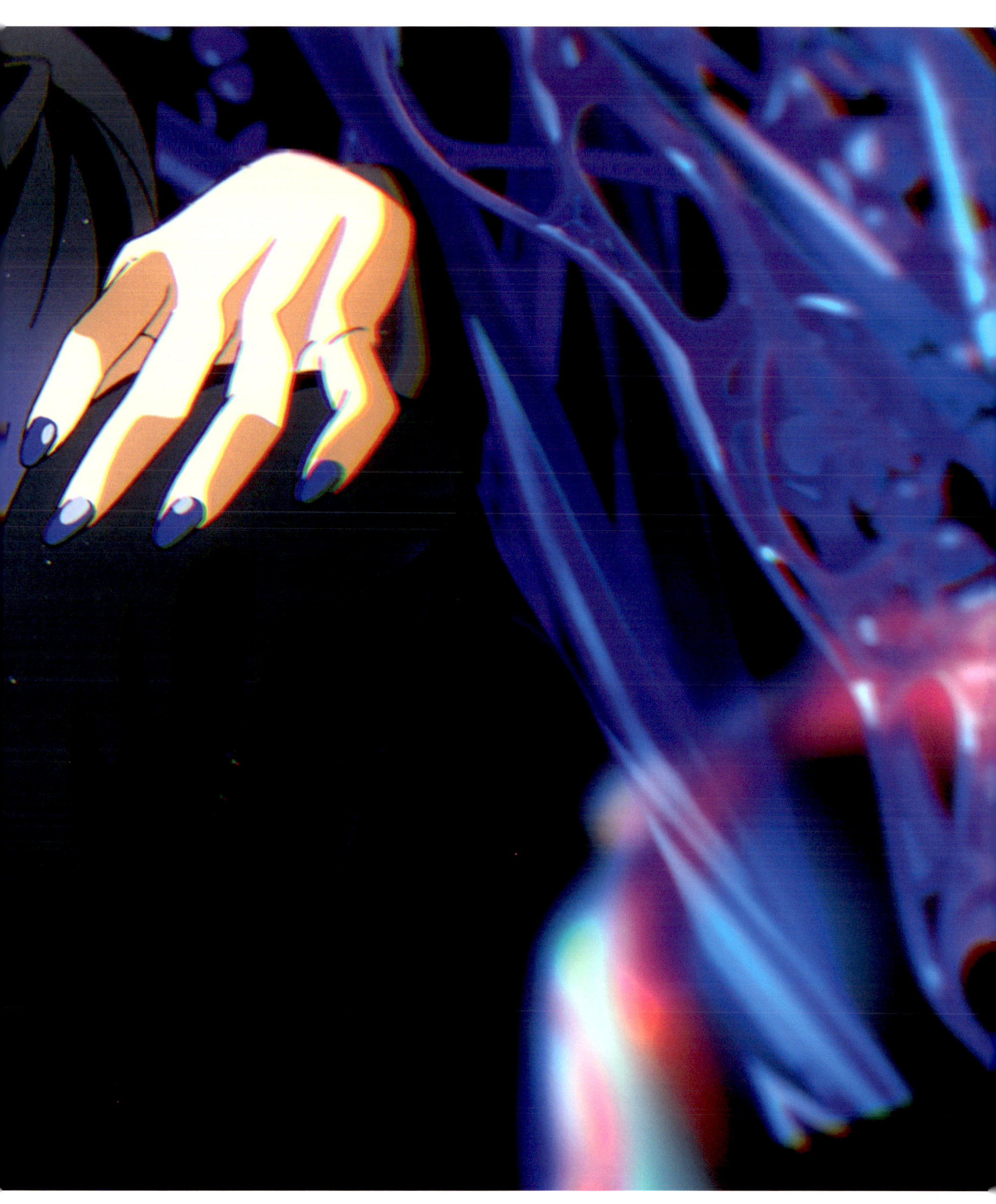

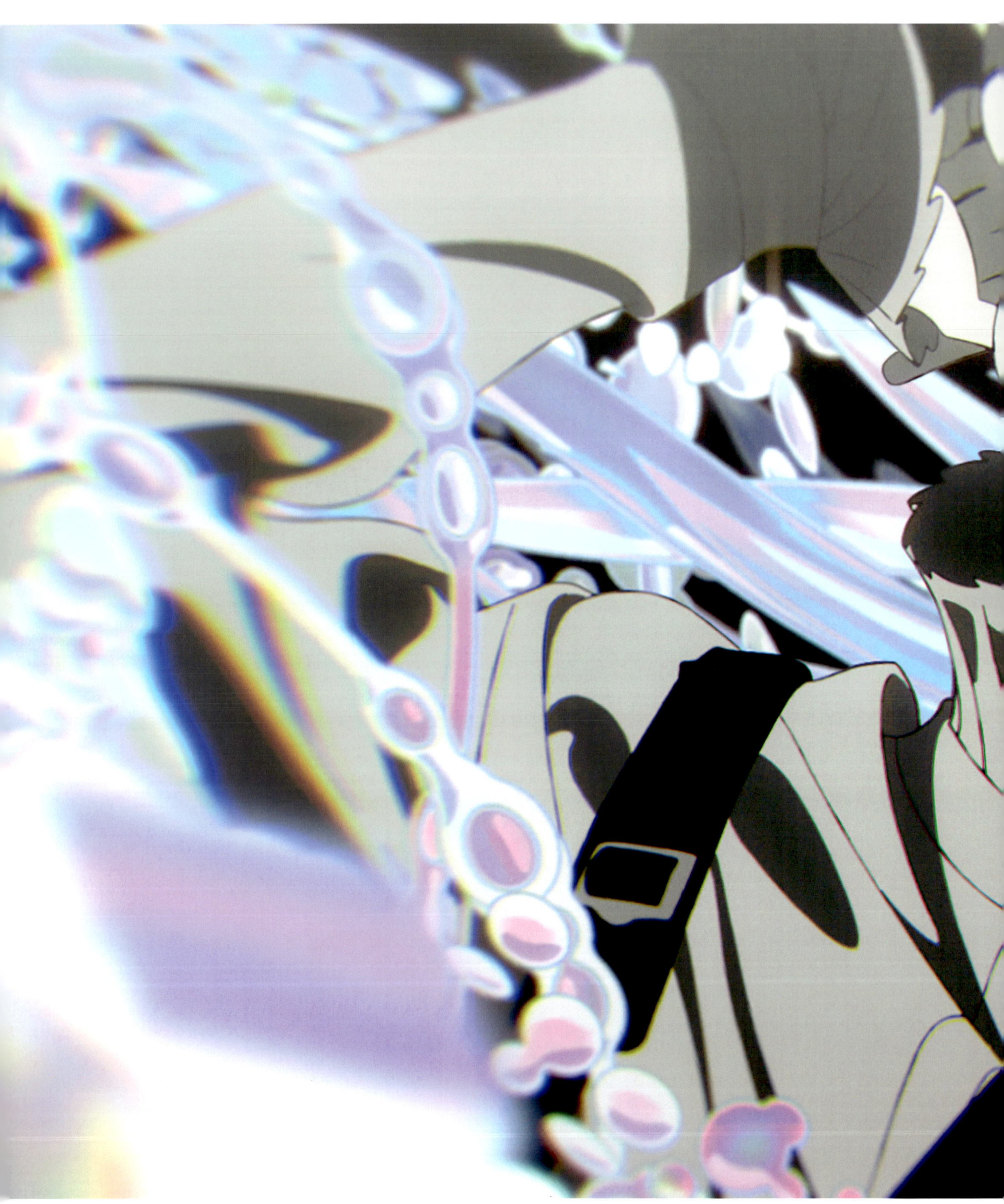

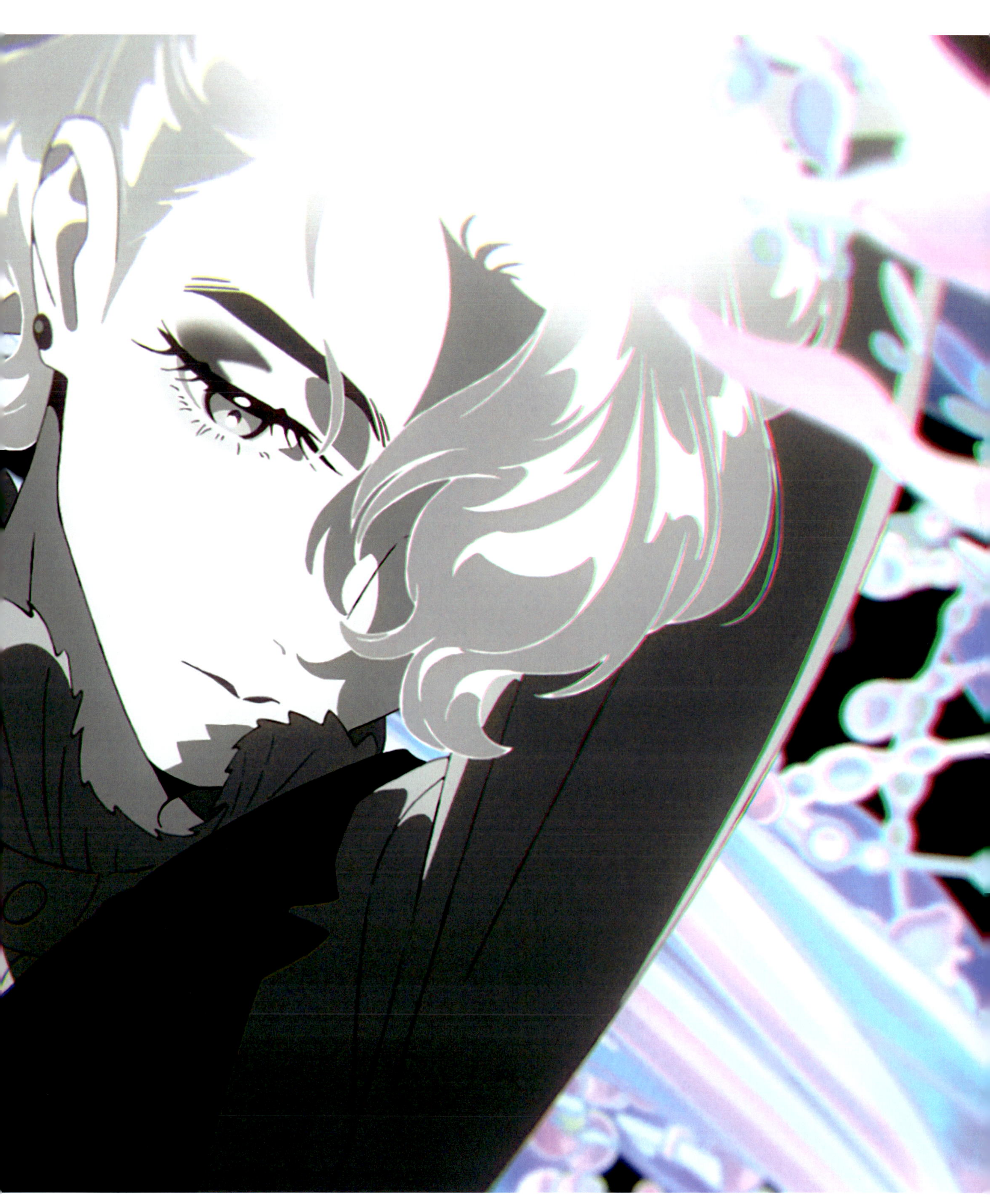

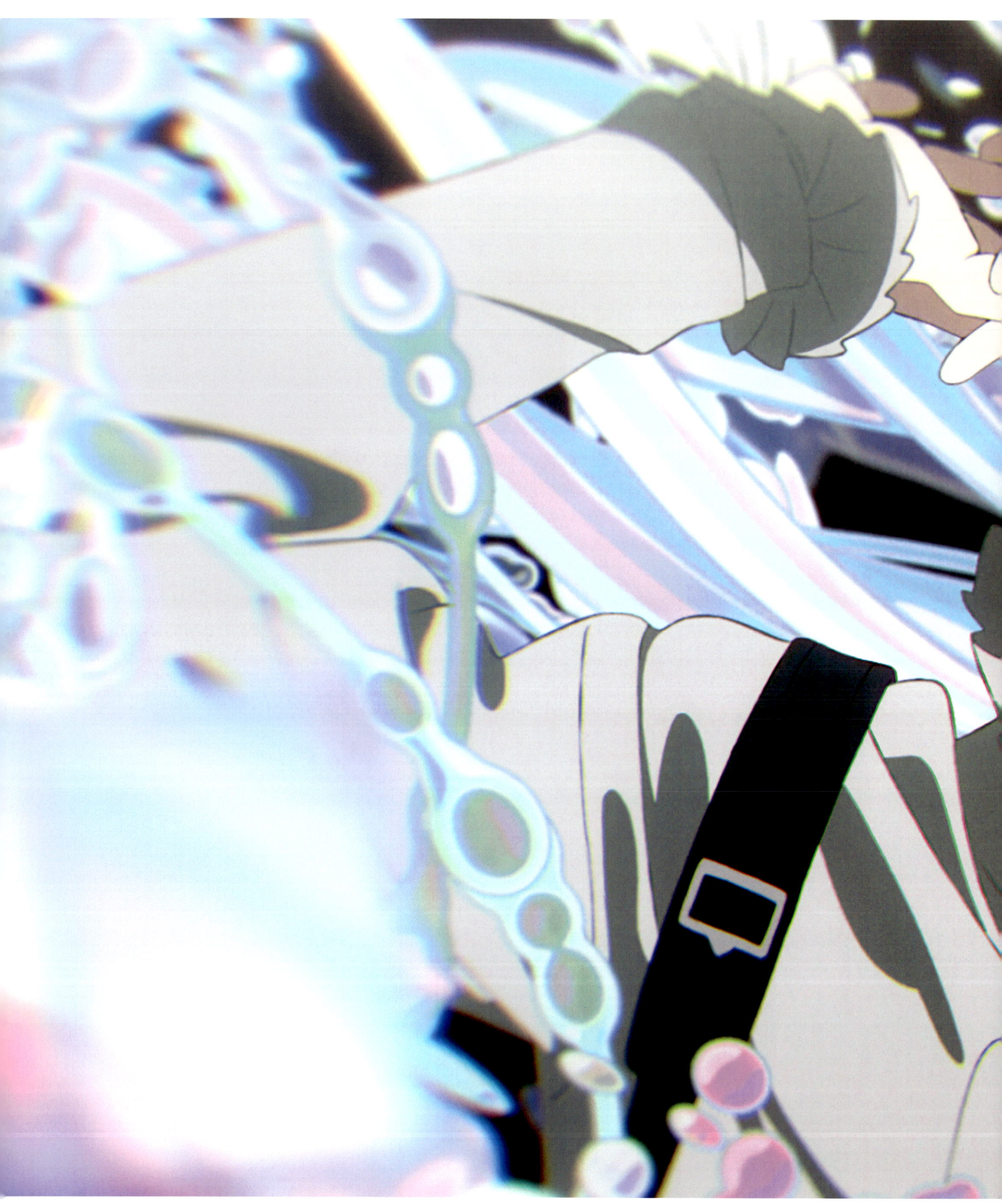

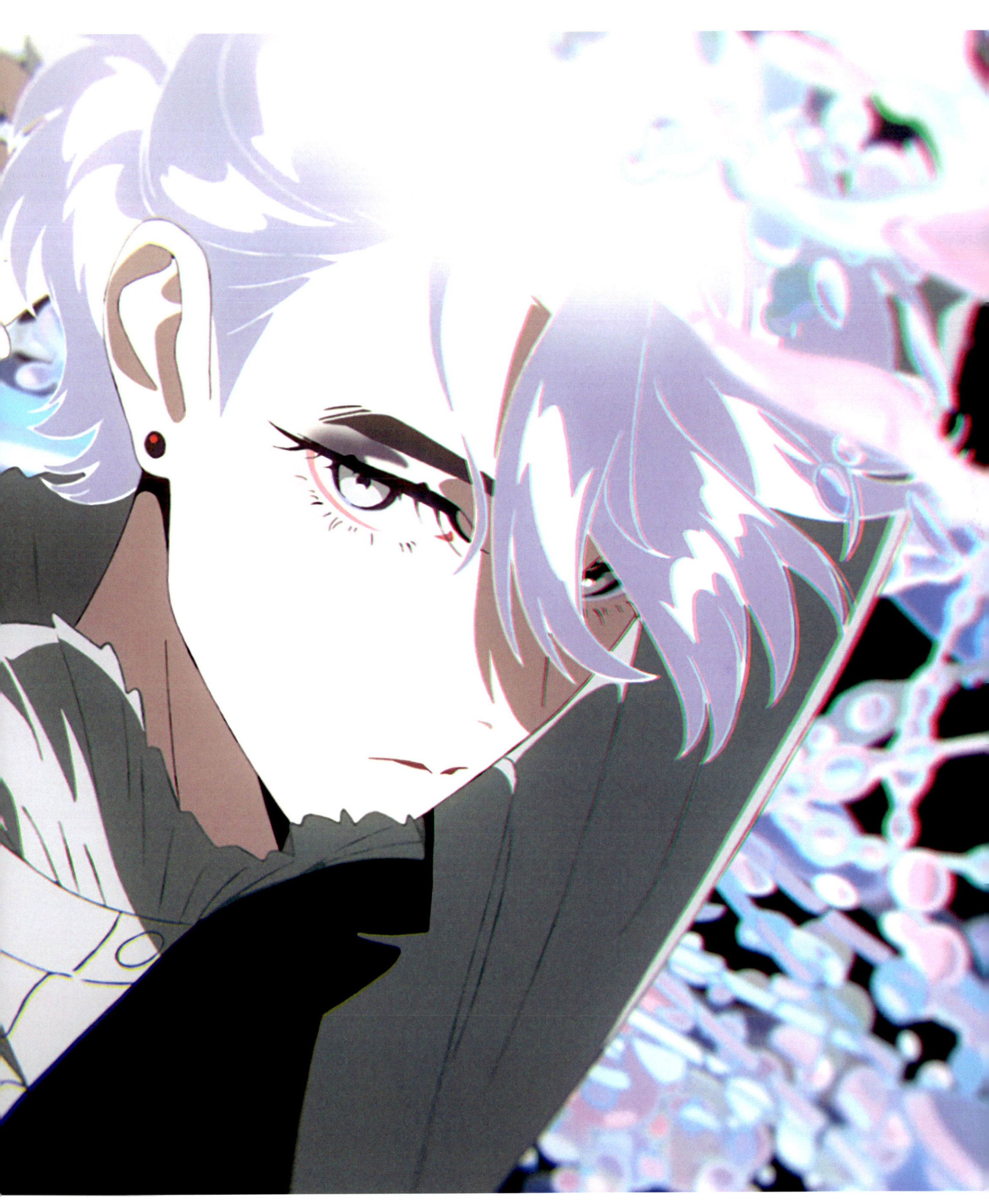

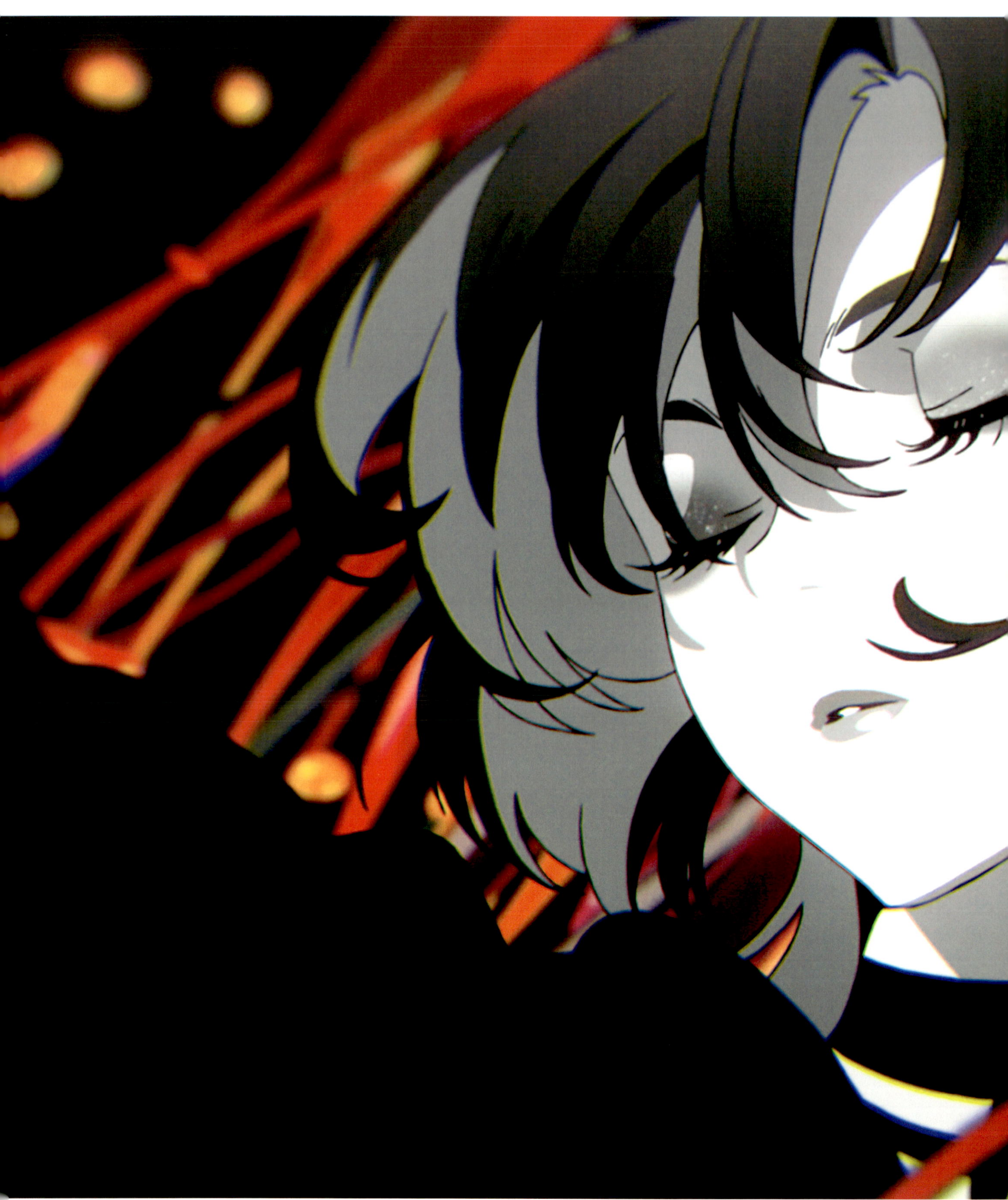

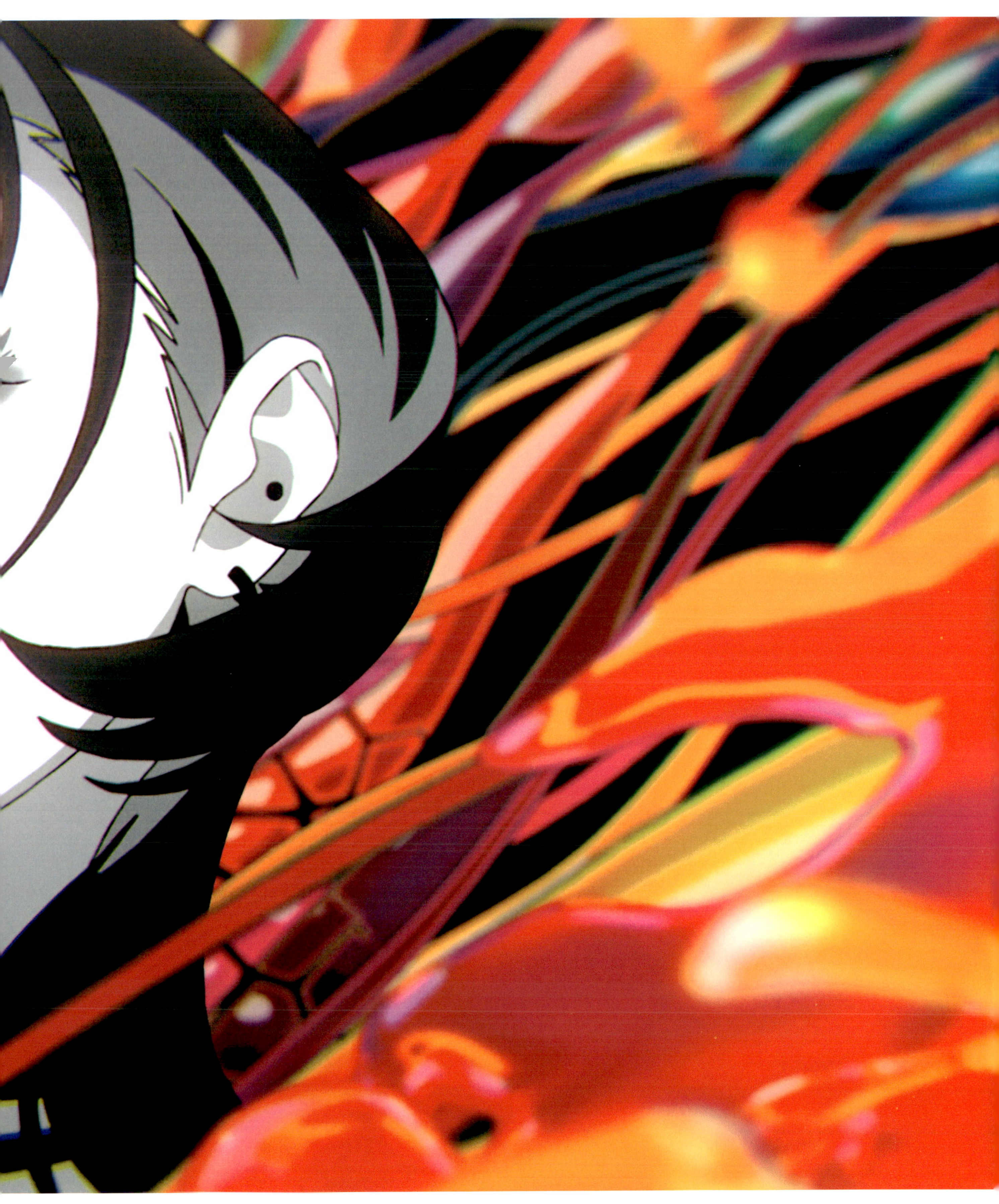

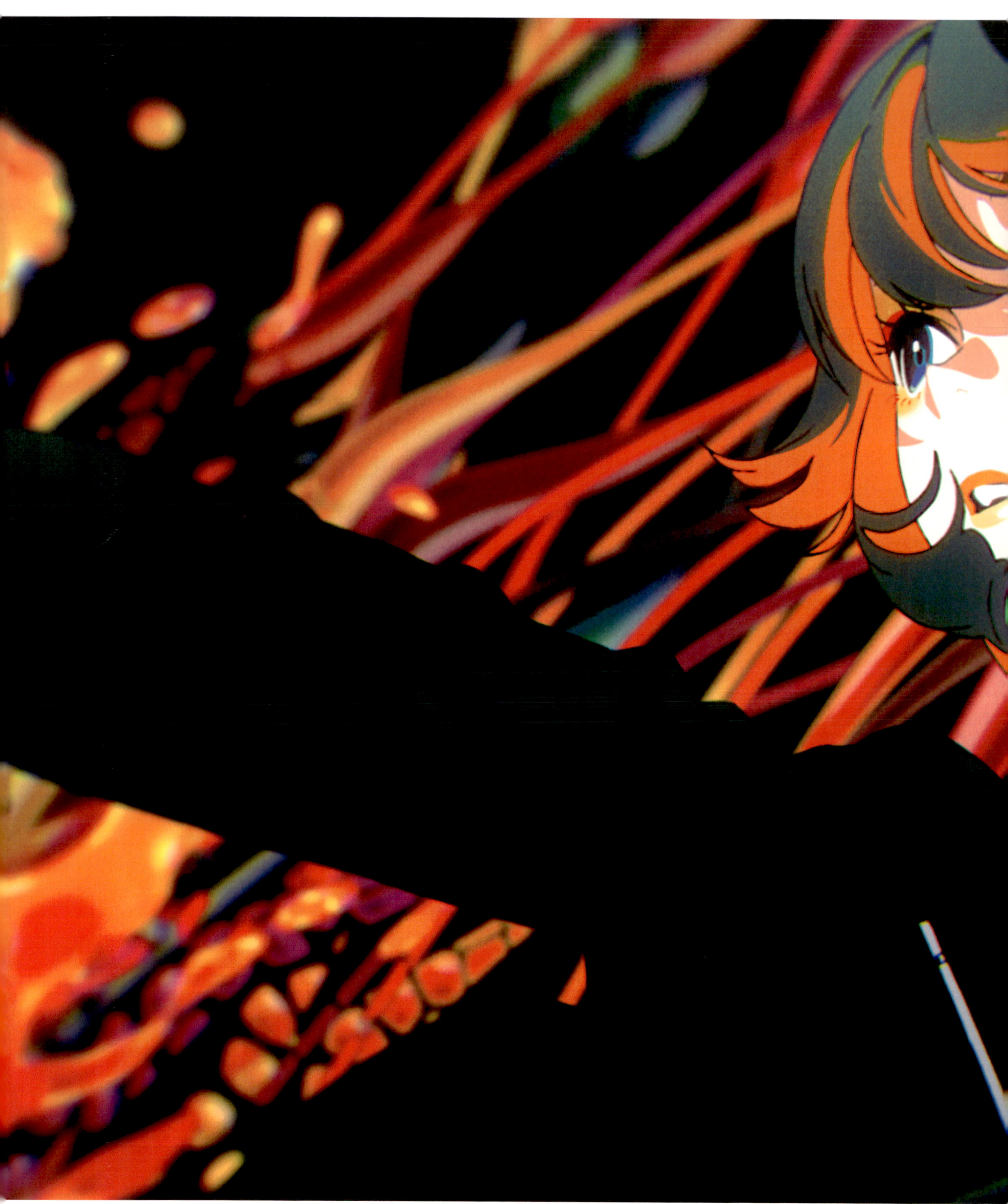

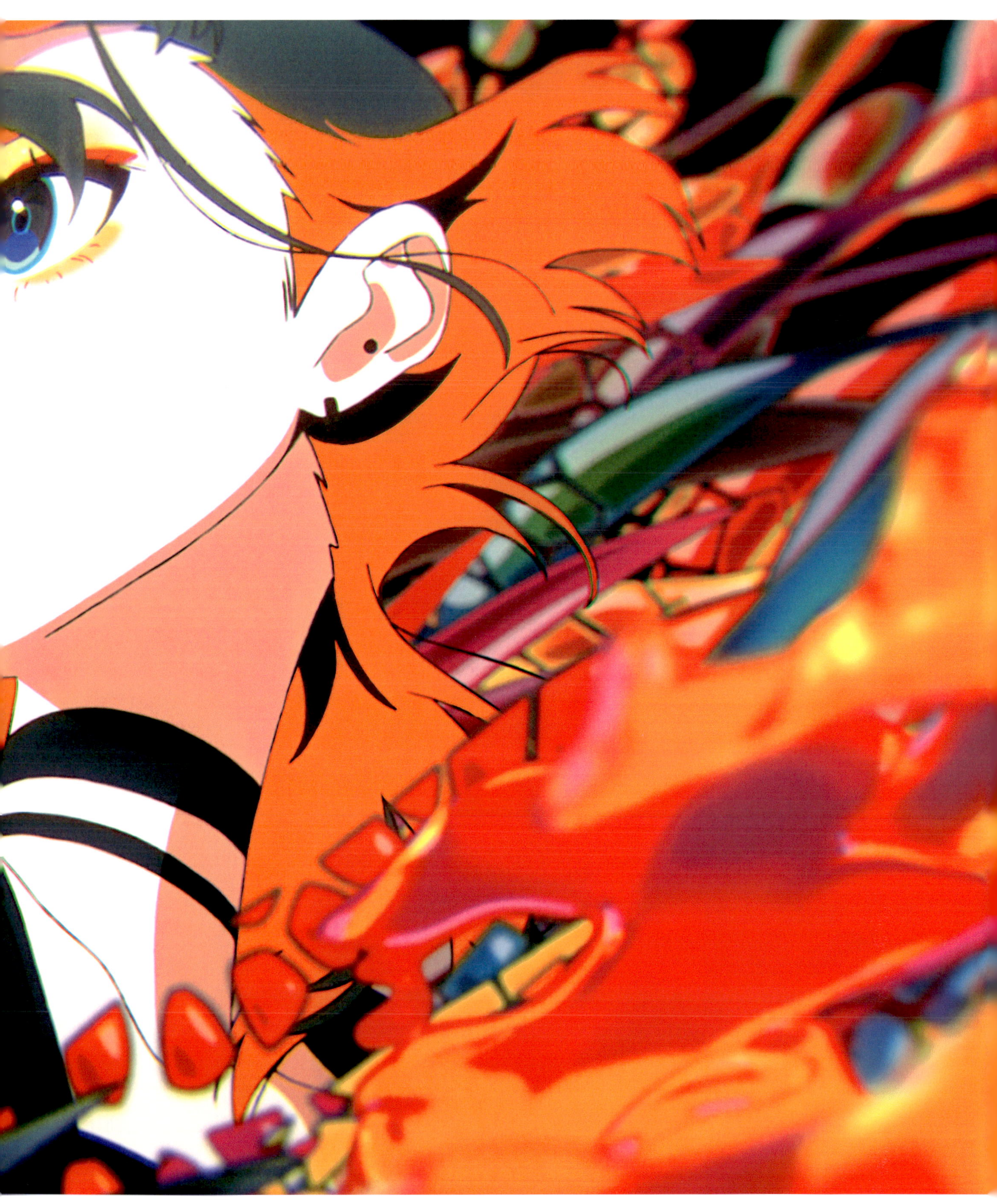

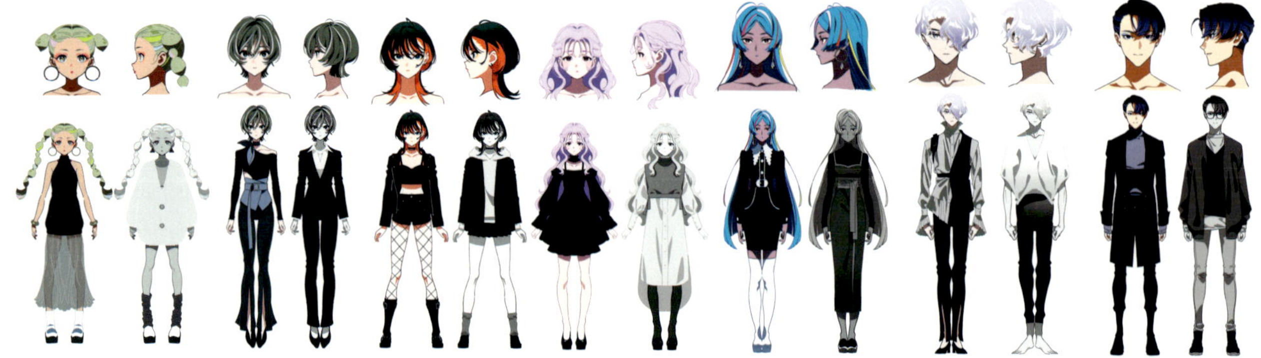

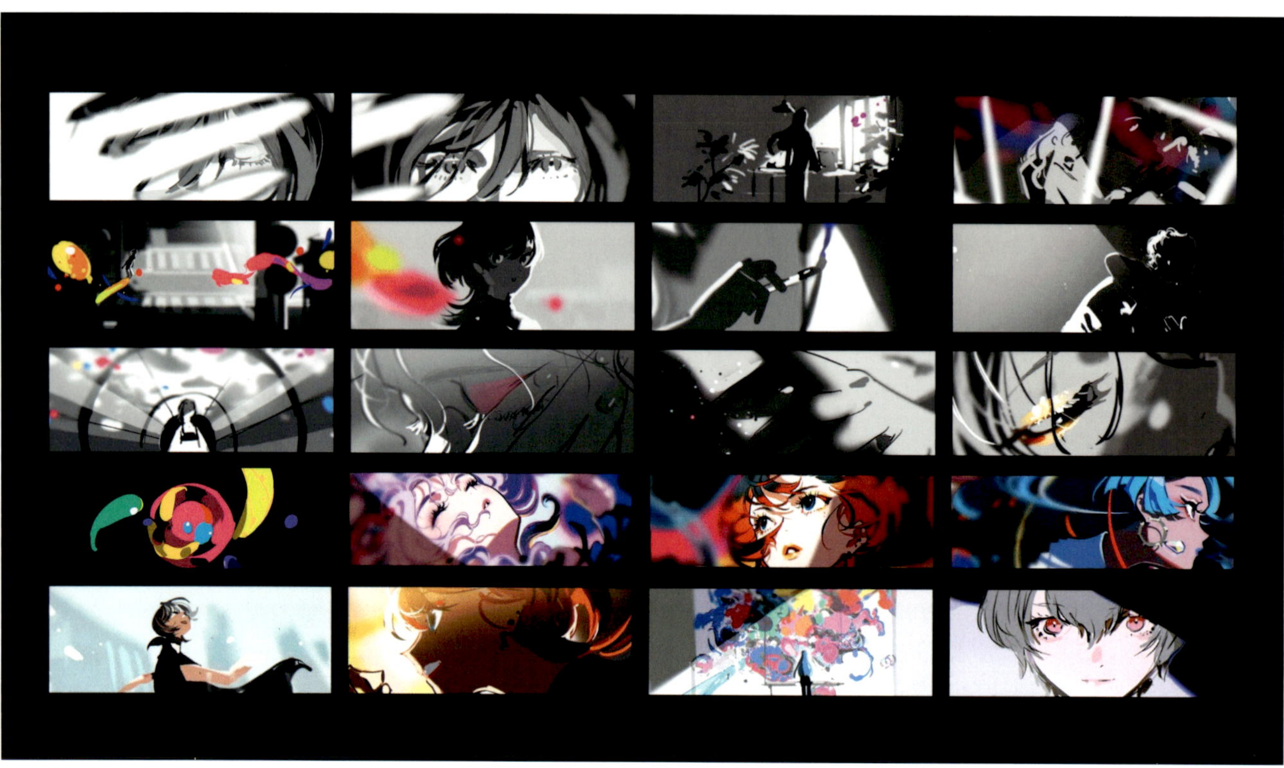

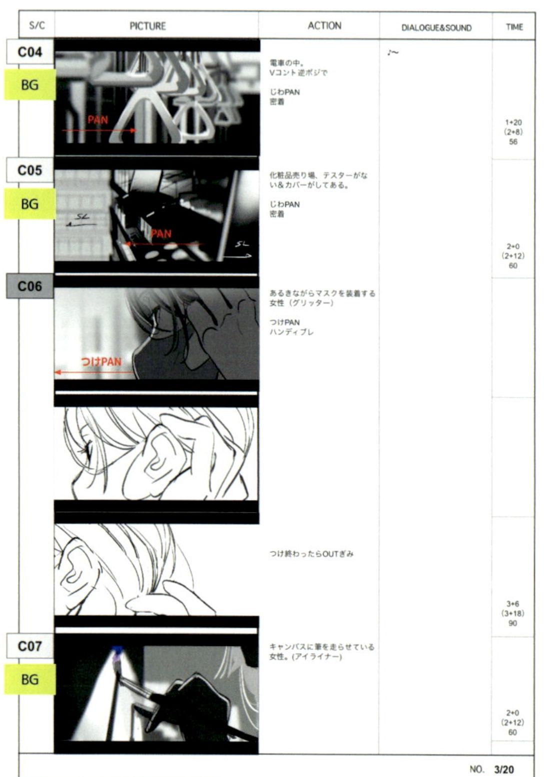

S/C	PICTURE	ACTION	DIALOGUE&SOUND	TIME
C04 BG	PAN	電車の中。 Vコント逆ポジで じわPAN 密着	♪～	1+20 (2+8) 56
C05 BG	SL PAN SL	化粧品売り場、テスターがない&カバーがしてある。 じわPAN 密着		2+0 (2+12) 60
C06	つけPAN	あるきながらマスクを装着する女性（グリッター） つけPAN ハンディブレ		
		つけ終わったらOUTぎみ		3+6 (3+18) 90
C07 BG		キャンバスに筆を走らせている女性。(アイライナー)		2+0 (2+12) 60

NO. 3/20

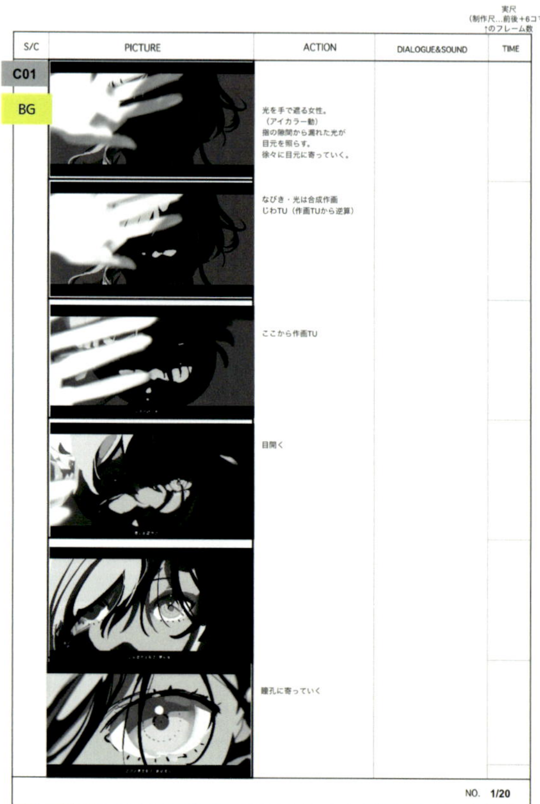

実尺
（制作尺…前後+6コマ）
↑のフレーム数

S/C	PICTURE	ACTION	DIALOGUE&SOUND	TIME
C01 BG		光を手で遮る女性。 （アイカラー動） 指の隙間から漏れた光が 目元を照らす。 徐々に目元に寄っていく。		
		なびき・光は合成作画 じわTU（作画TUから逆算）		
		ここから作画TU		
		目開く		
		瞳孔に寄っていく		

NO. 1/20

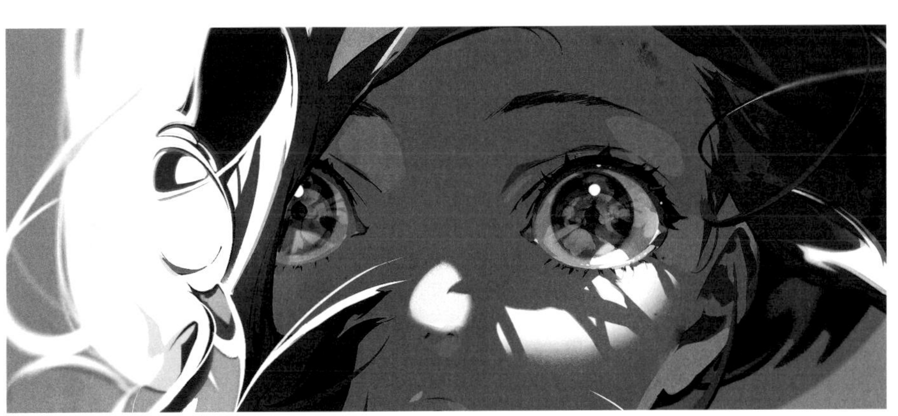

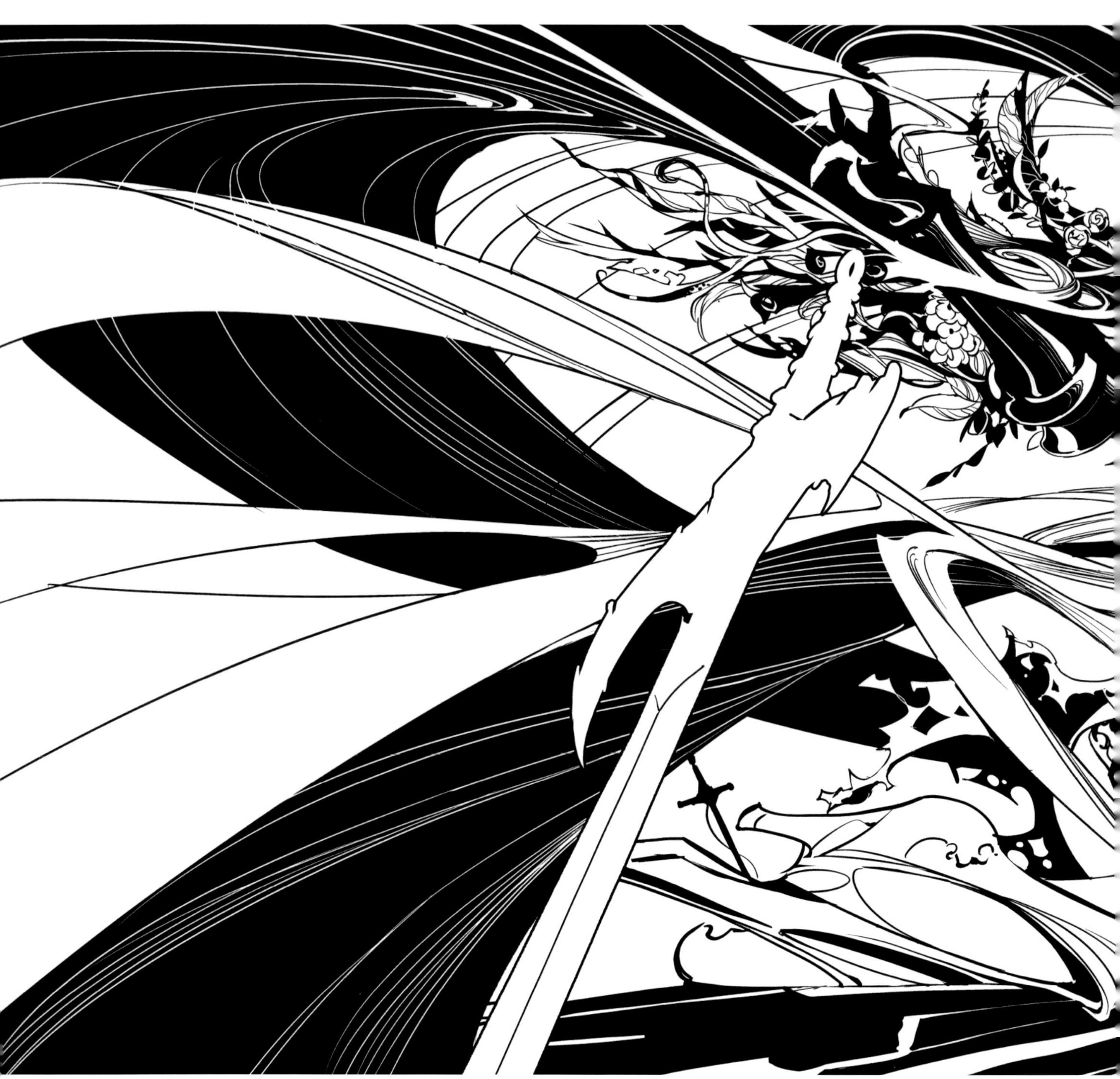

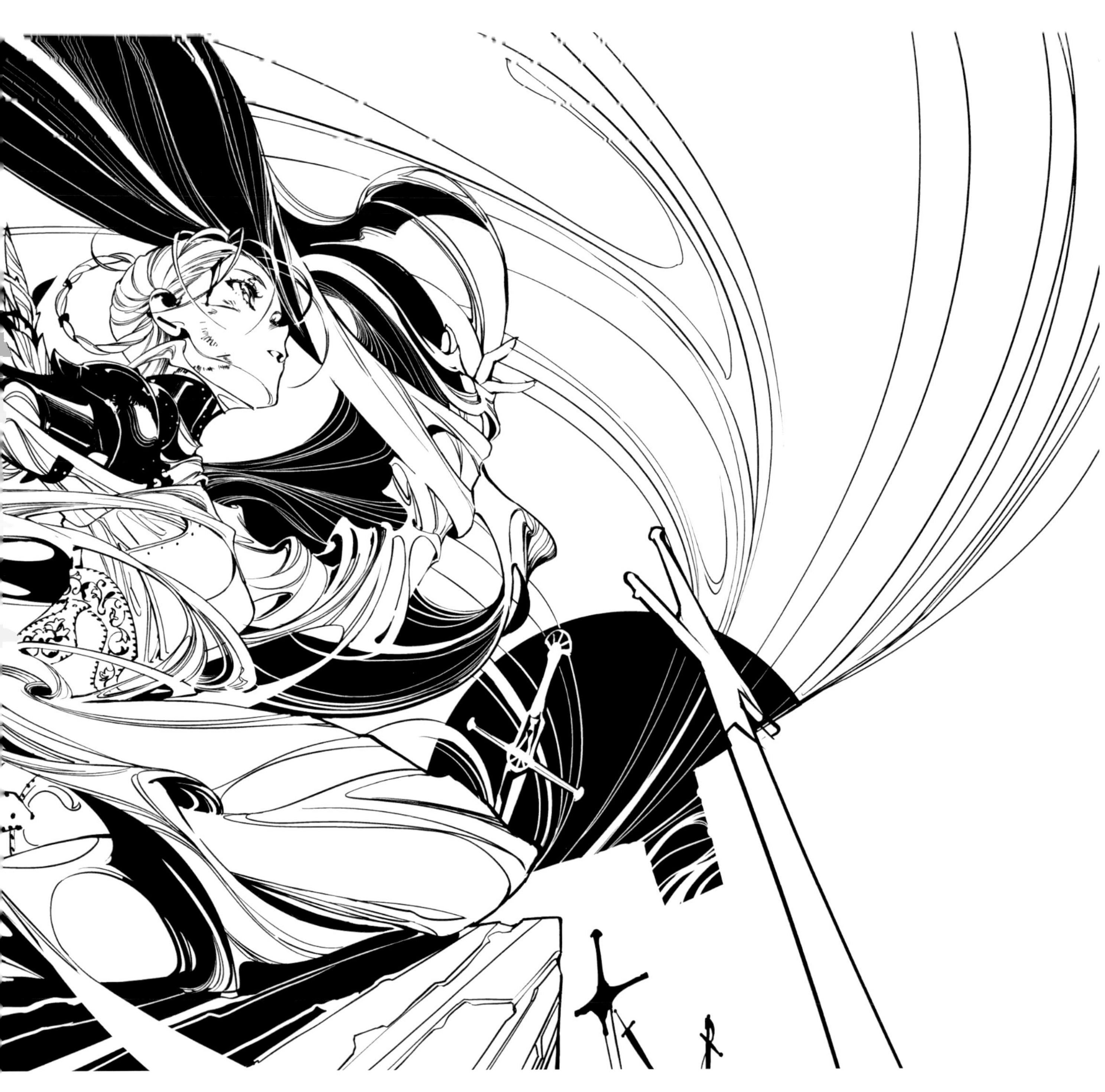

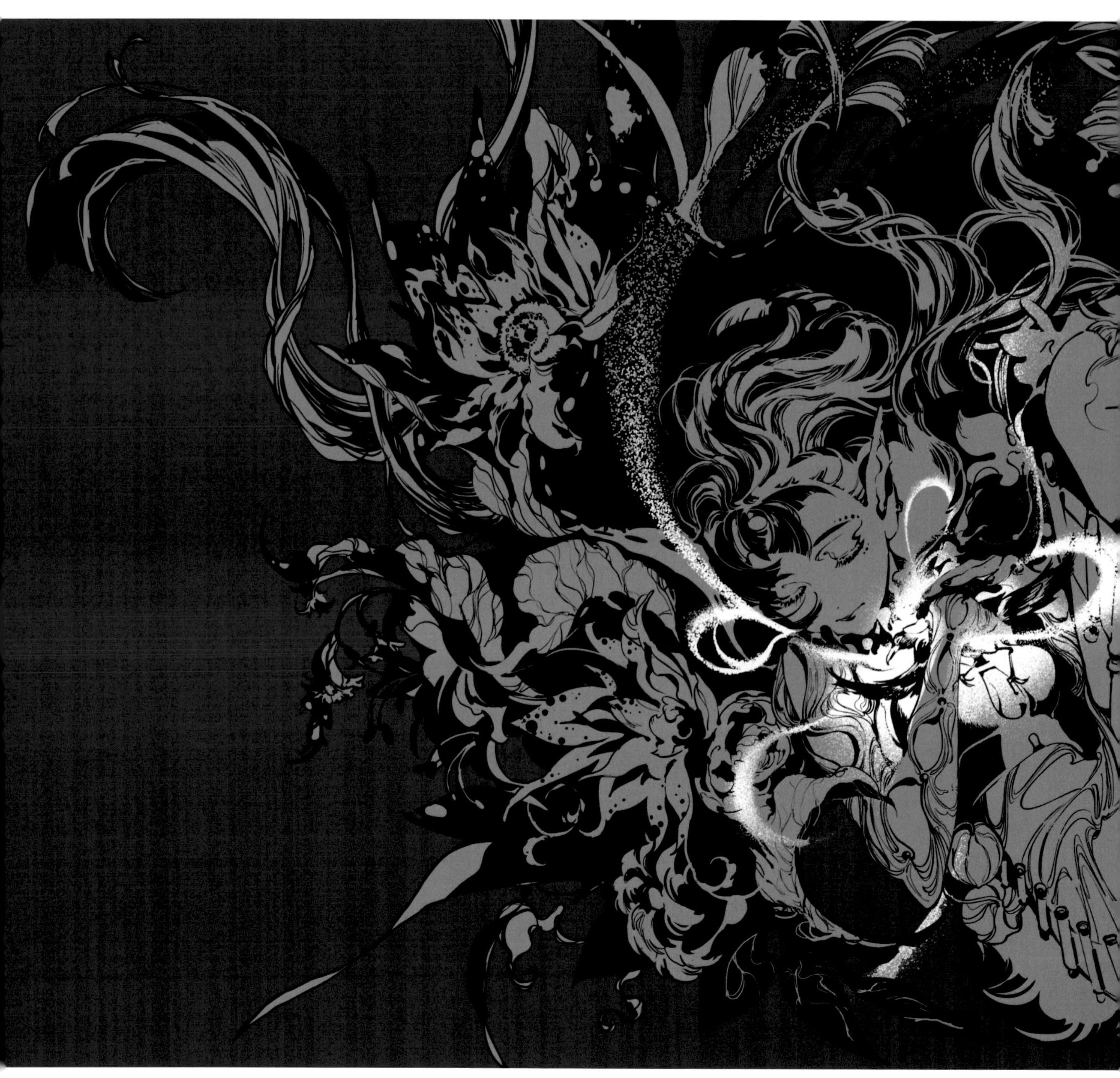

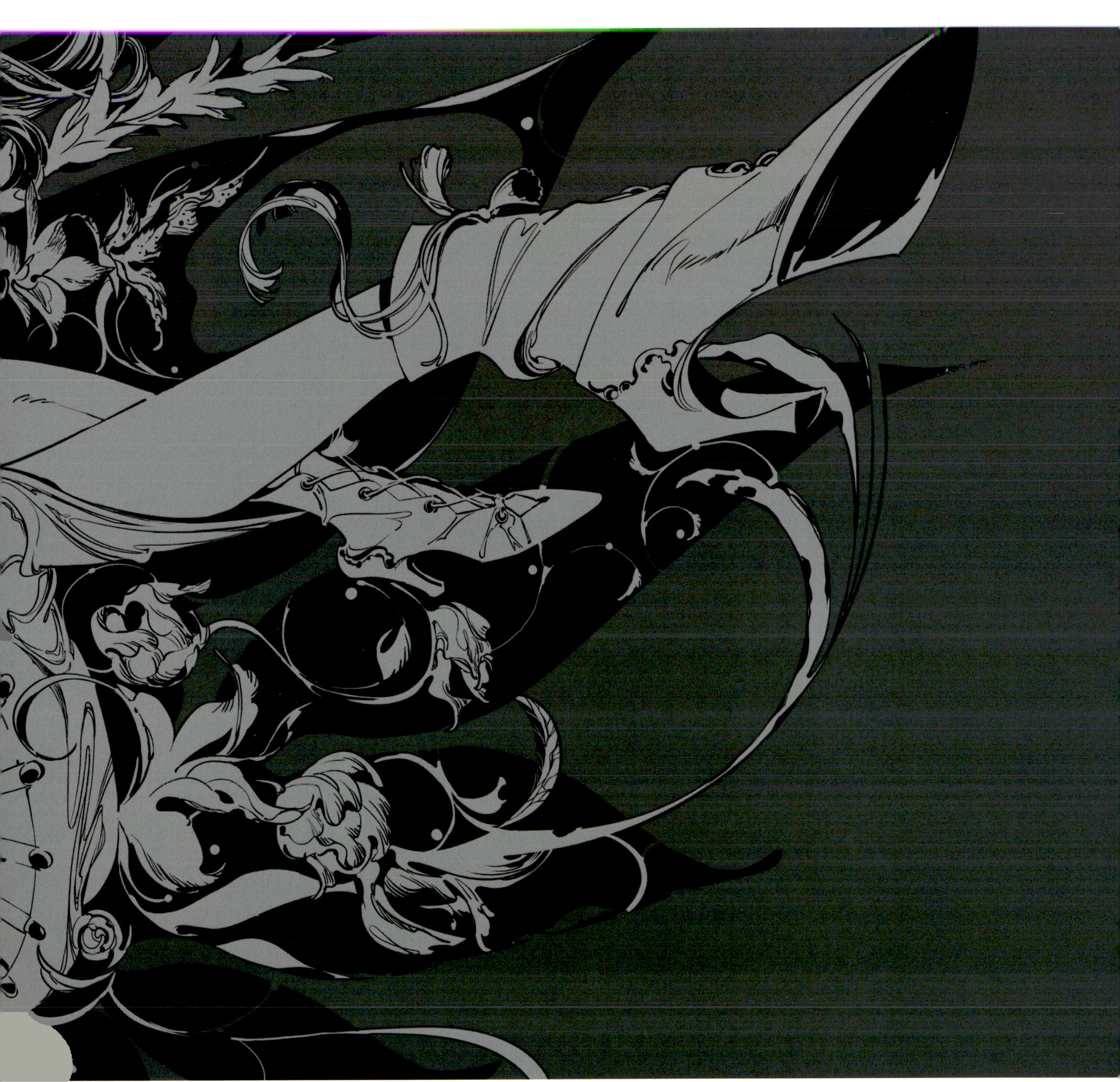

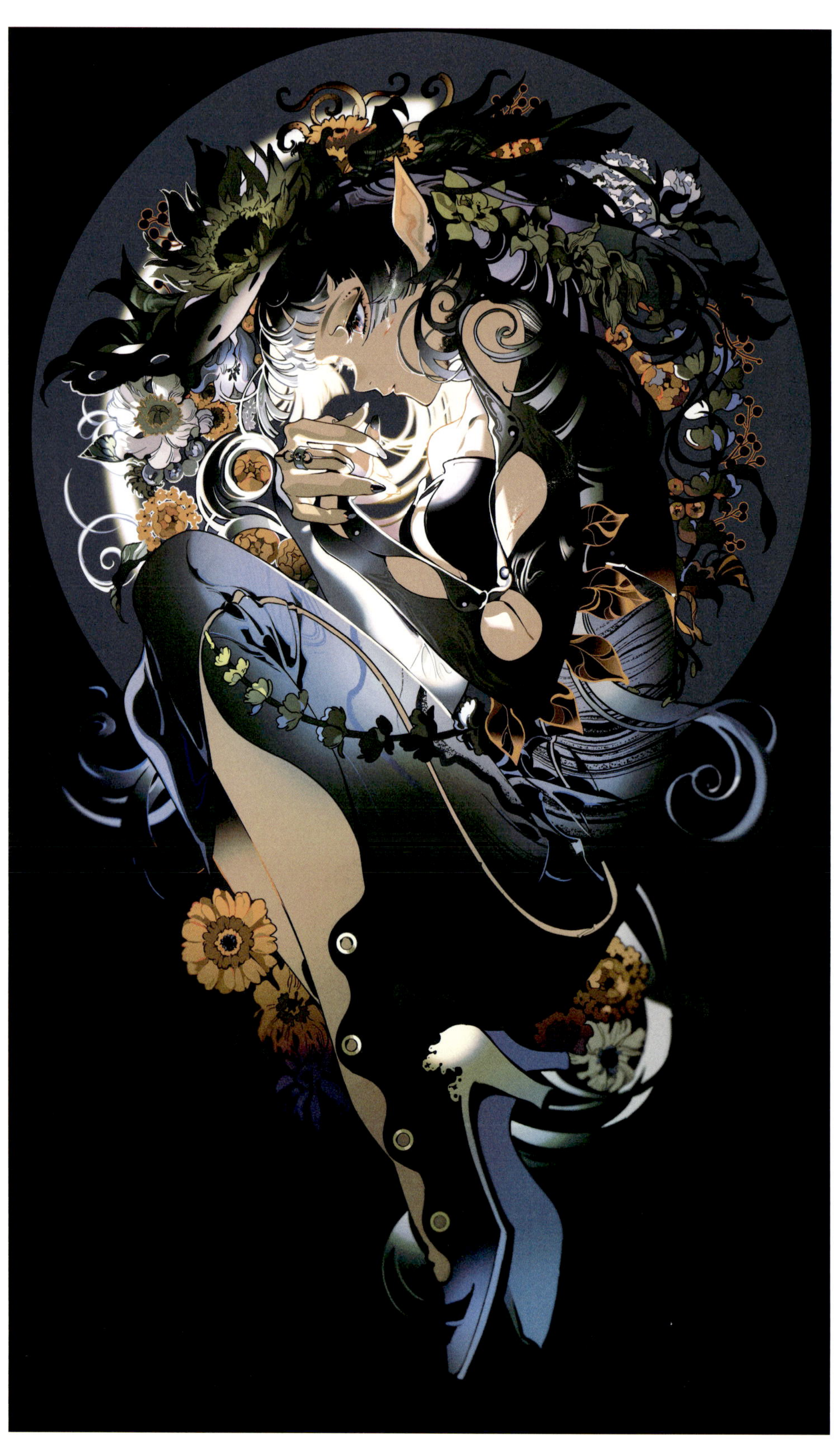

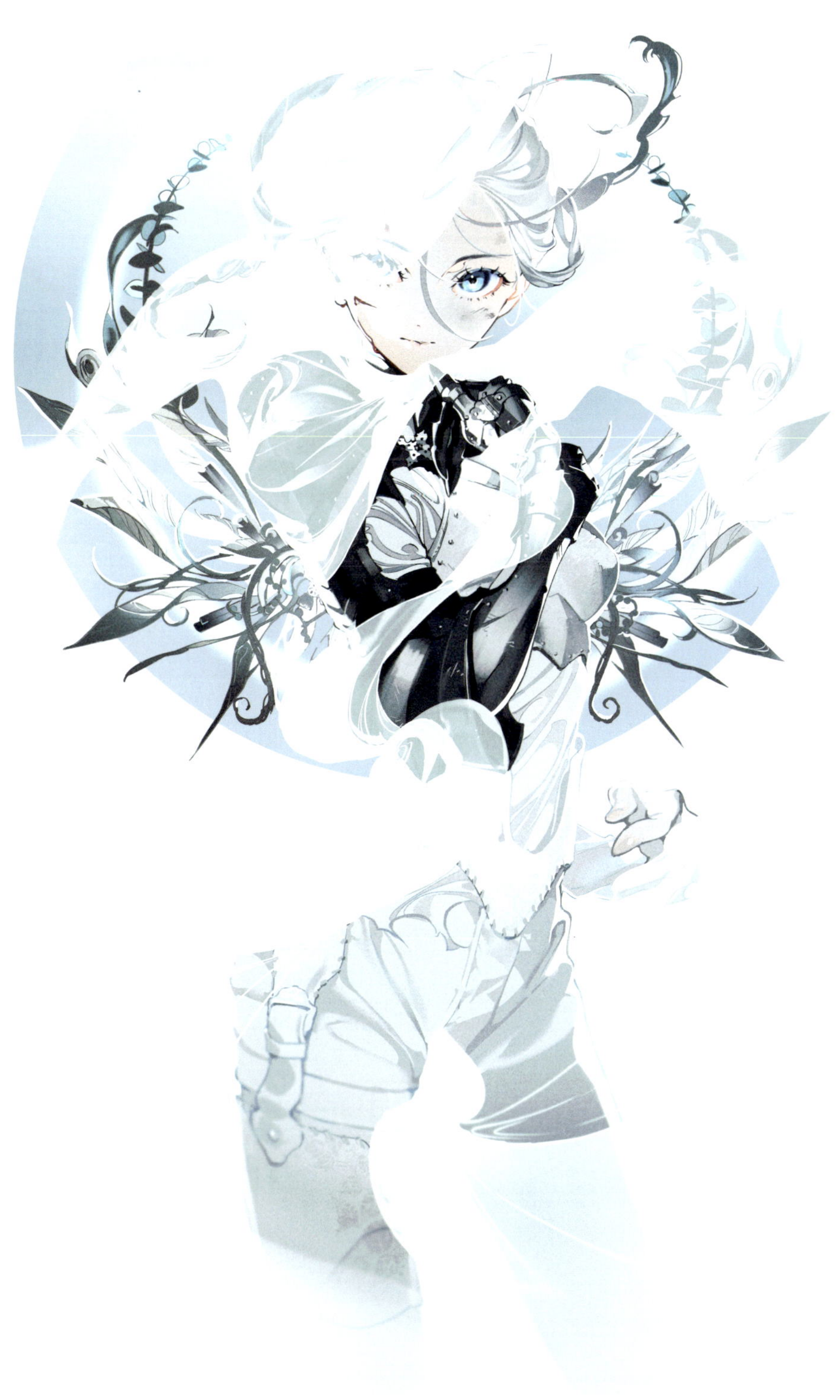

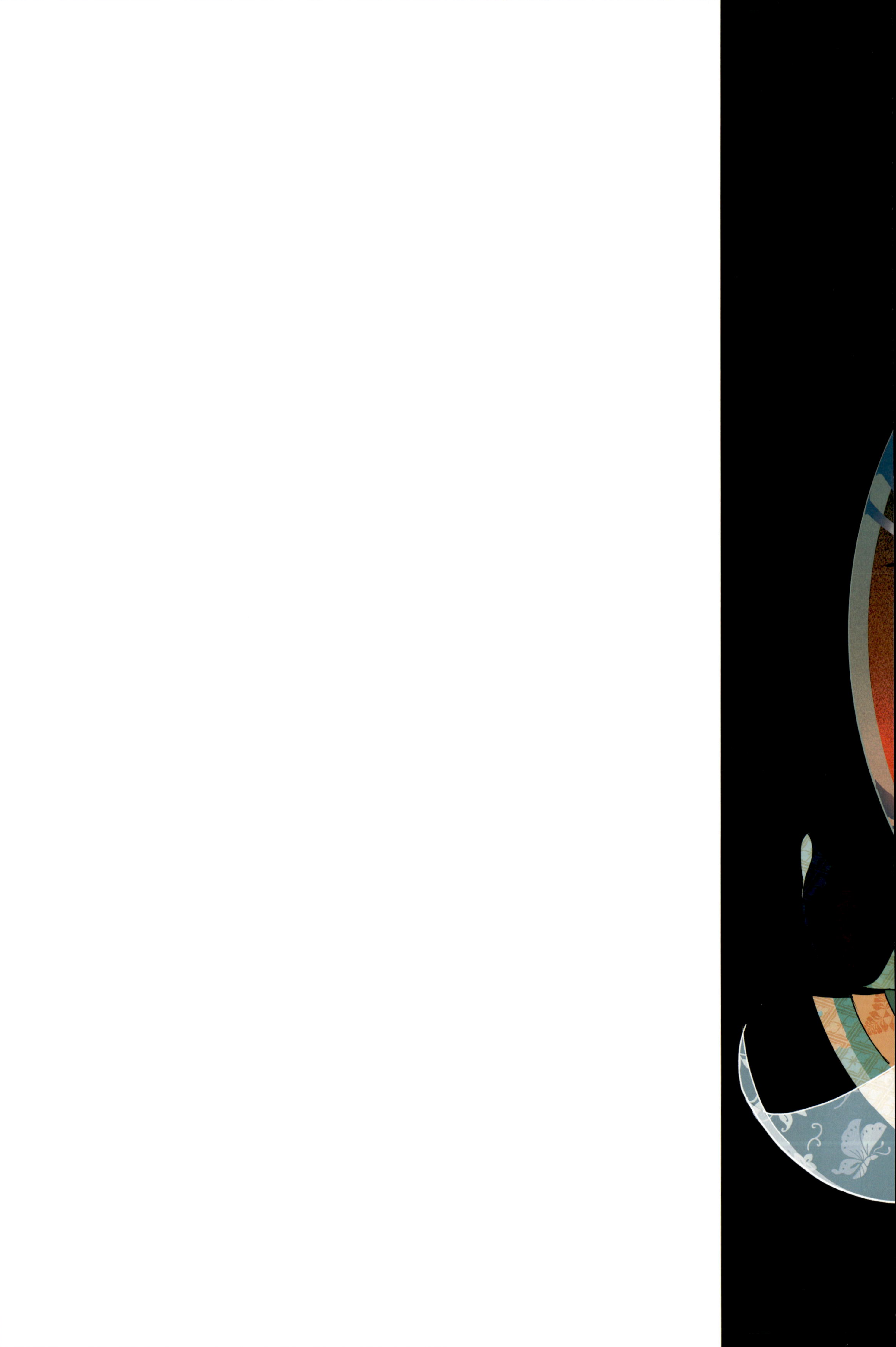

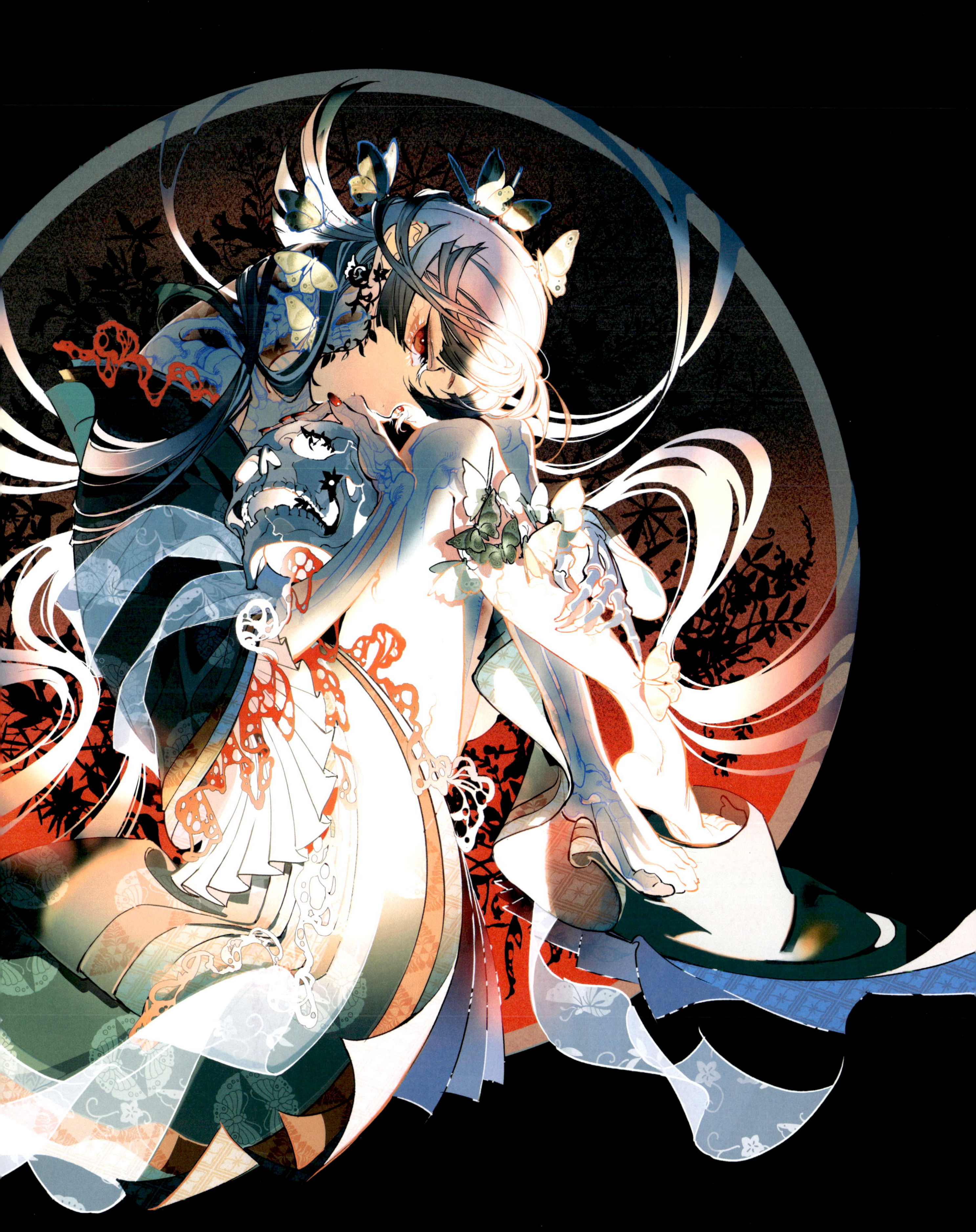

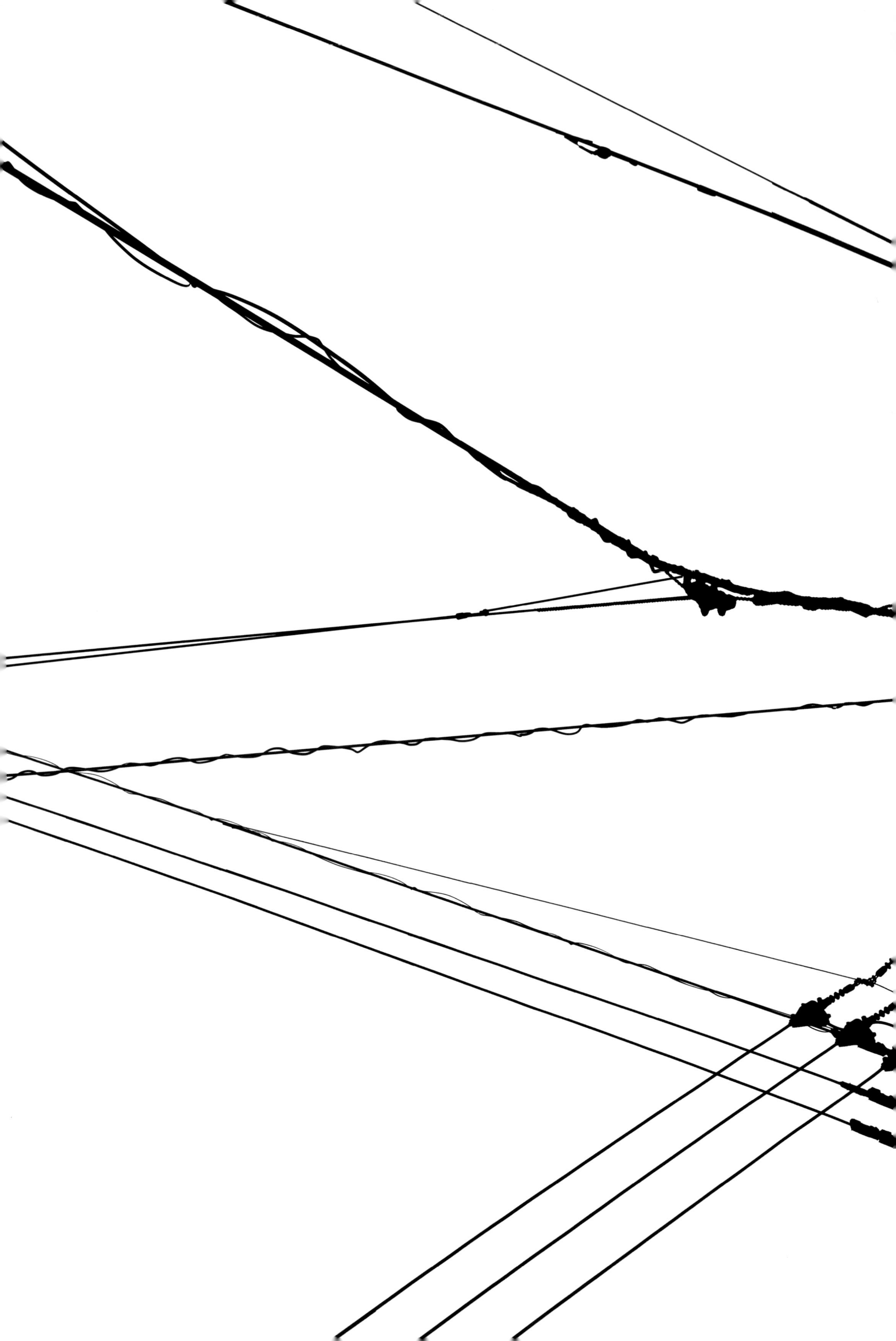

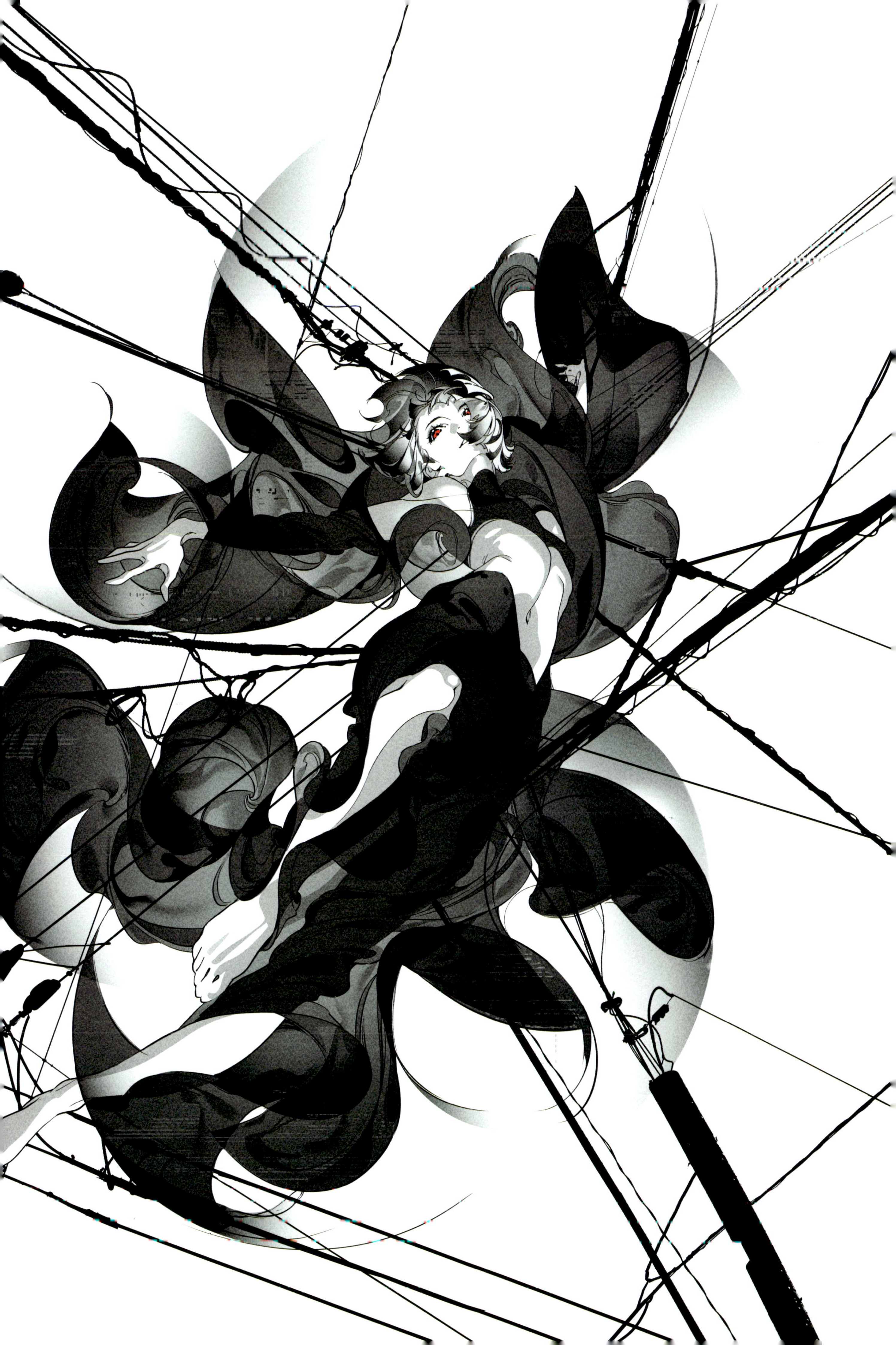

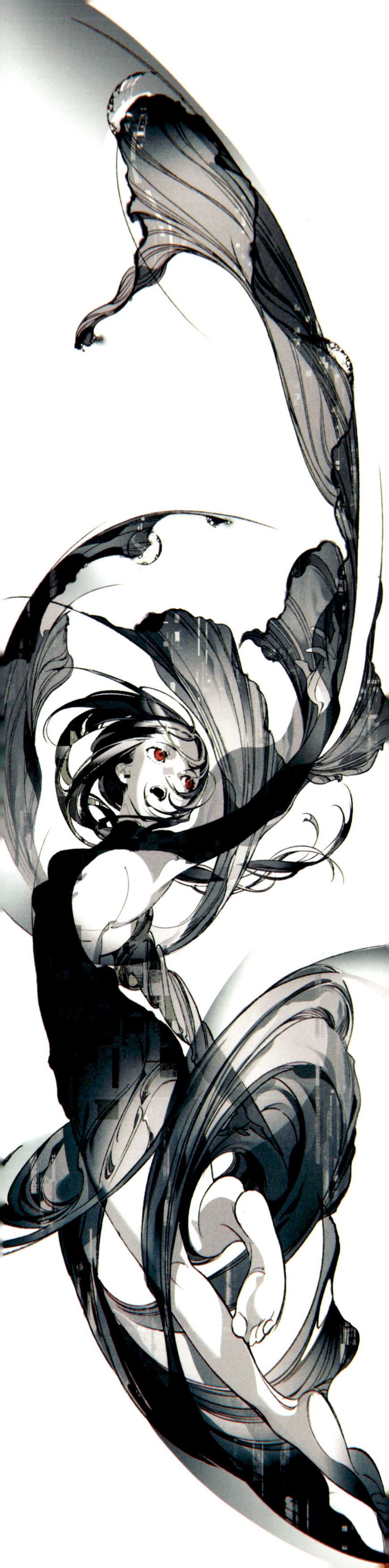

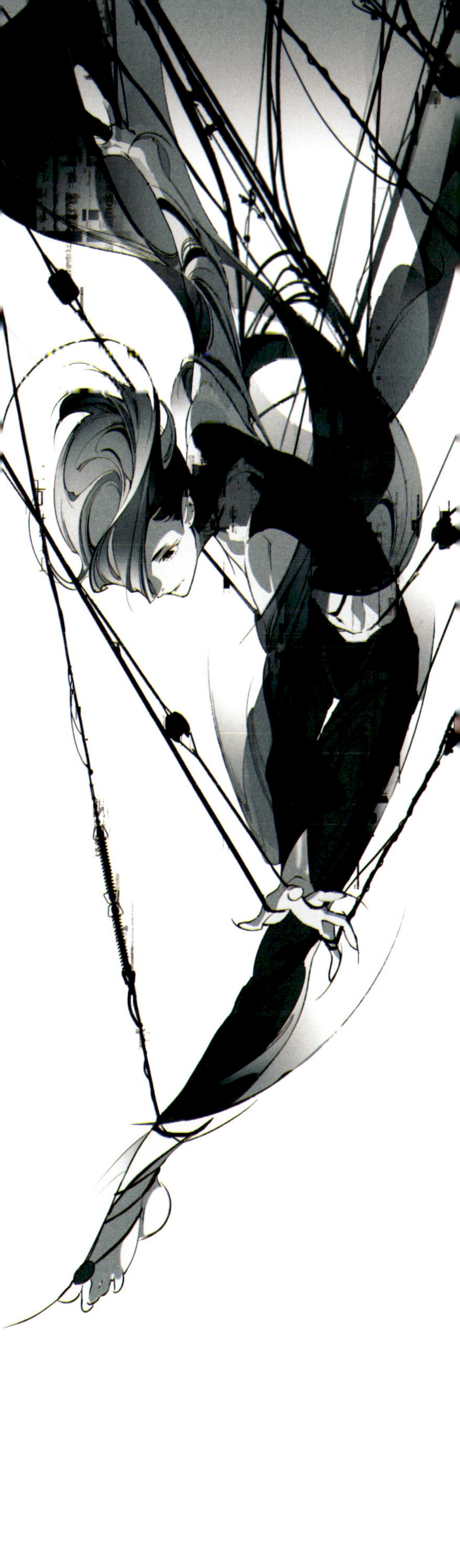

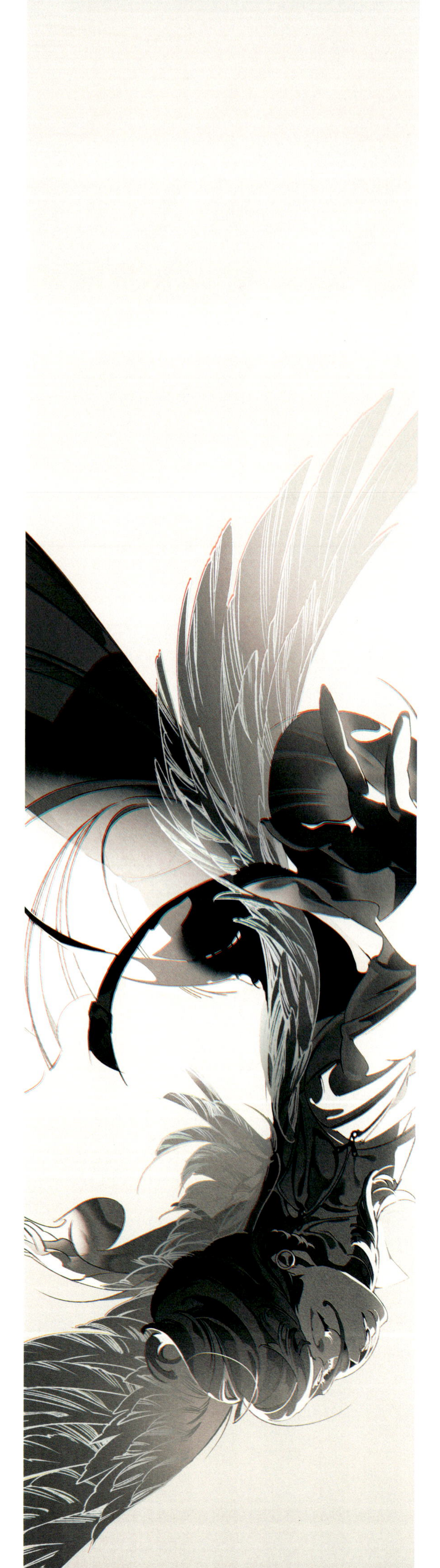

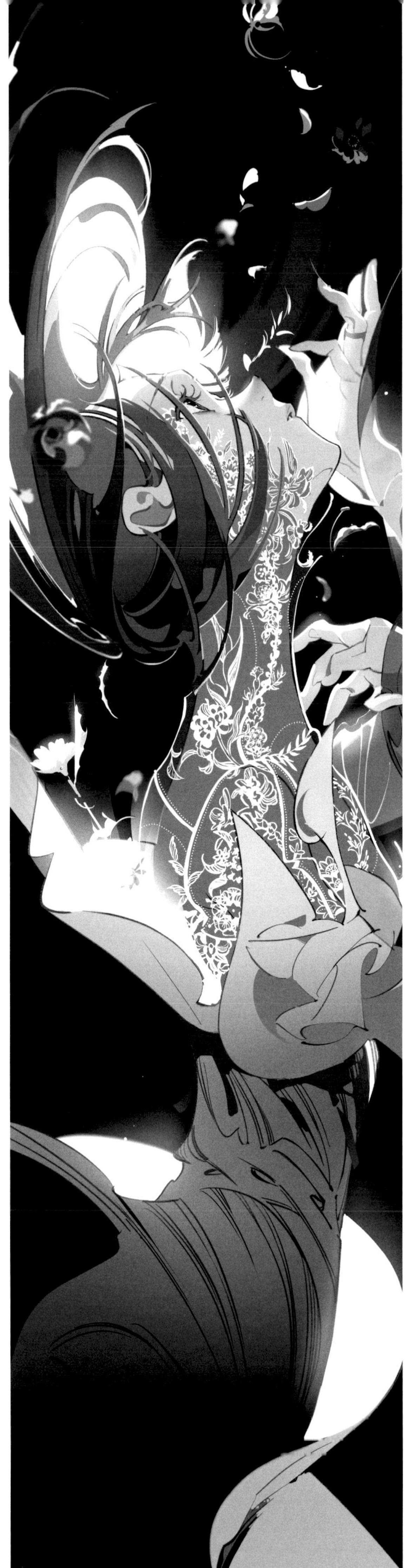

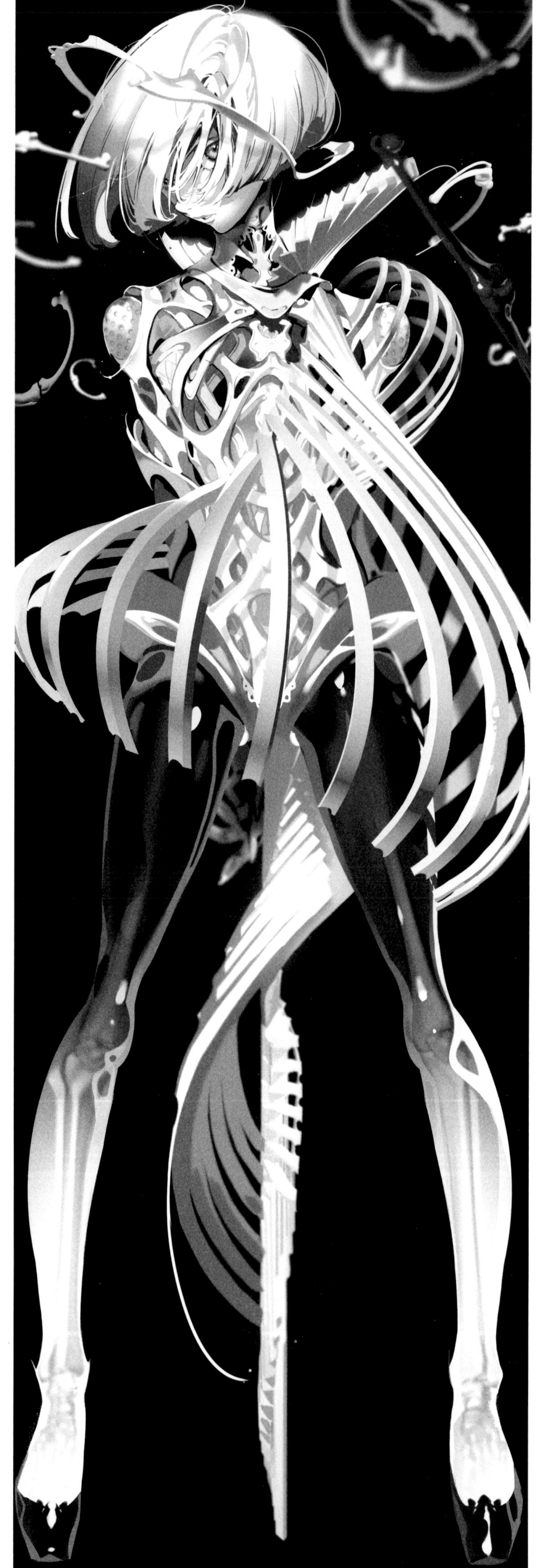

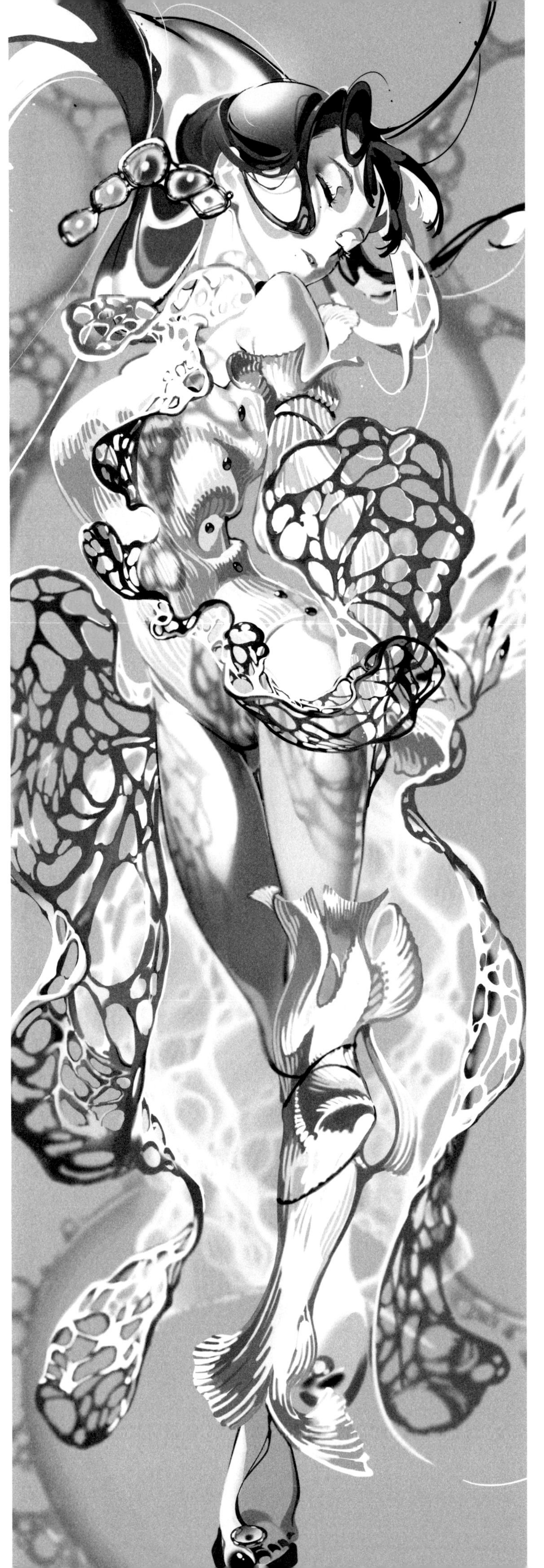

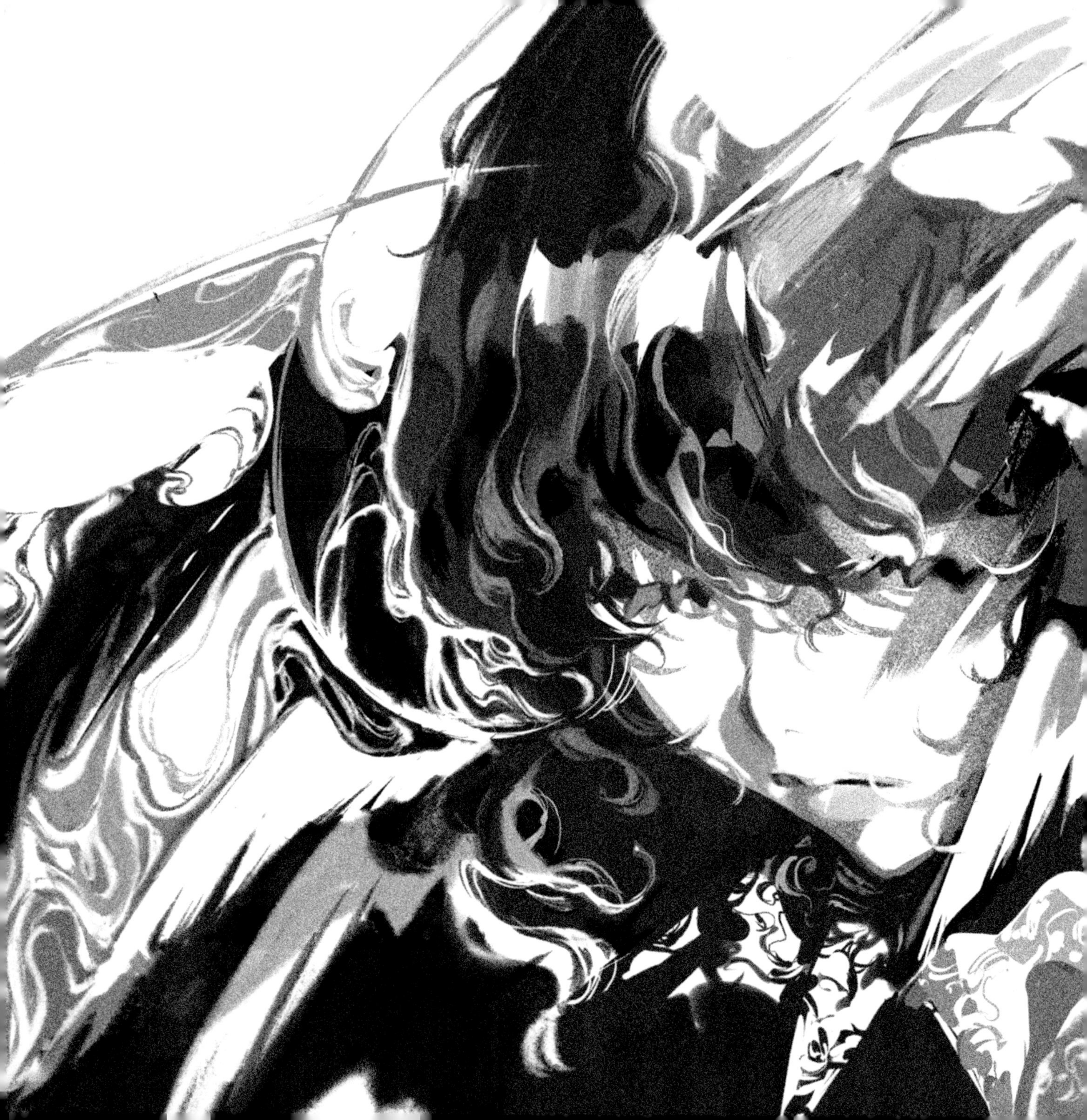

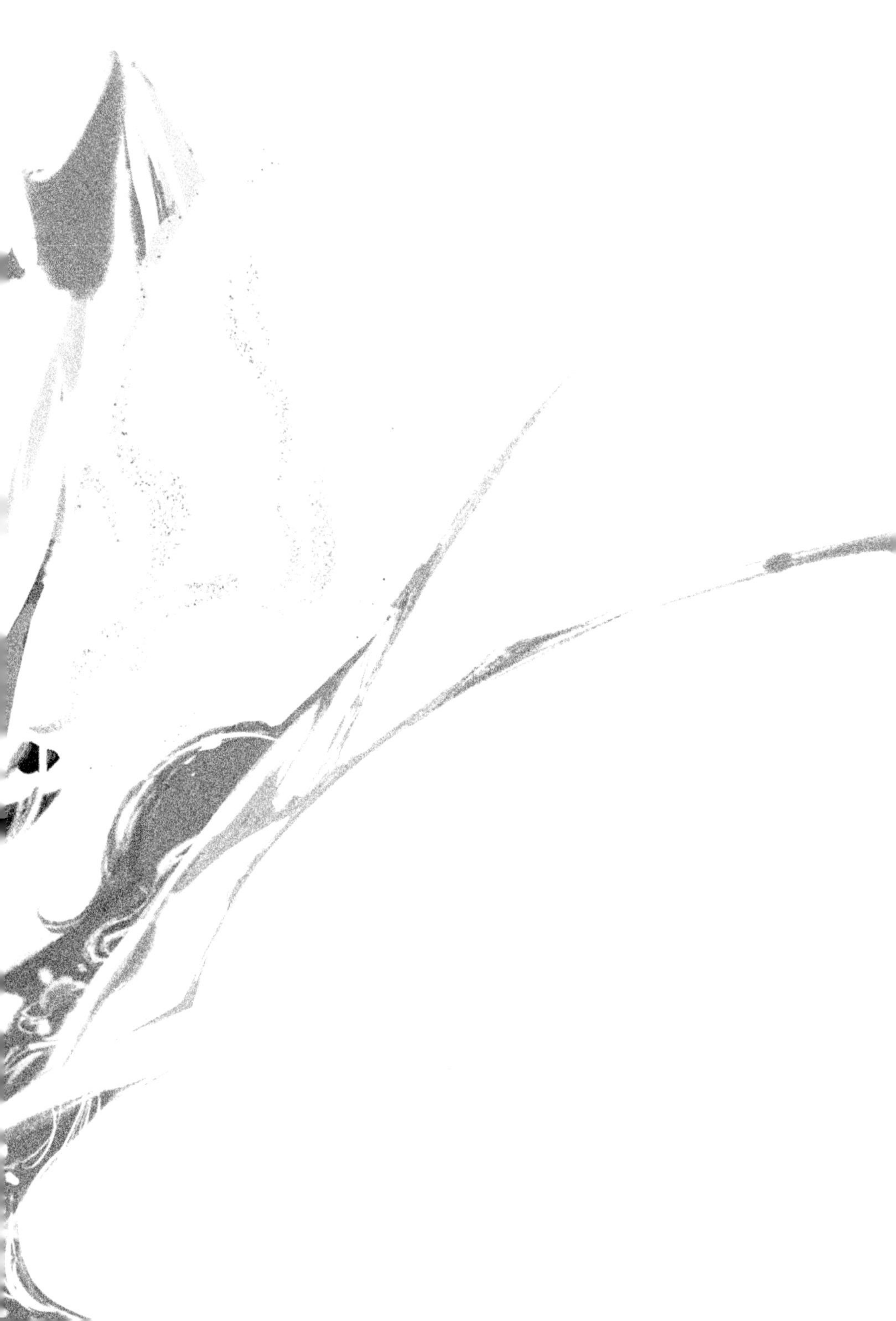

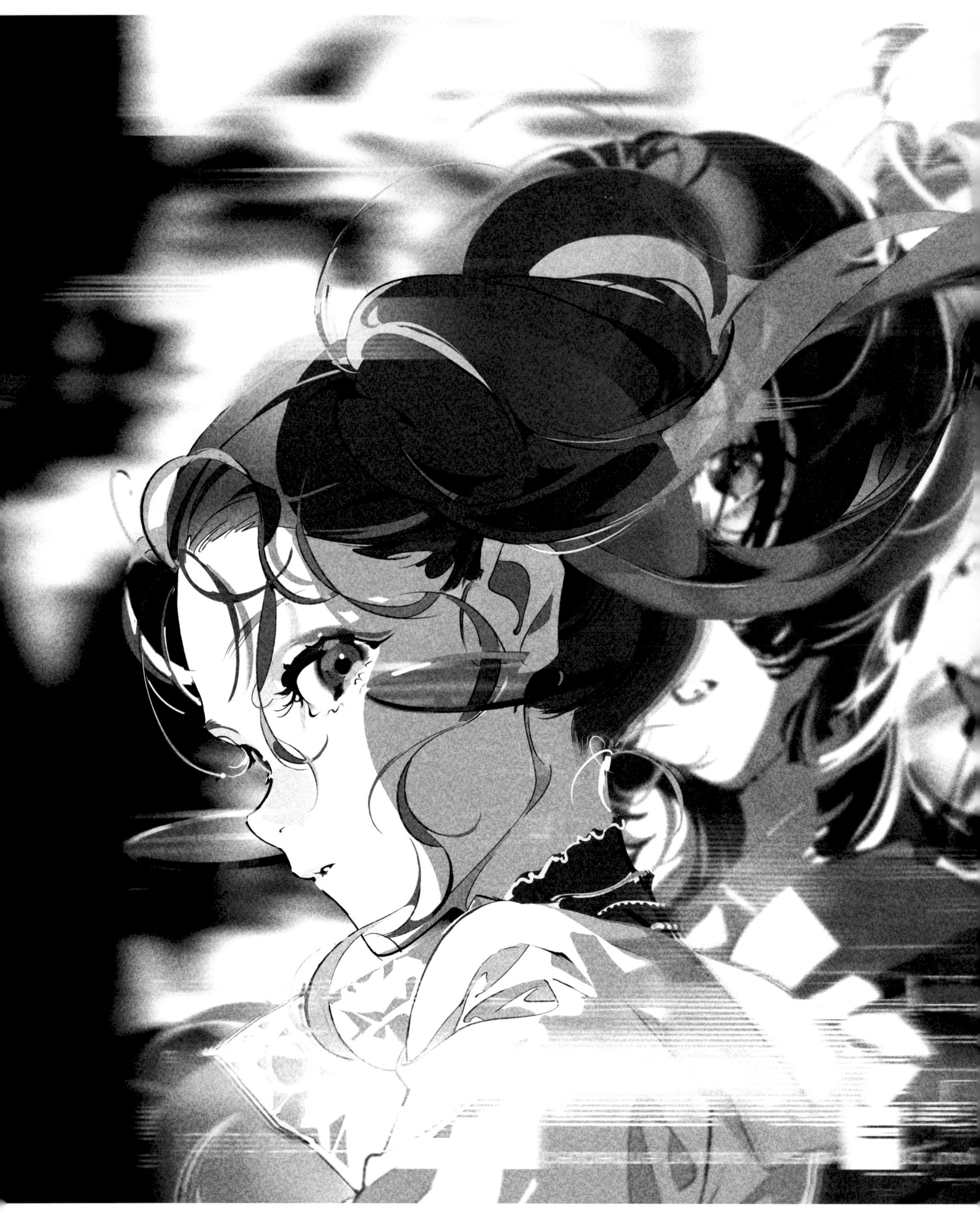

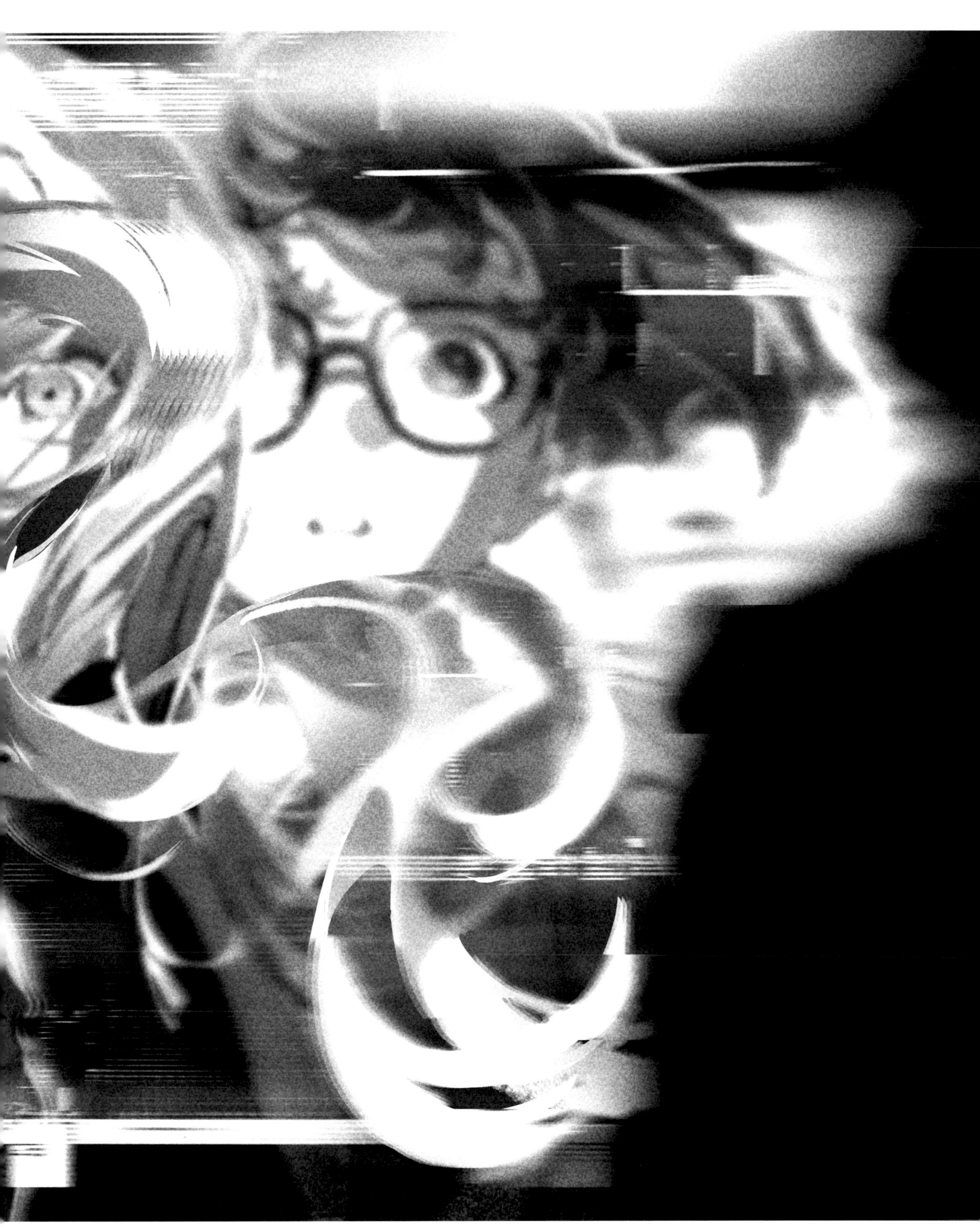

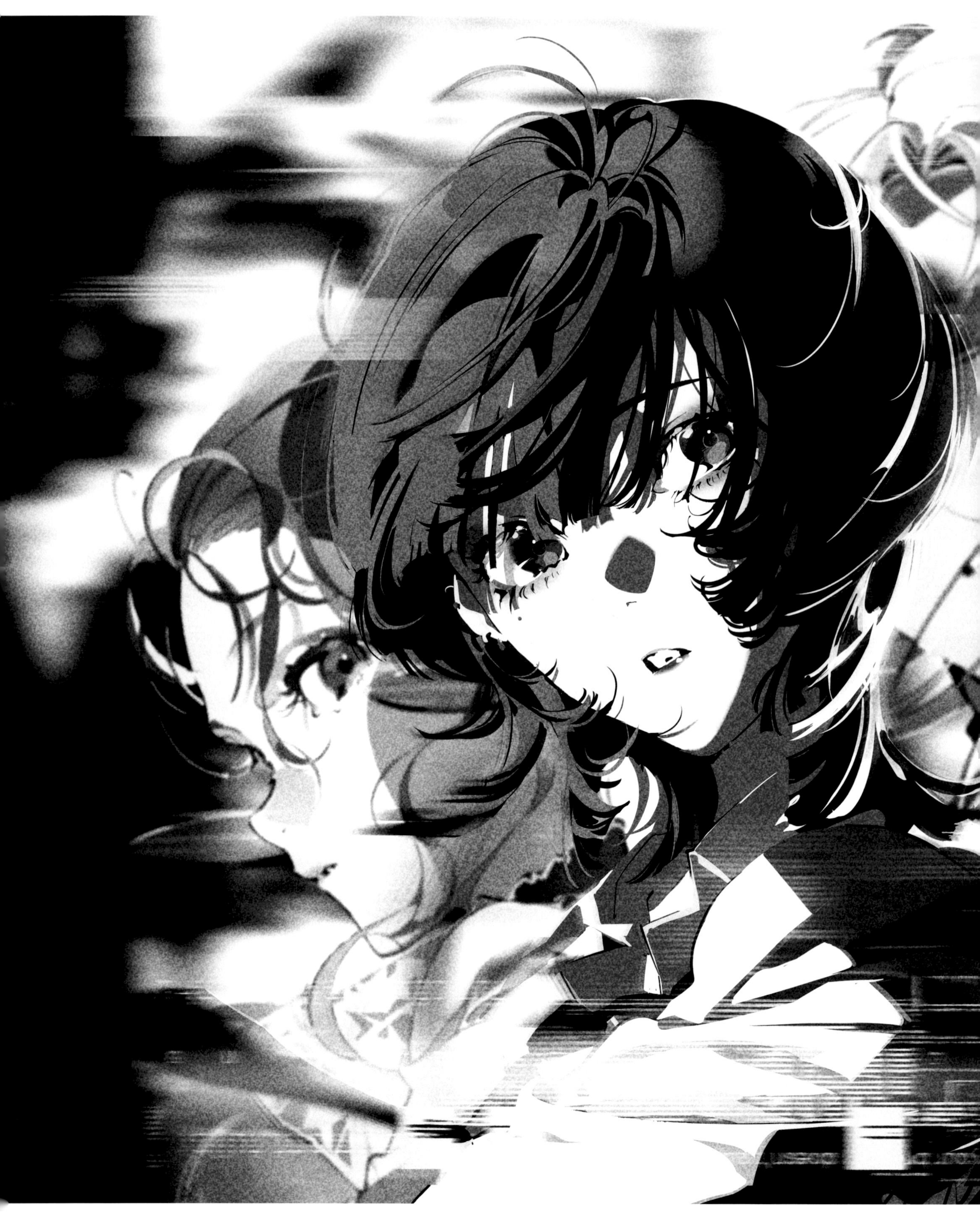

174　etc.
175

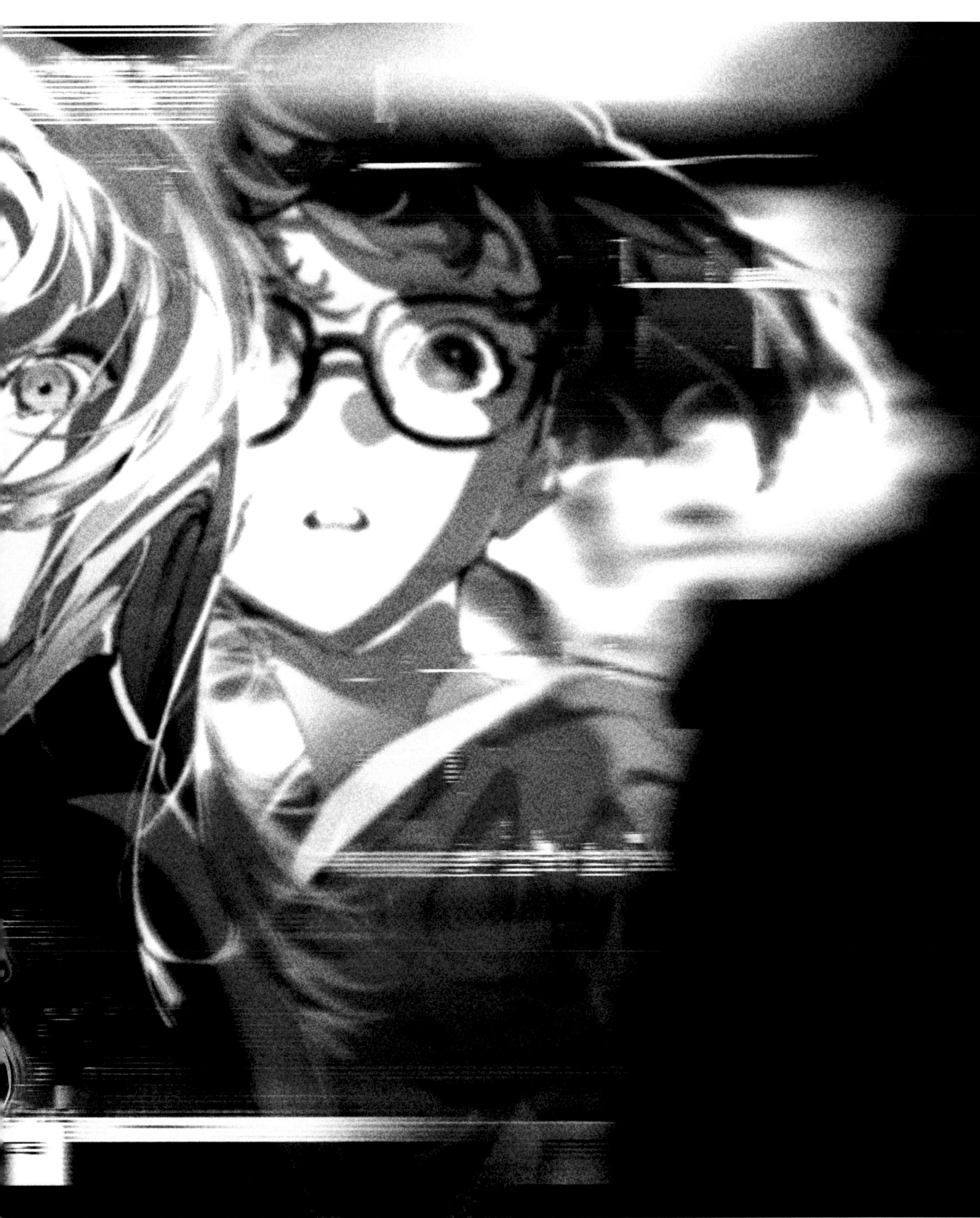

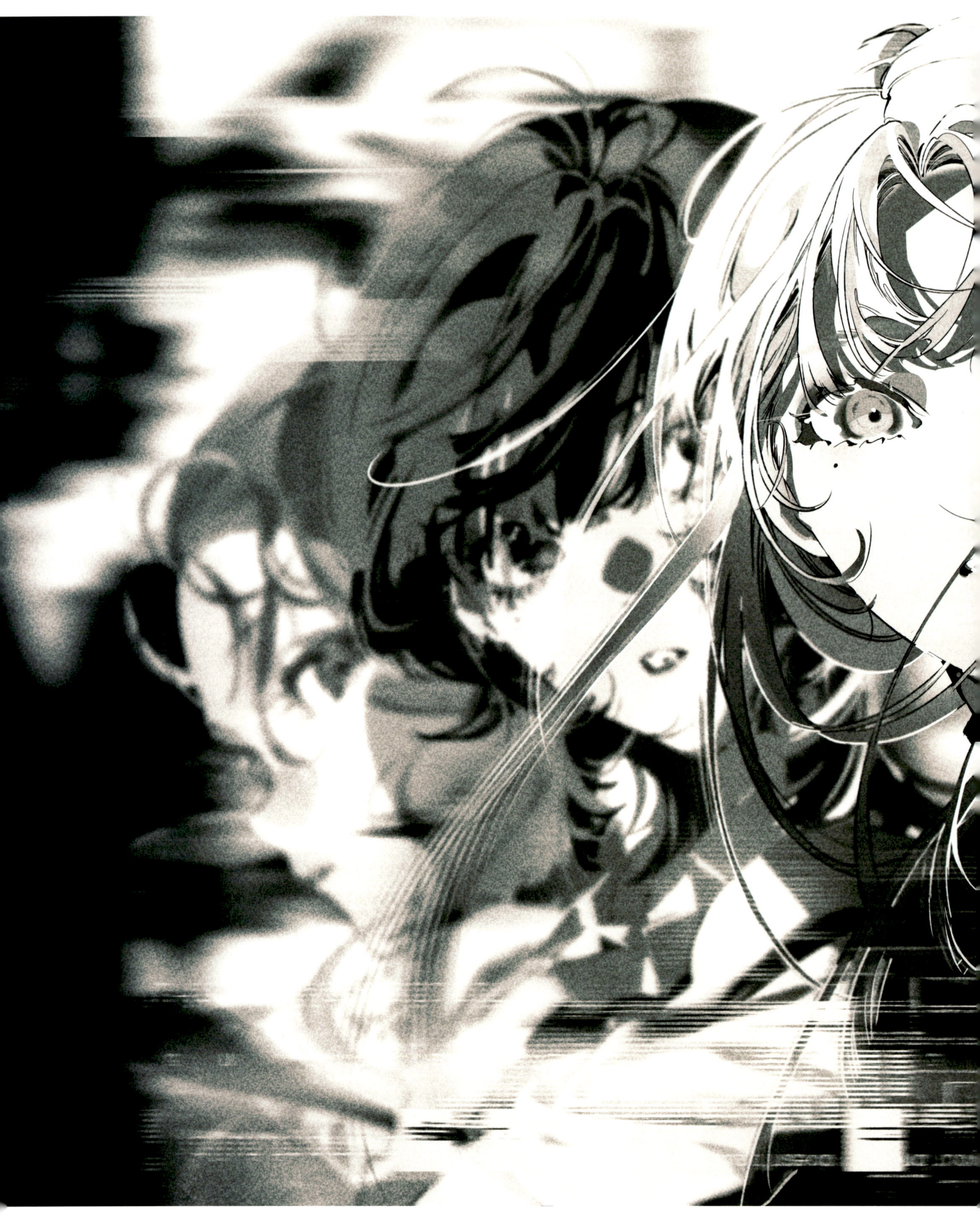

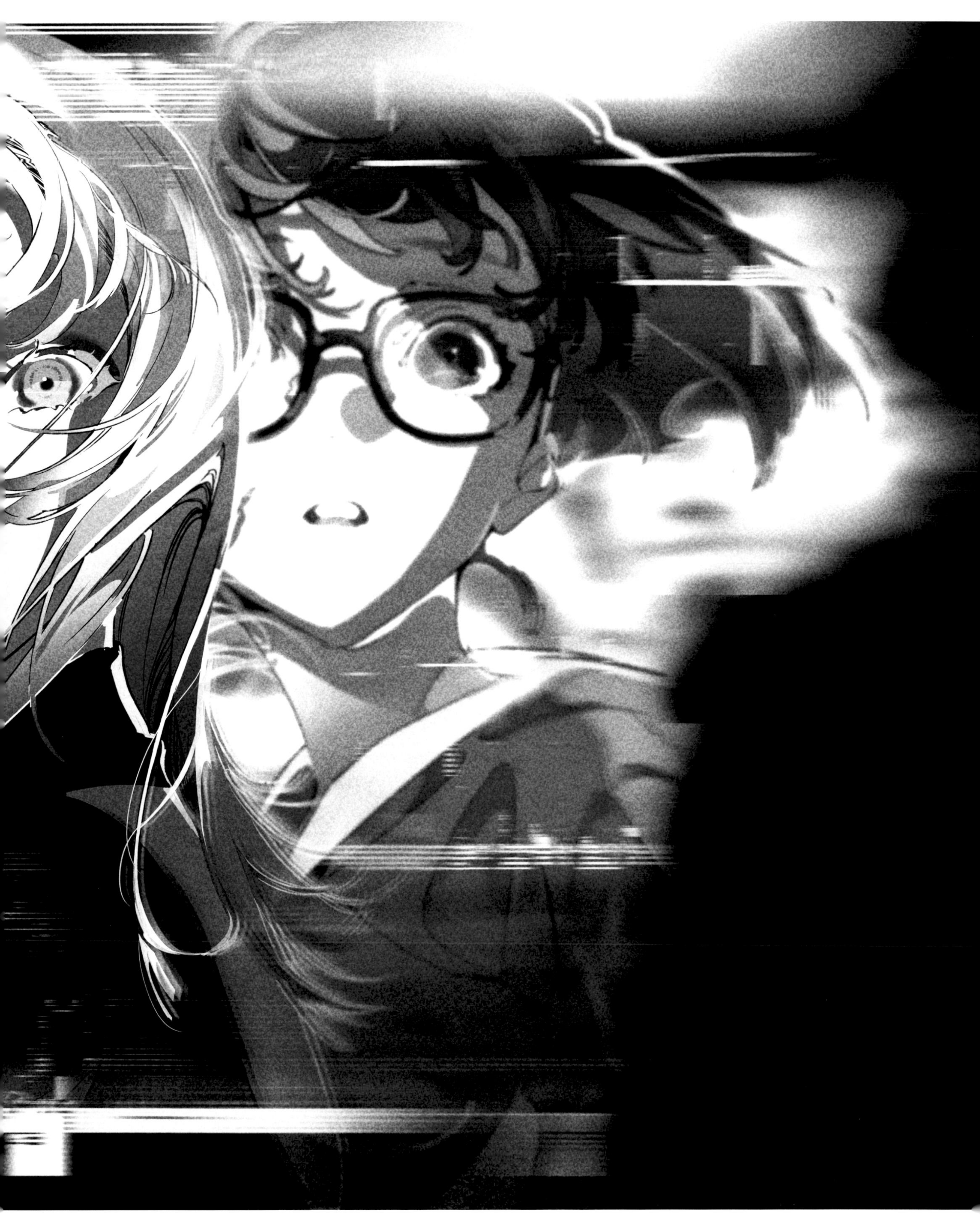

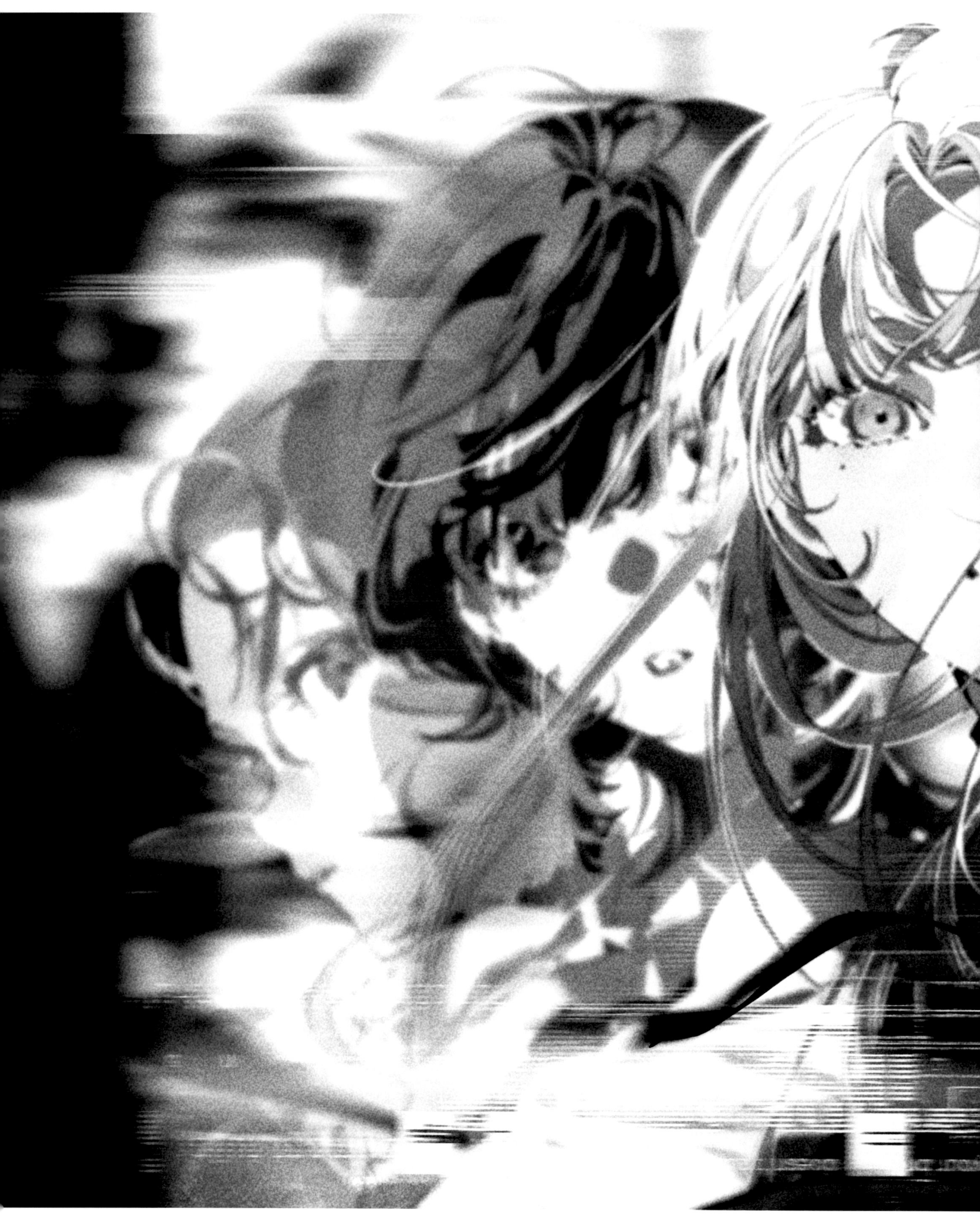

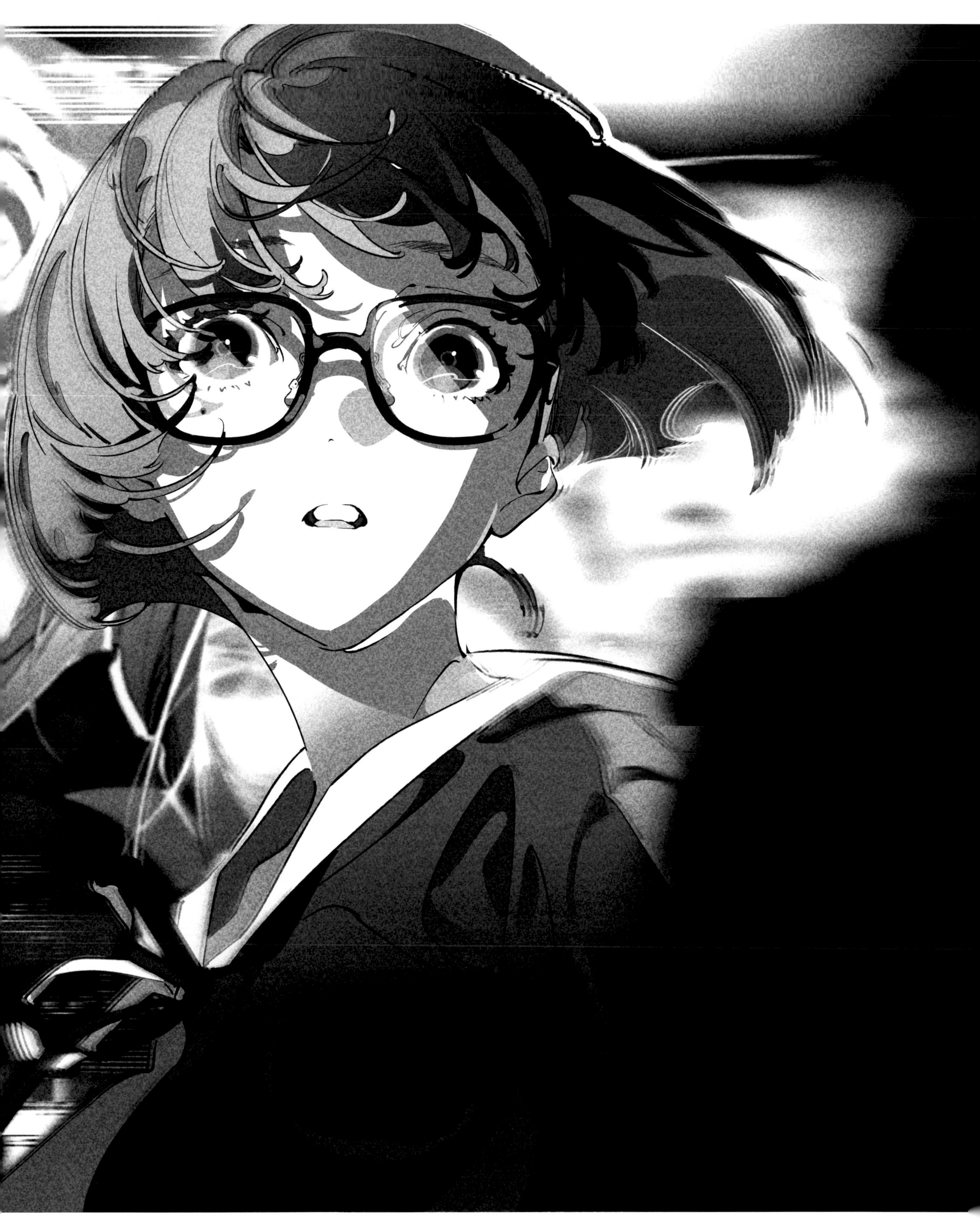

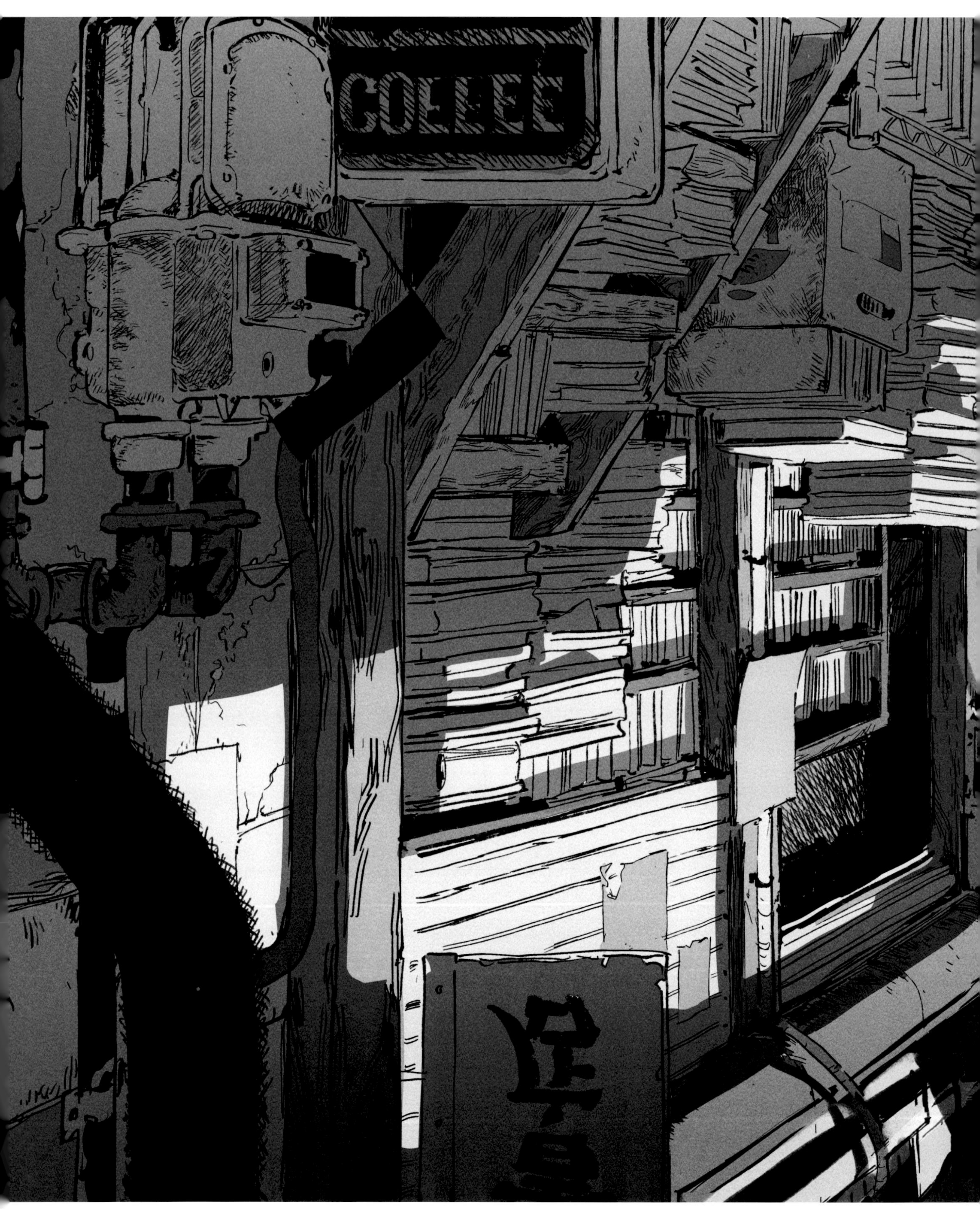
COFFEE

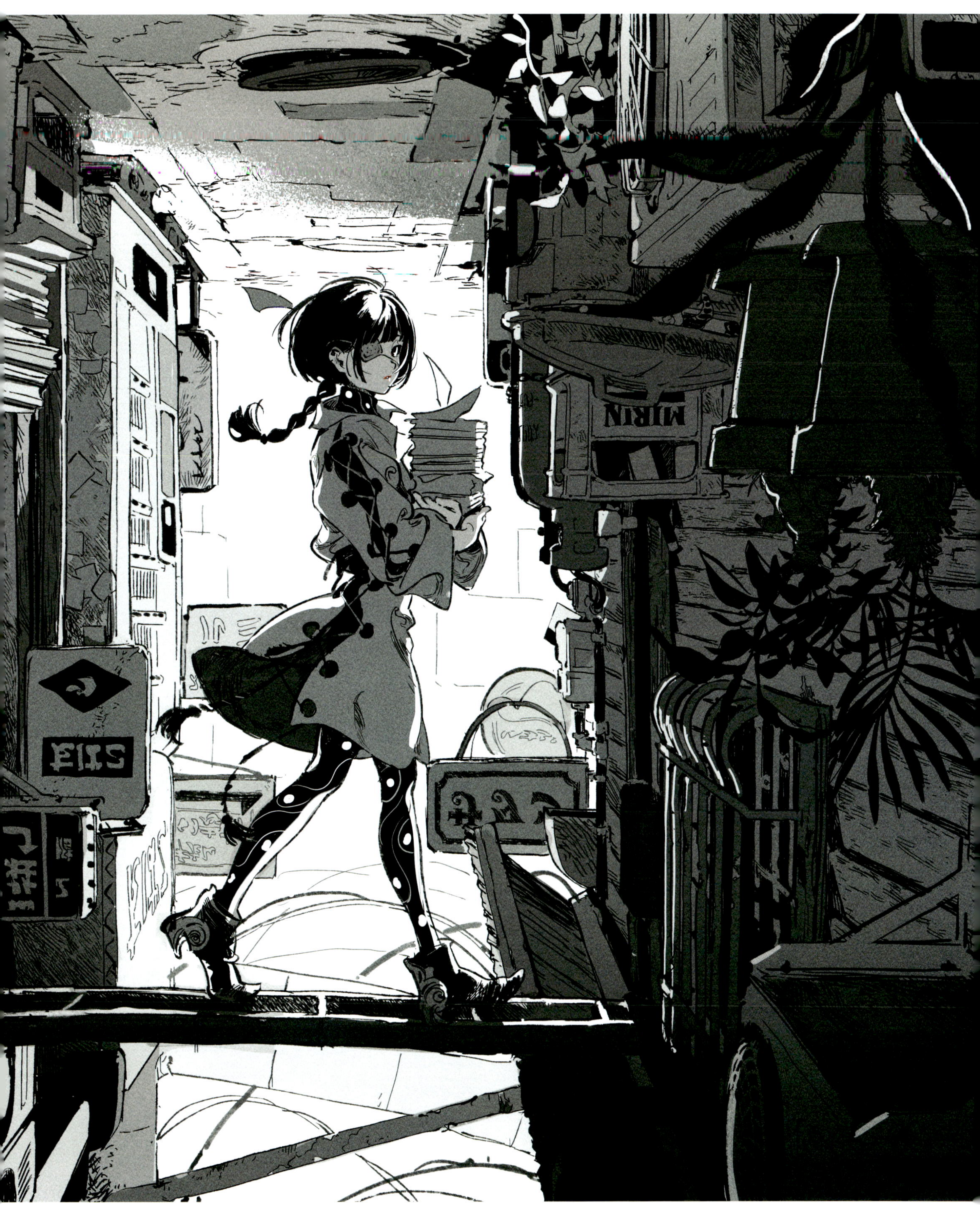

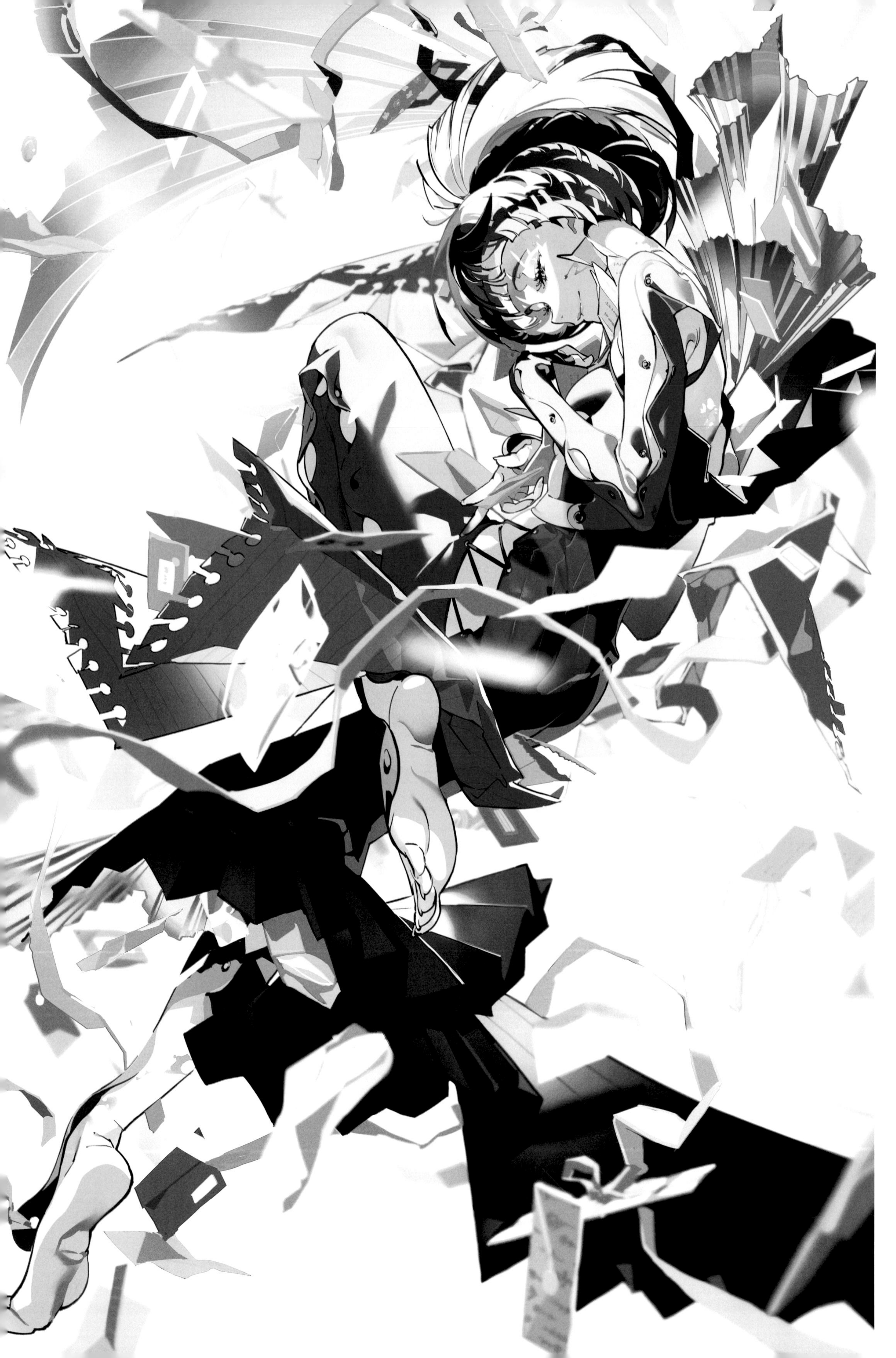

182 etc.
183

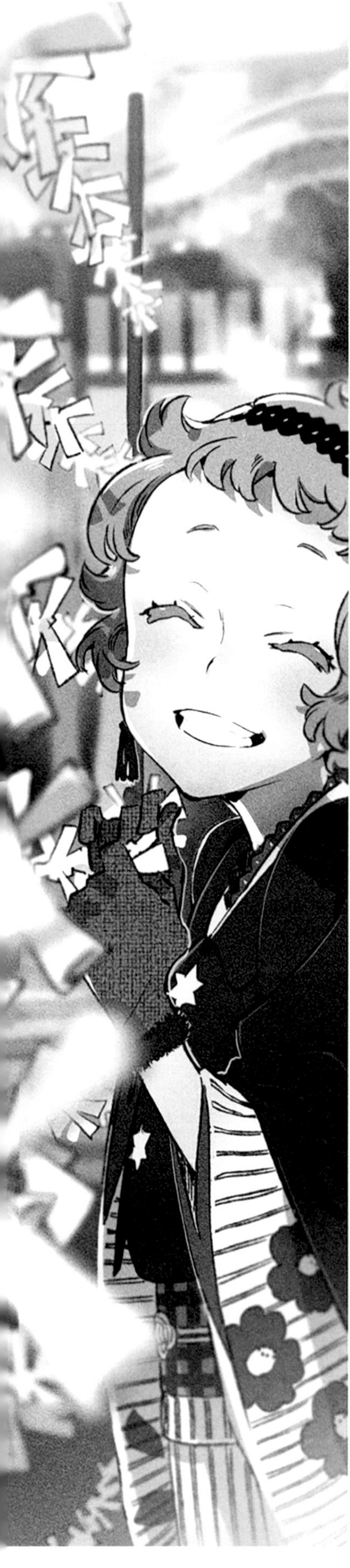
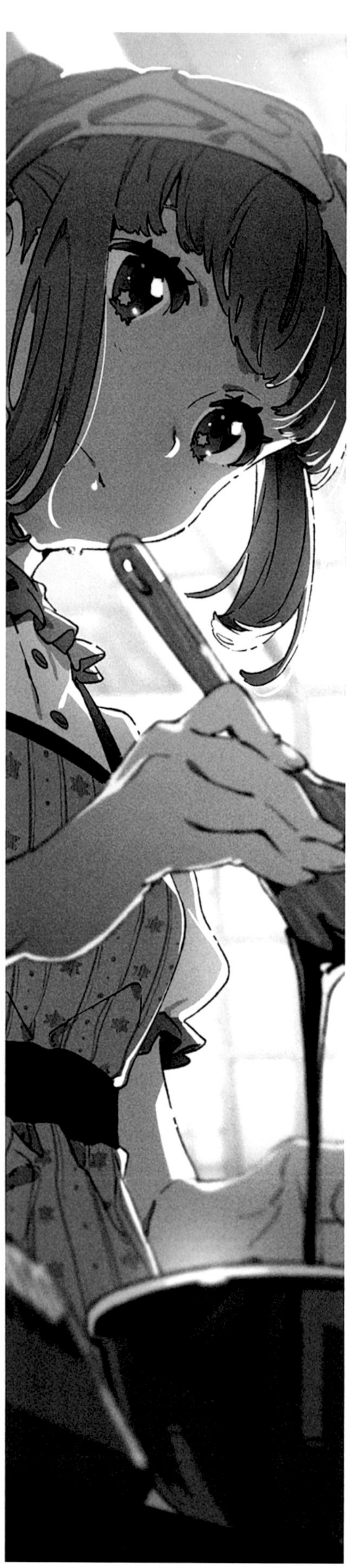
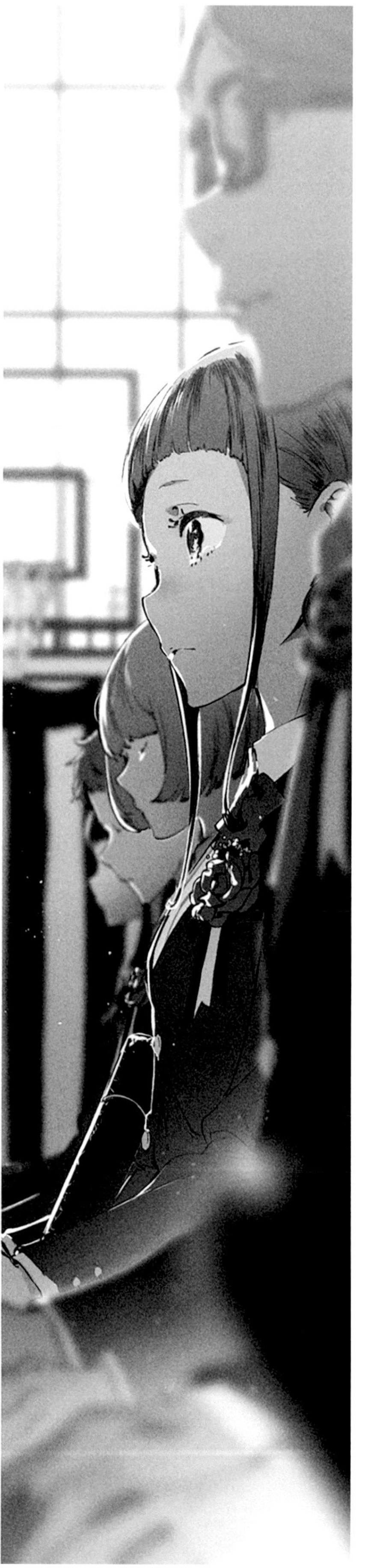

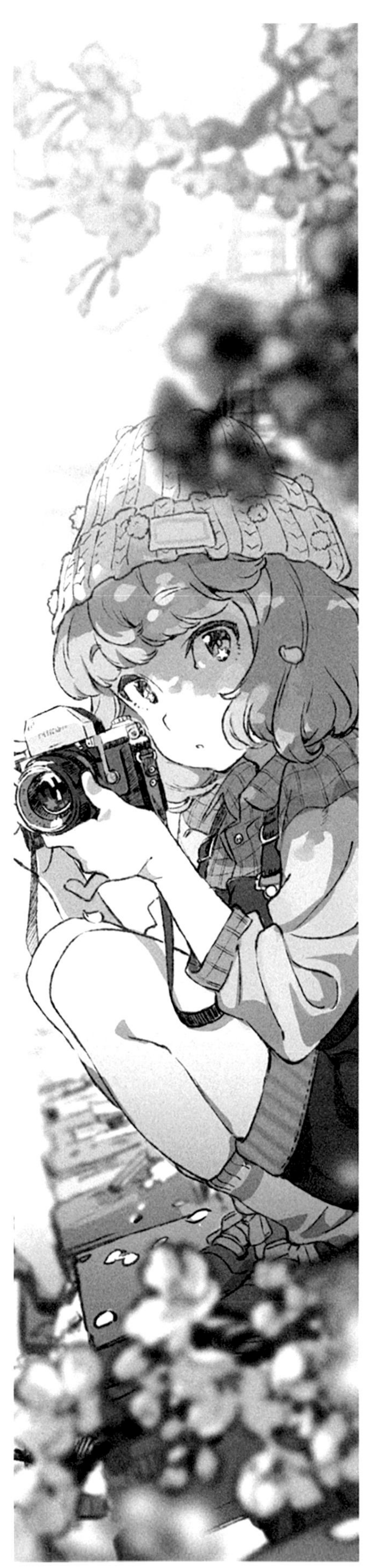

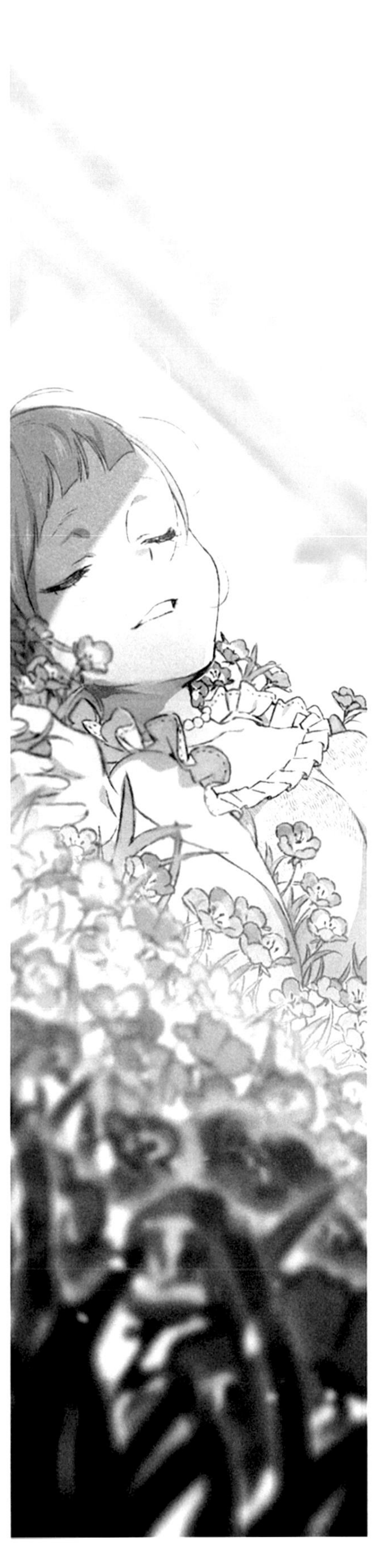

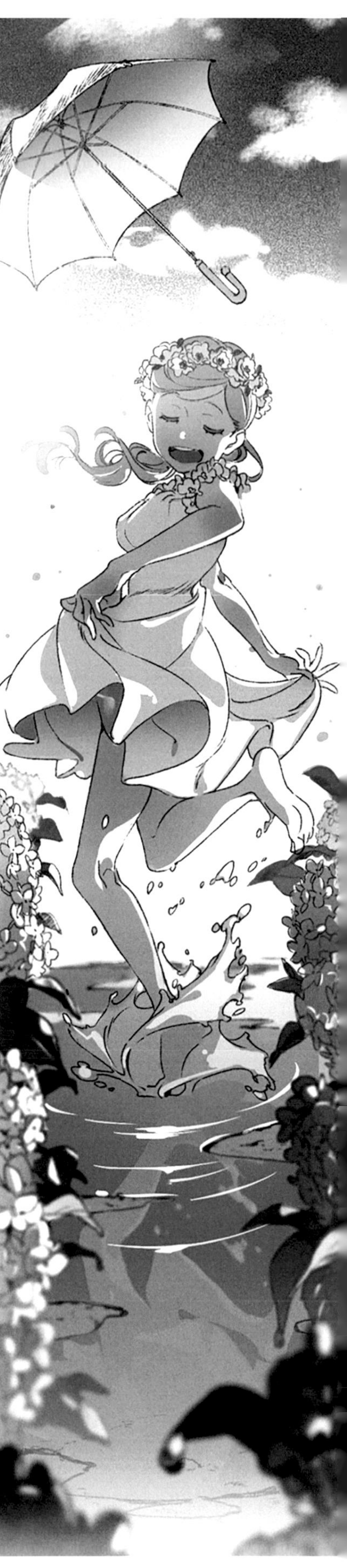

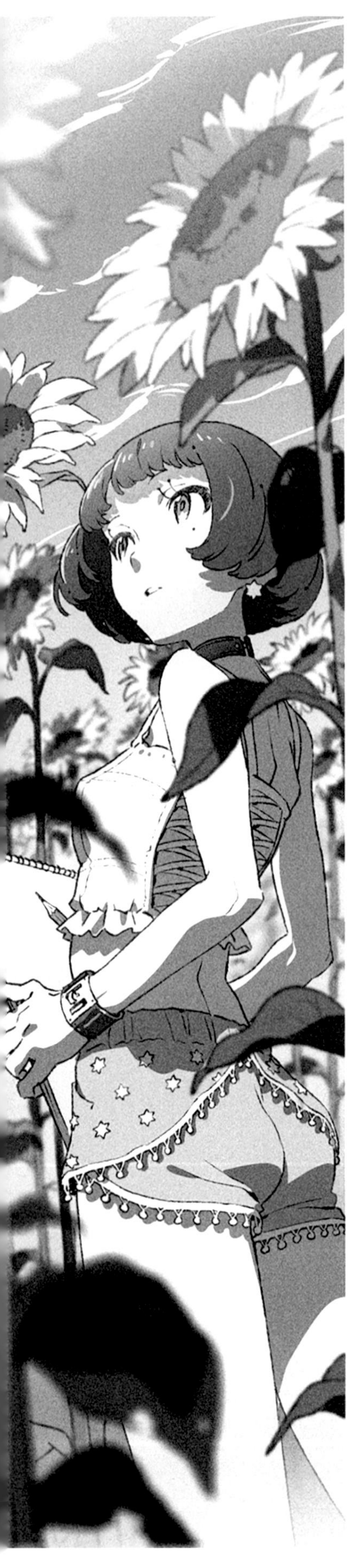

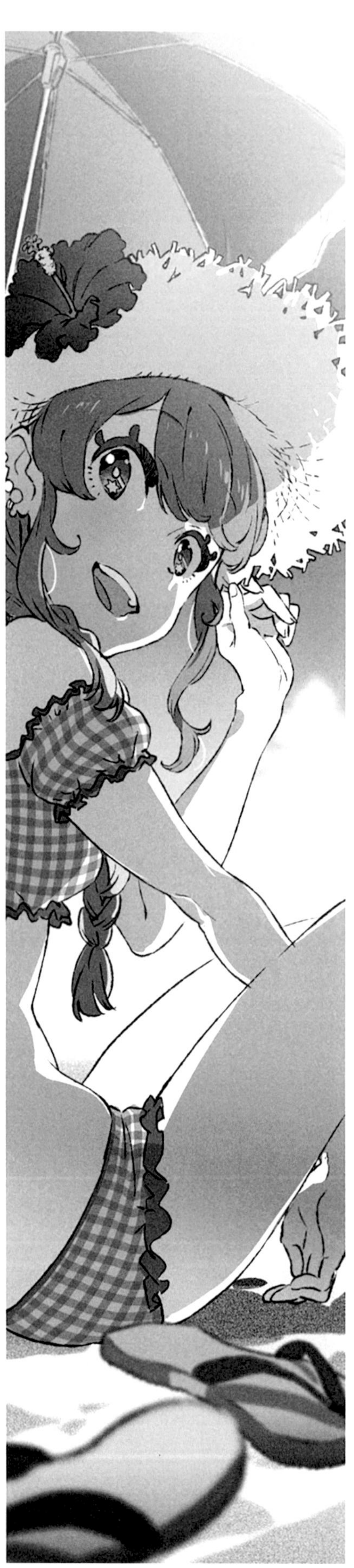

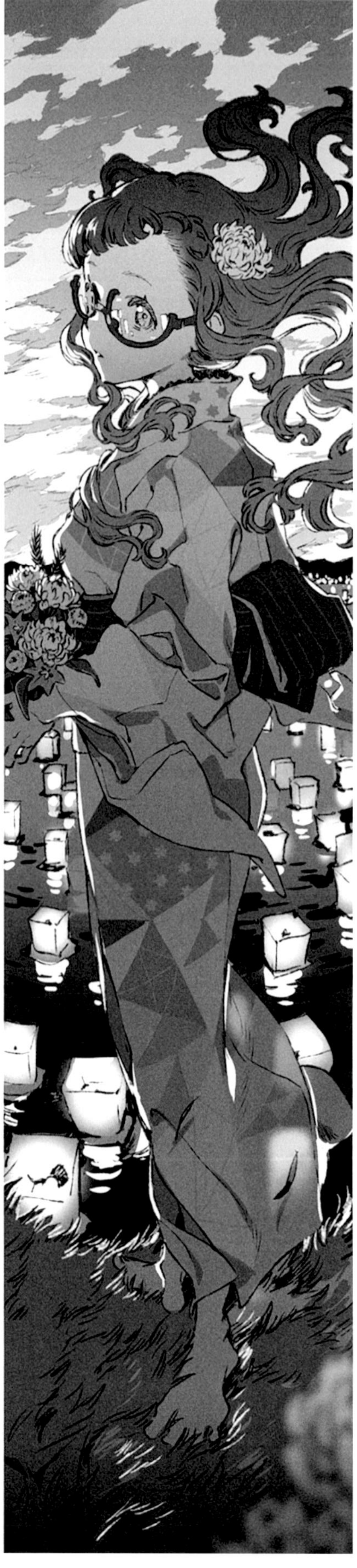

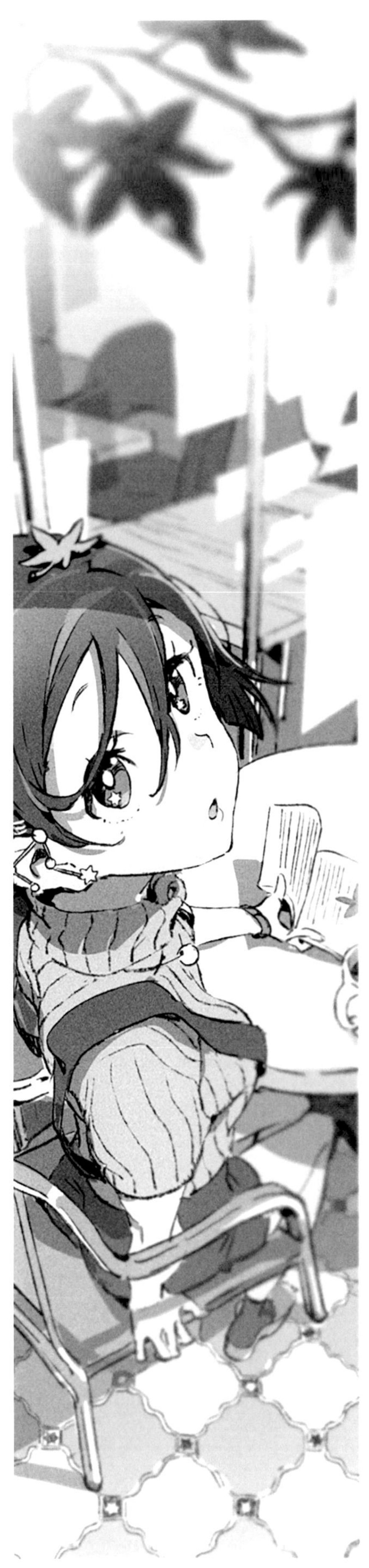

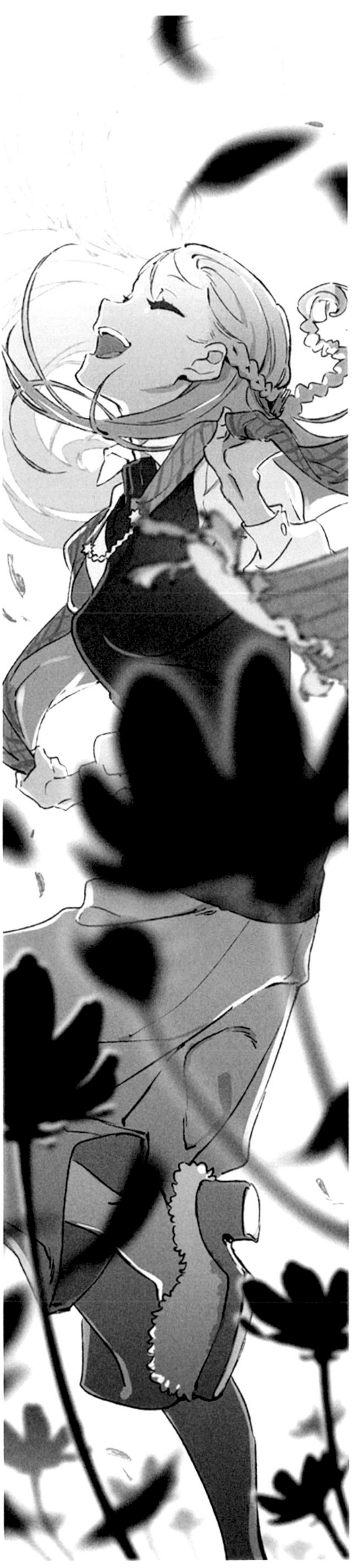

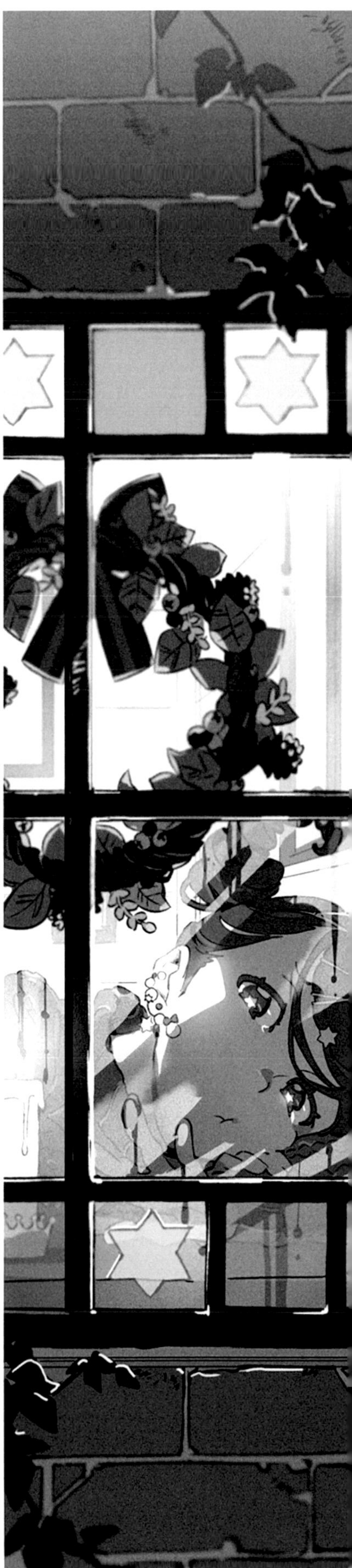

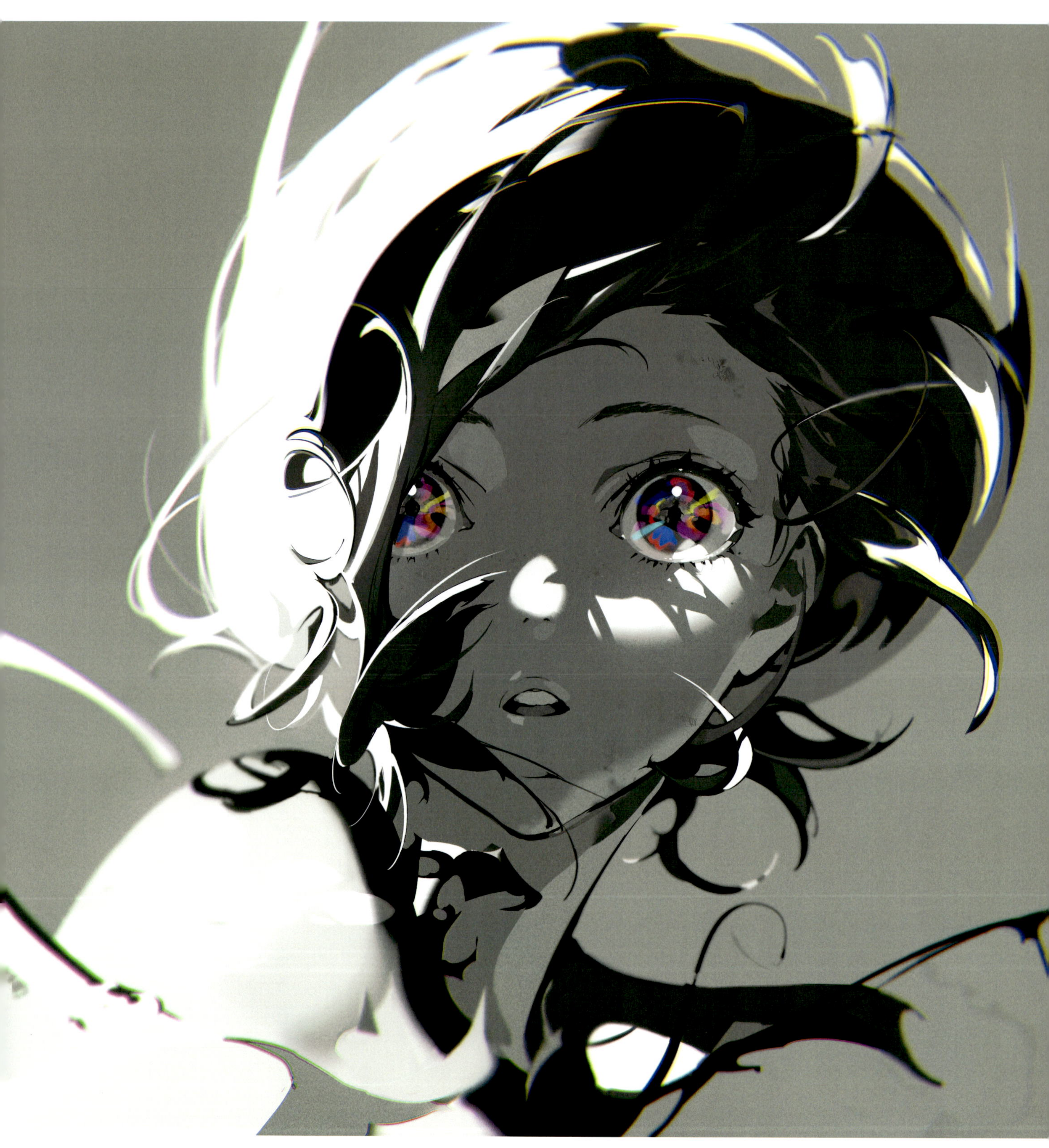

188 etc.
189

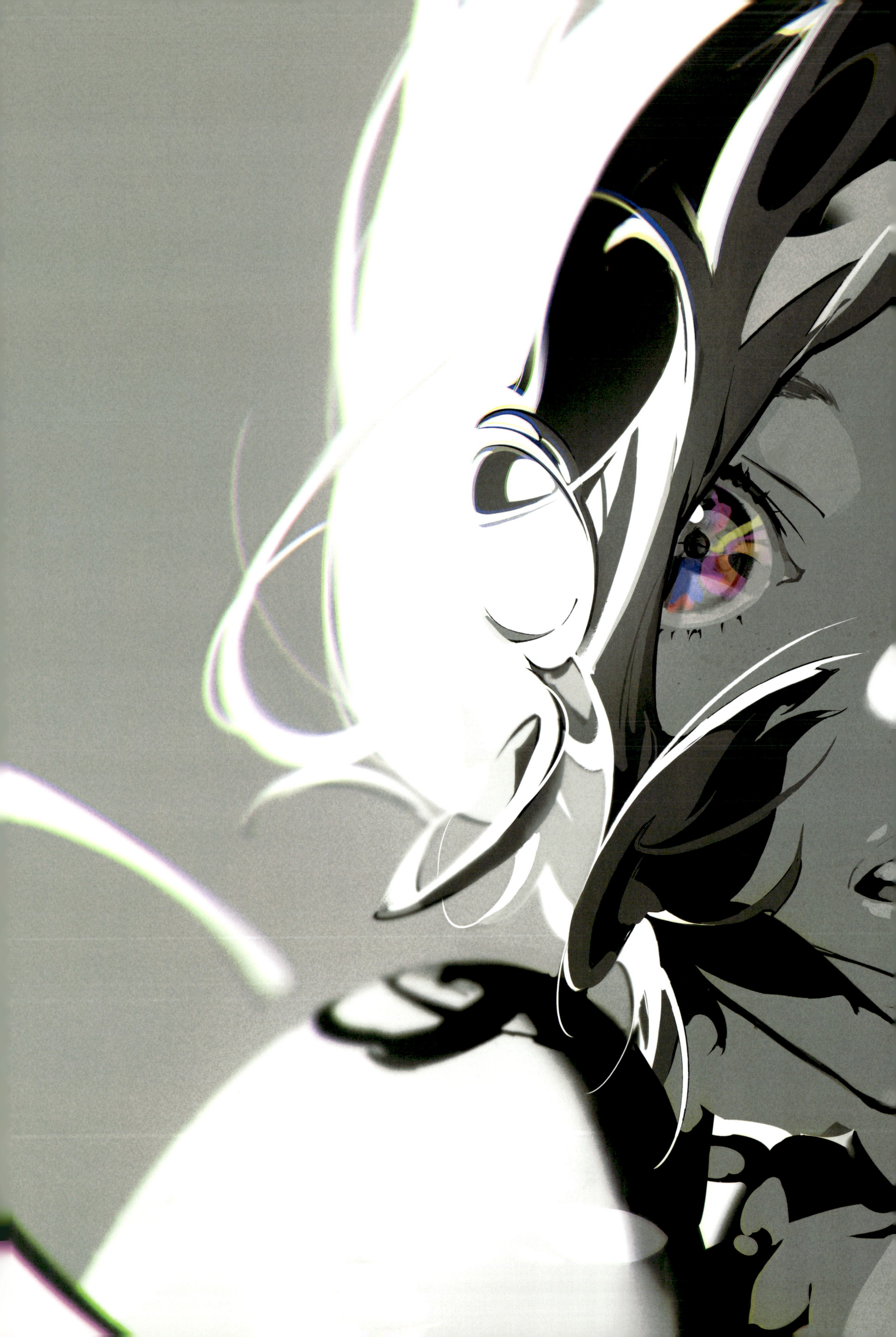

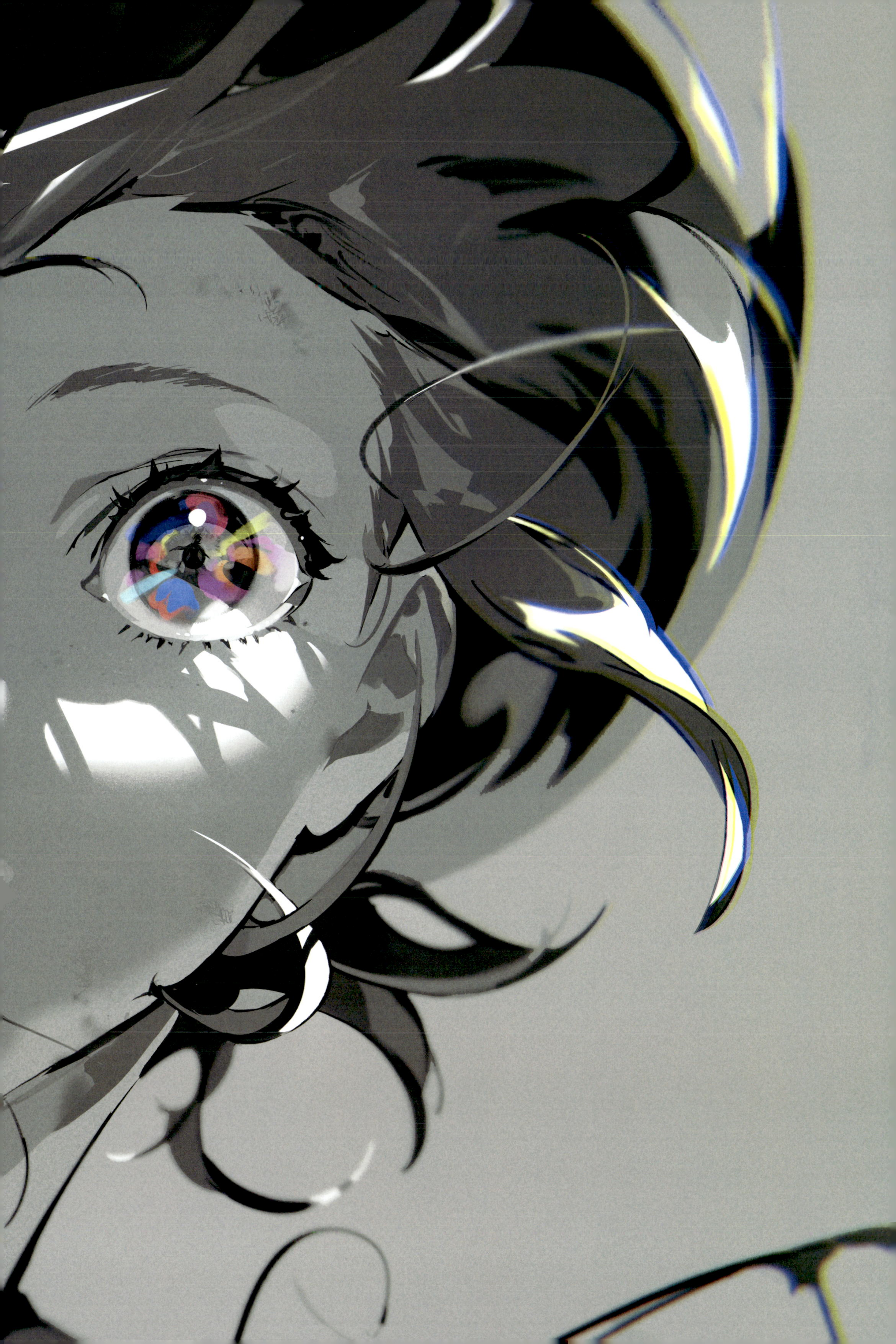

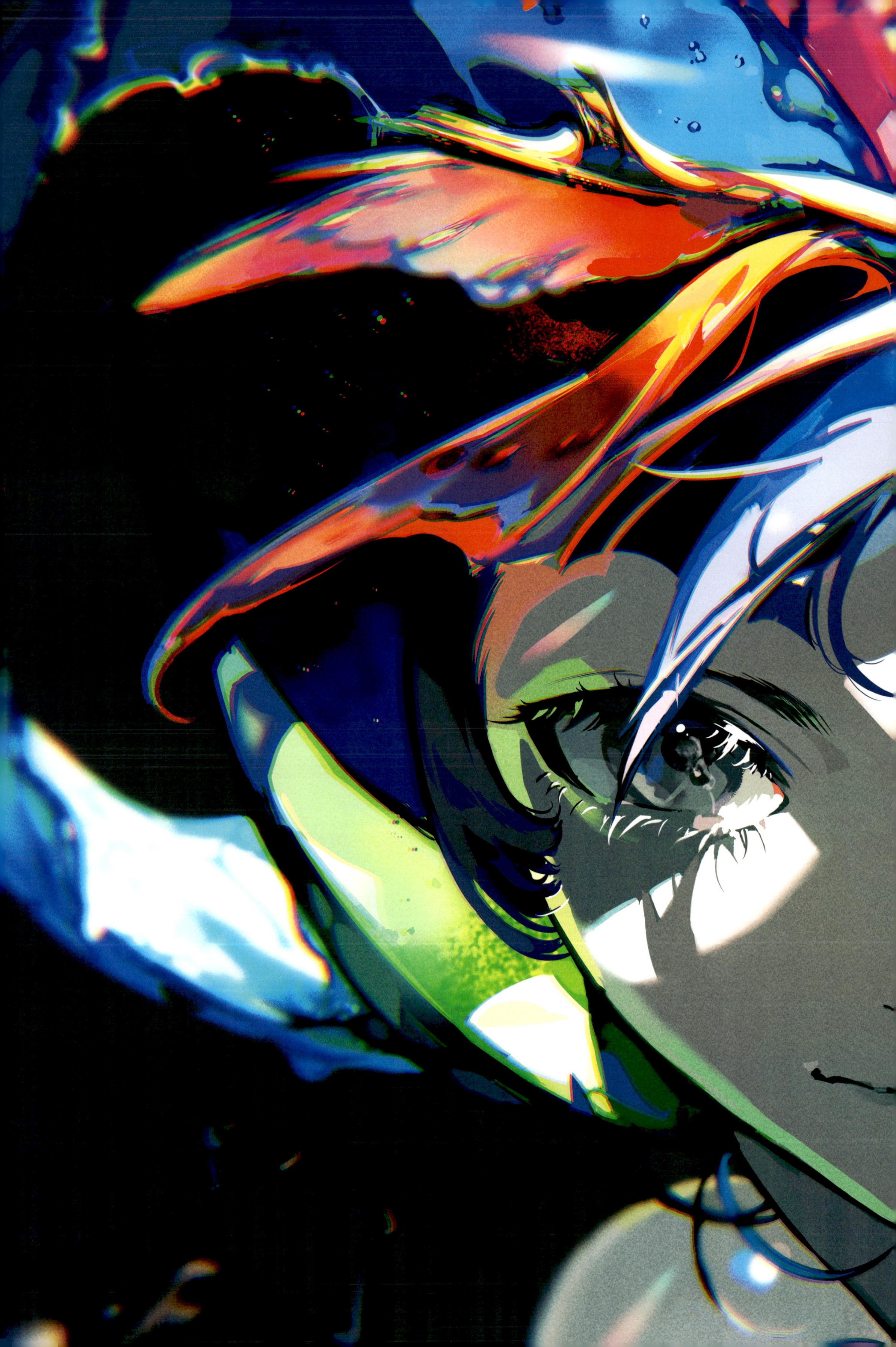

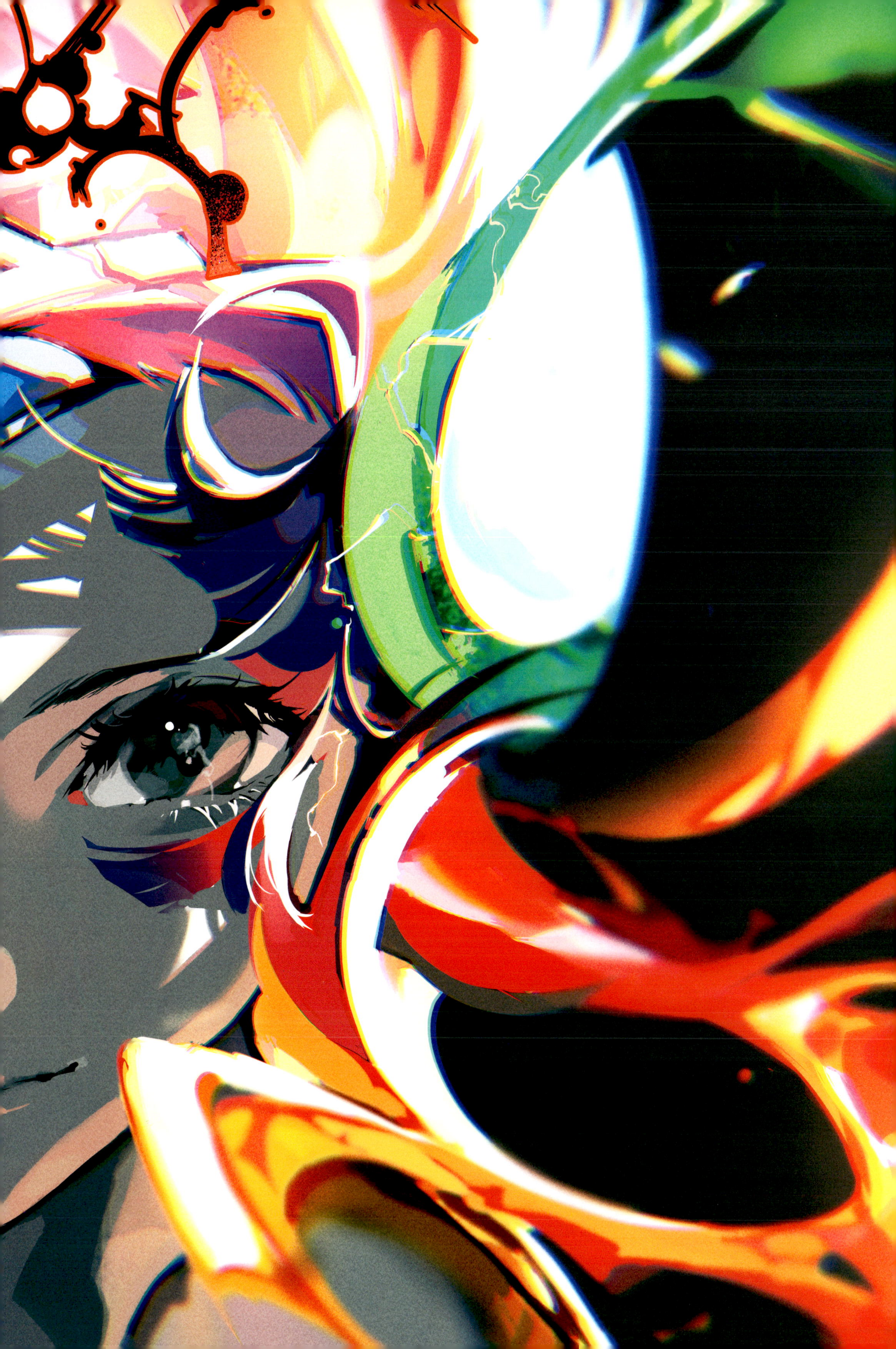

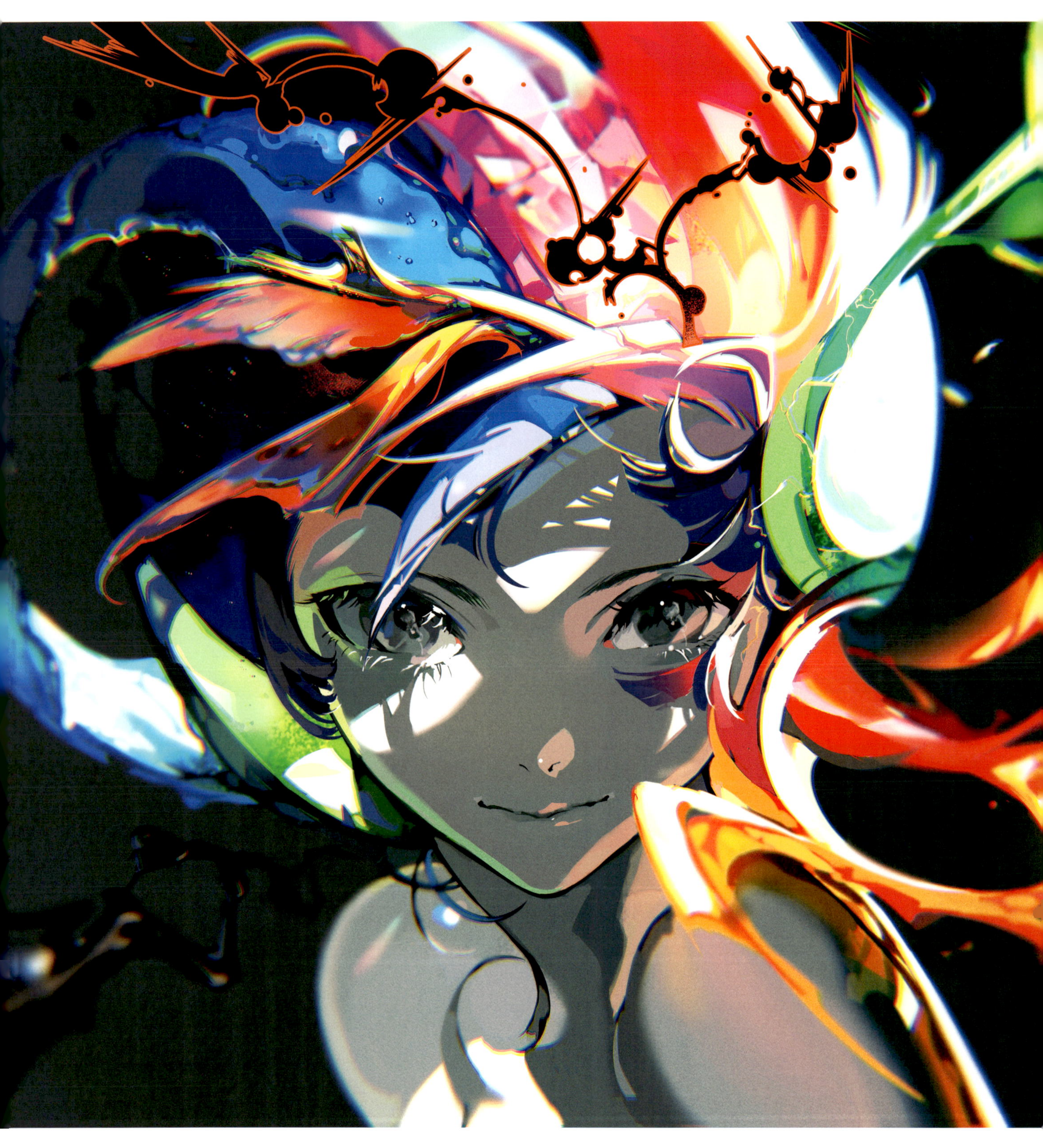

194 etc.
195

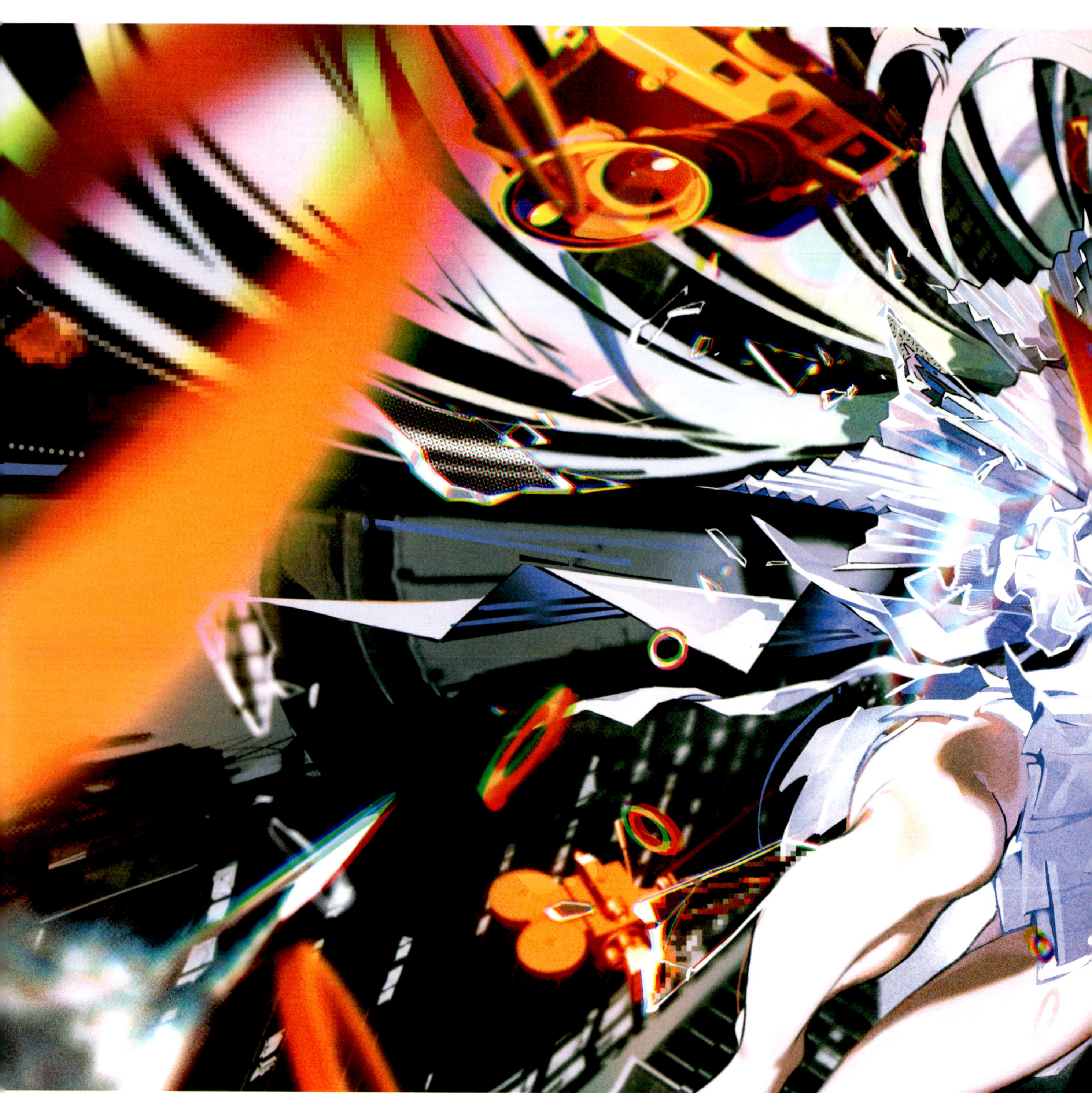

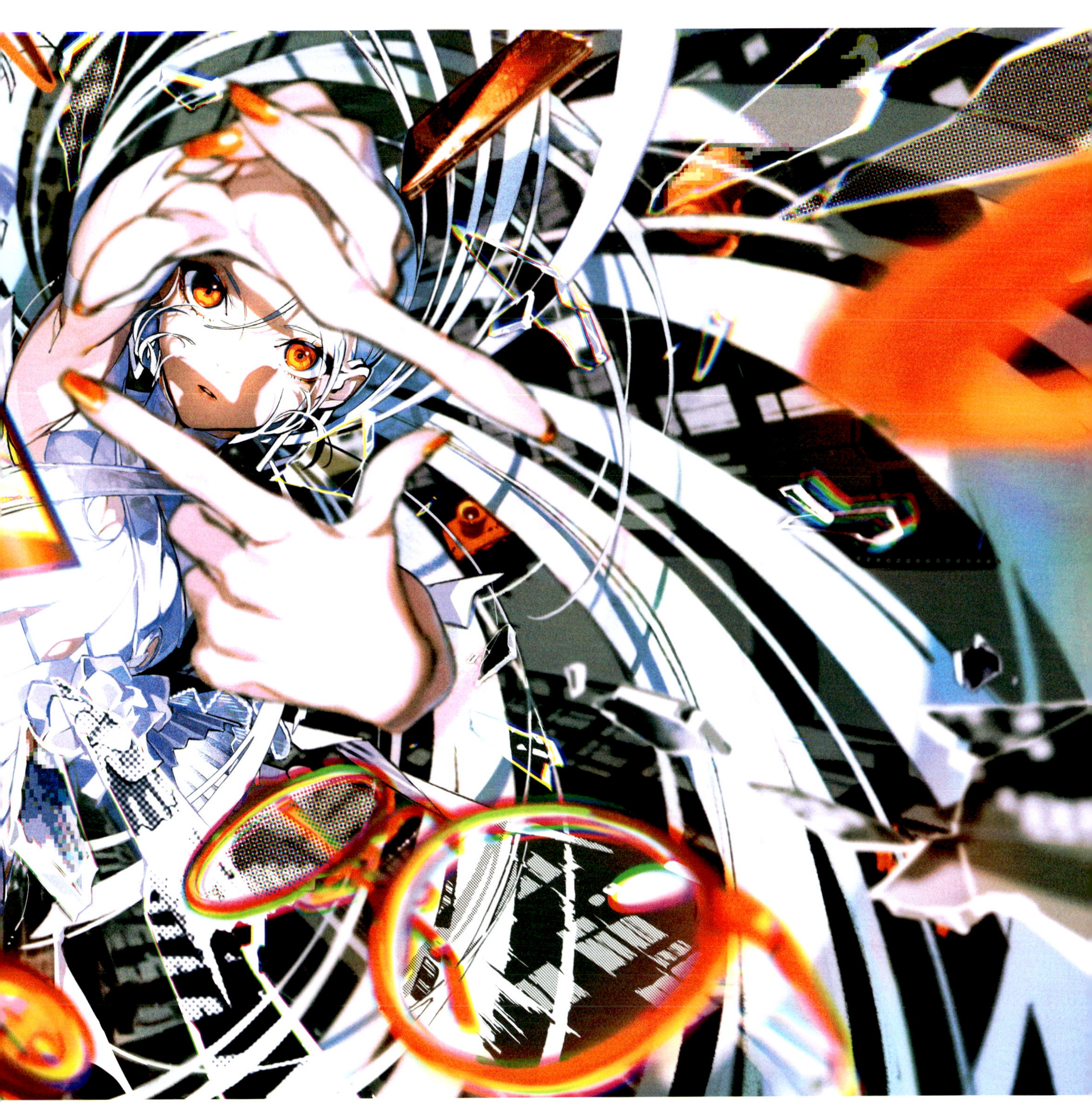

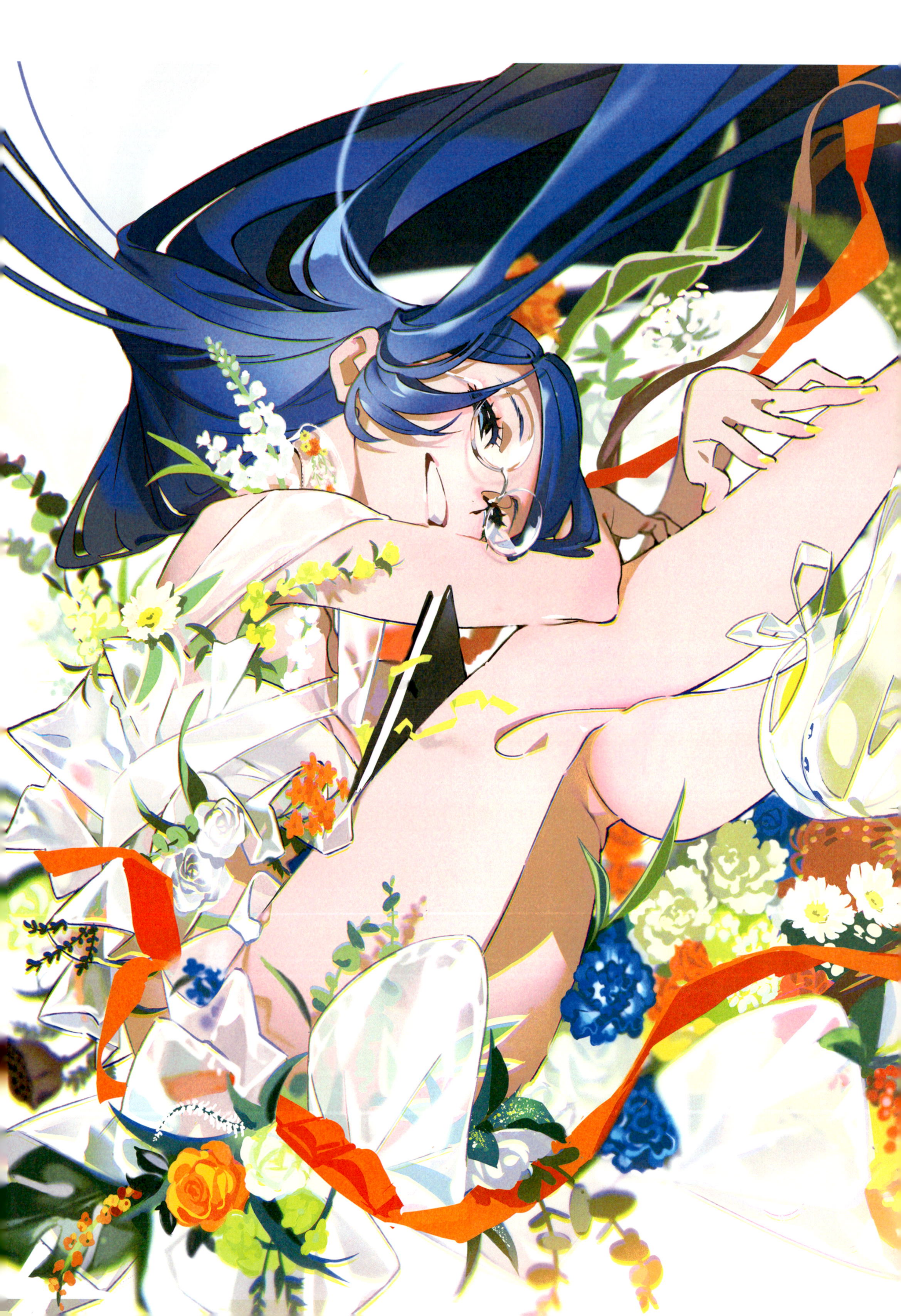

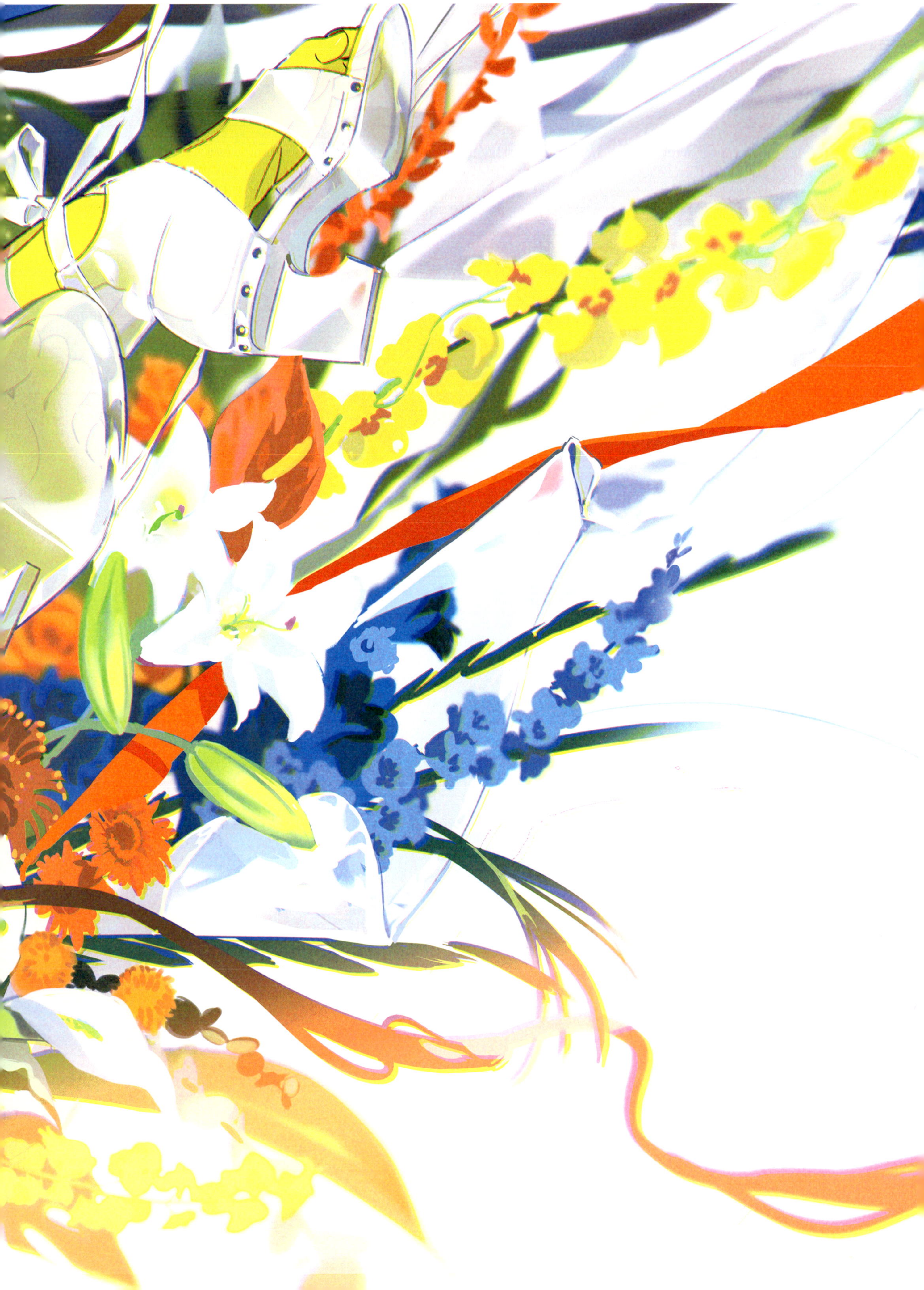

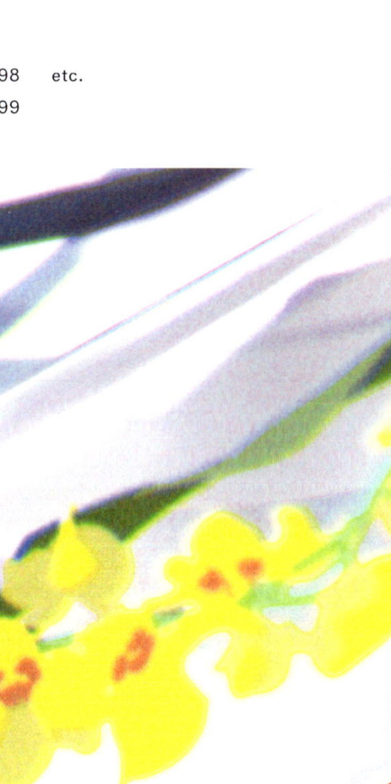

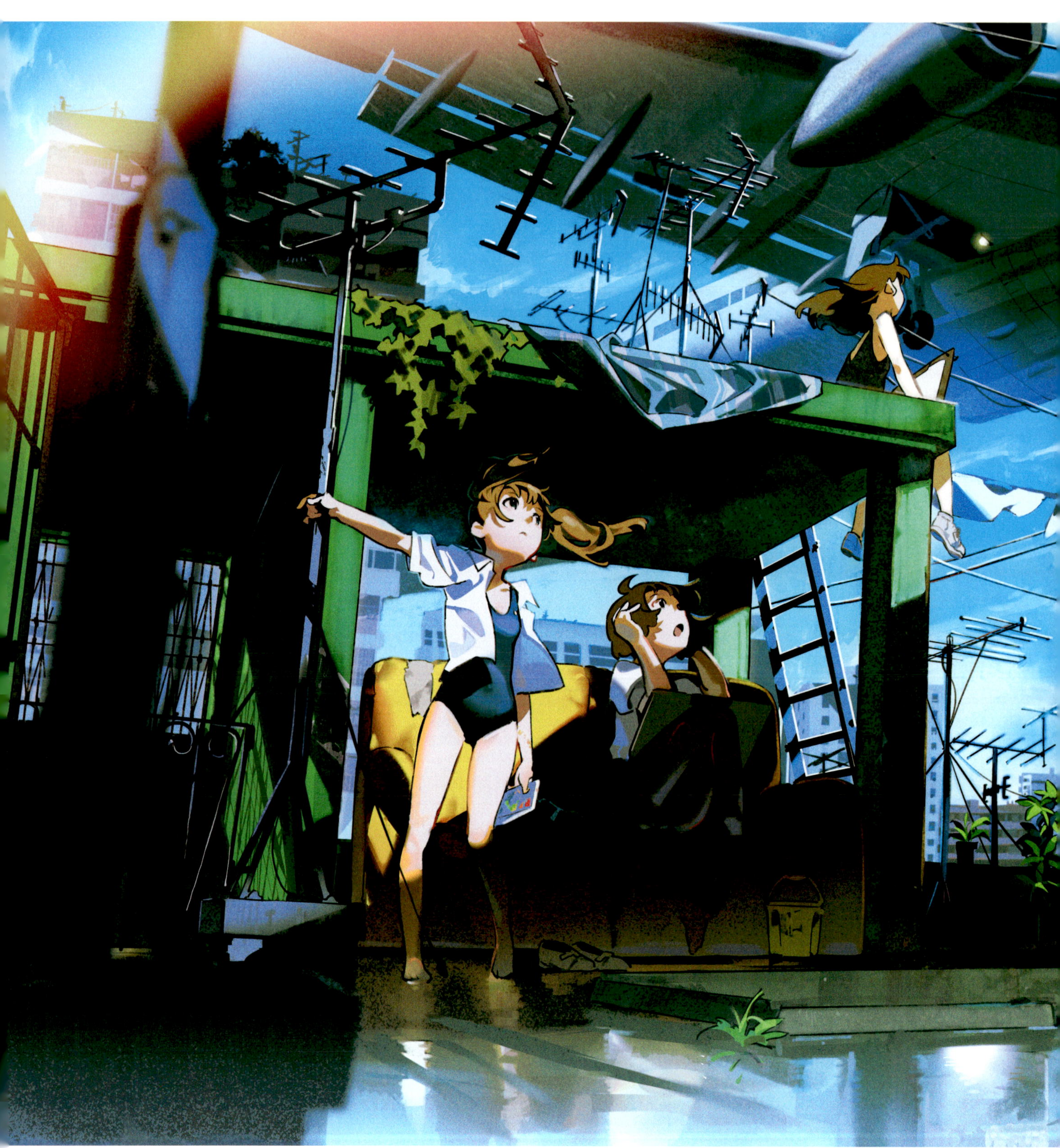

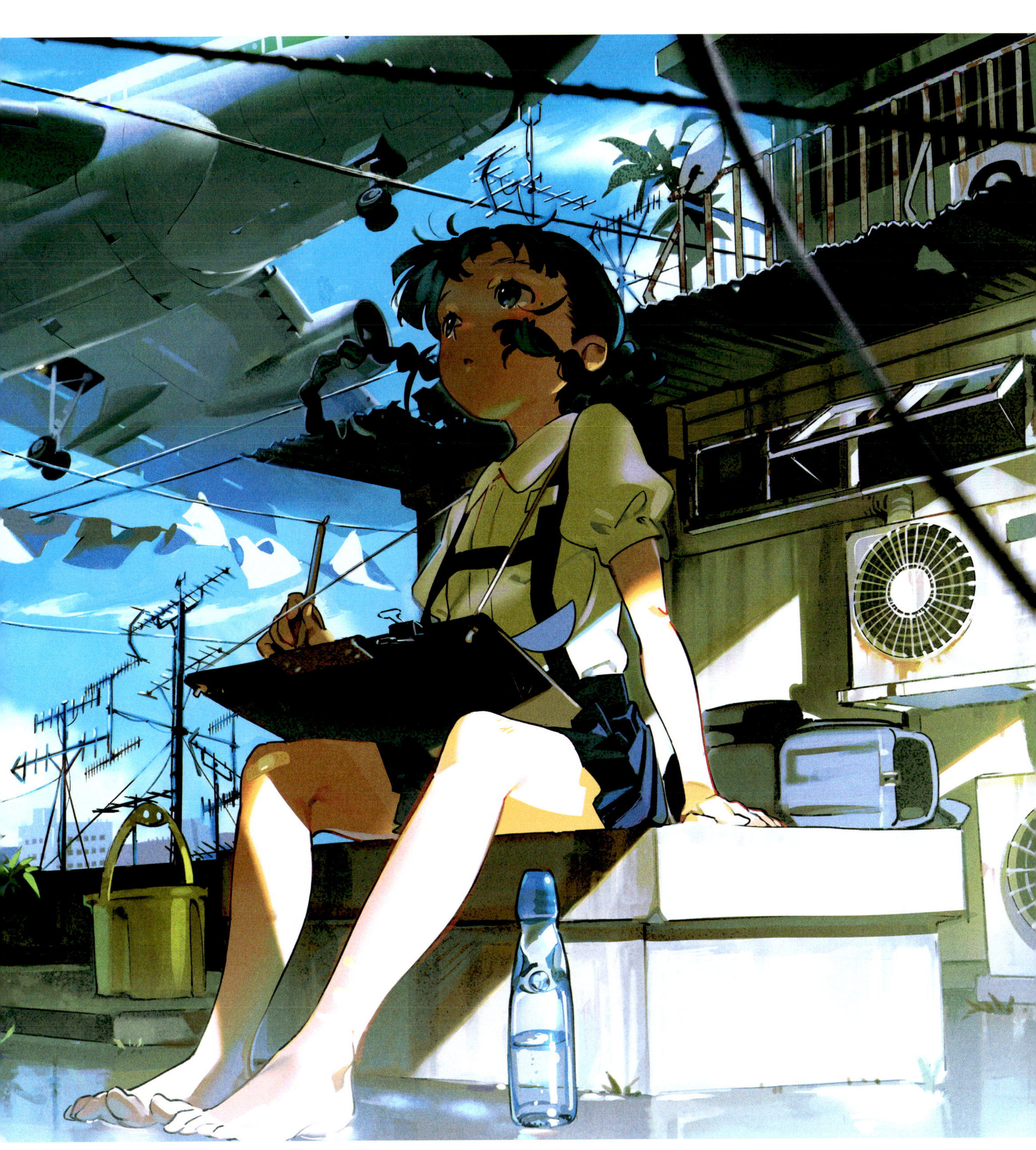

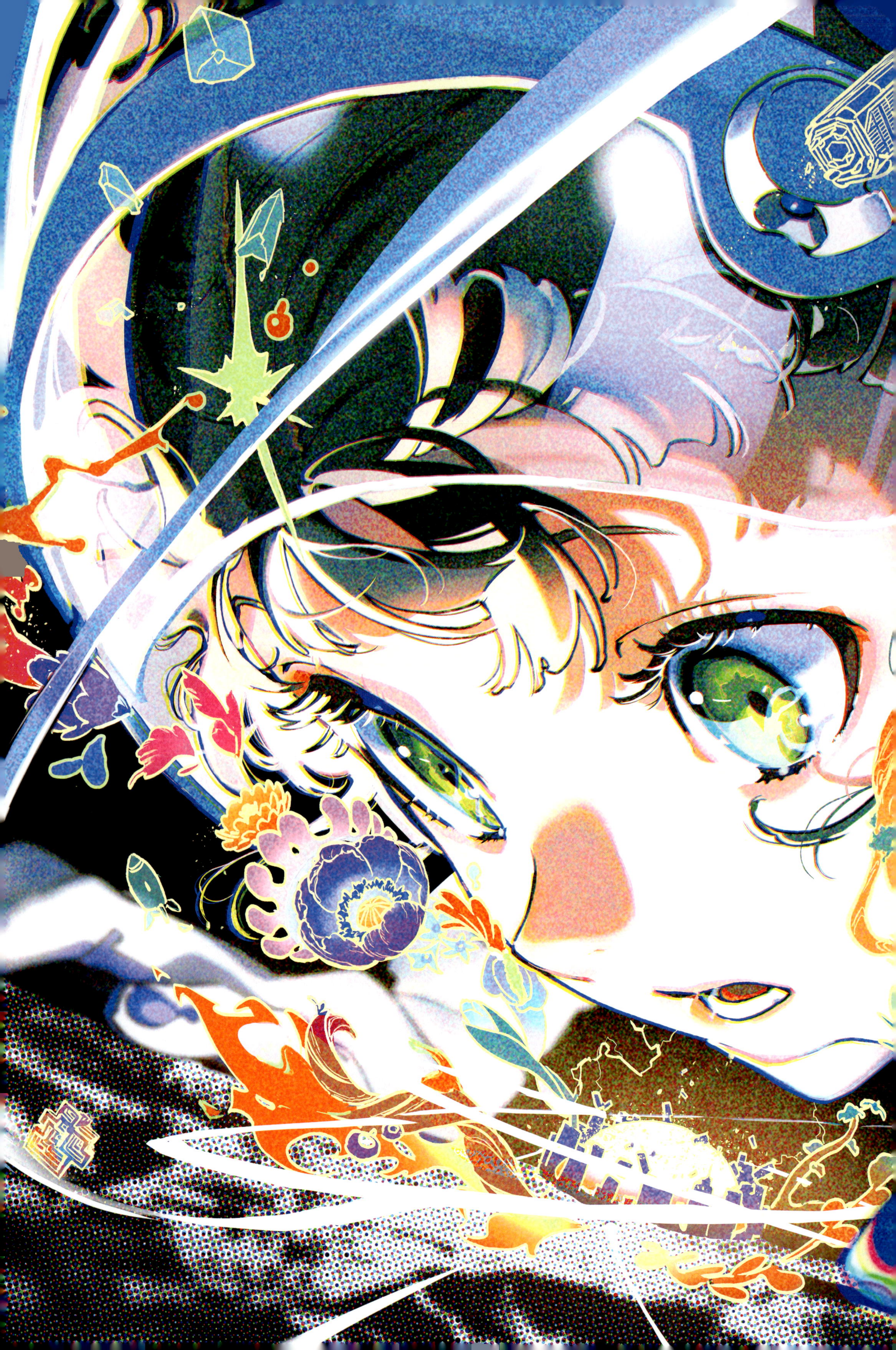

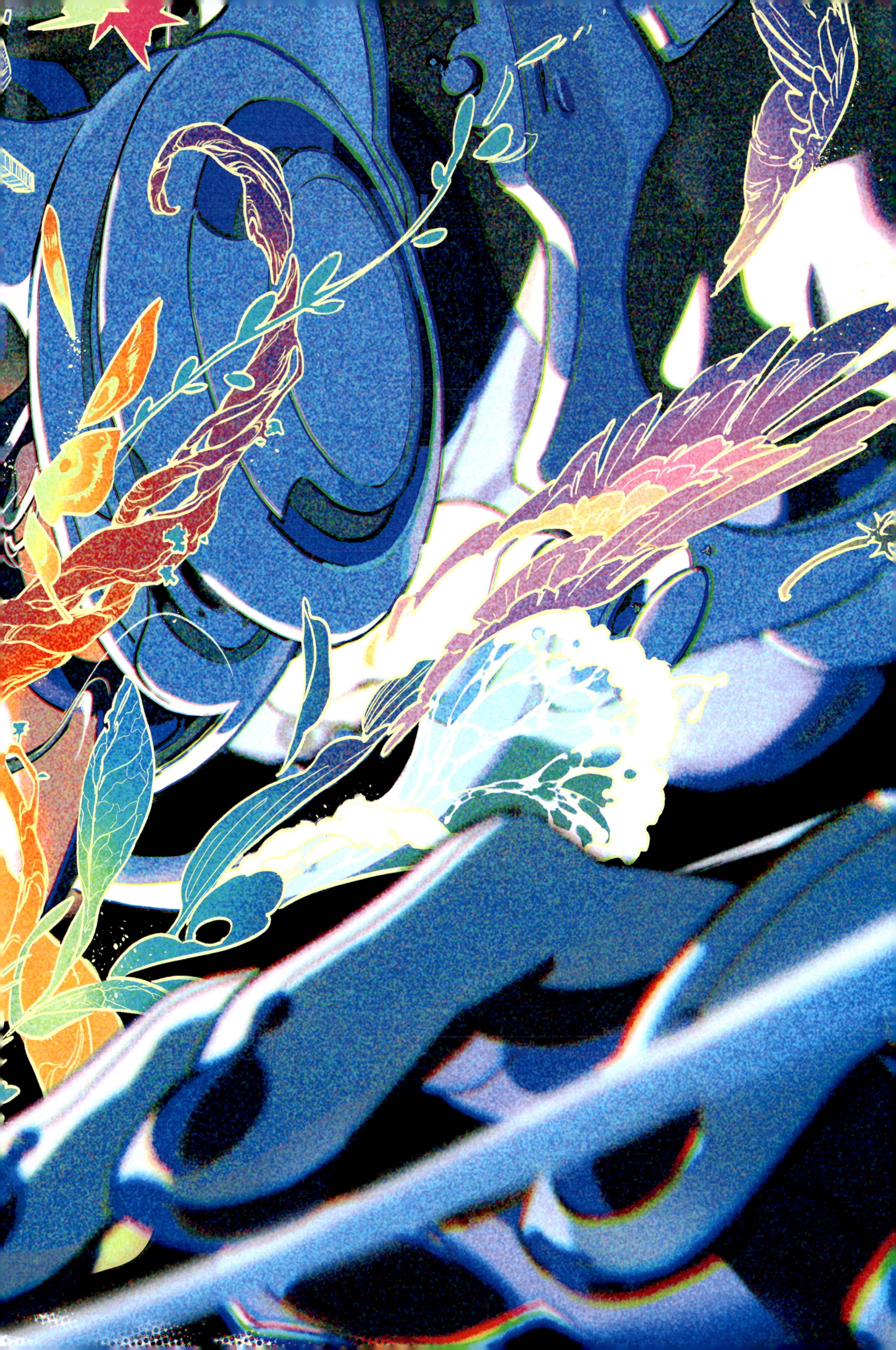

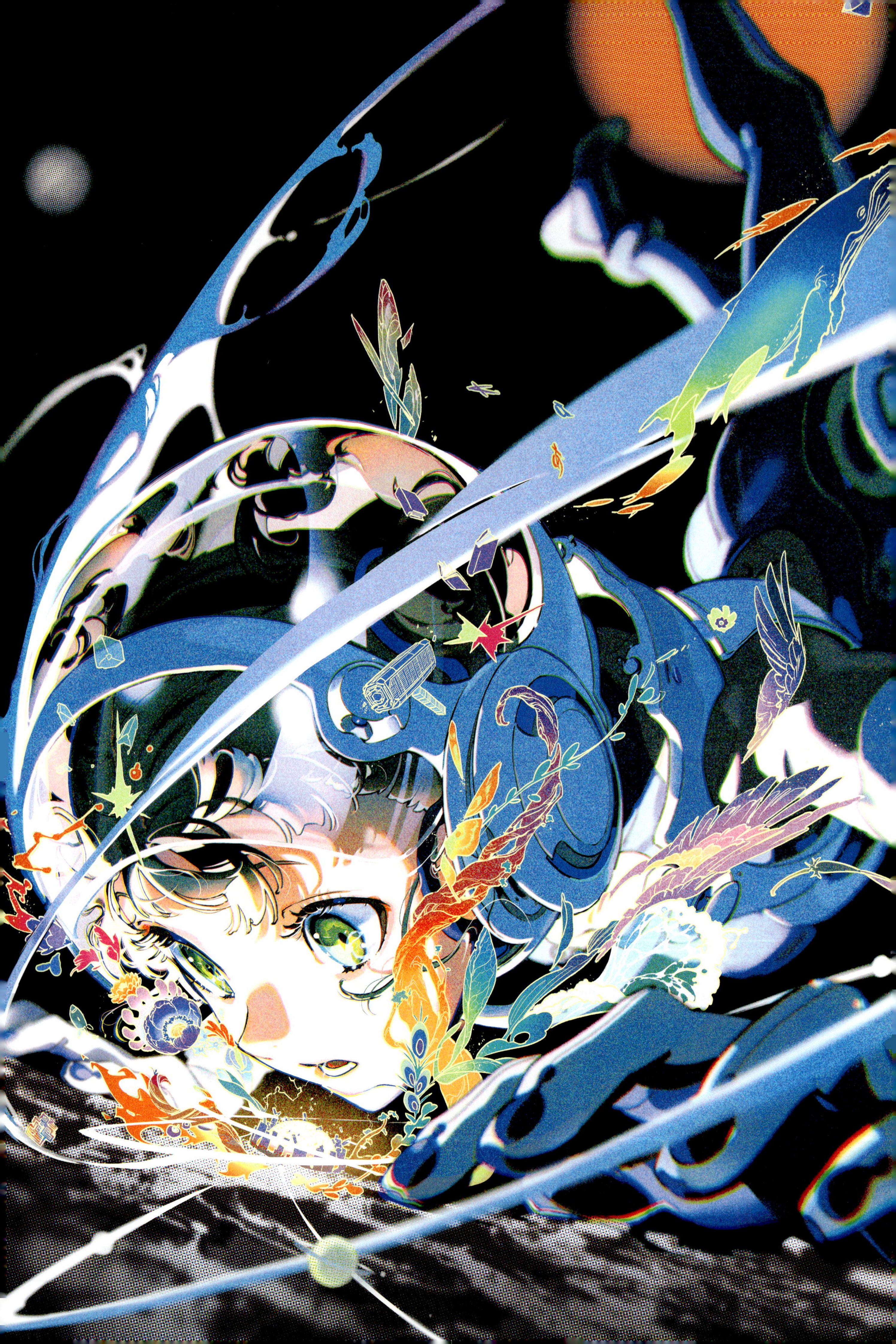

204 etc.
205

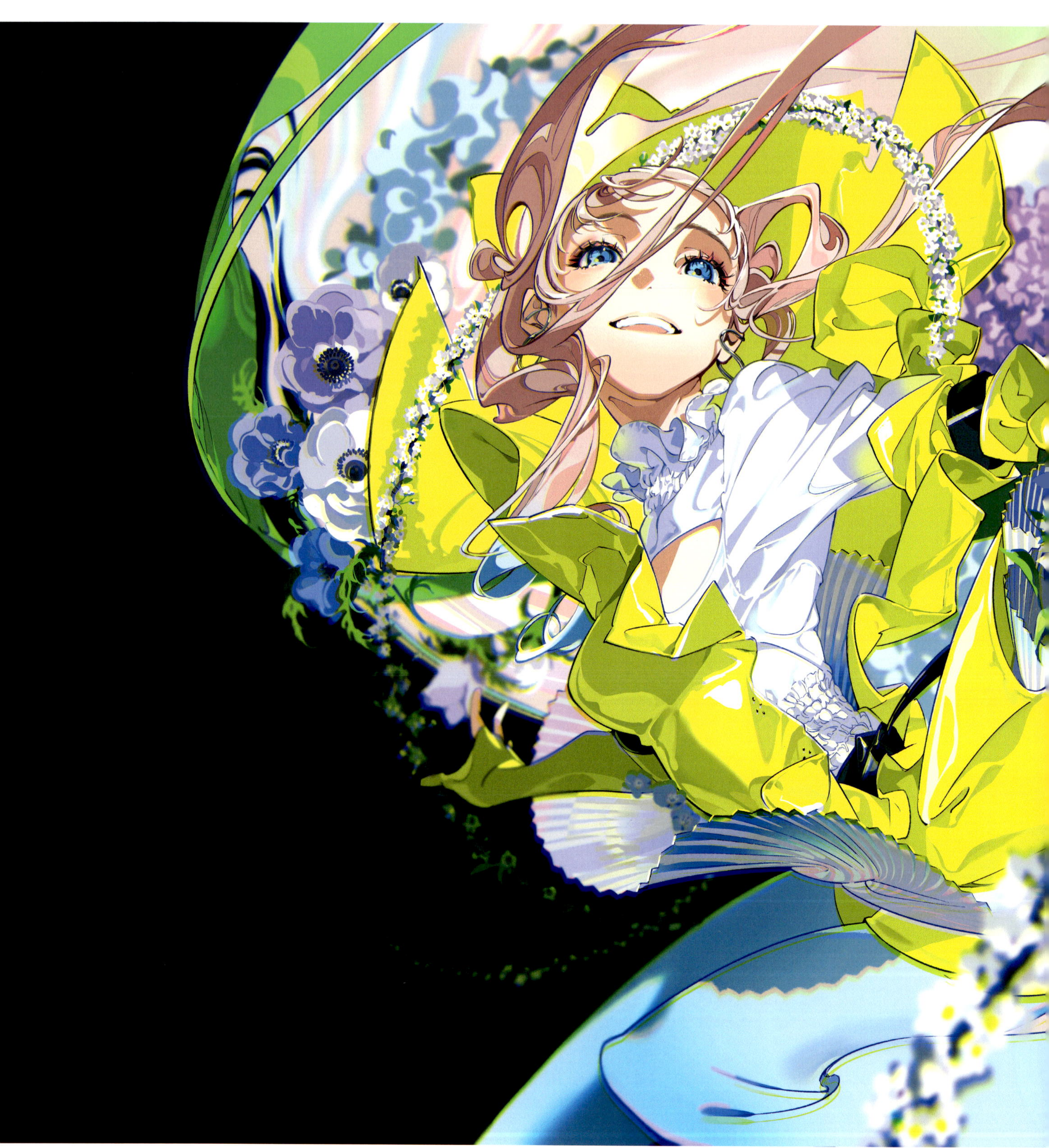

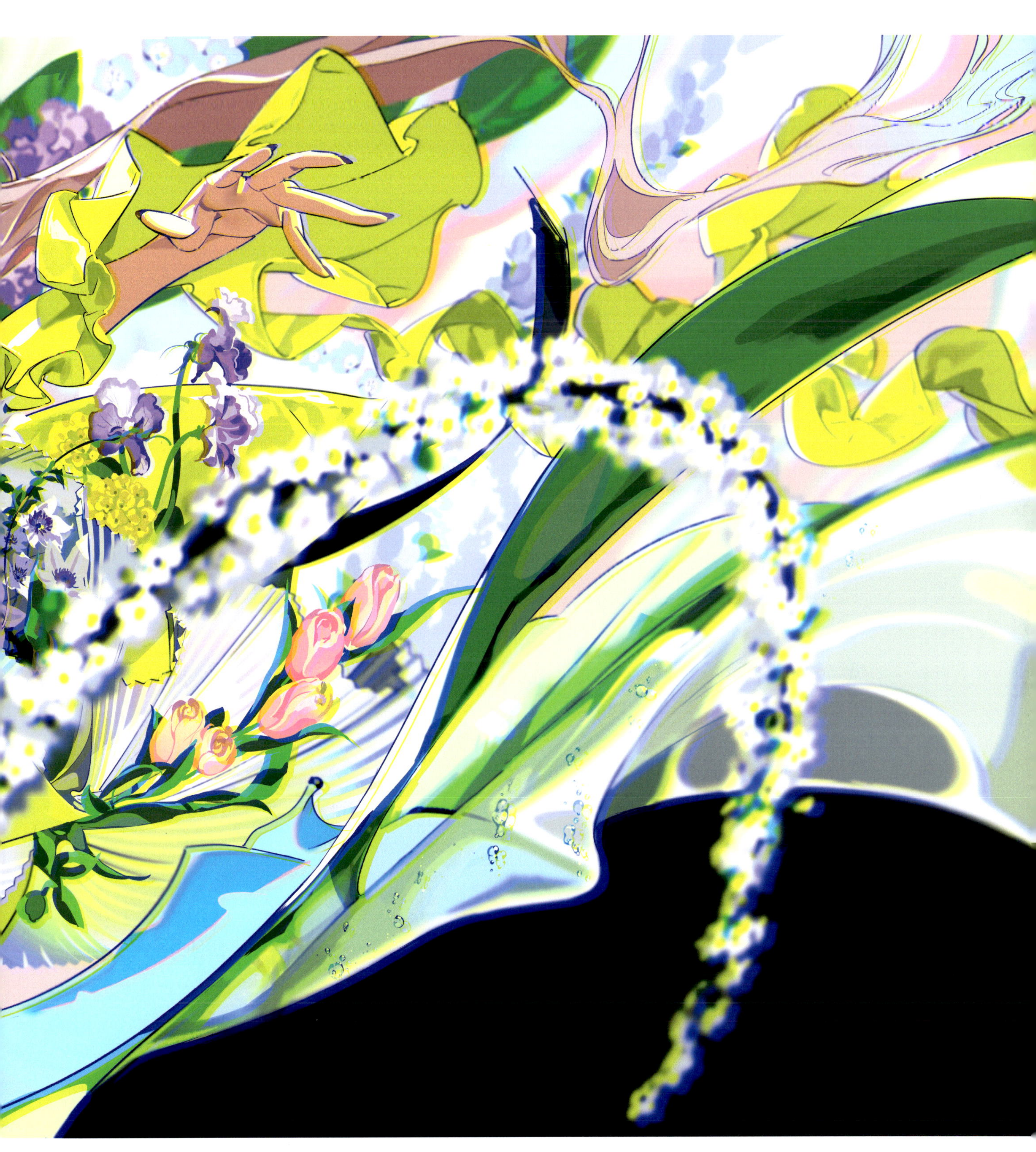

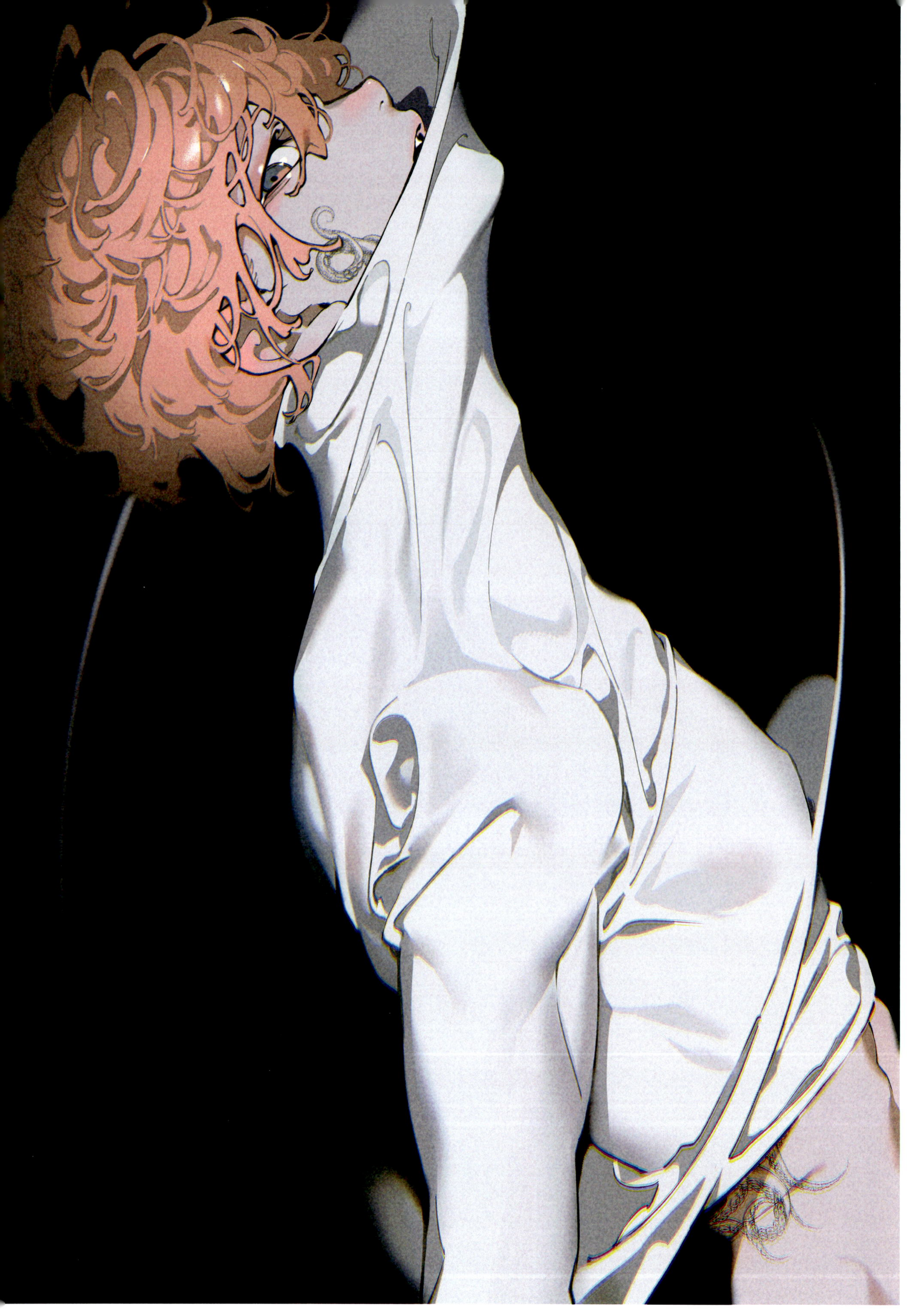

208 etc.

209

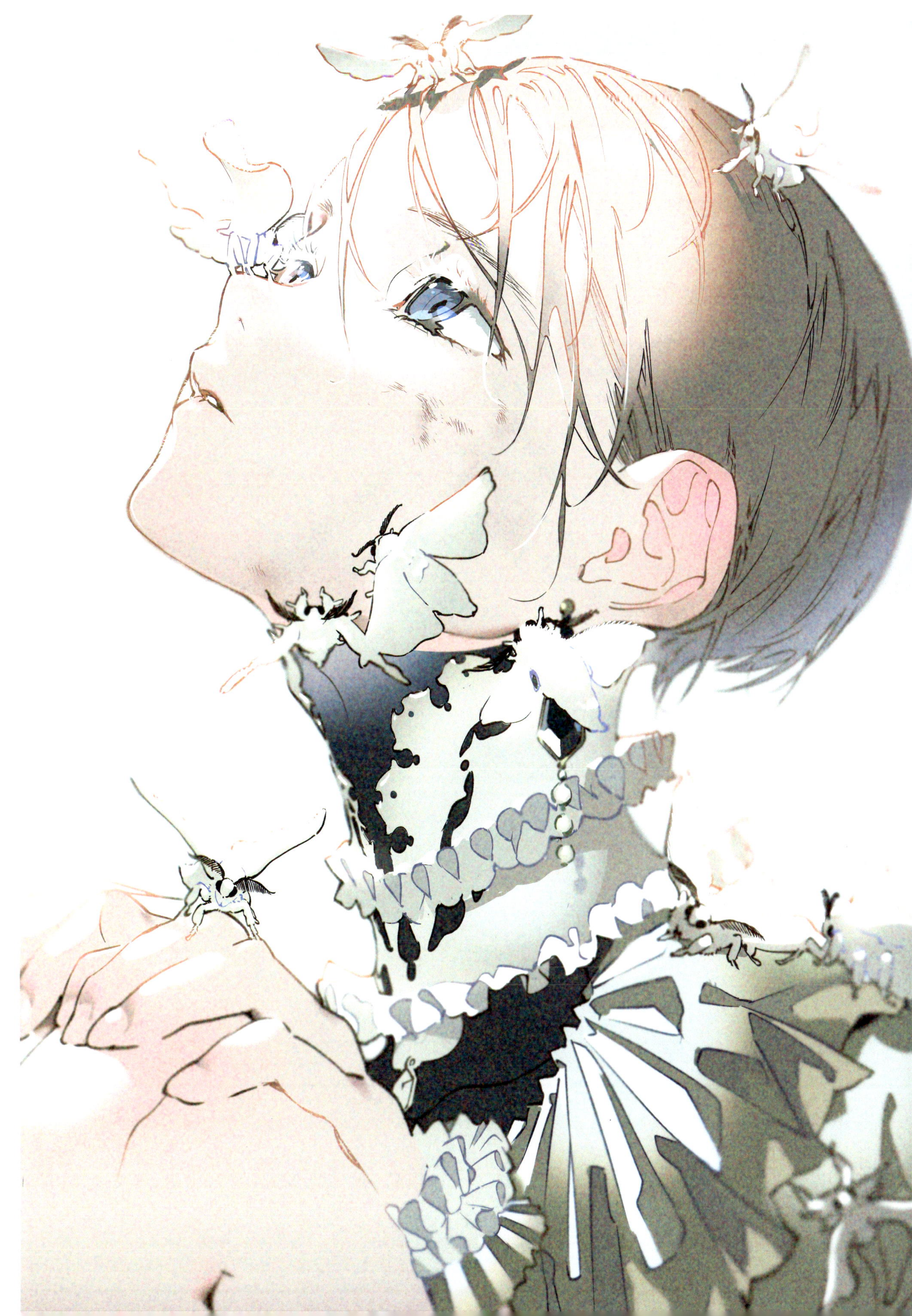

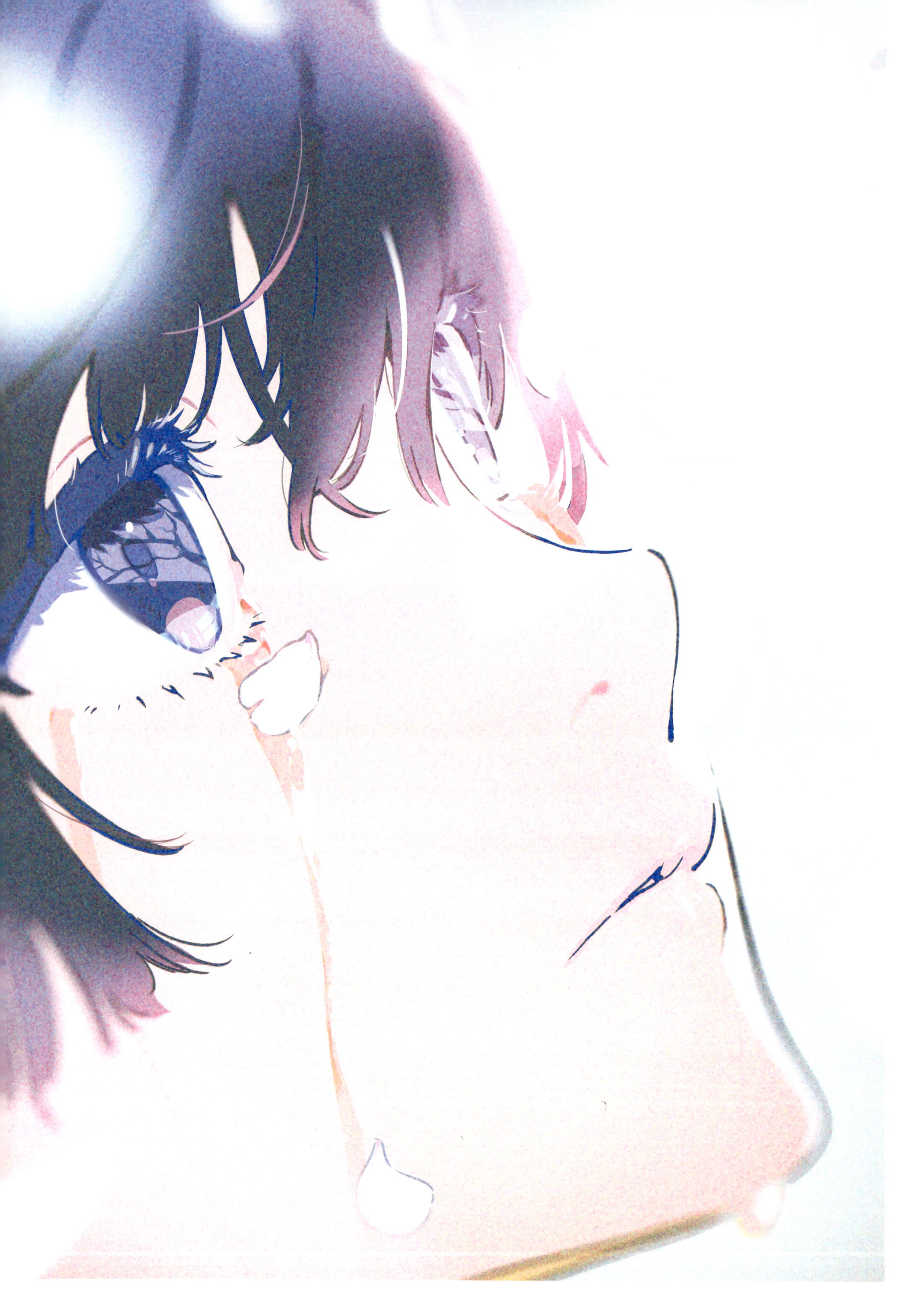

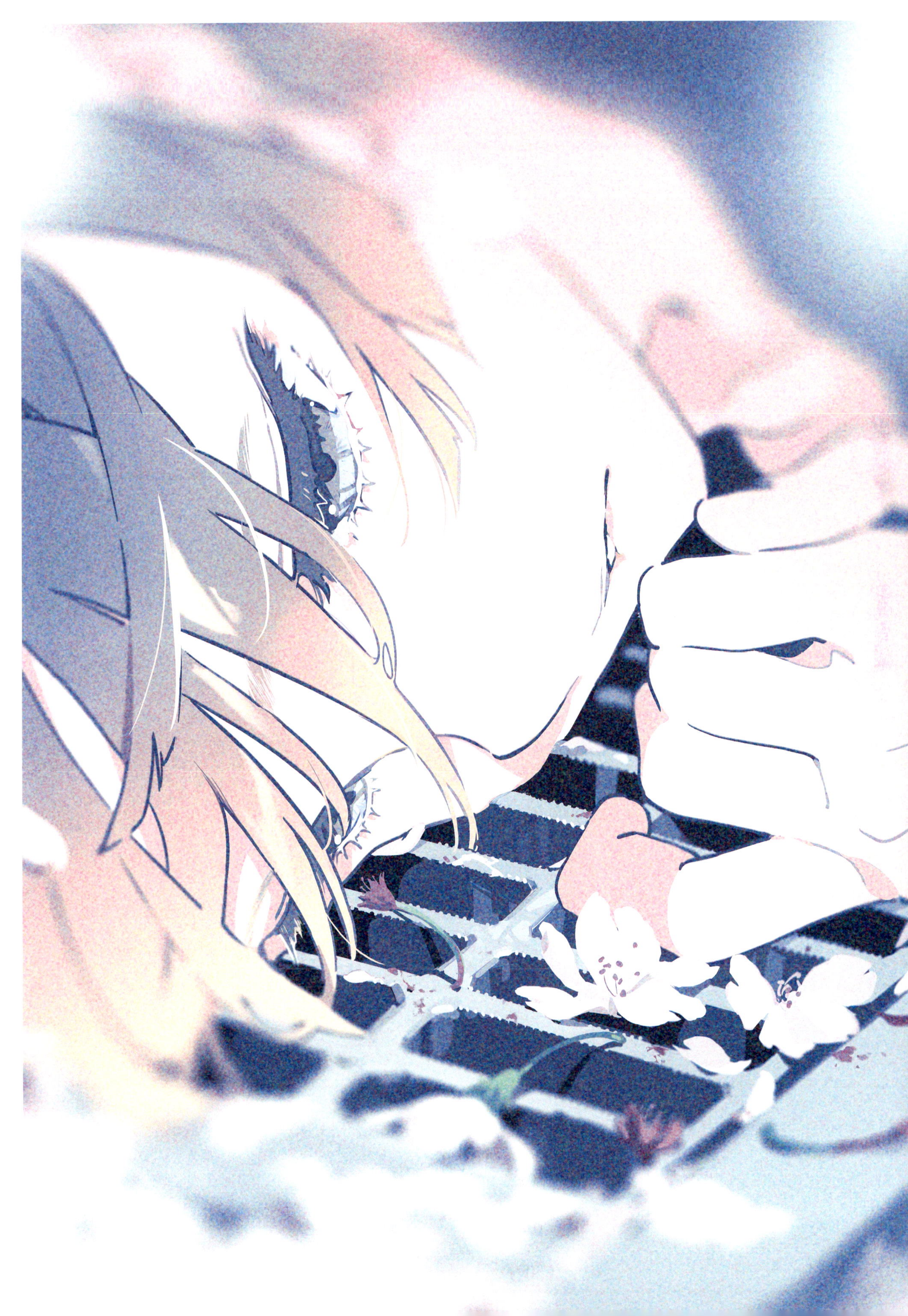

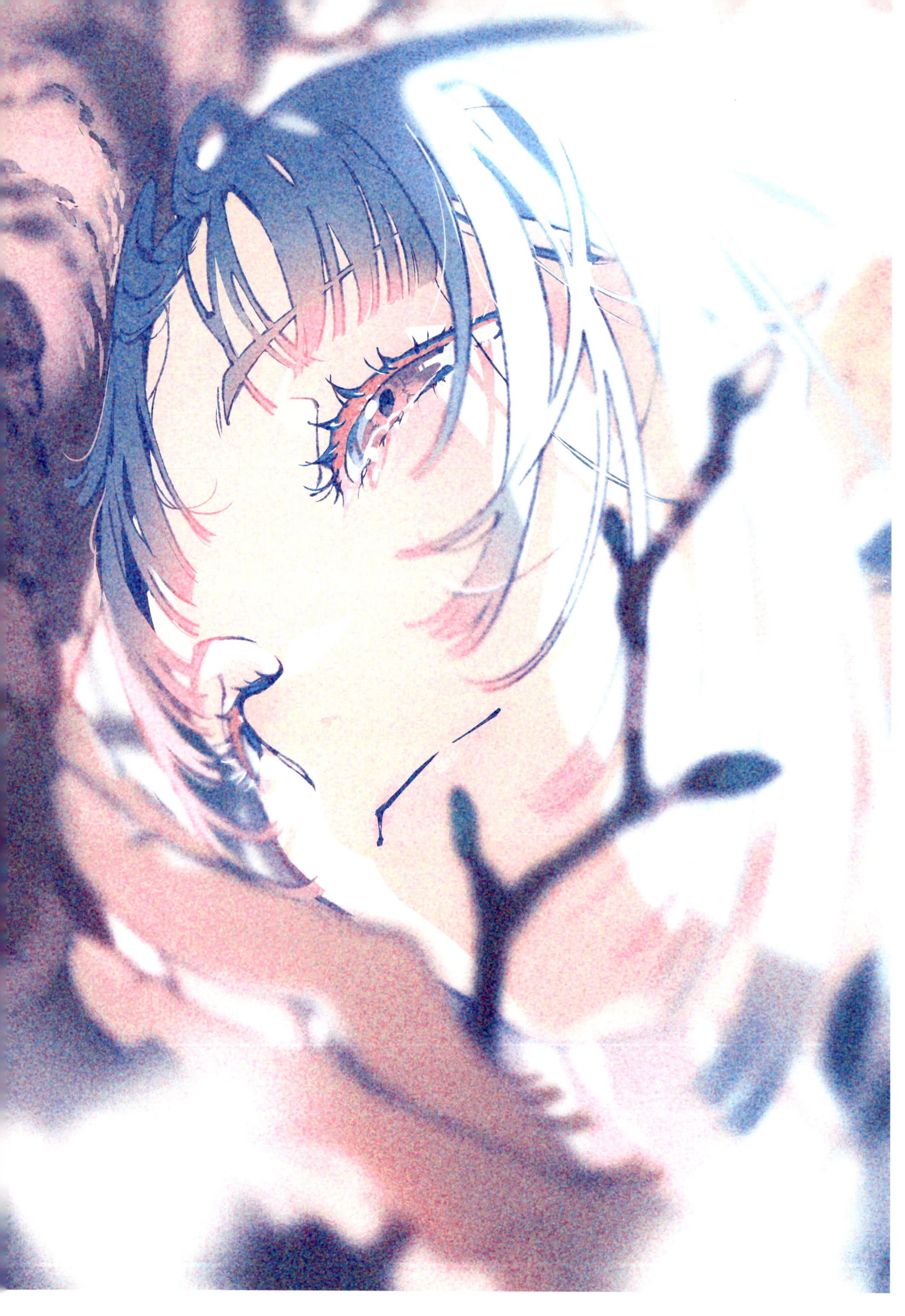

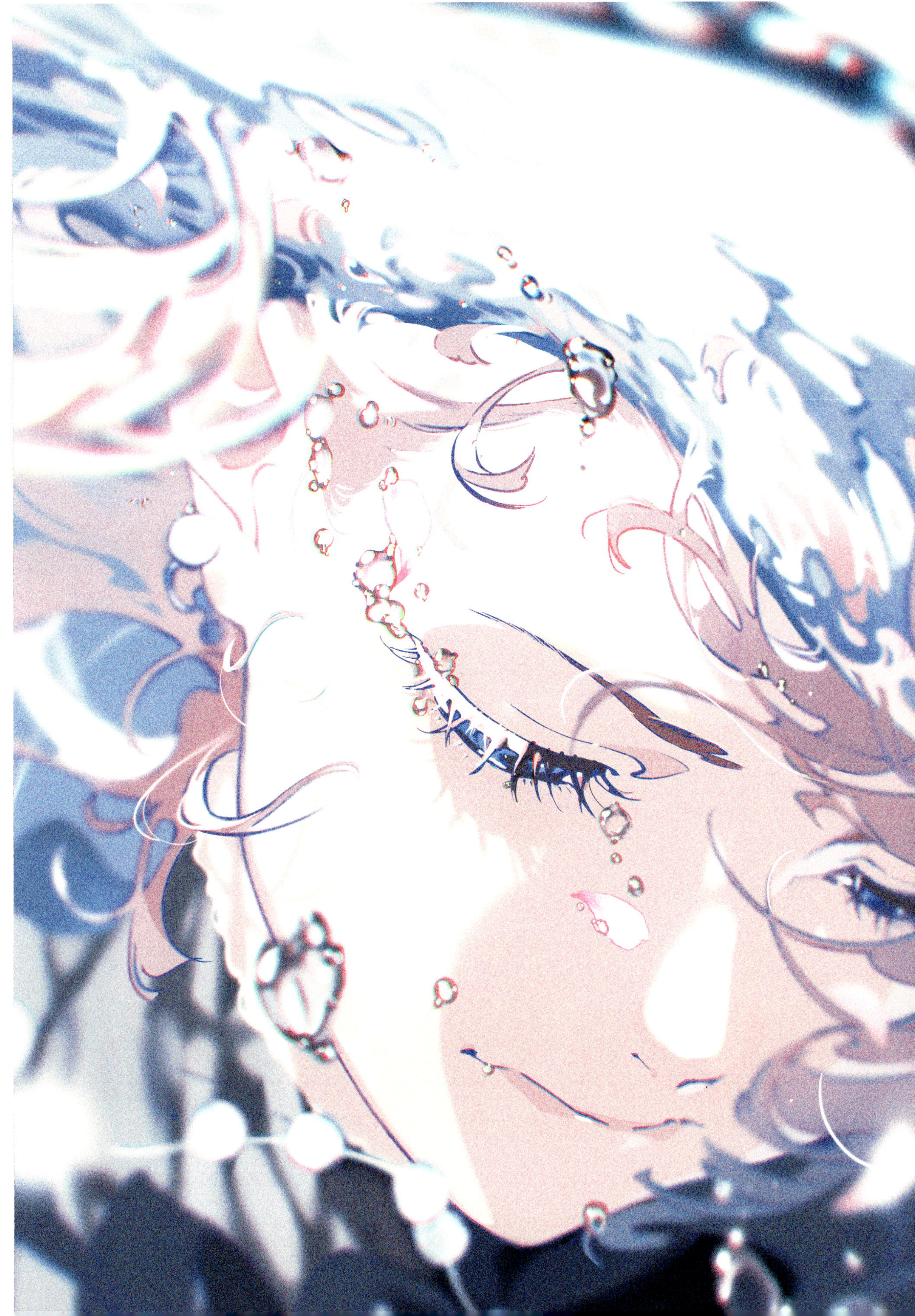

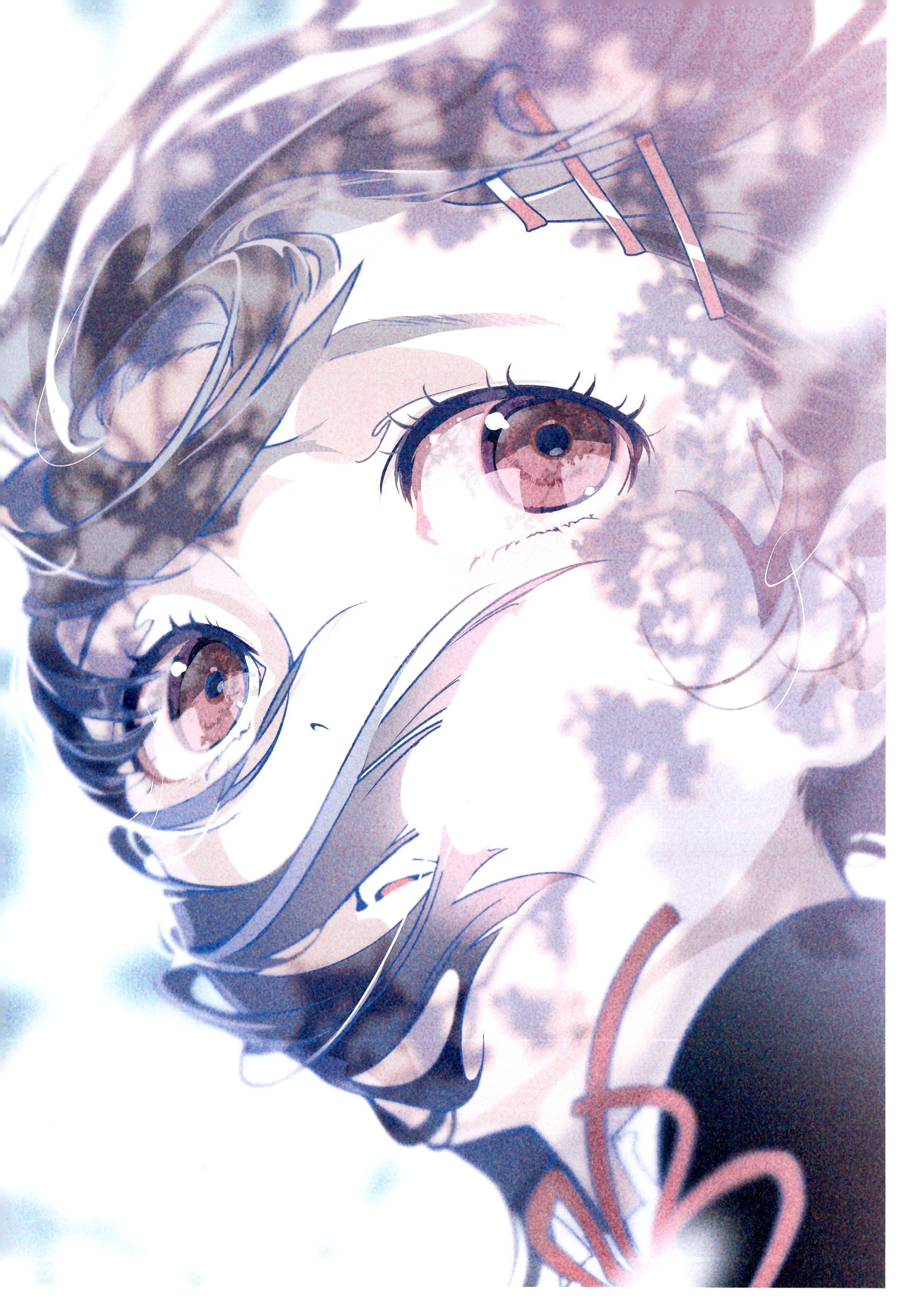

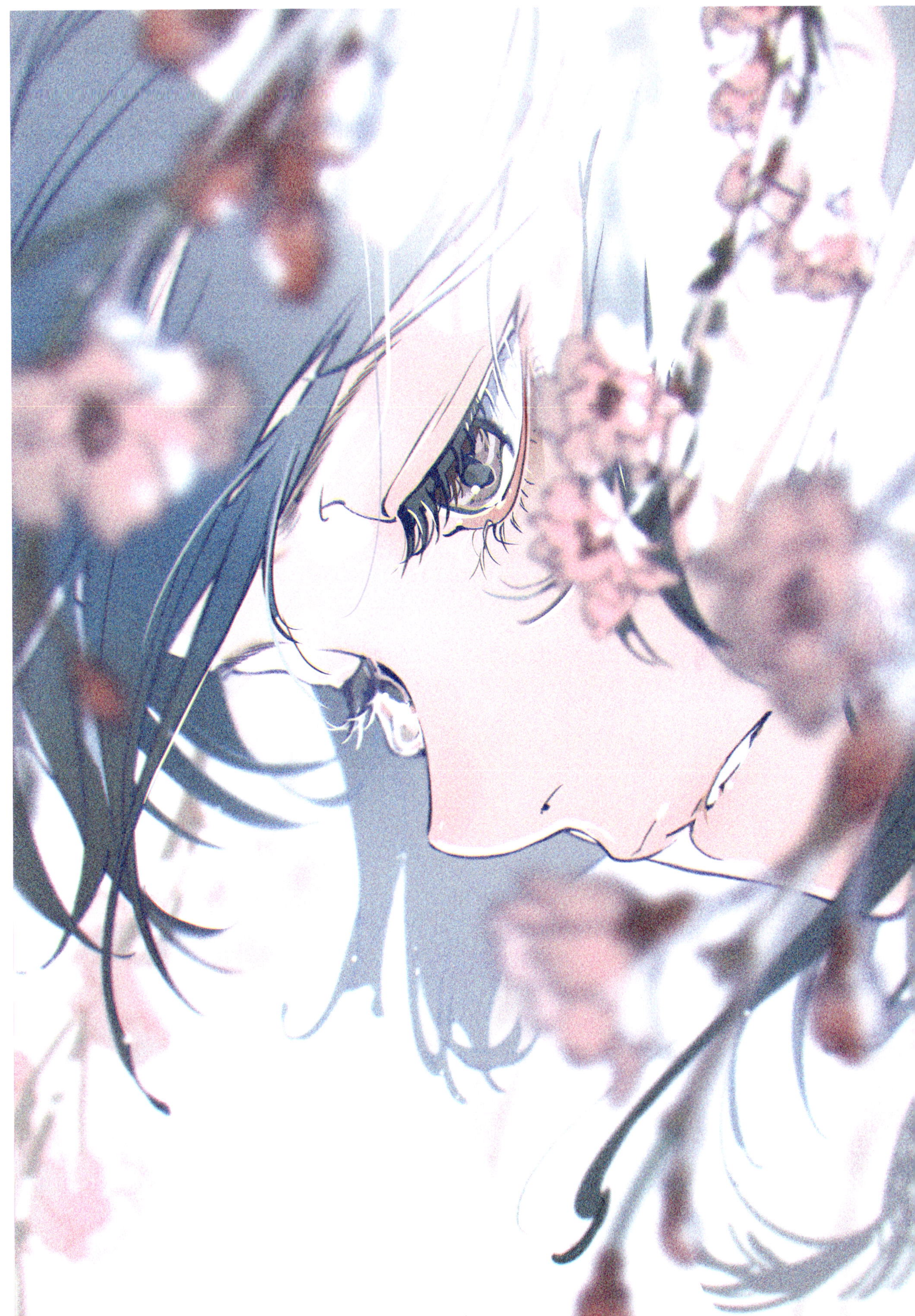

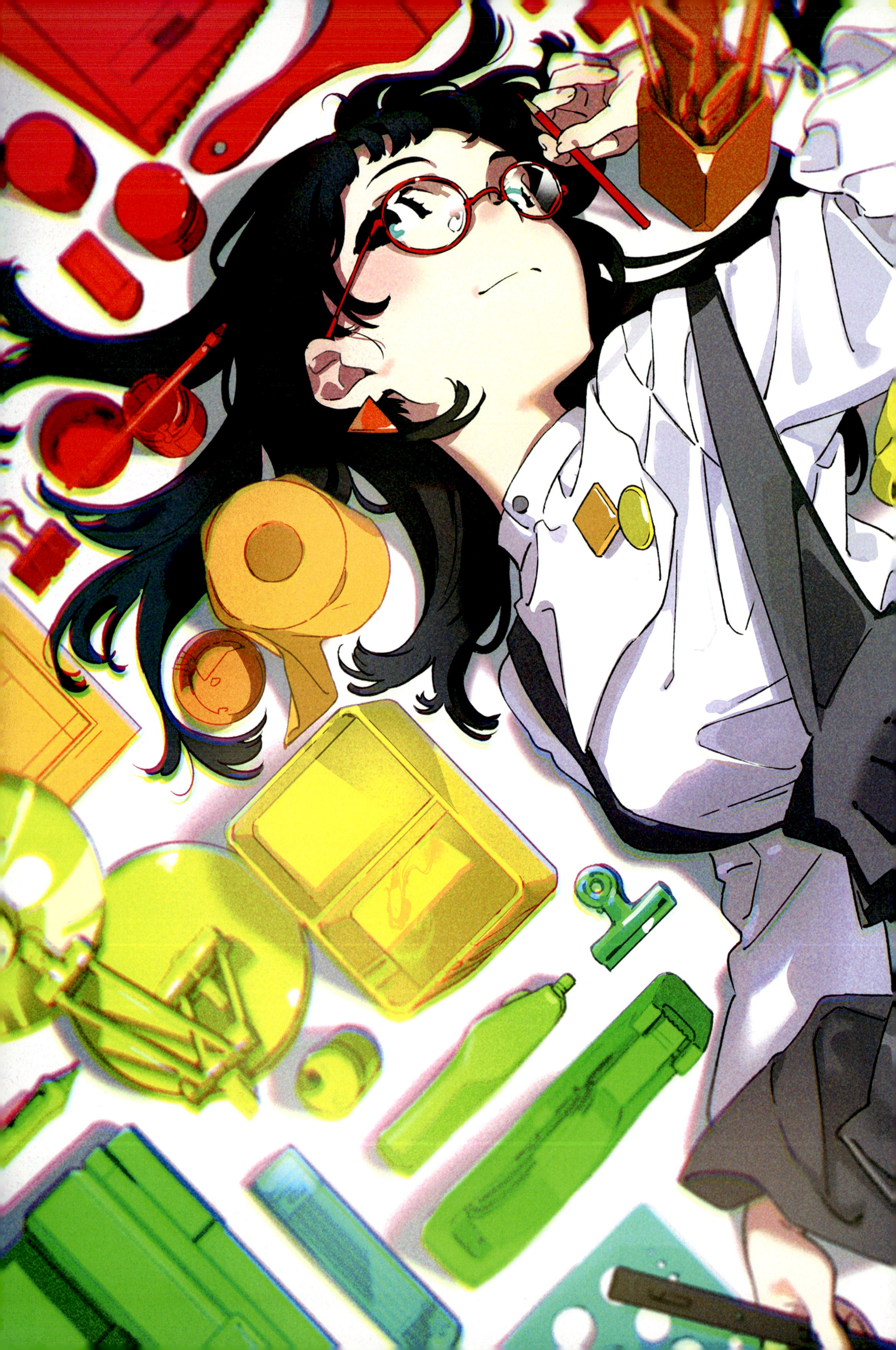

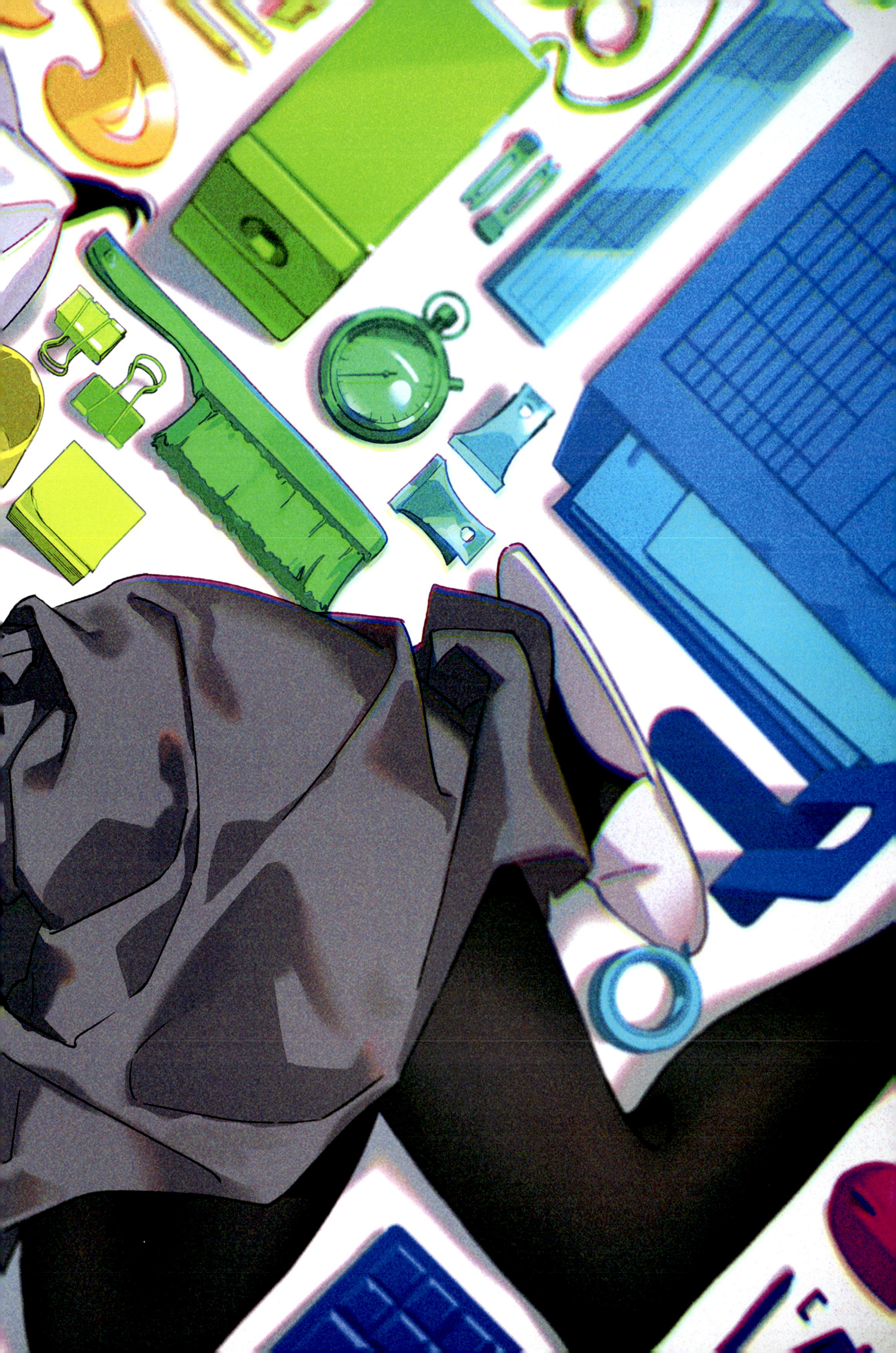

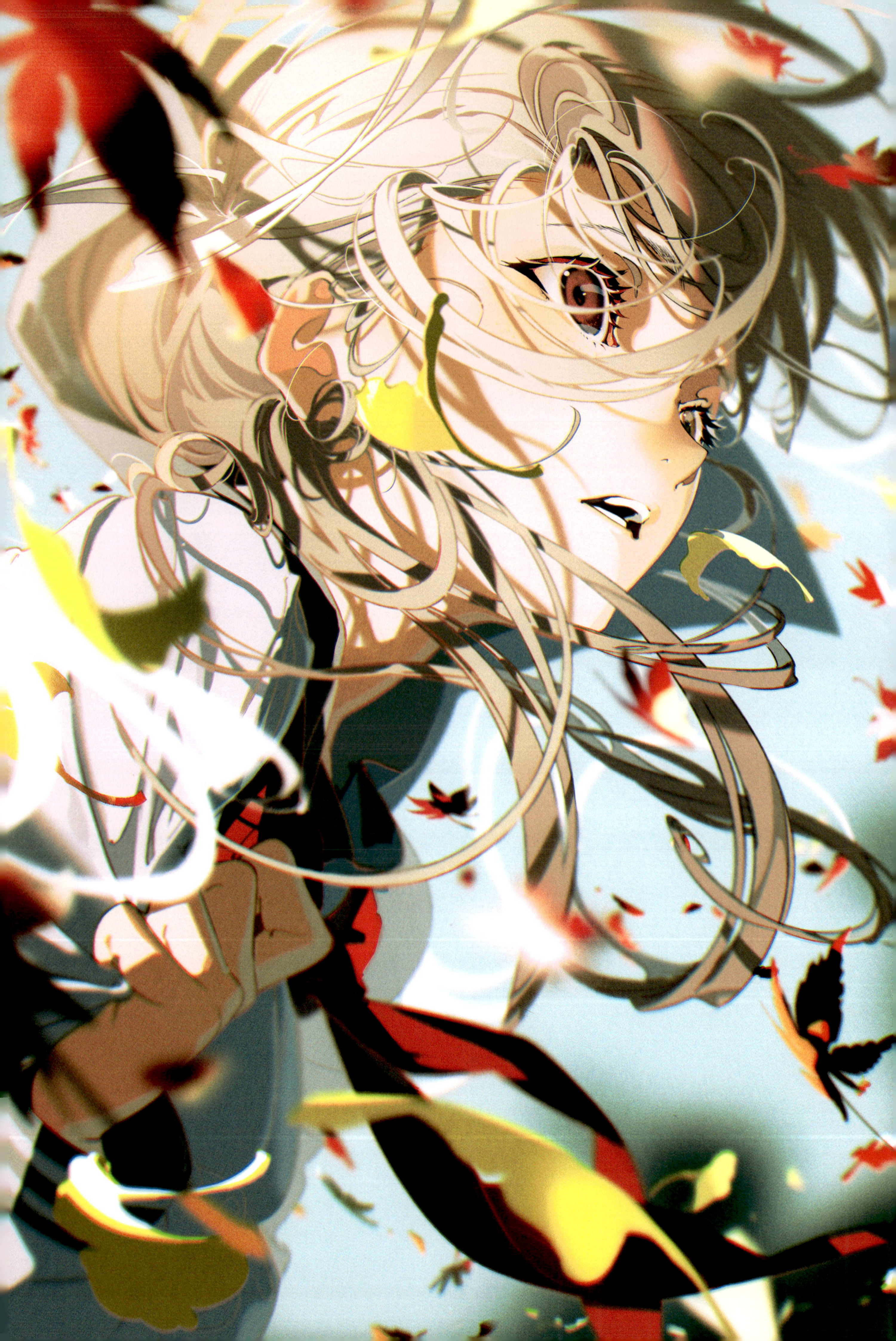

220　etc.
221

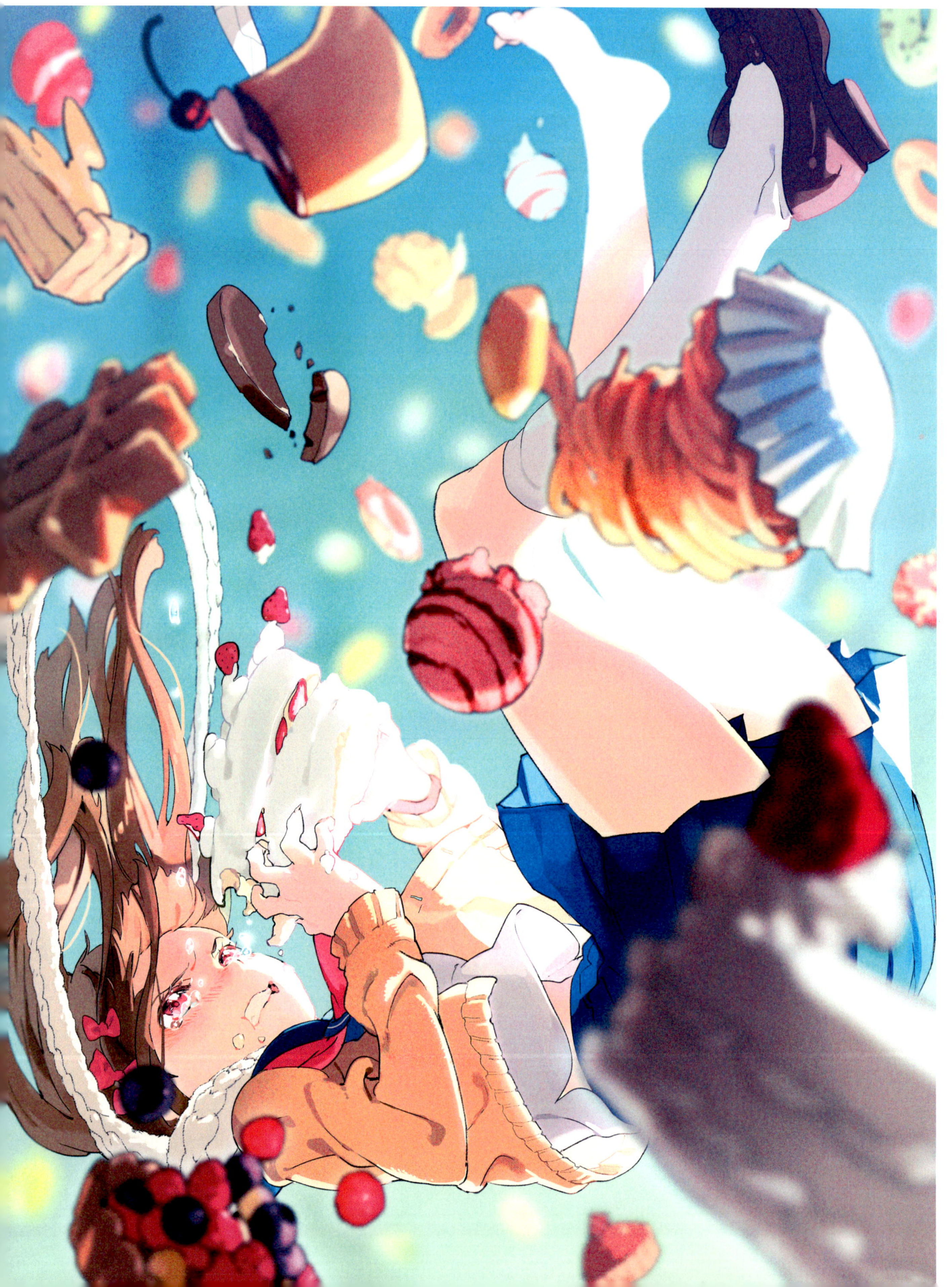

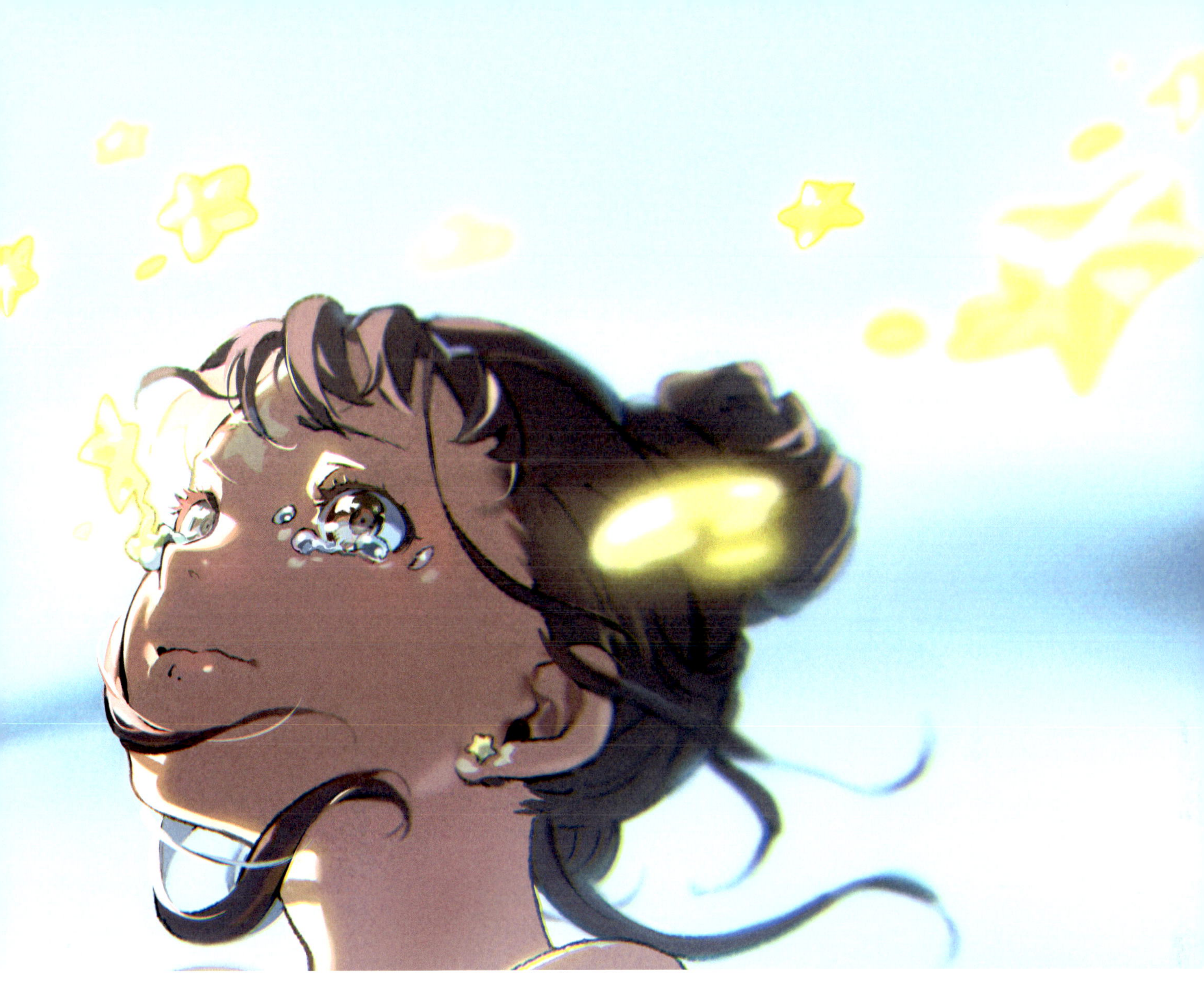

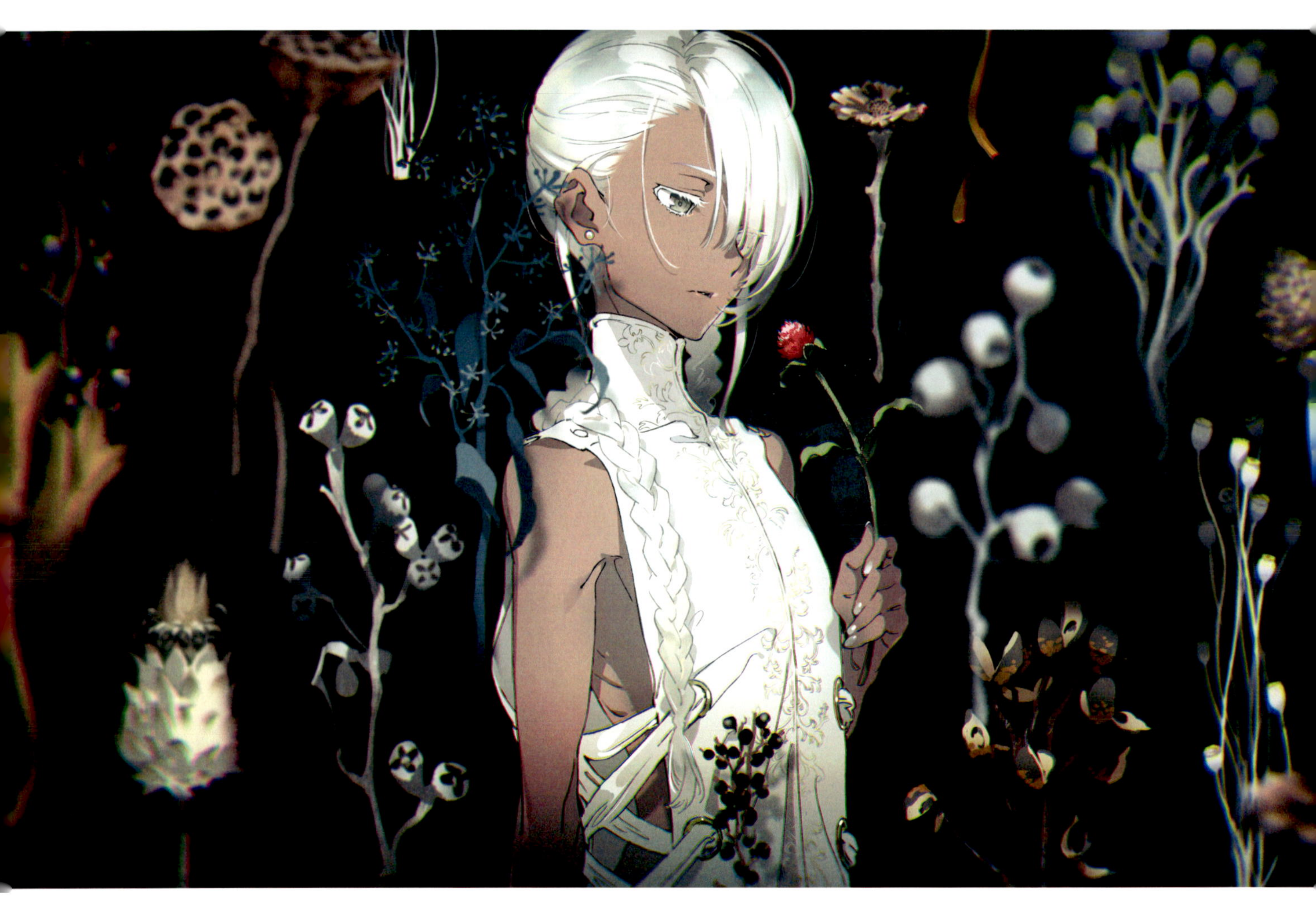

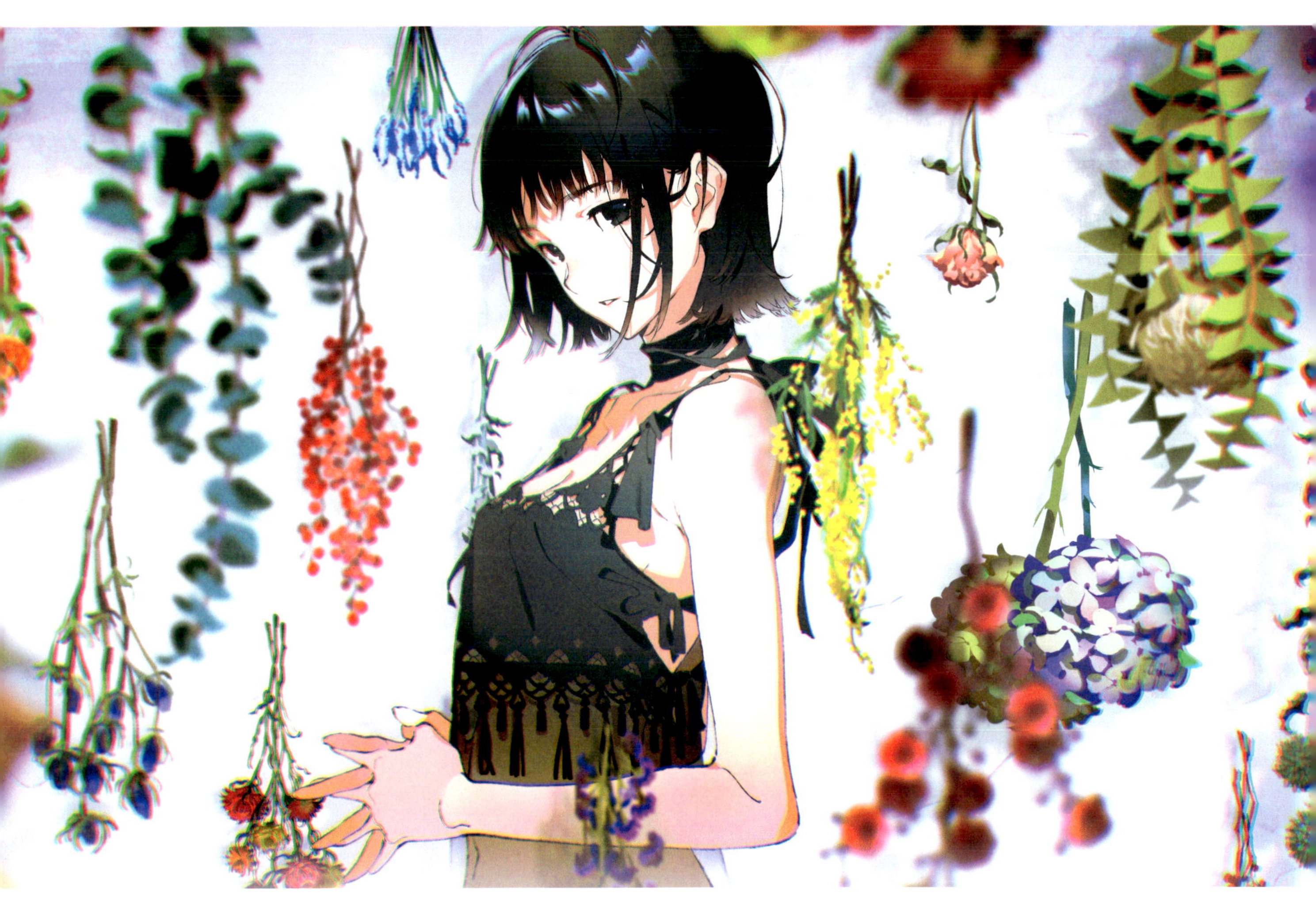

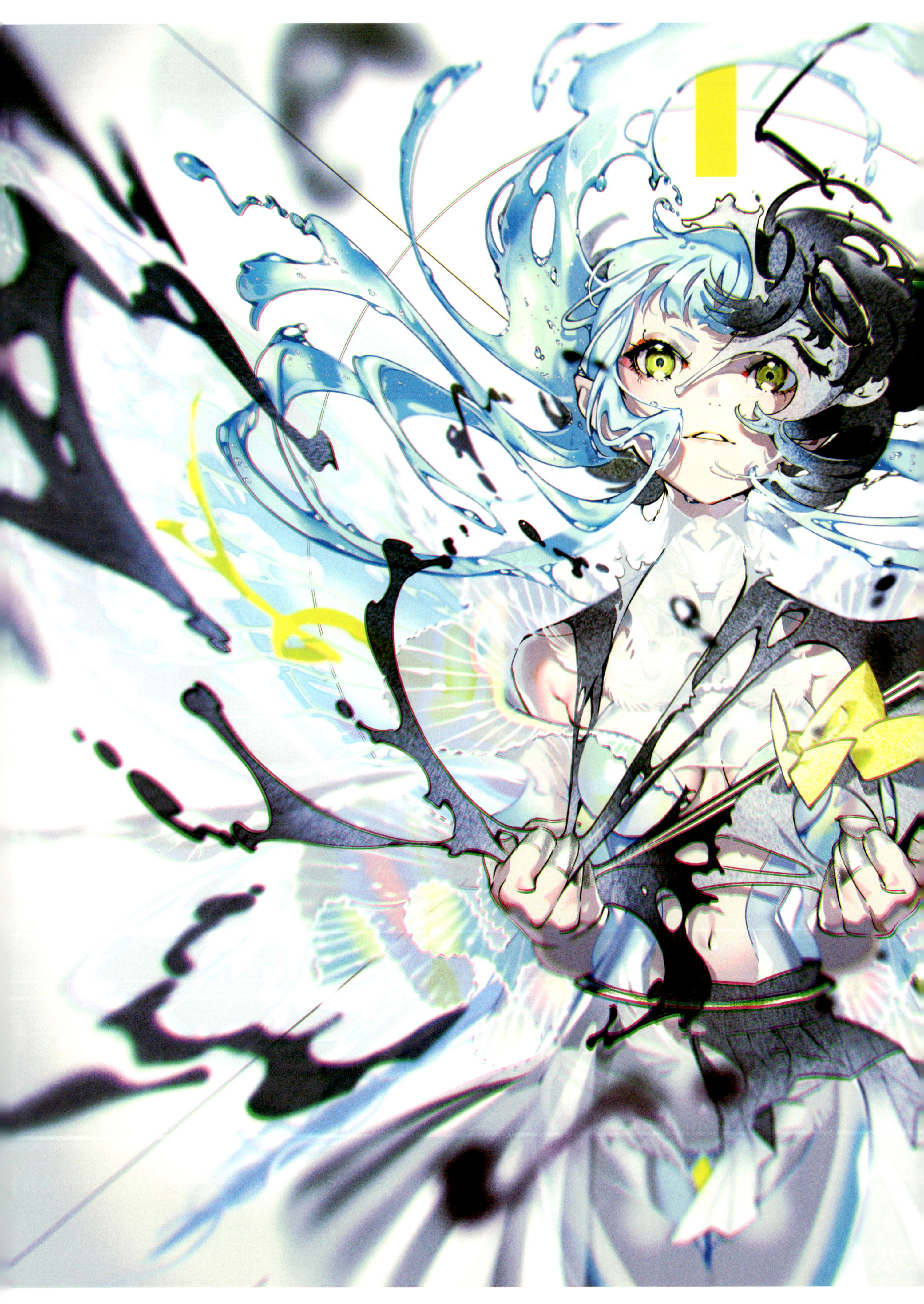

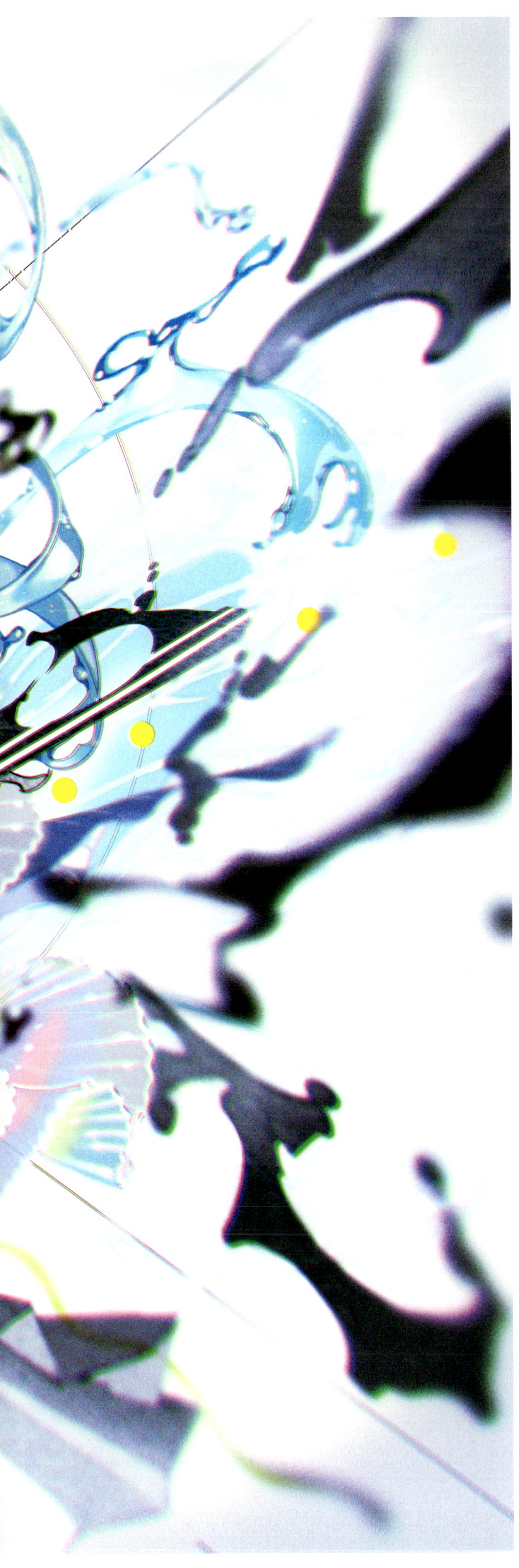

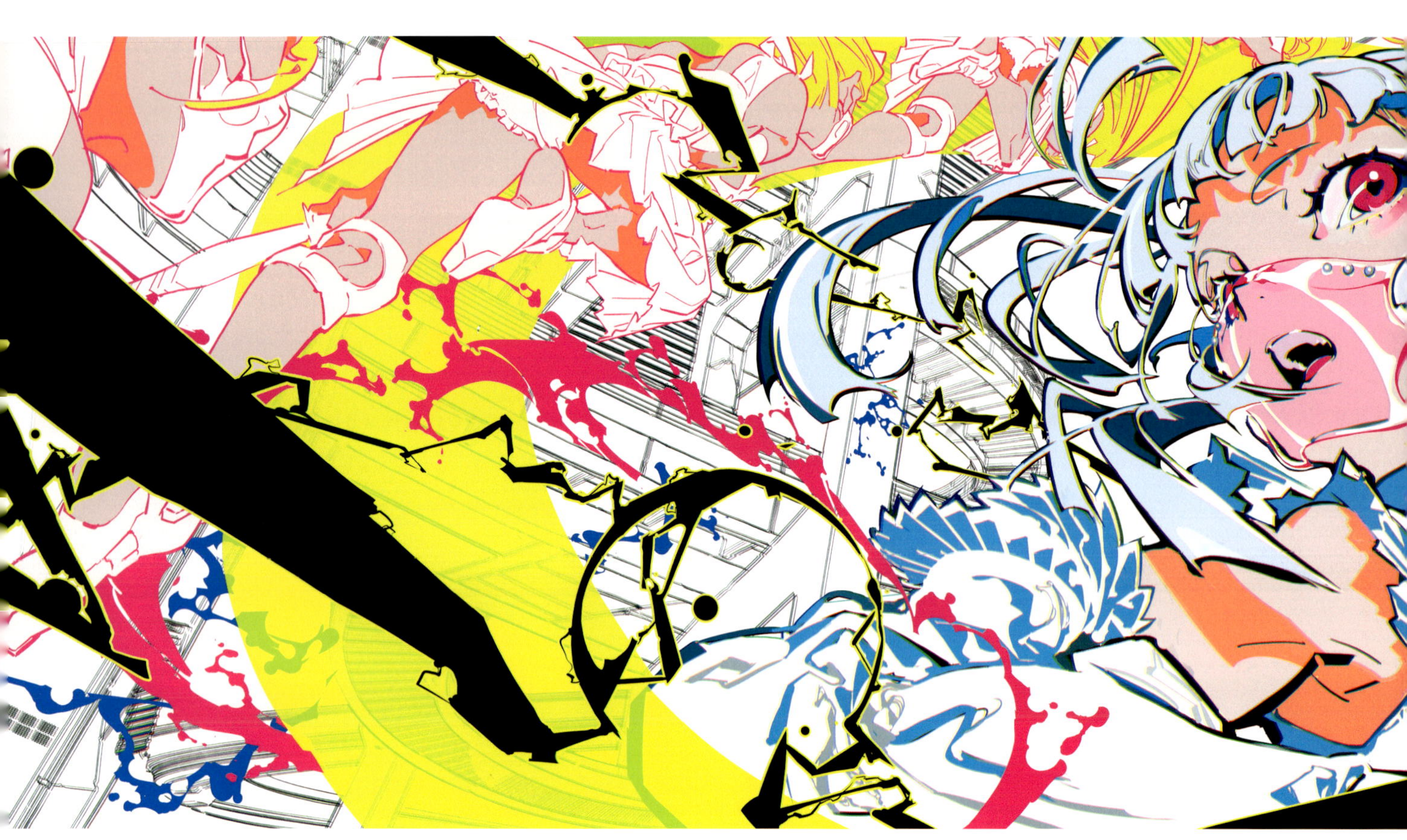

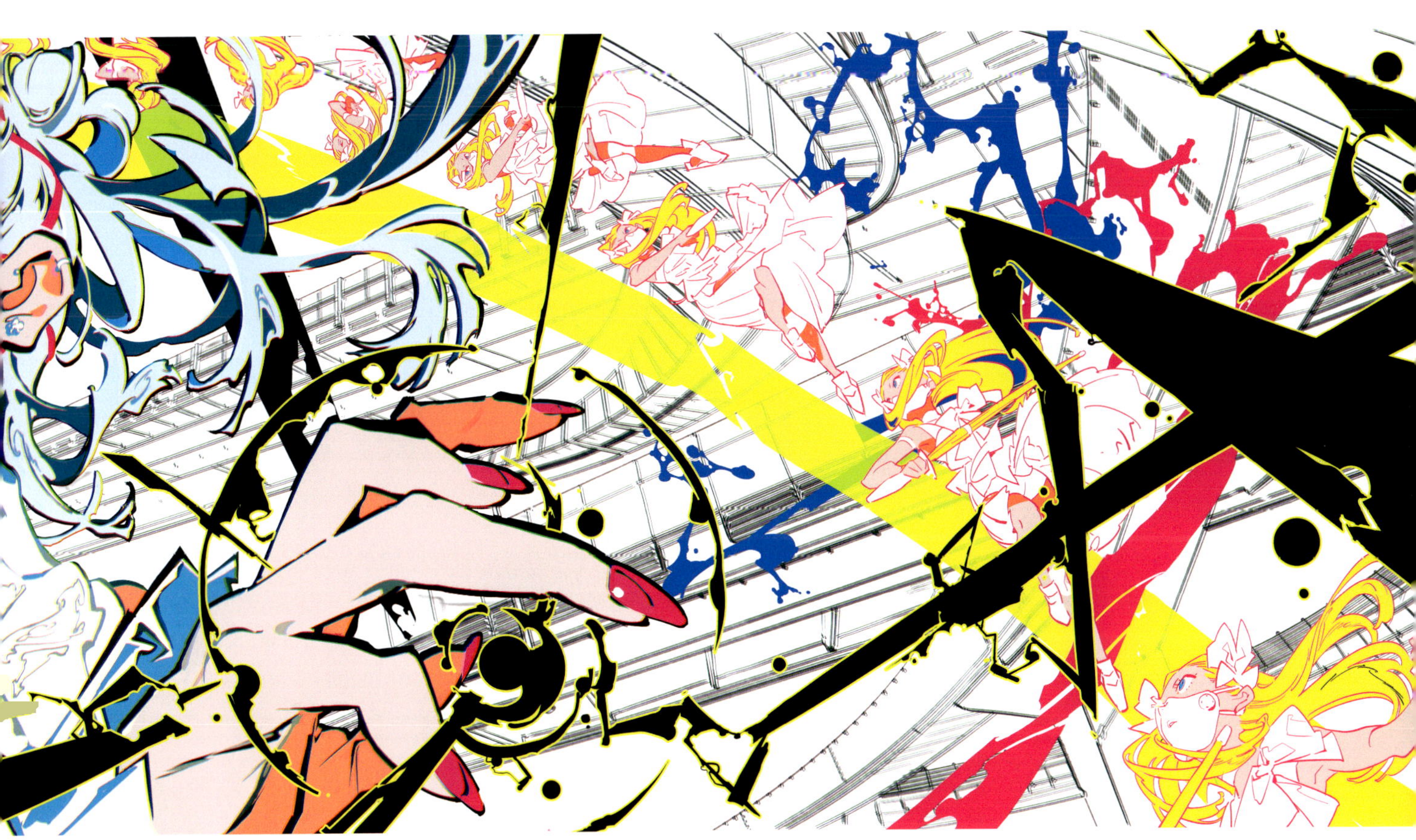

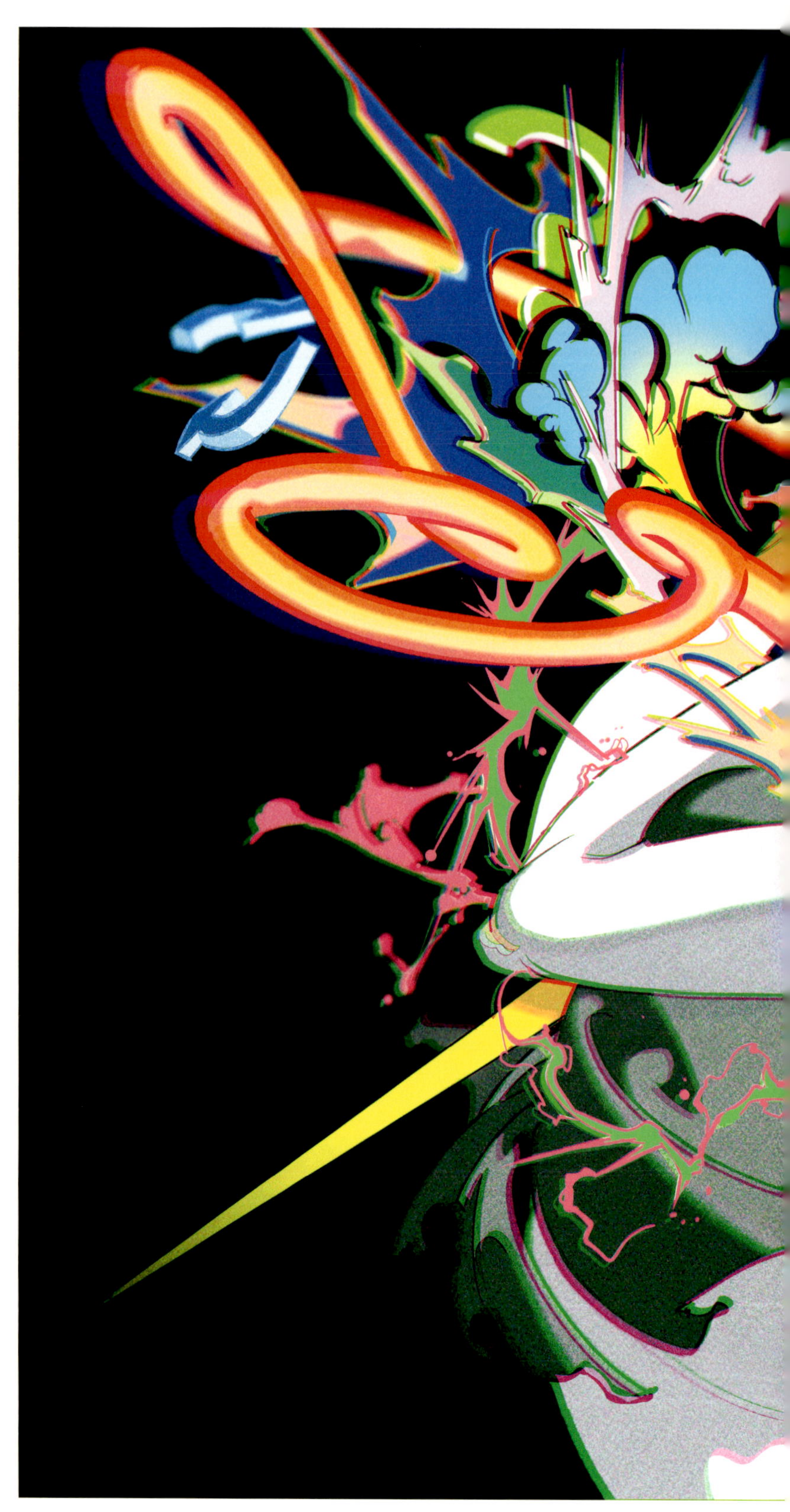

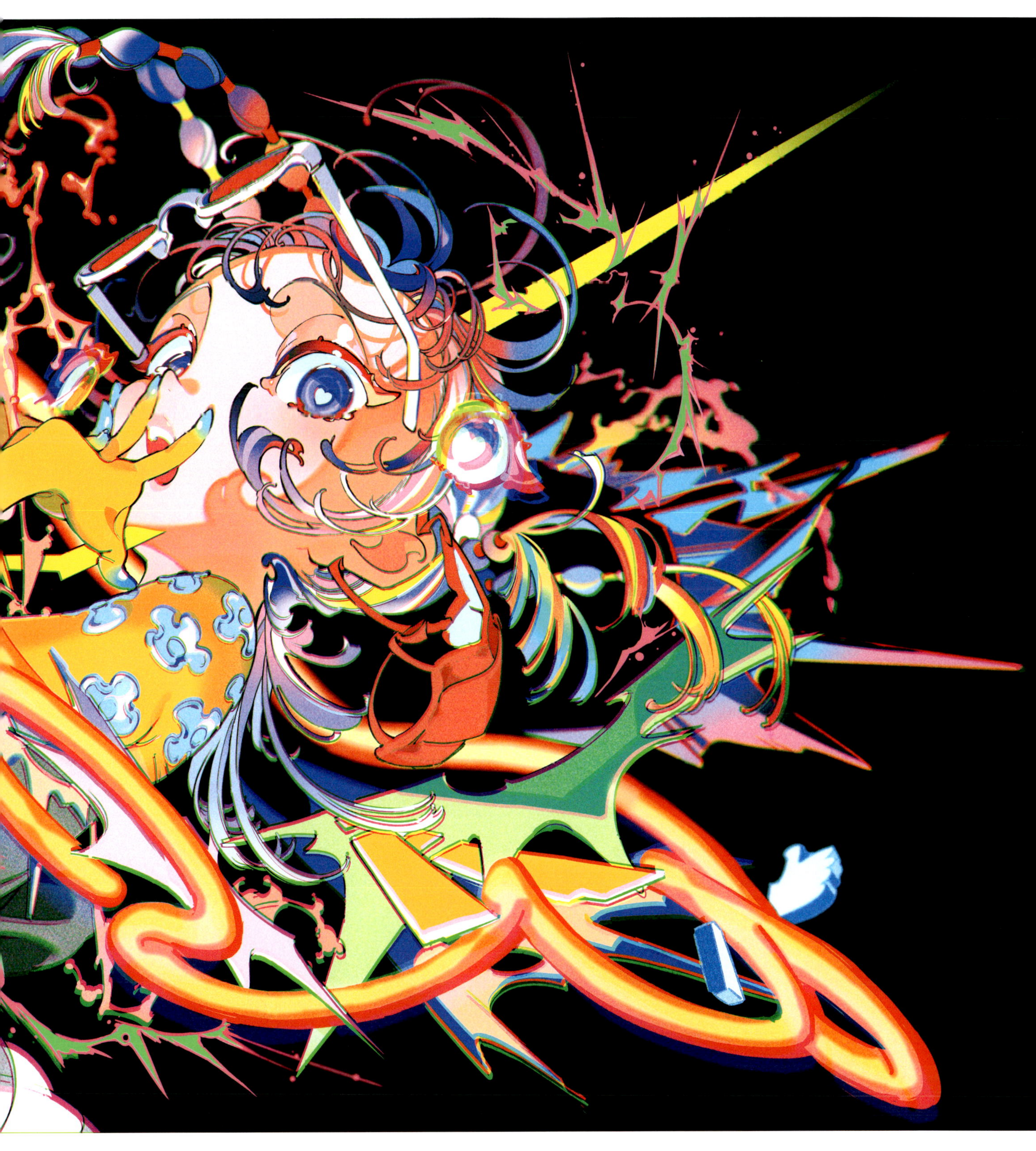

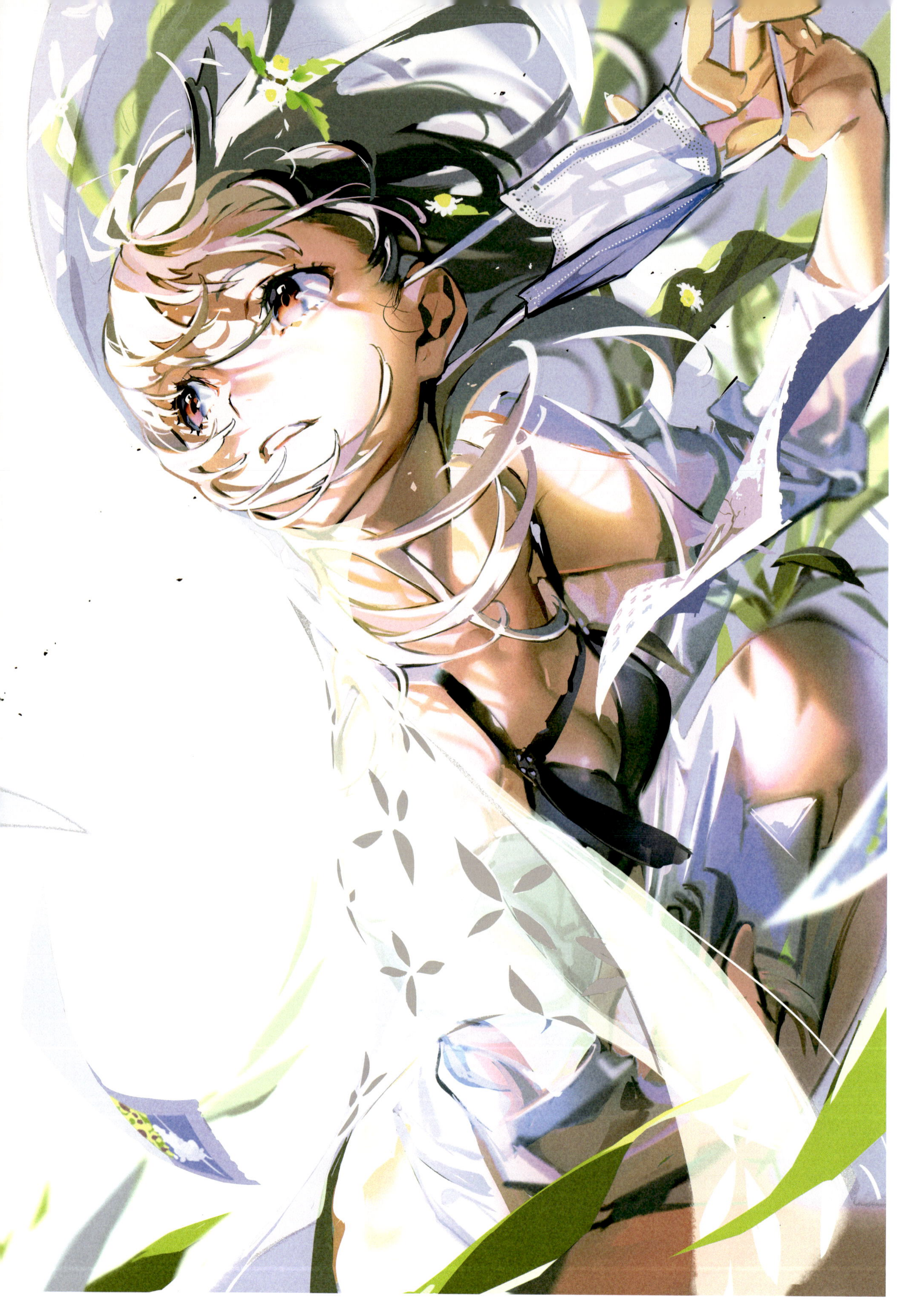

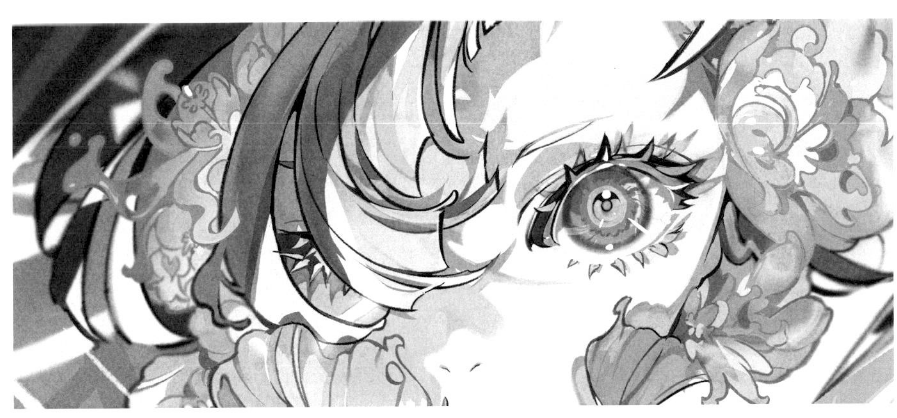

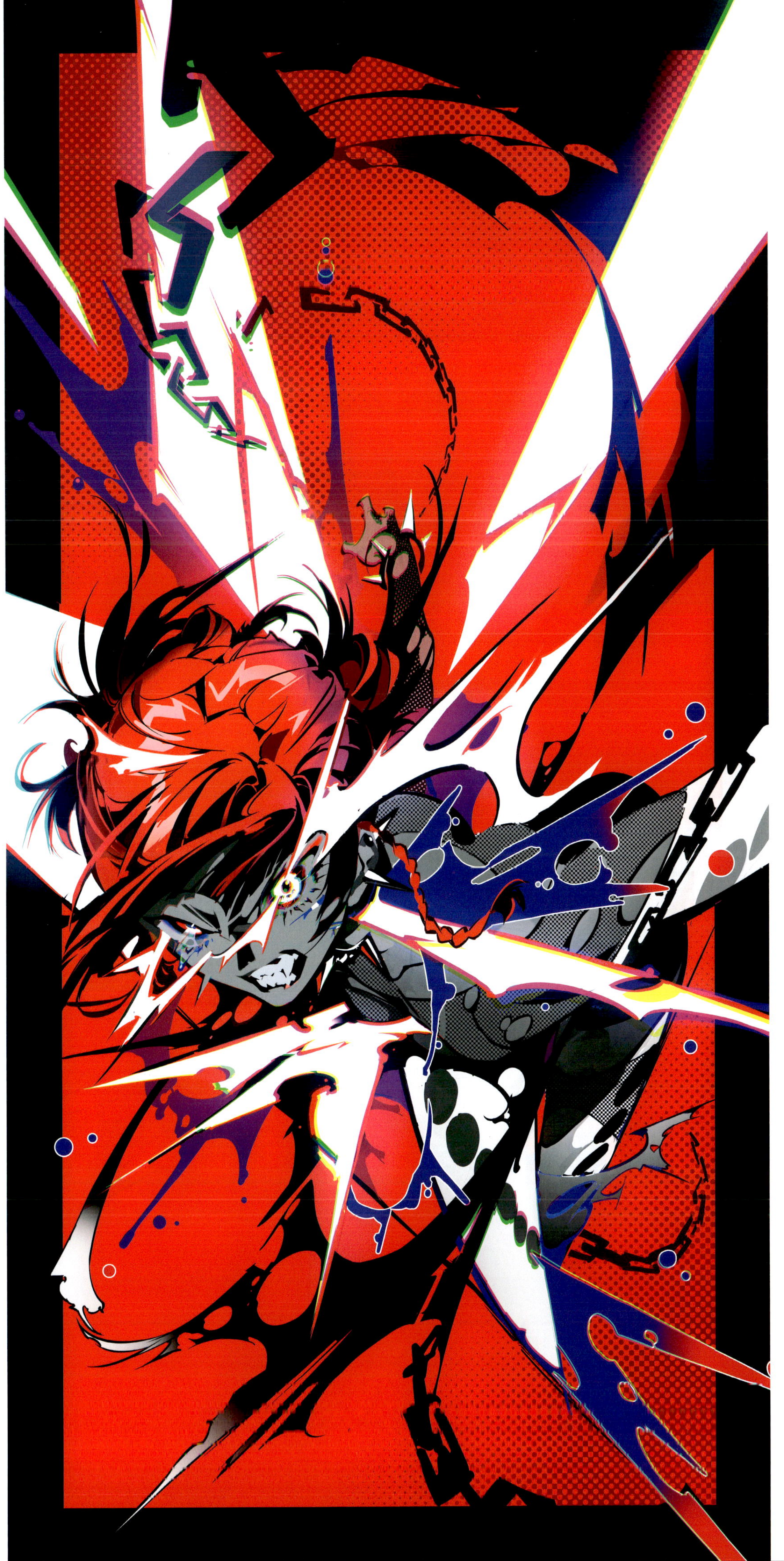

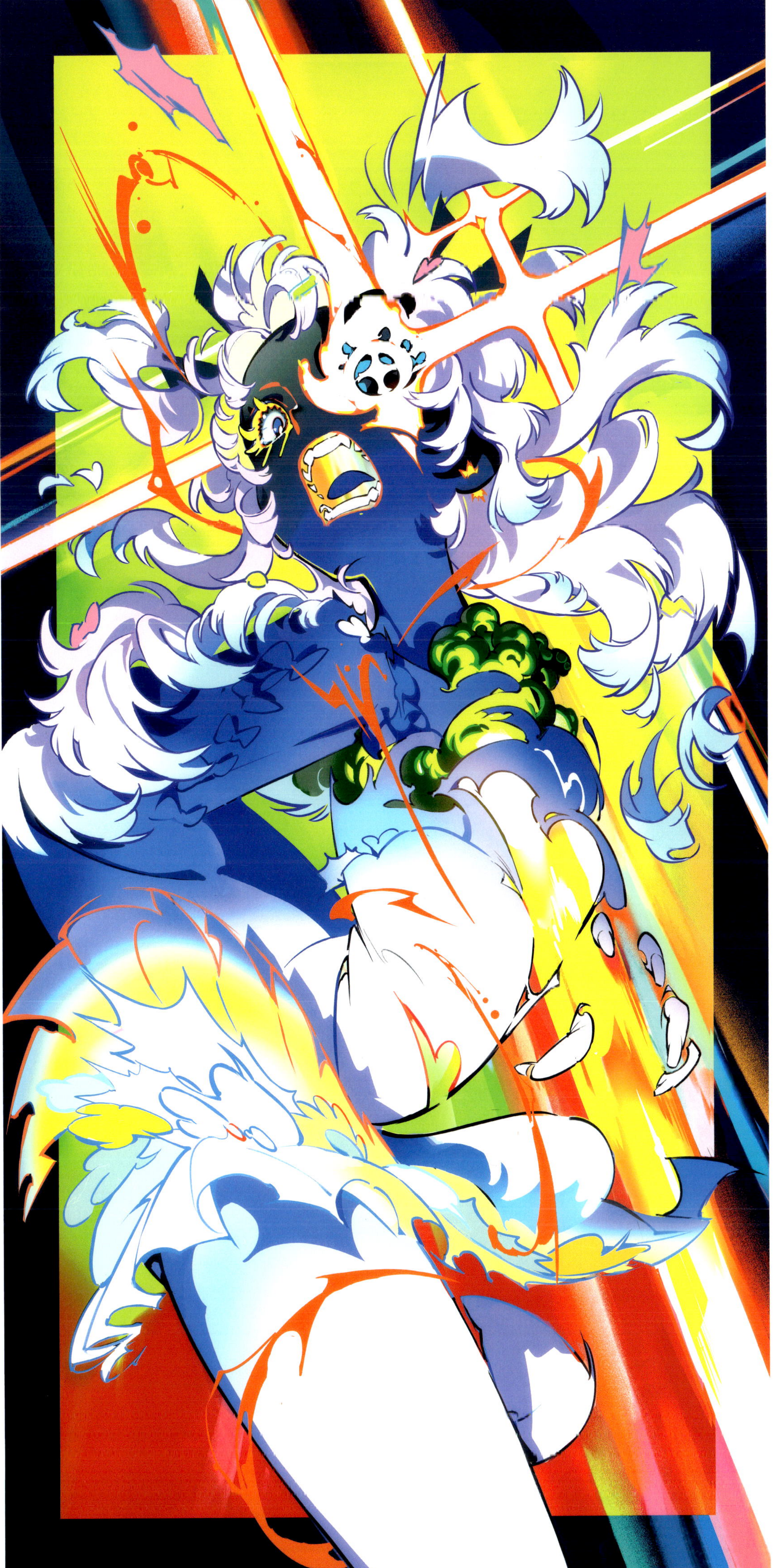

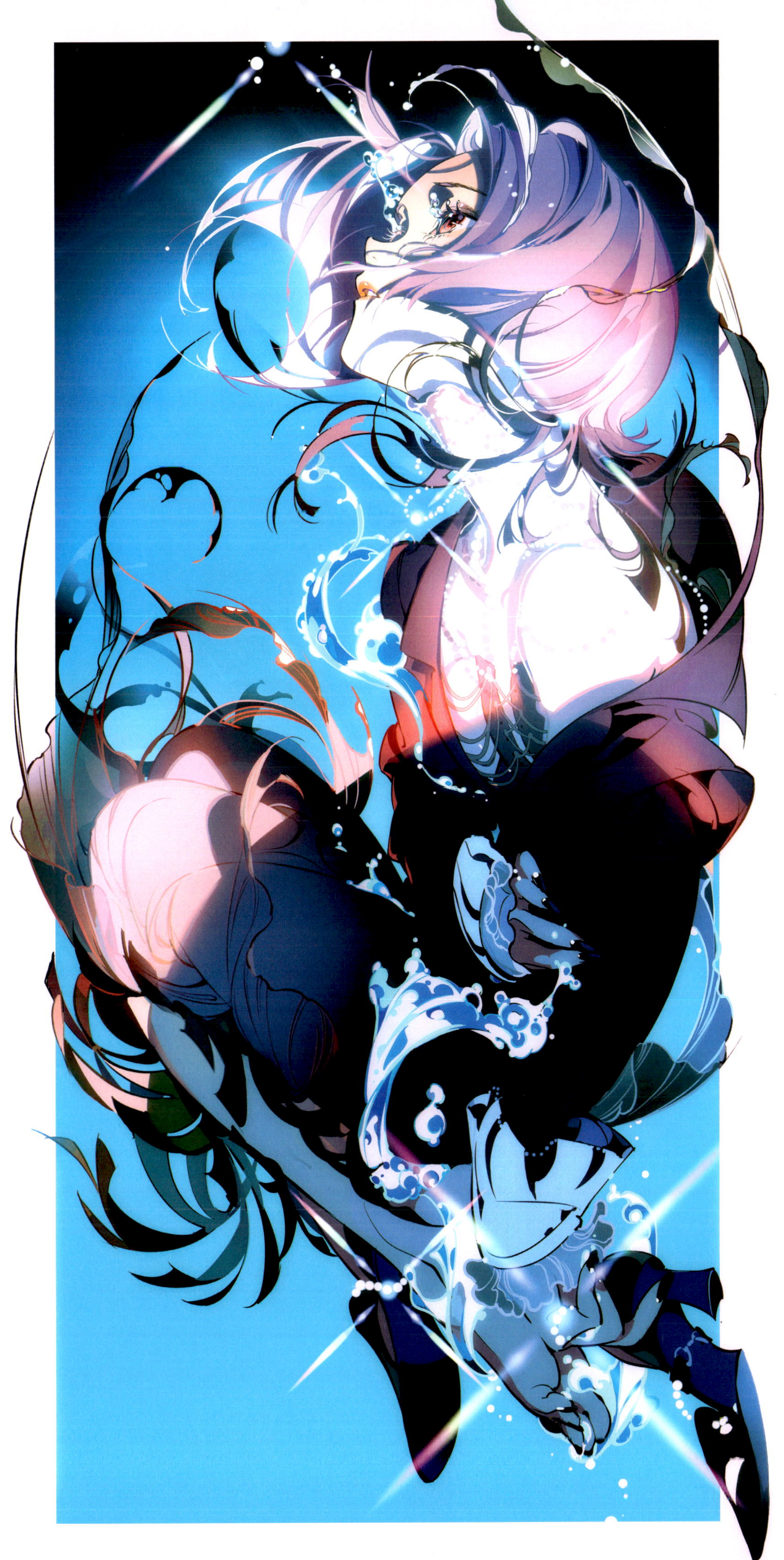

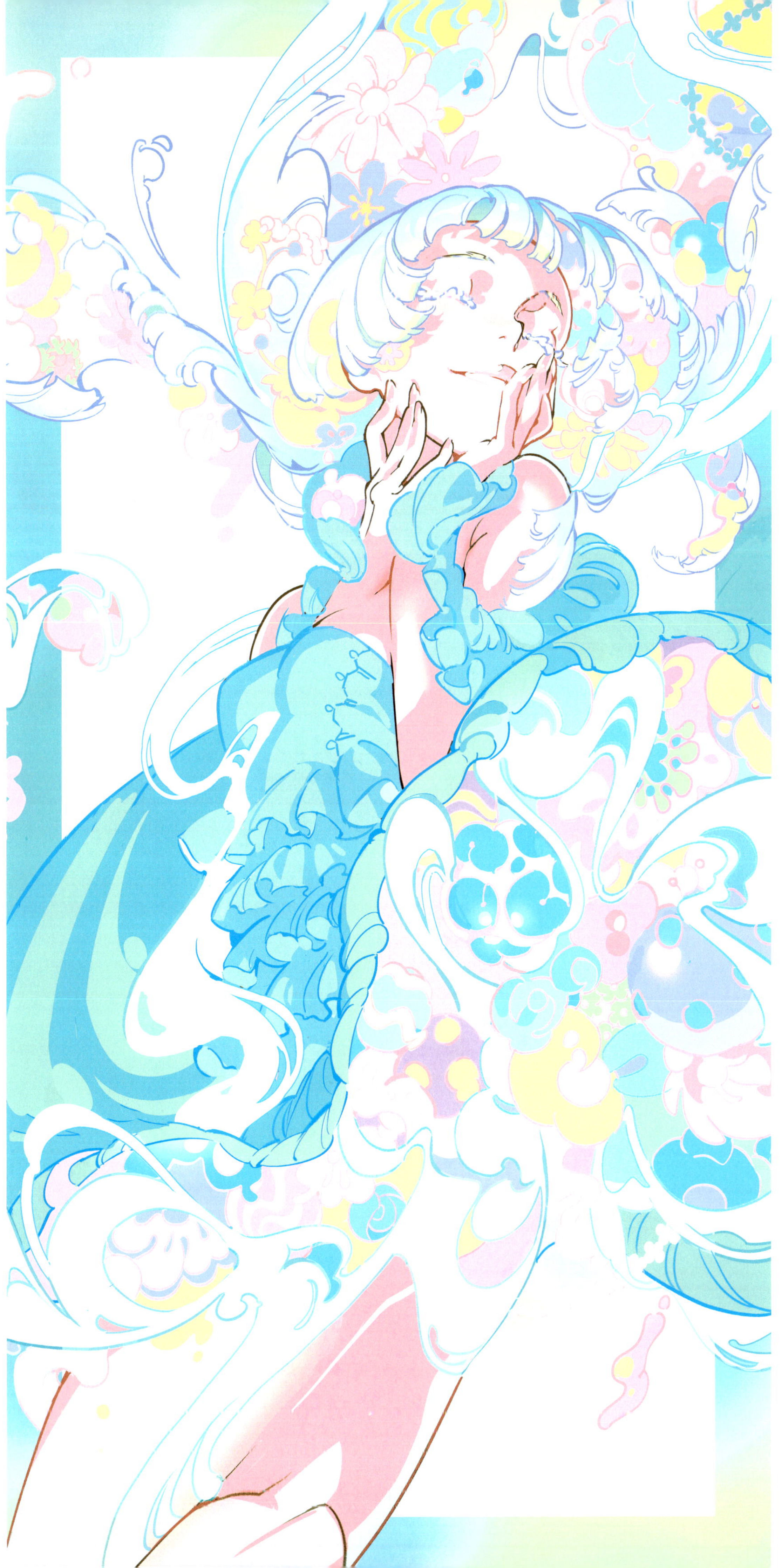

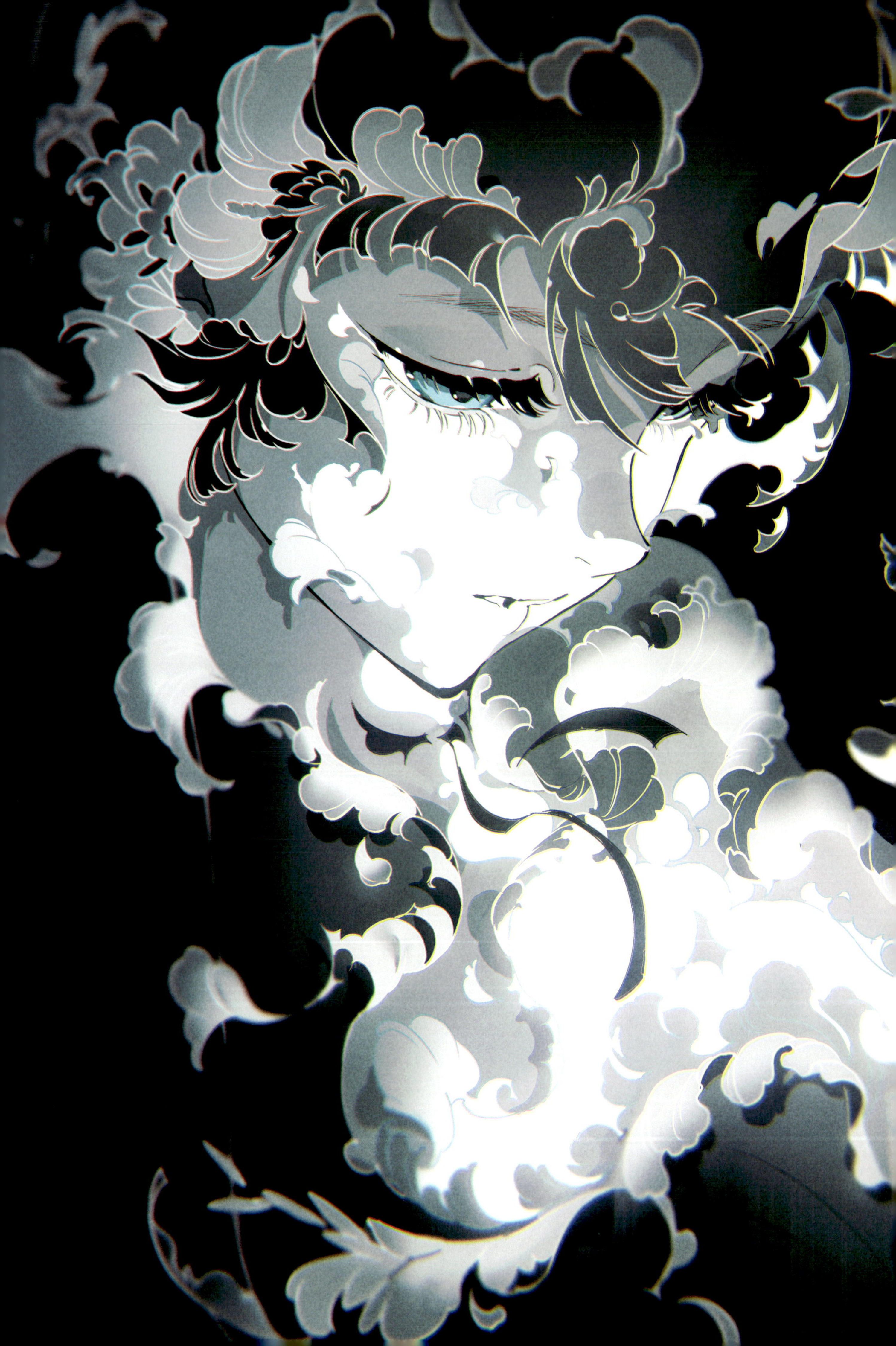

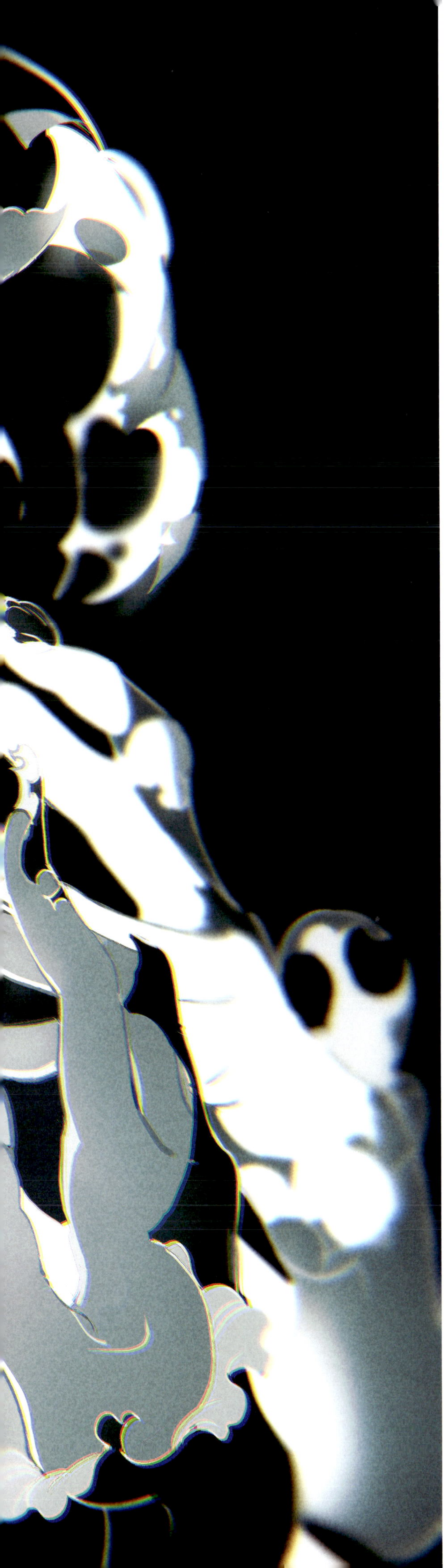

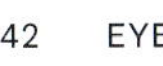

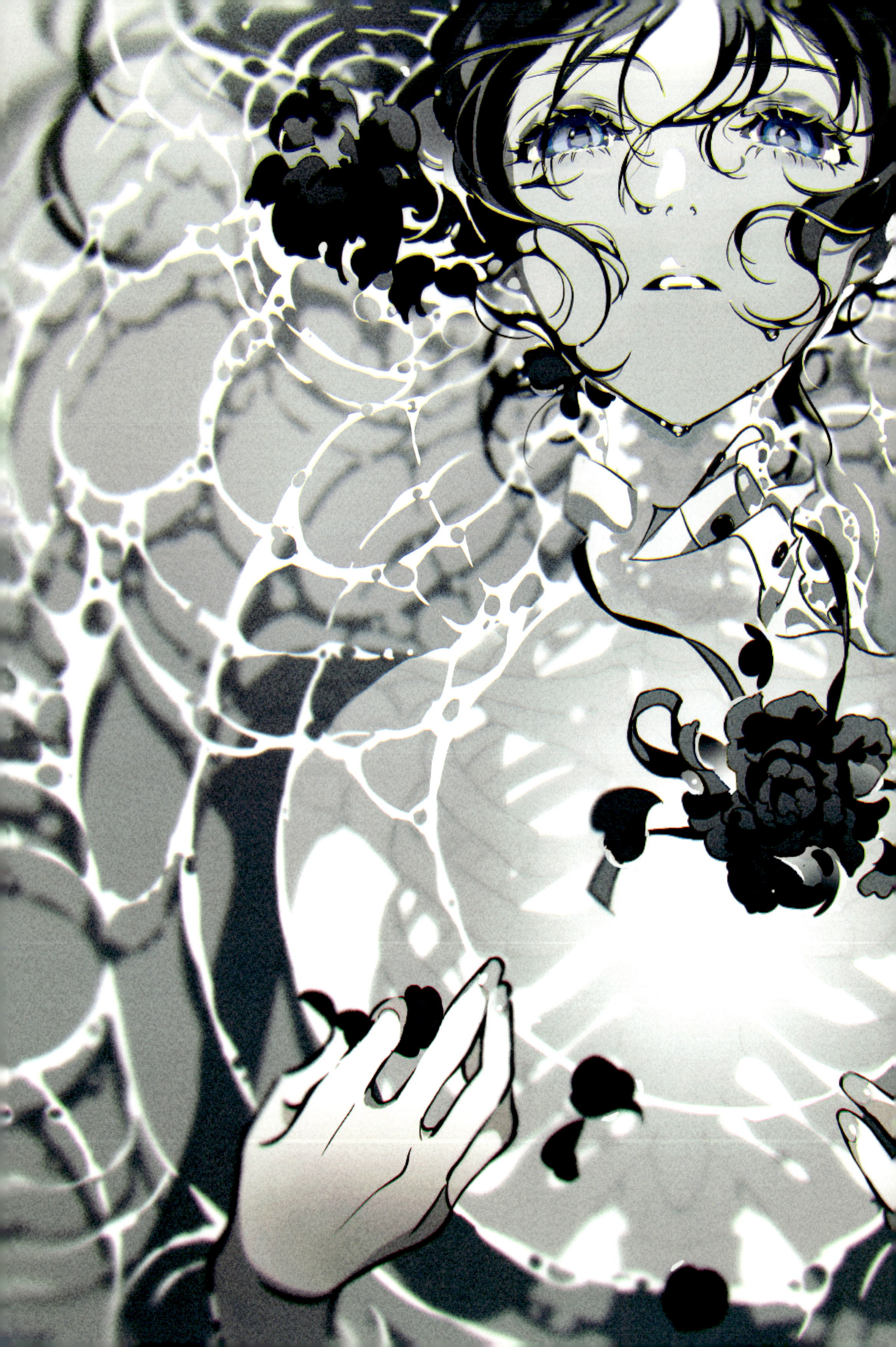

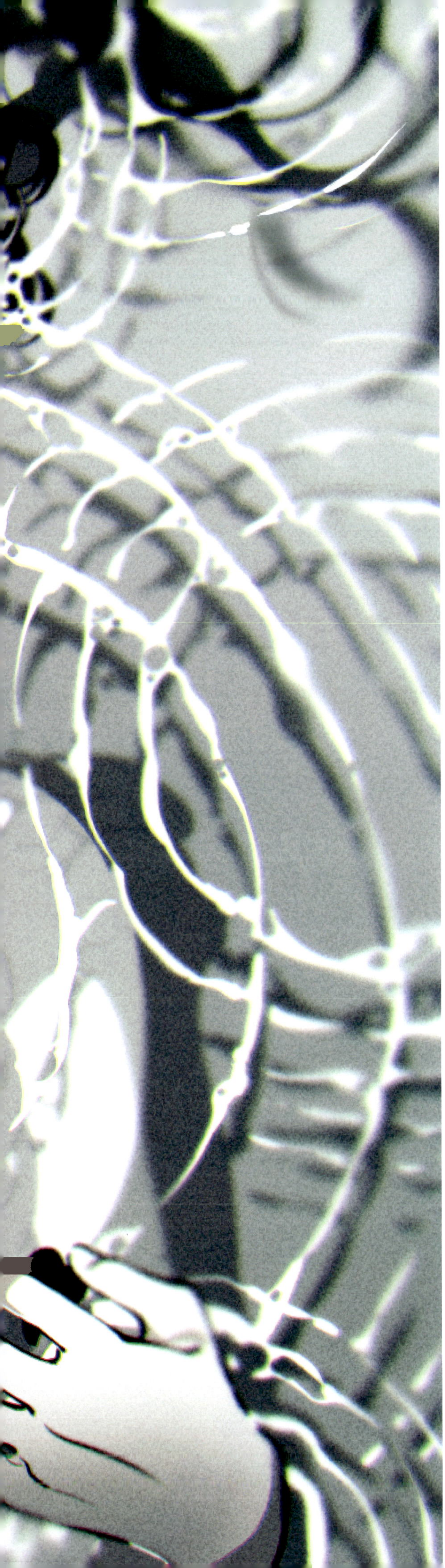

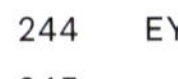

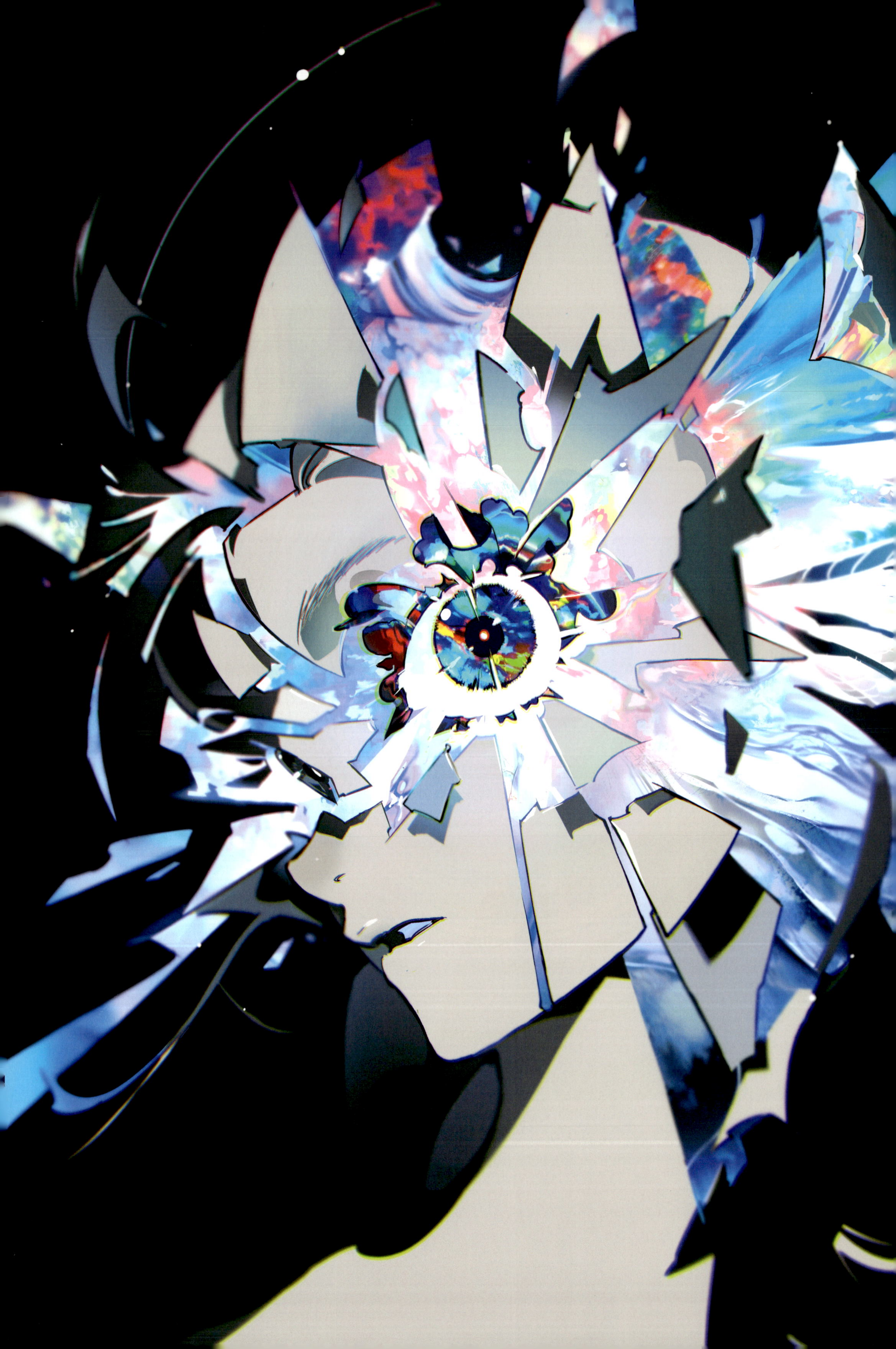

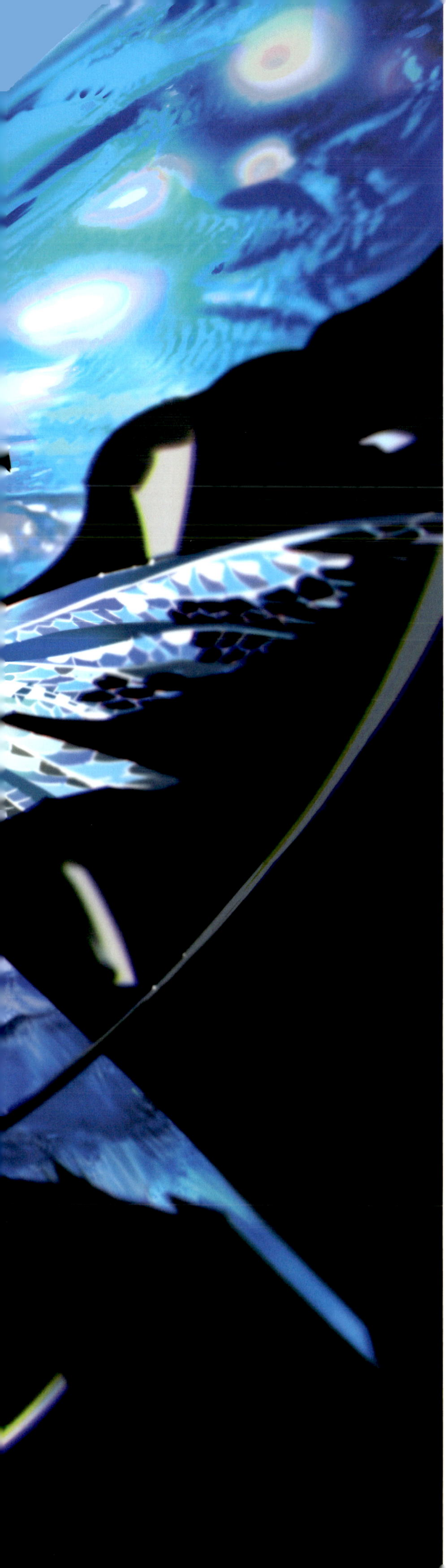

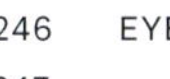

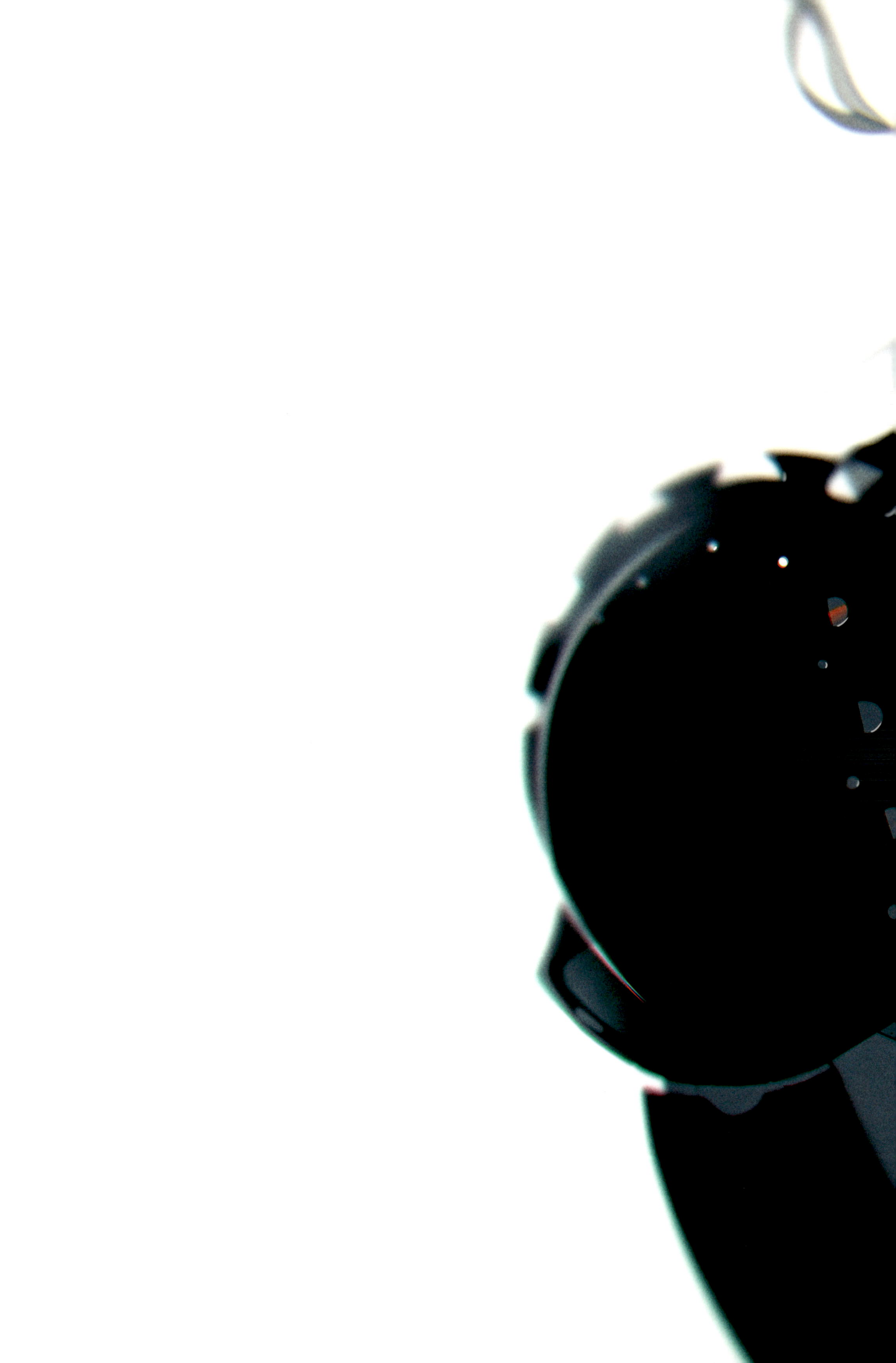

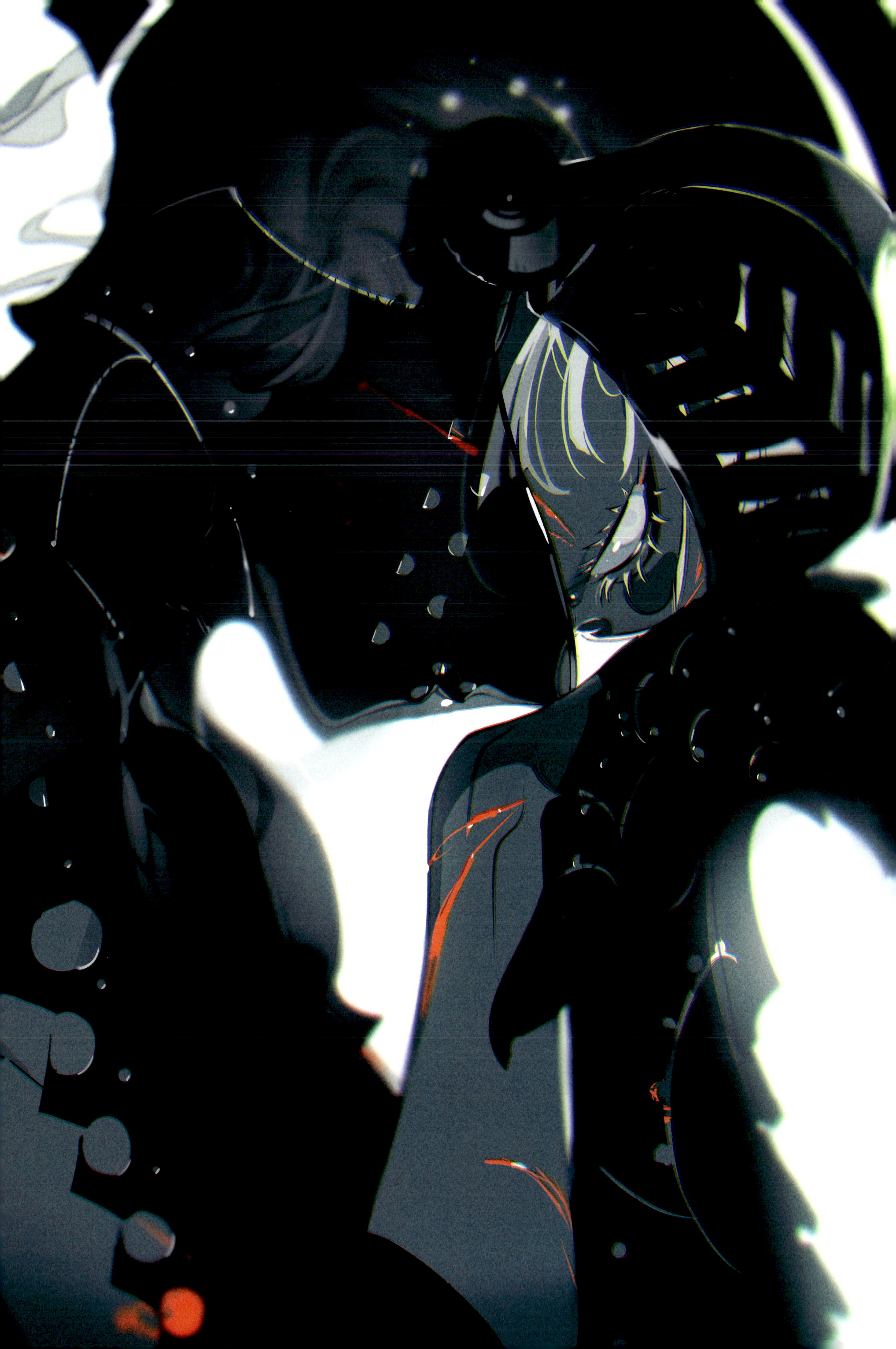

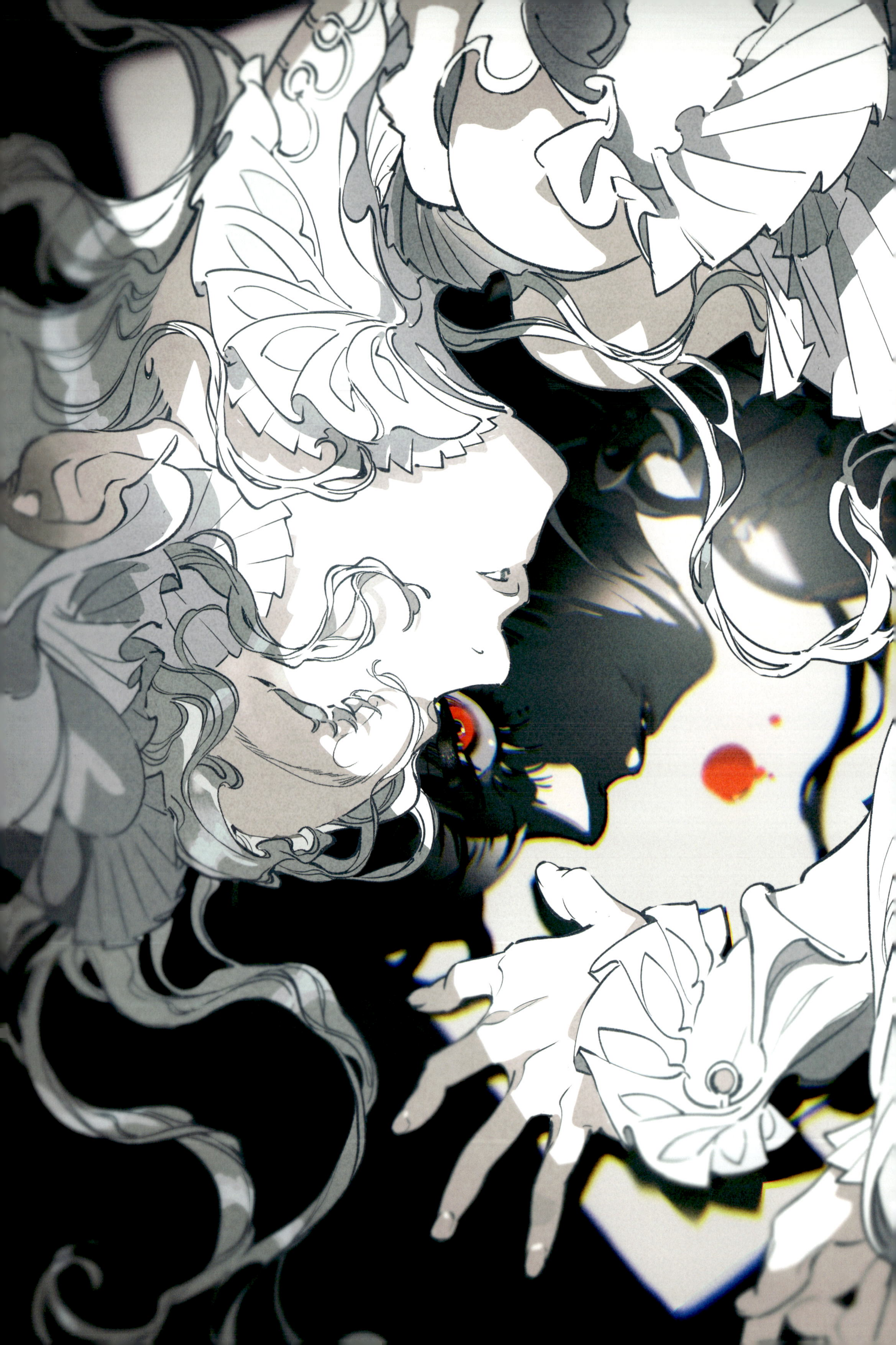

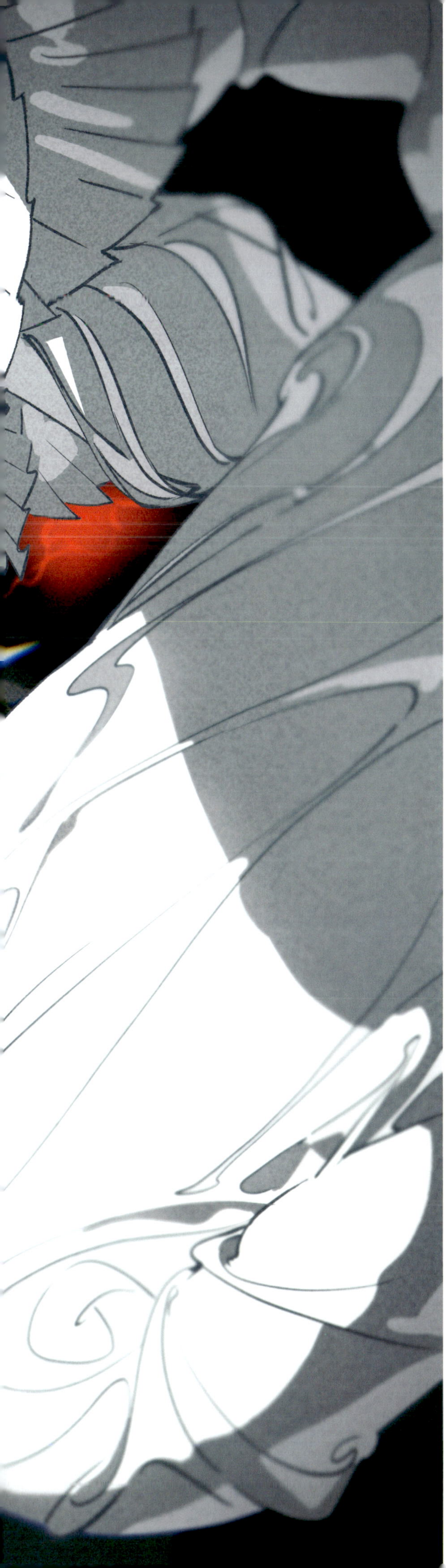

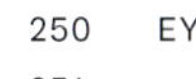

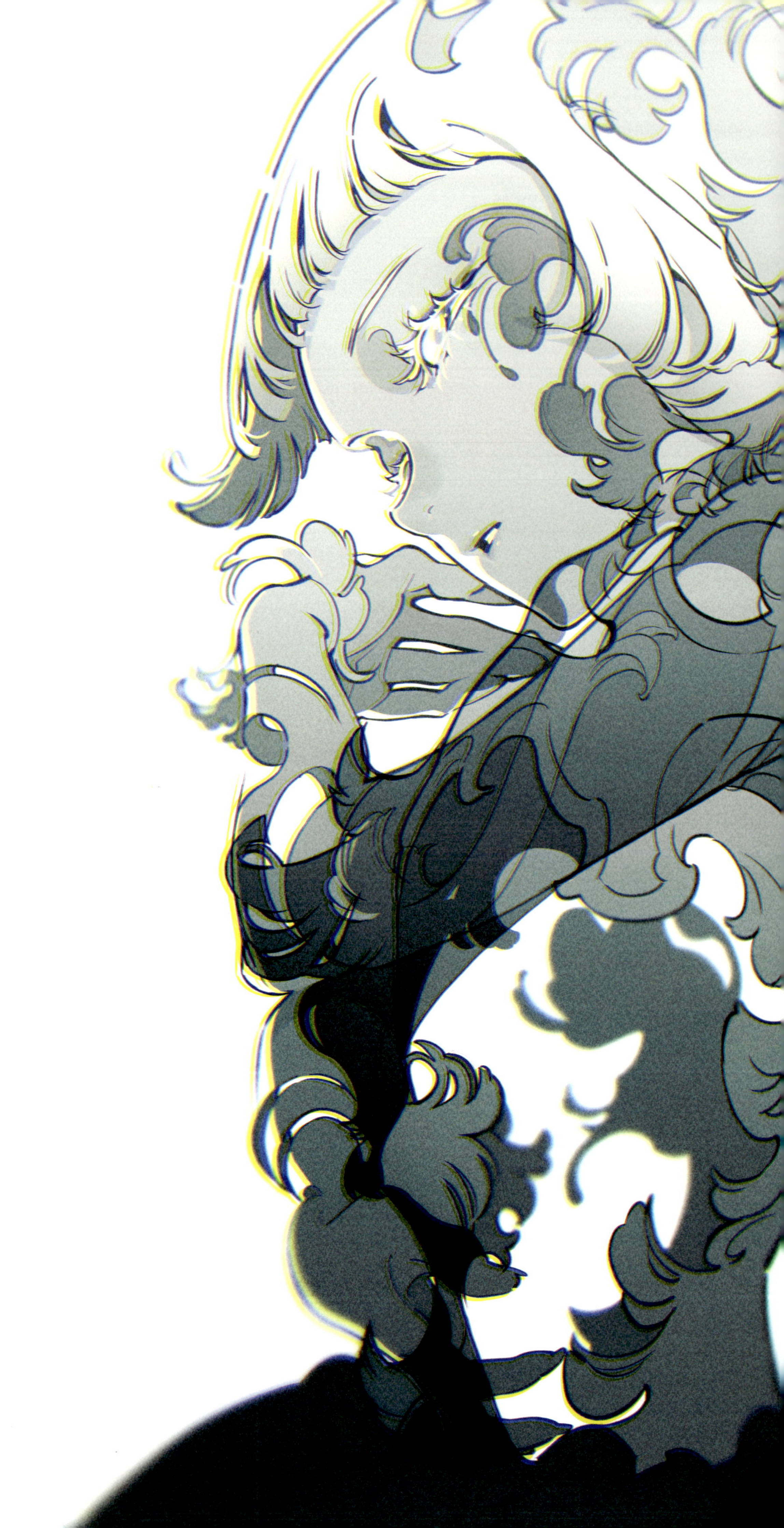

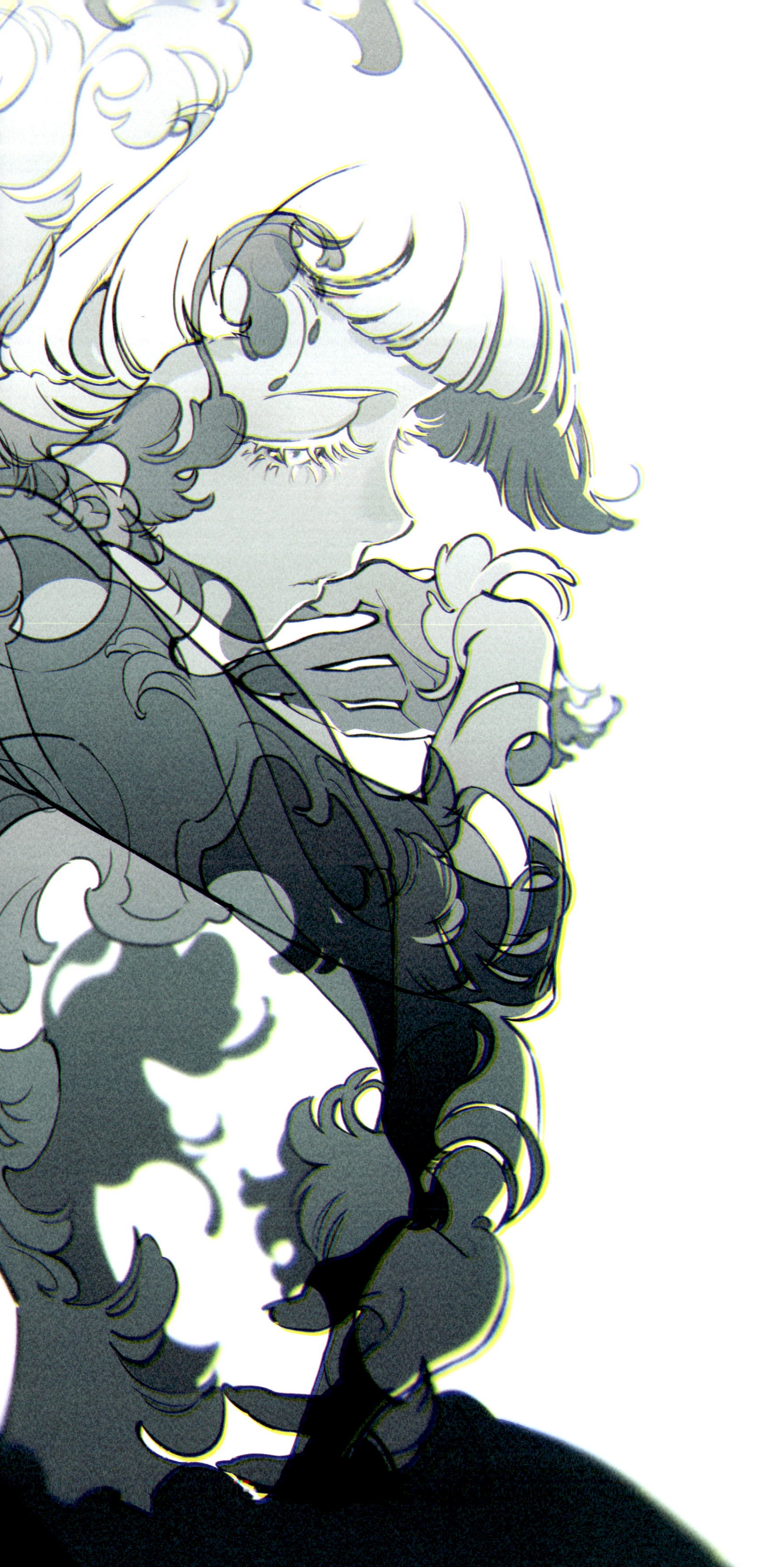

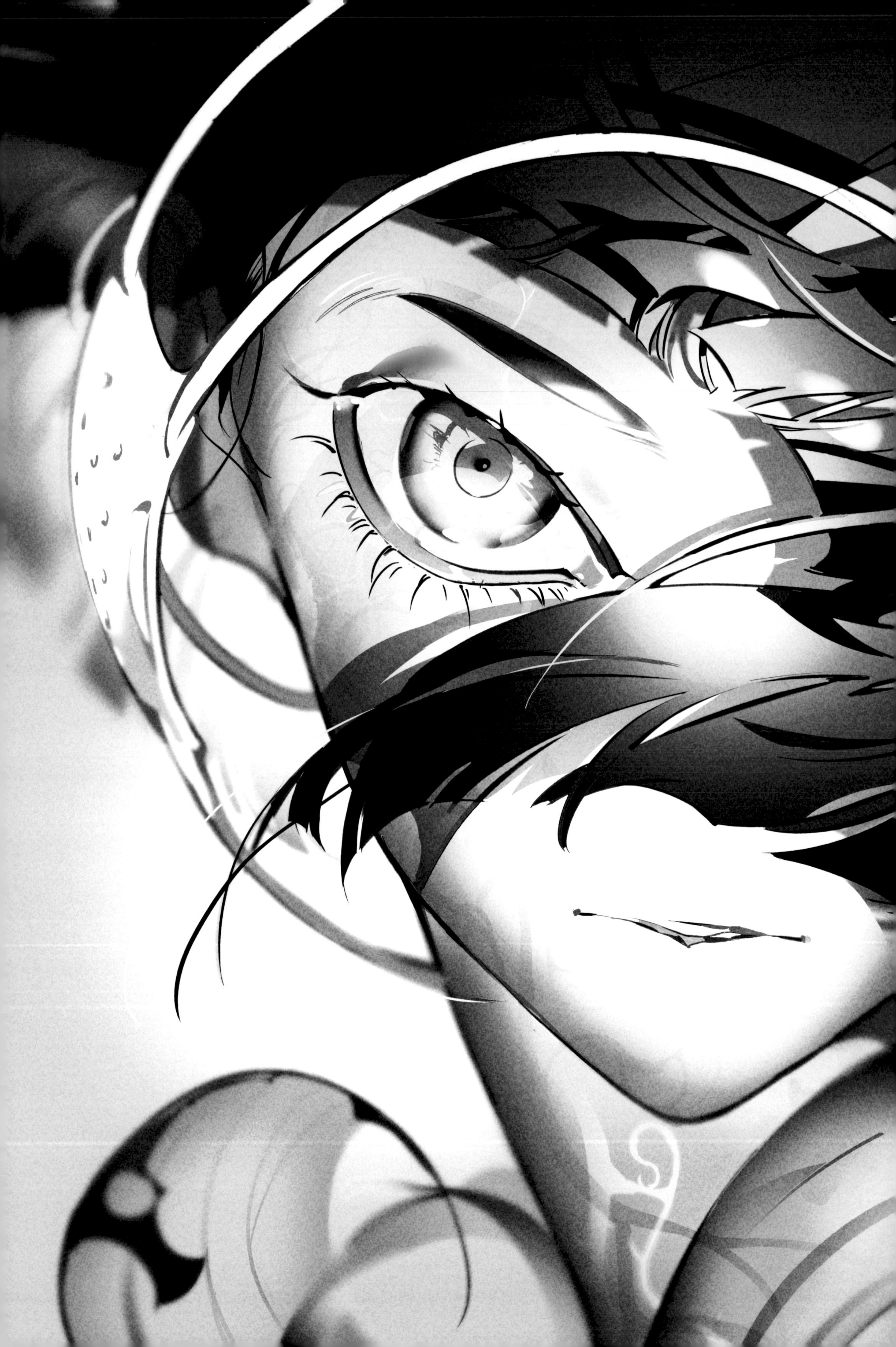

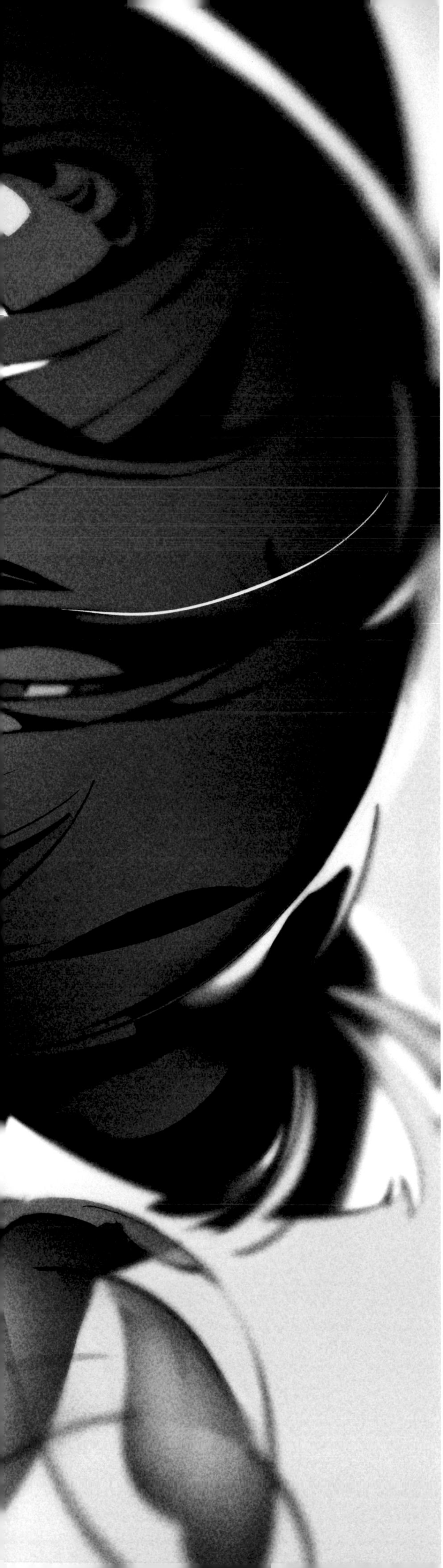

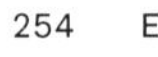

254　EYE
255

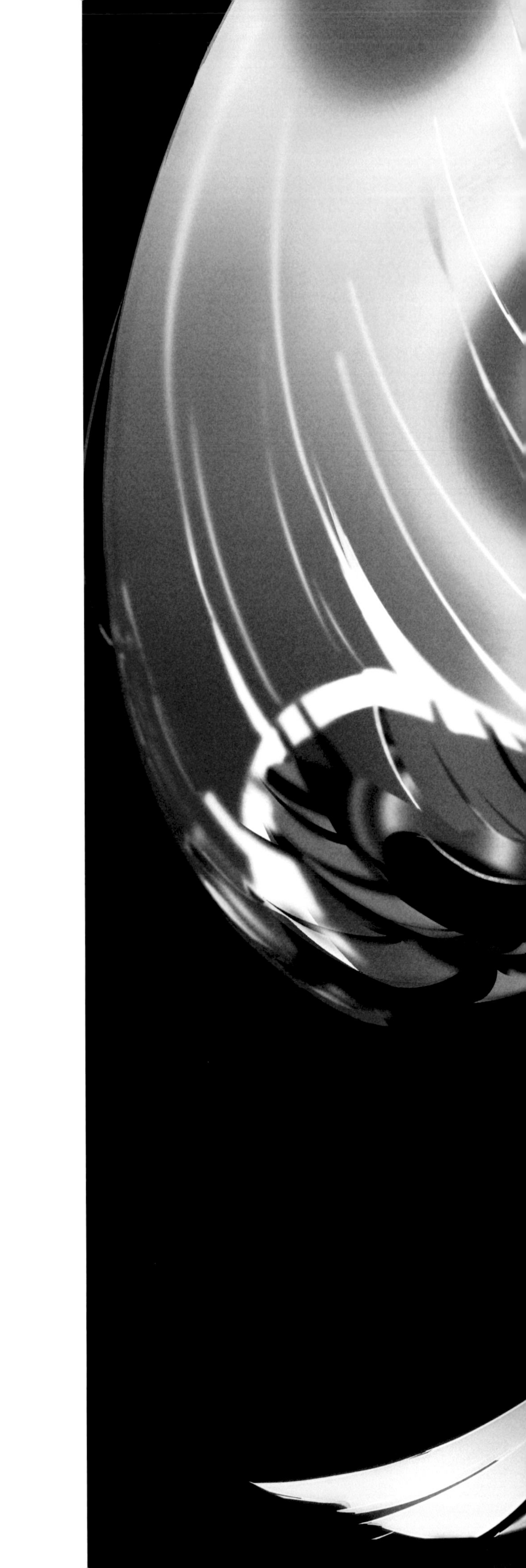

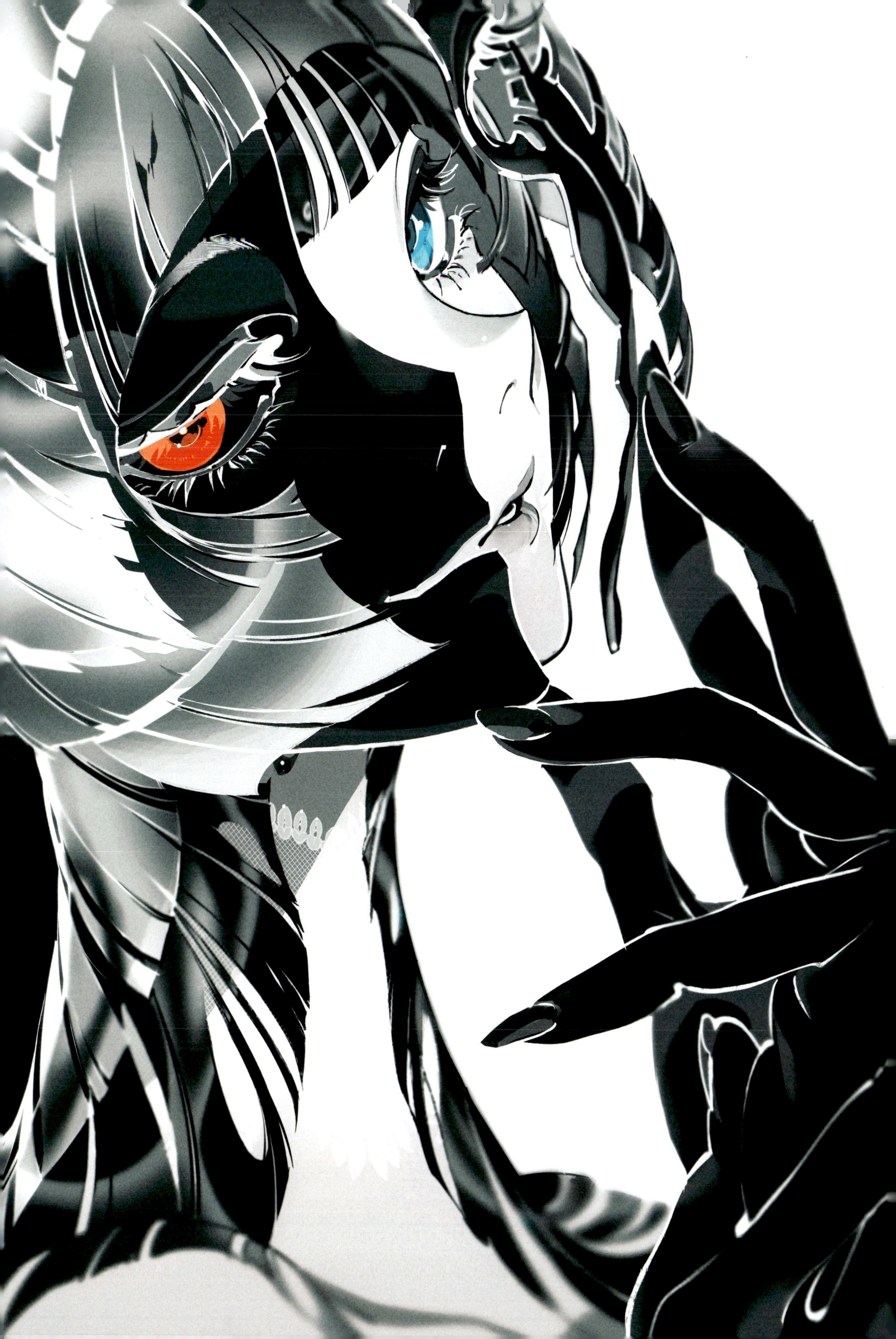

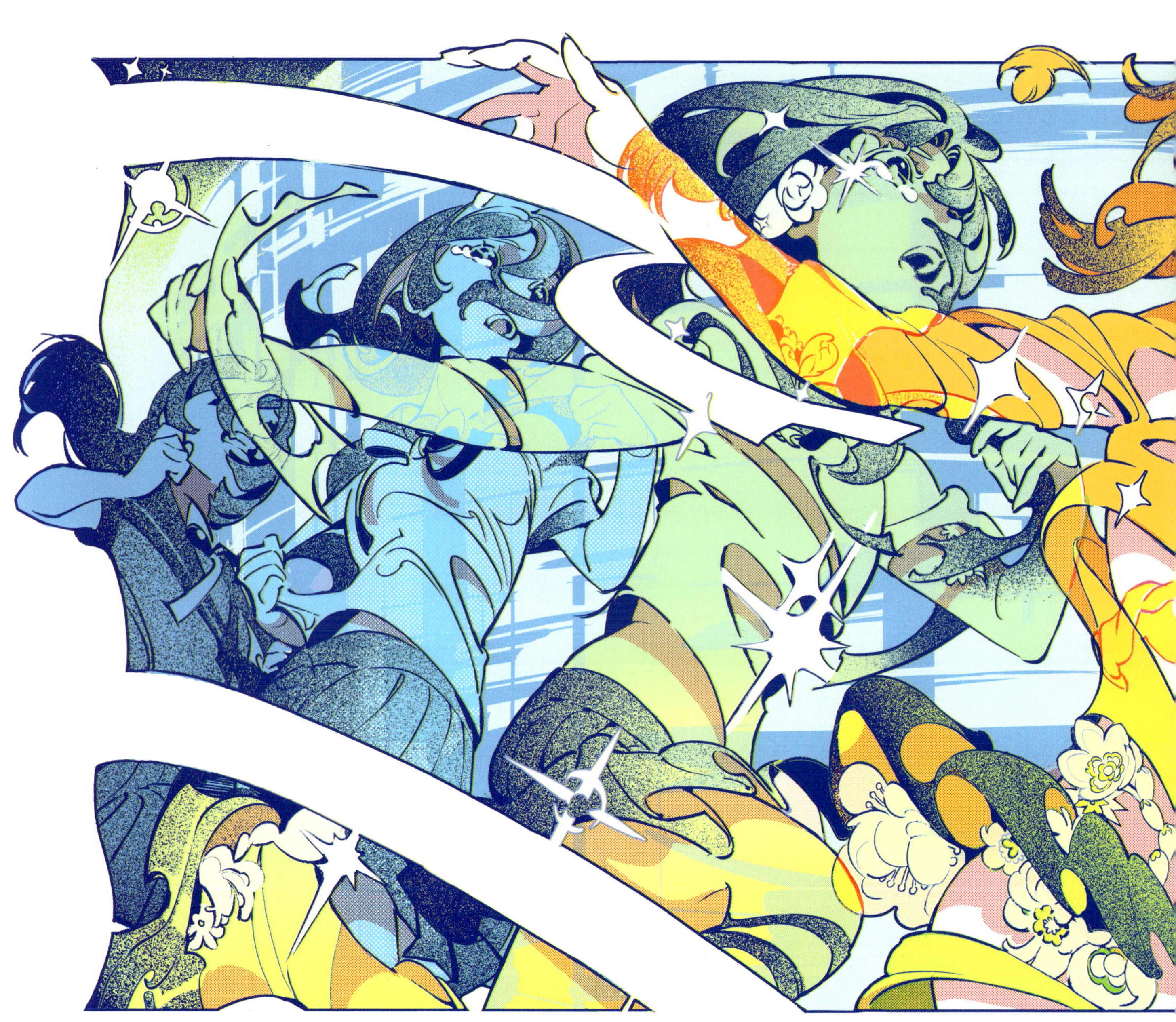

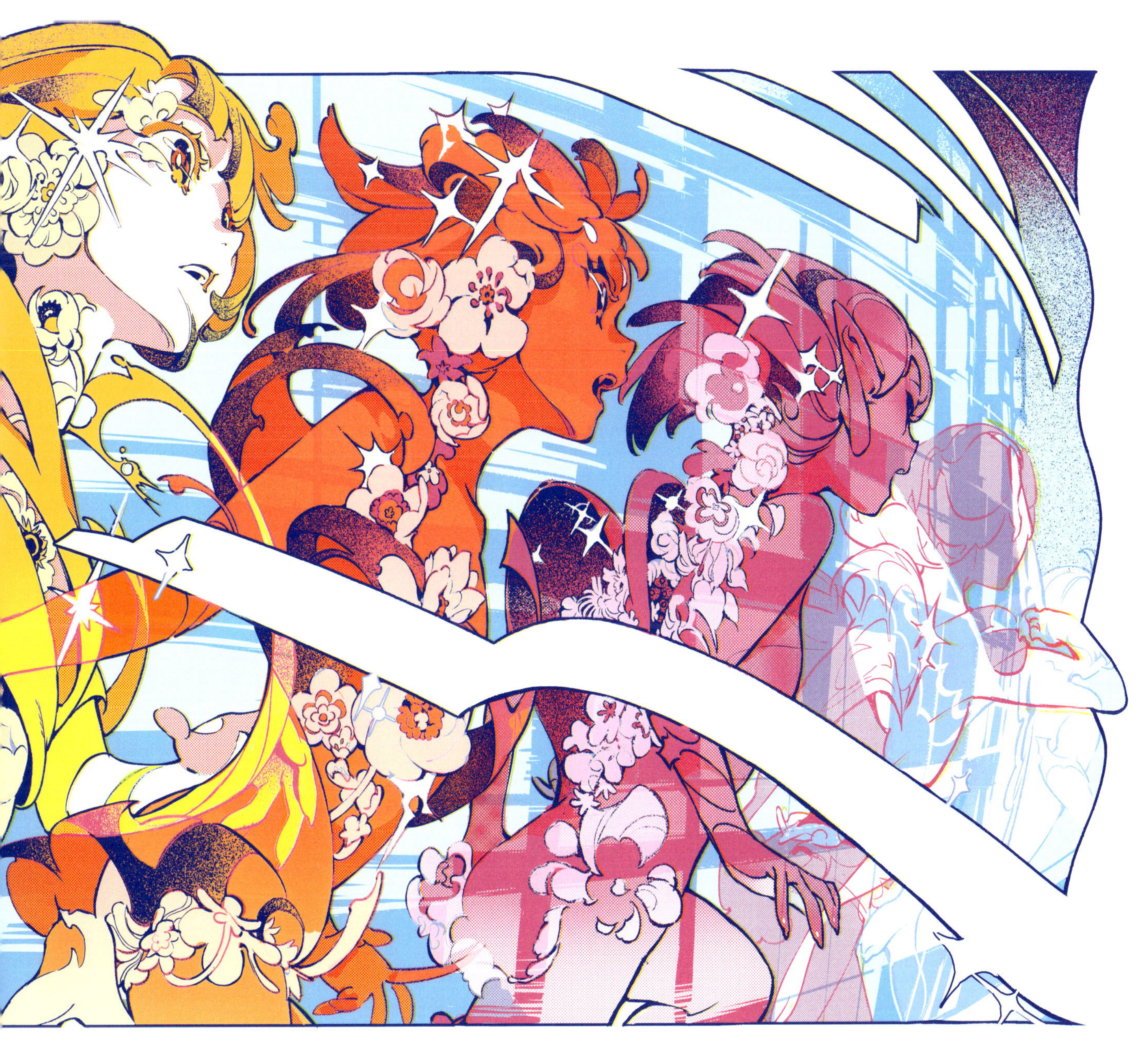

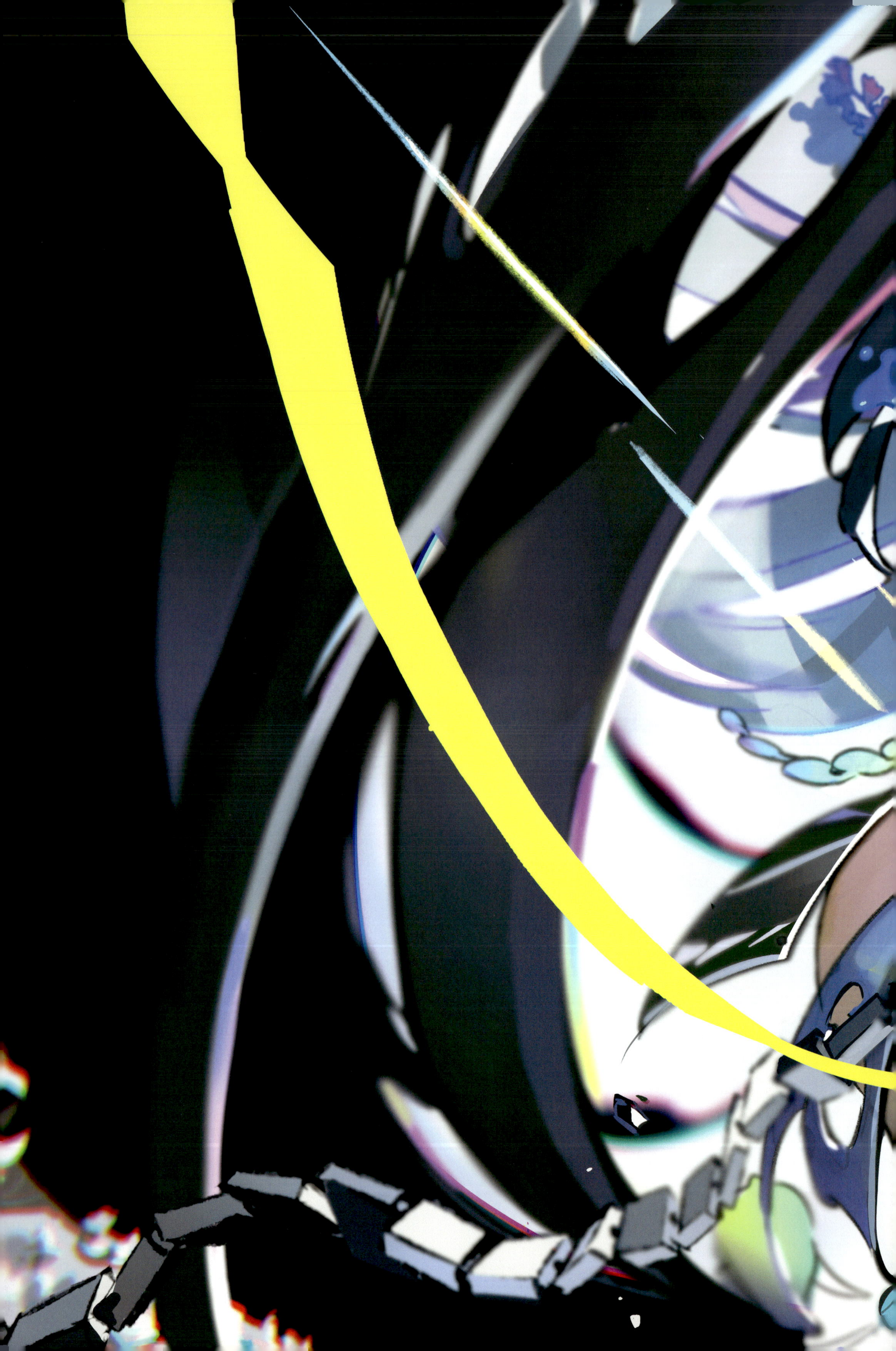

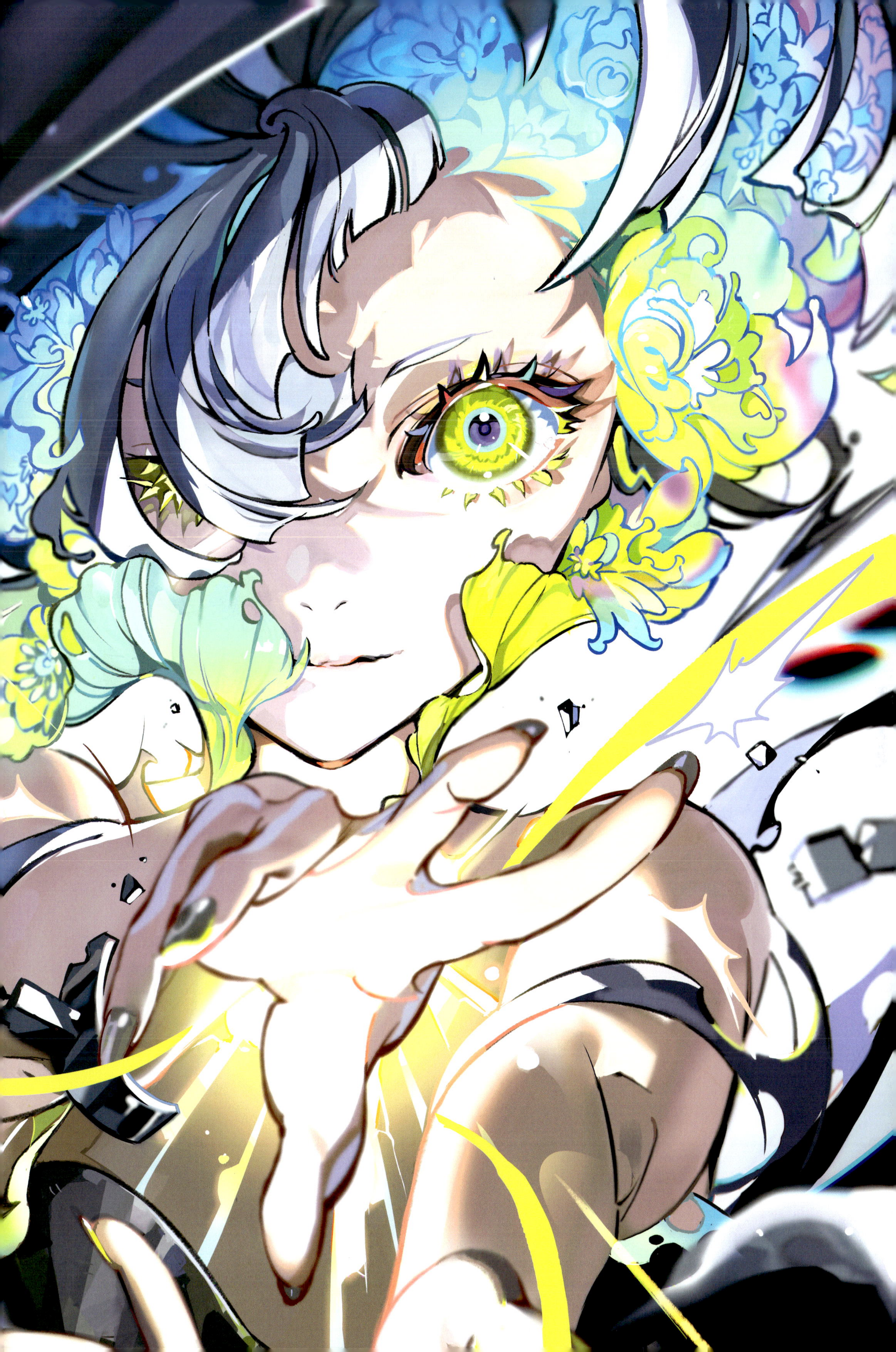

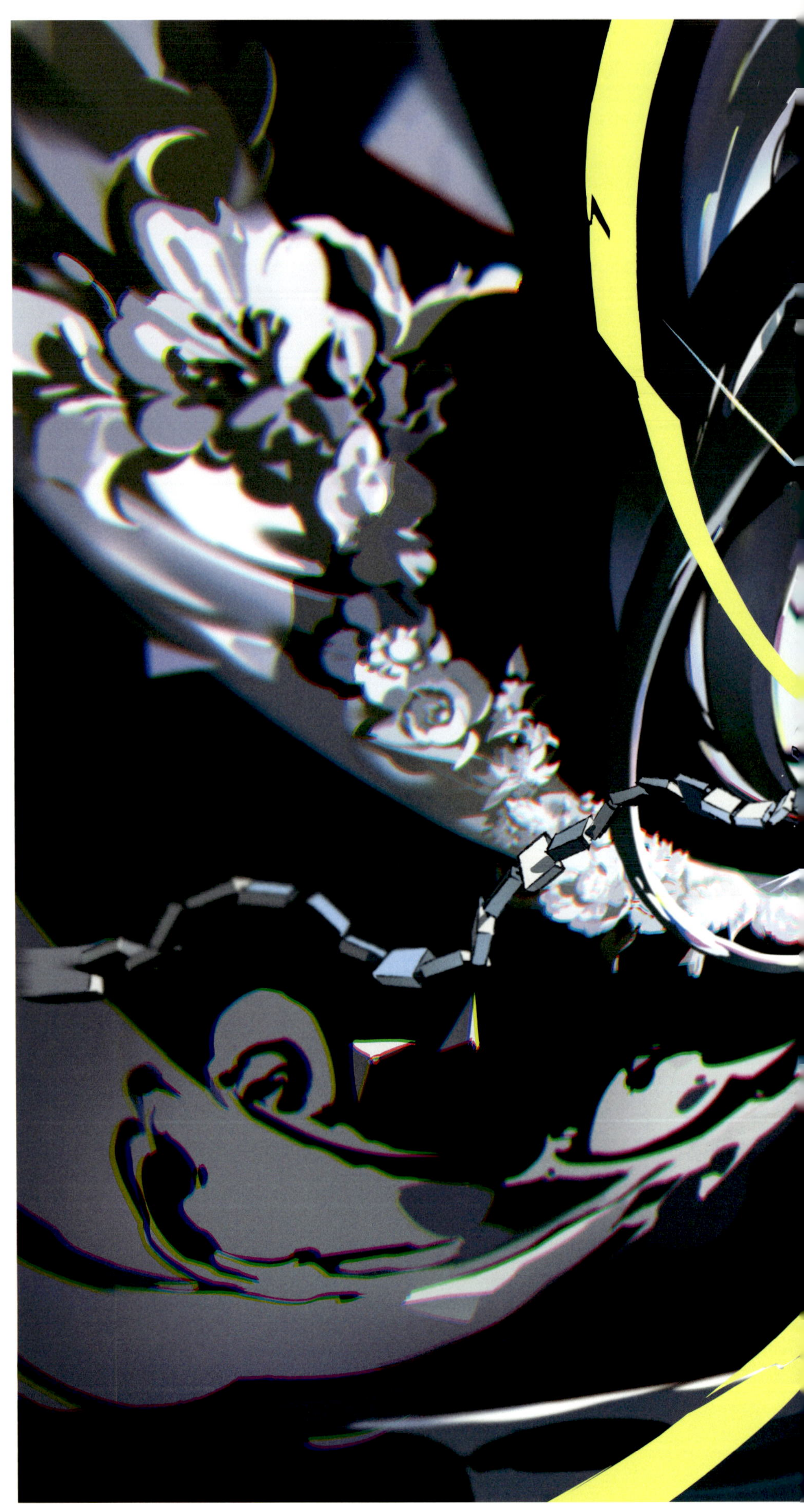

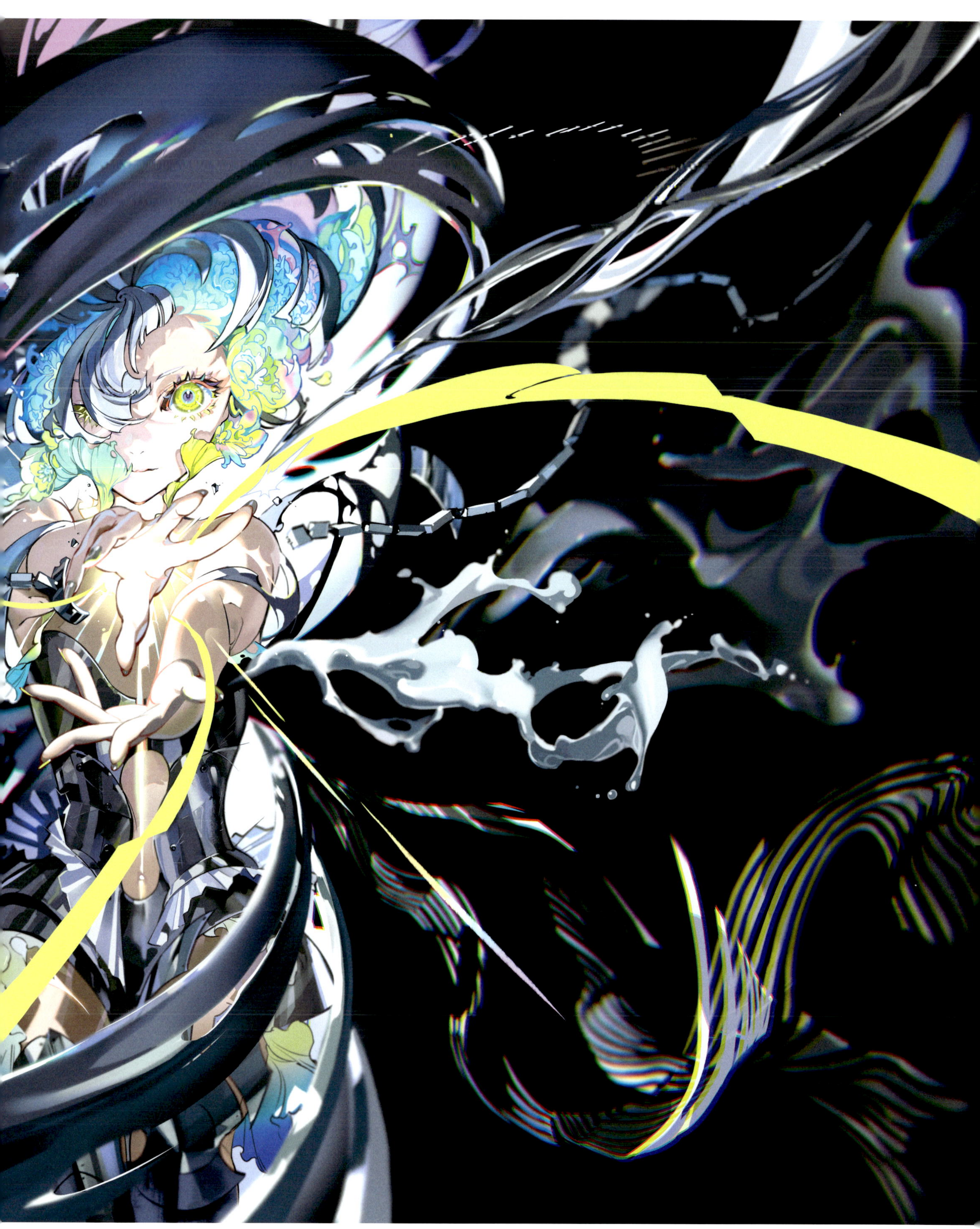

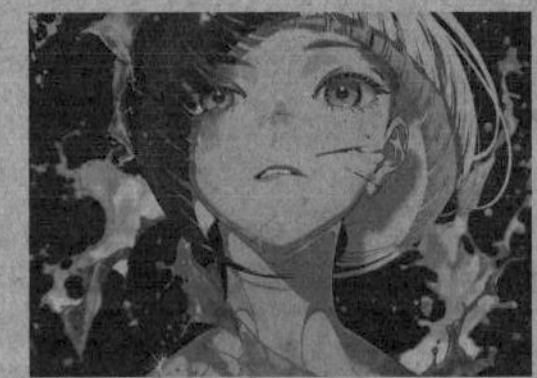

58
EGO - Es
2021

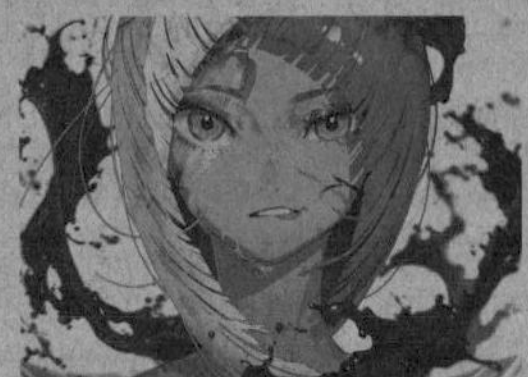

60-61
EGO - Id
2021

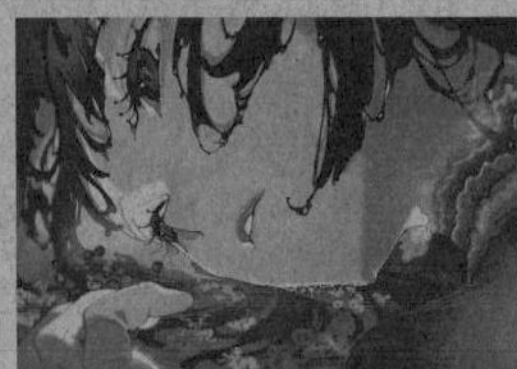

62
EGO - MELT
2021

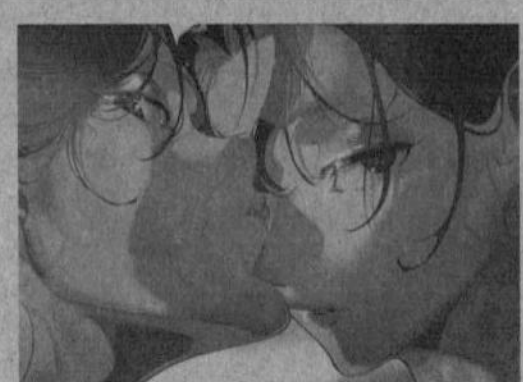

64
EGO - DNA
2021

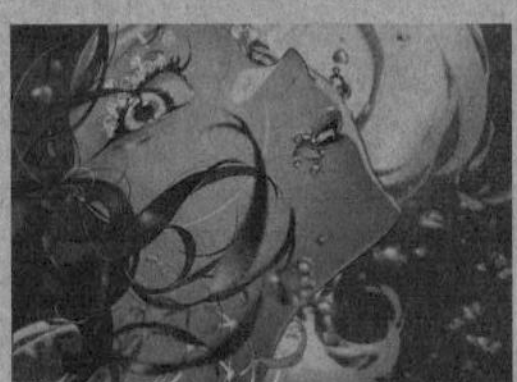

66
EGO - FLOW
2021

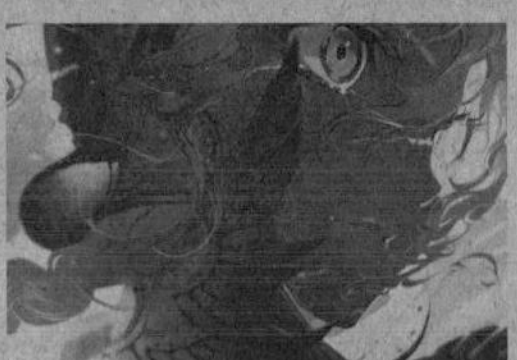

68
EGO - SCAR
2021

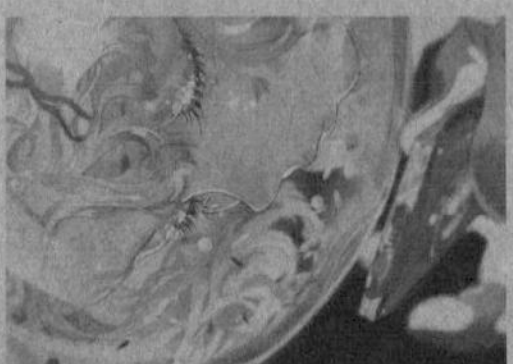

70
EGO - BEAT
2021

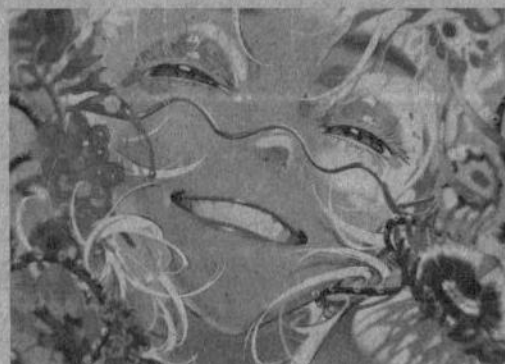

72
EGO - GRIN
2021

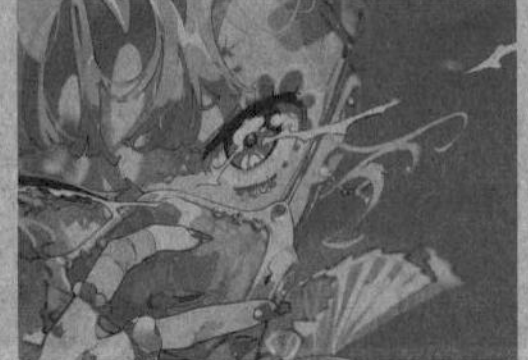

74
EGO - BRUISE
2021

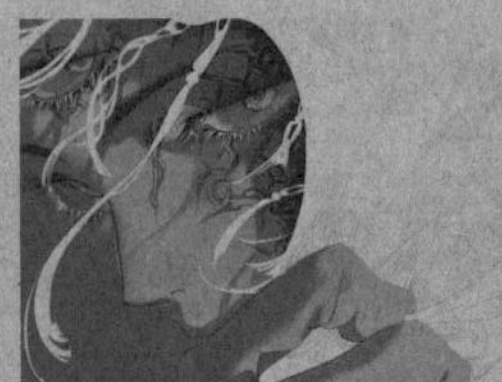

76
EGO - THIRD
2021

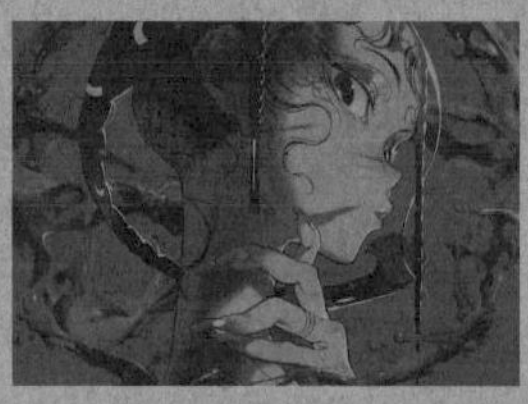

78-79
EGO - RED
2021

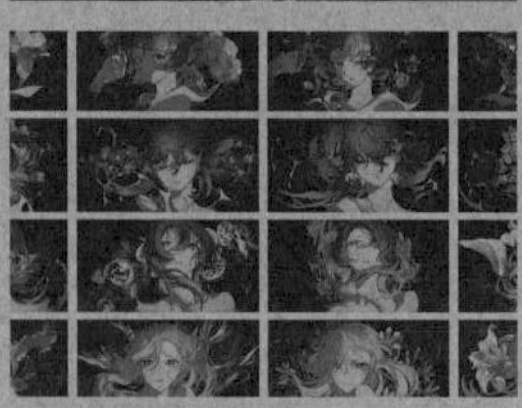

80-111
00:00:00:00
2020

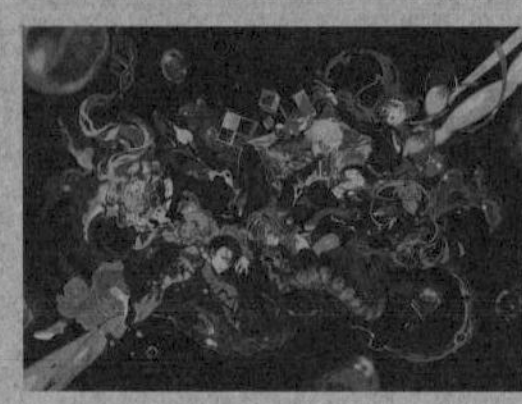

114-152
YOKU
2022

楽曲名：KATE「欲コレクション」インスパイアソング 「YOKU」
アーティスト名：Eve

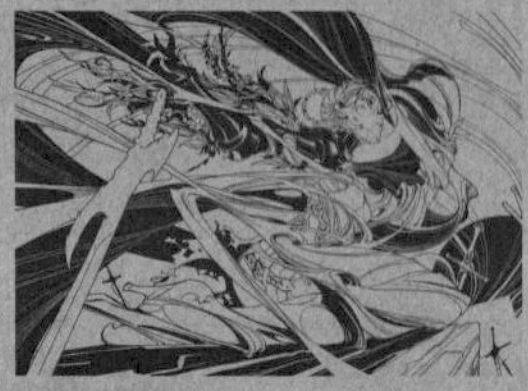

154-155
DAWN
2022

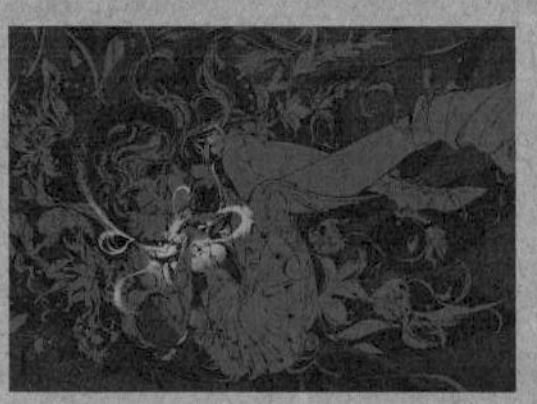

156-157
DUSK
2022

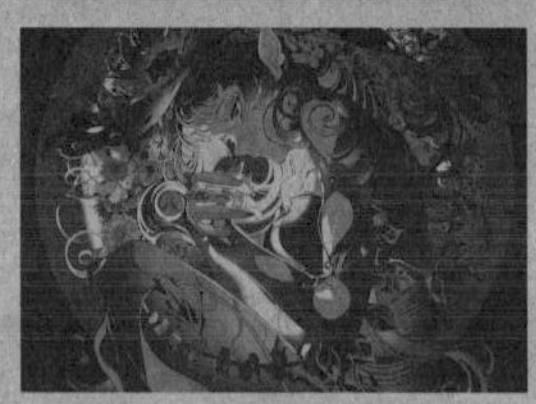

158
RAY - DUSK
2022

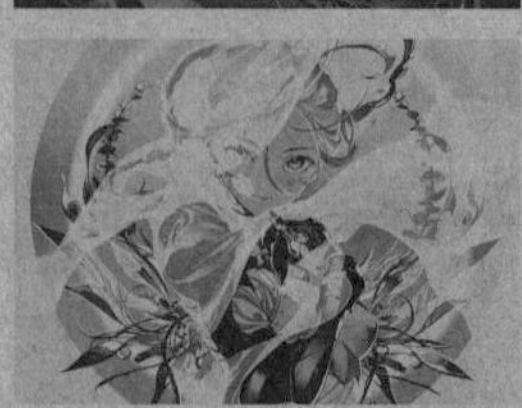

159
RAY - DAWN
2022

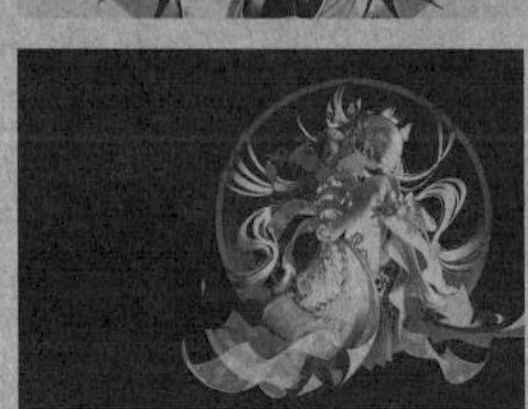

160-161
RAY - TWILIGHT
2023

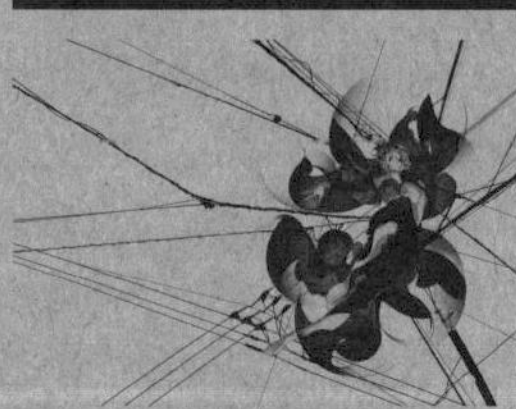

162-163
FLOW
2022

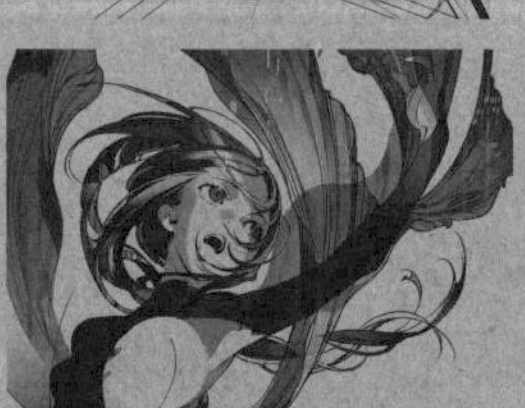

164
PARTITION - stream
2022

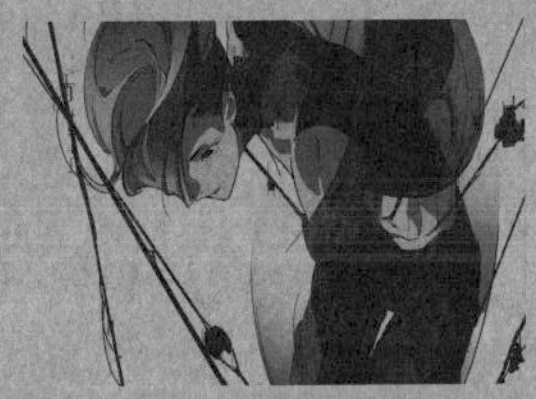

165
PARTITION - current
2022

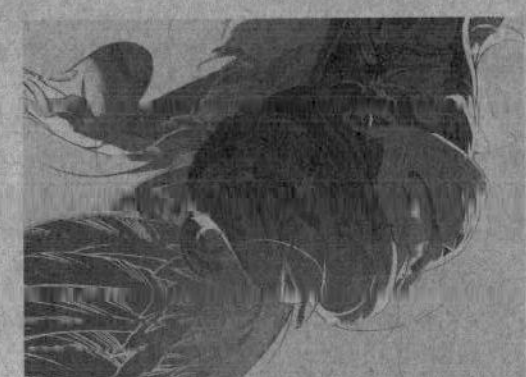

166
PARTITION - parting
2022

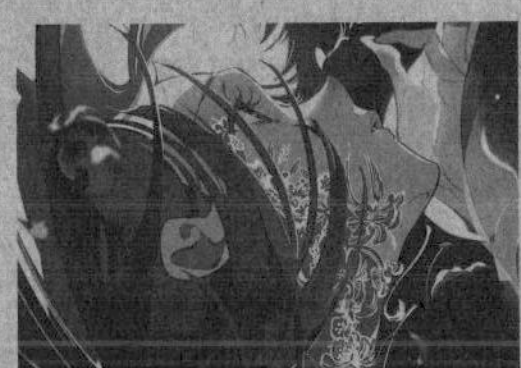

167
PARTITION - offering
2022

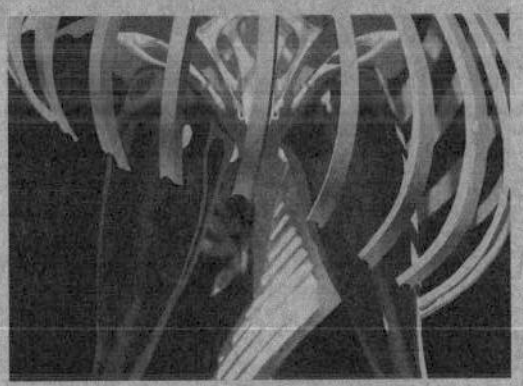

168
BONE
2021

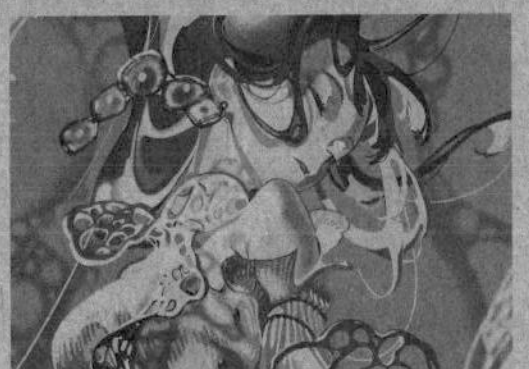

169
CELL
2021

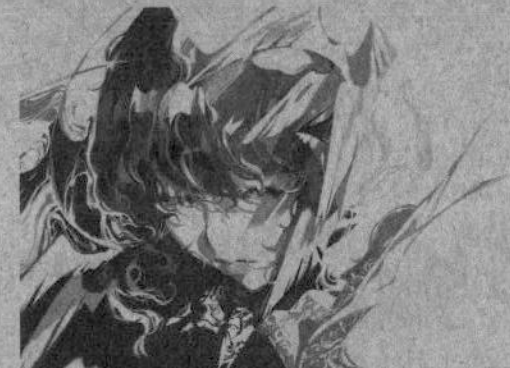

170-171
doodle
2021

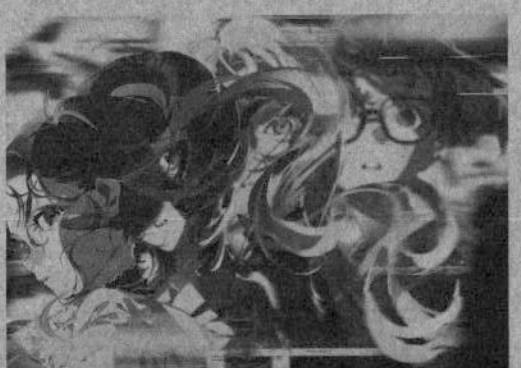

172-179
LAYER
2022

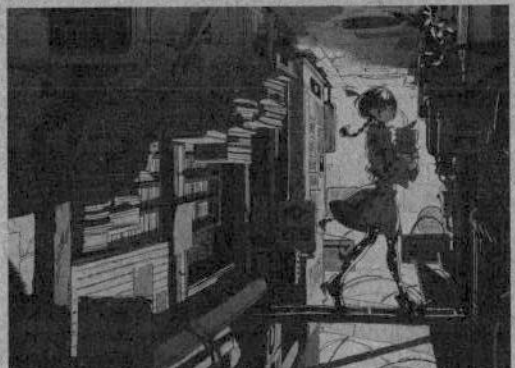

180-181
ゆぶね／青虫
2021

青虫 [AYUNi D] illustration

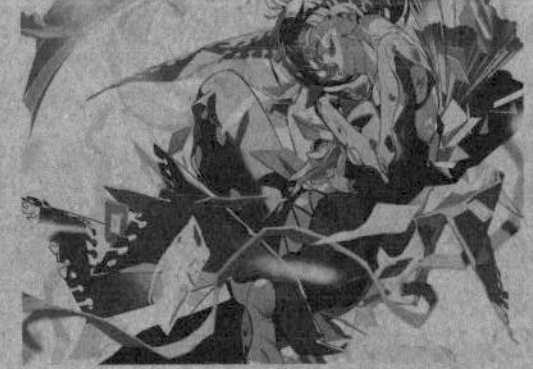

182
ONE BY ONE
2021

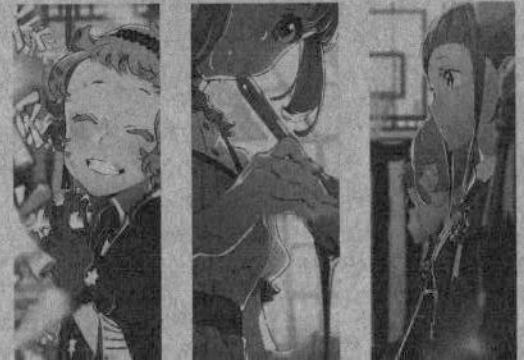

184
NewType horoscope 1-3
2016

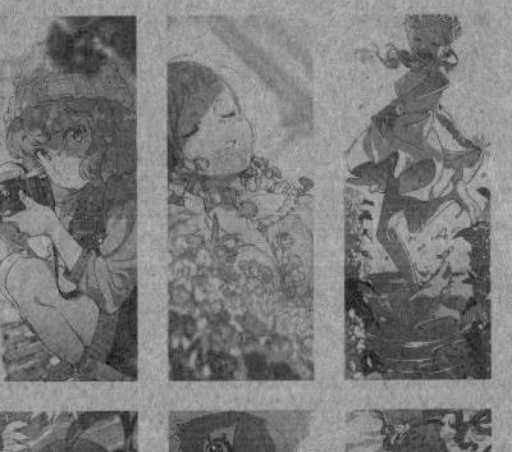

185
NewType horoscope 4-6
2015

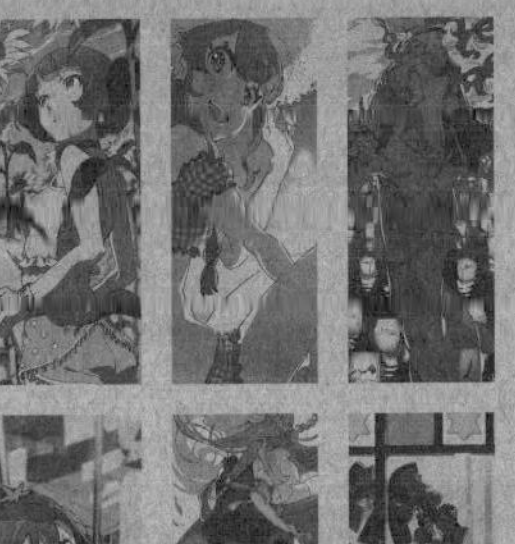

186
NewType horoscope 7-9
2015

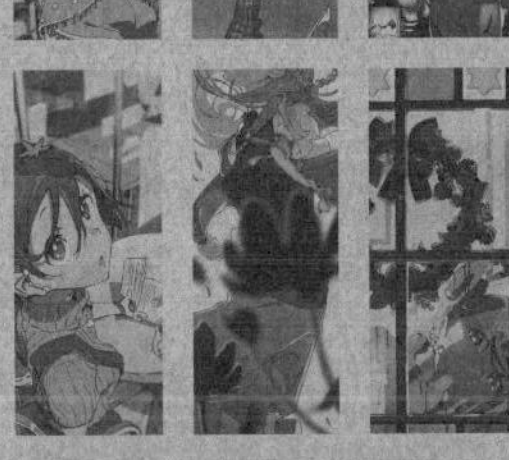

187
NewType horoscope 10-12
2015

p184-187　月刊ニュータイプ 2015年5月号～2016年4月号
「HOROSCOPE」イラスト

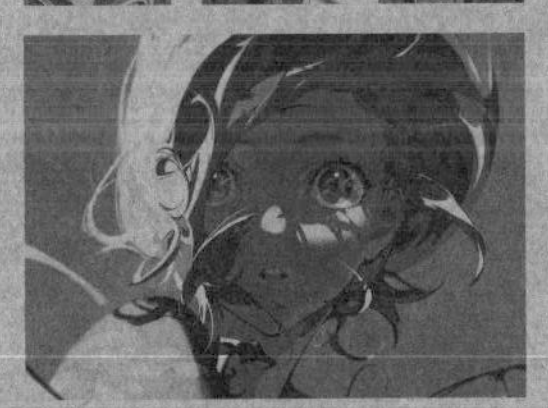

188-191
illume
2022

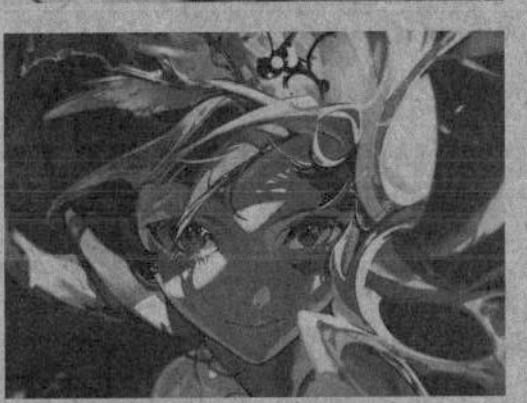

192-194
gift
2023

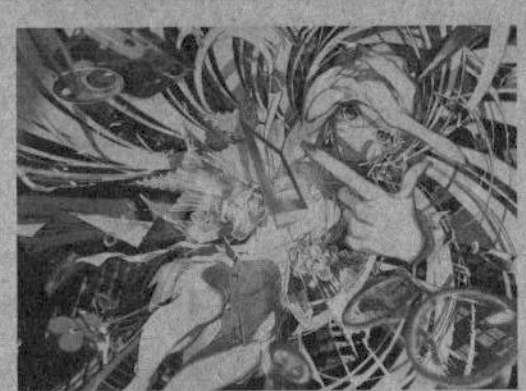

196-197
VISIONS
2020

VISIONS 2021 ILLUSTRATORS BOOK
pixiv KADOKAWA

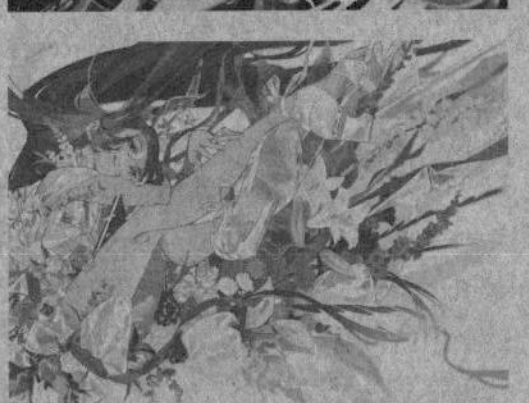

198-199
A LOT
2019

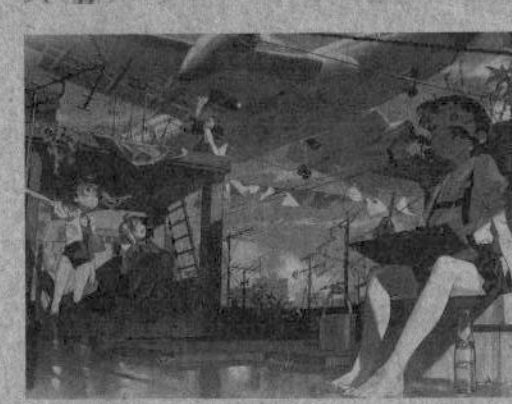

200-201
CHILDHOOD
2018

美しい情景イラストレーション
ノスタルジー編

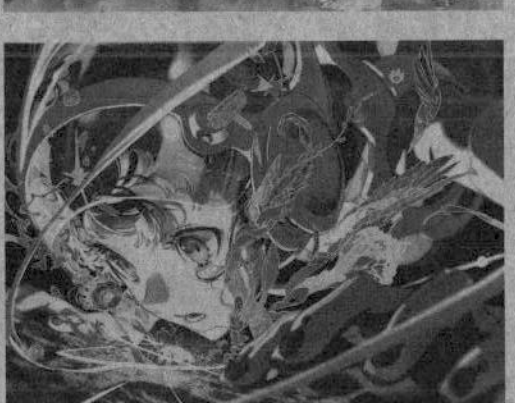

202-204
DISCOVER
2021

DISCOVERY 京都芸術大学 通信教育部
イラストレーションコース

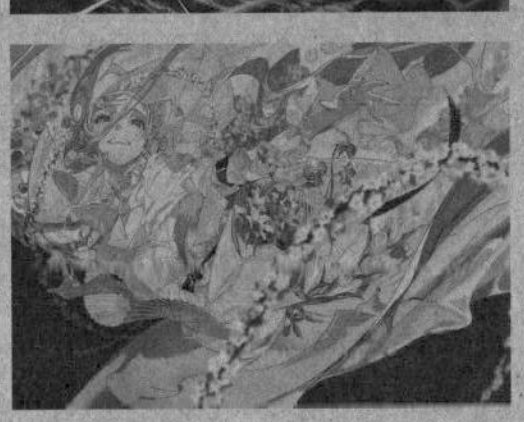

206-207
printemps
2022

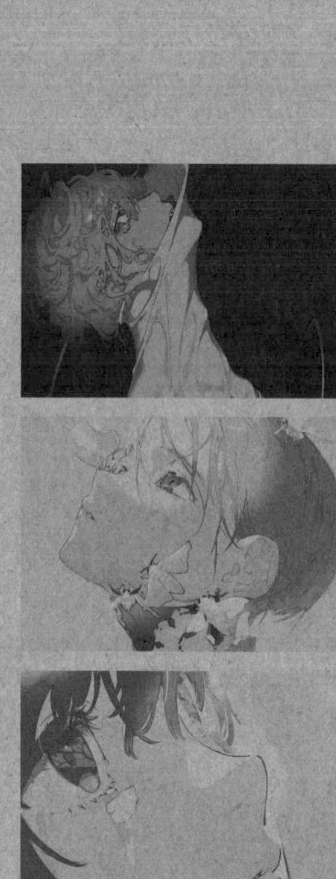

208
knit
2020

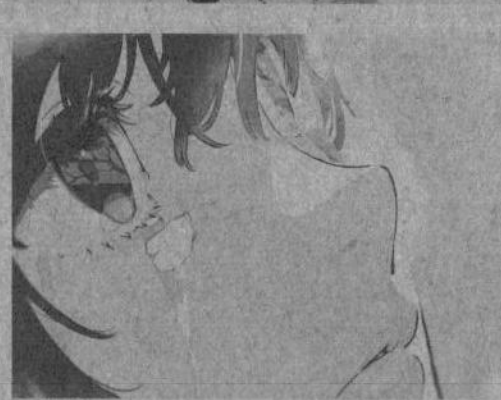

211
silk moss
2020

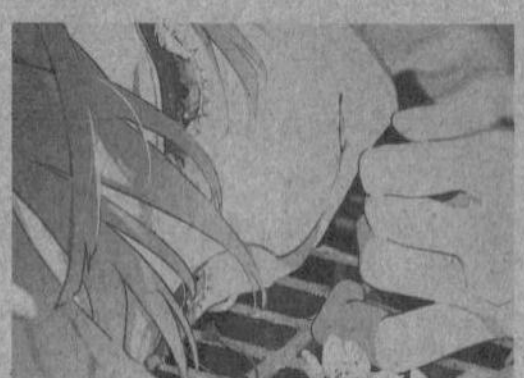

212
2018.04.13
2018

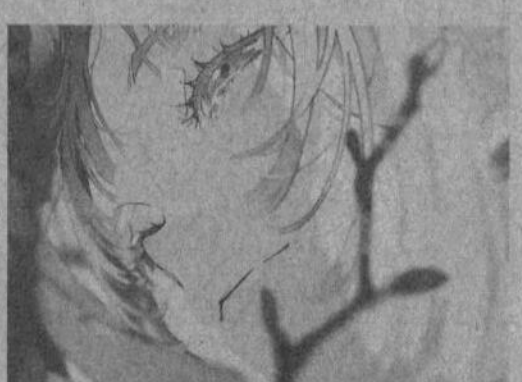

213
2019.04.13
2019

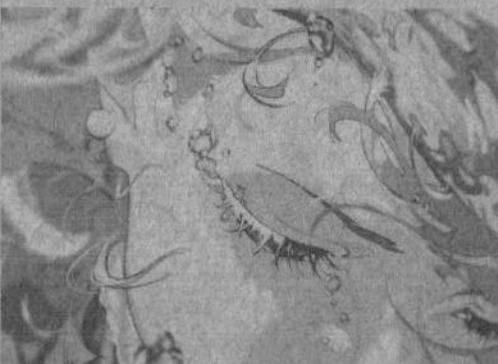

214
2020.04.13
2020

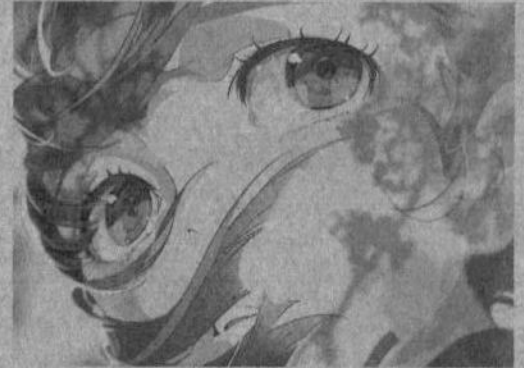

215
2021.04.13
2021

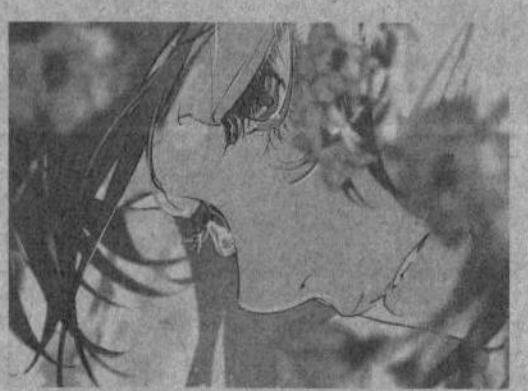

216
2022.04.13
2022

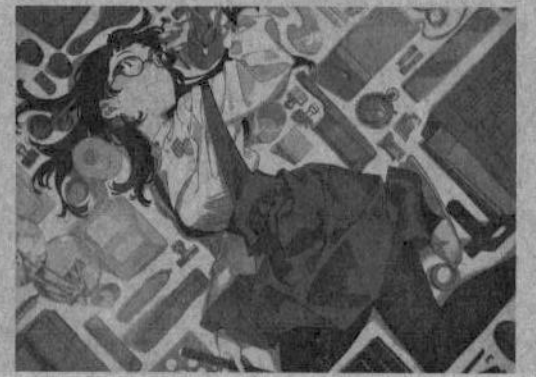

217
2023.04.13
2023

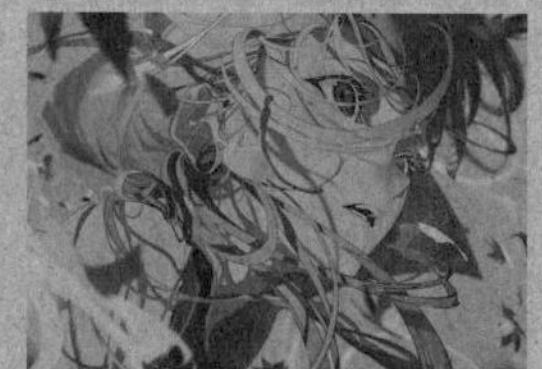

218-219
ANIMATION
2017
専門学校東京クールジャパン 2019年
入学案内書

220
Cyclone
2021

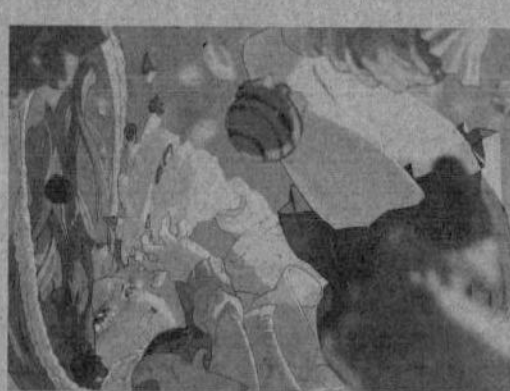

222
No more bitter
2013

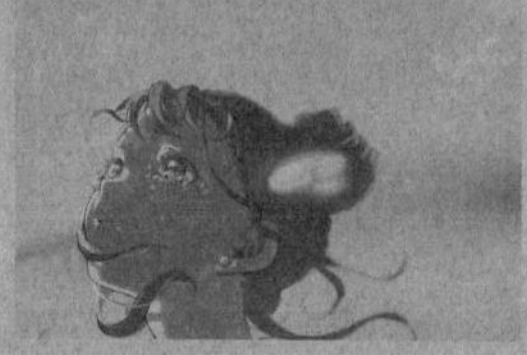

223
ぼろぼろ
2013

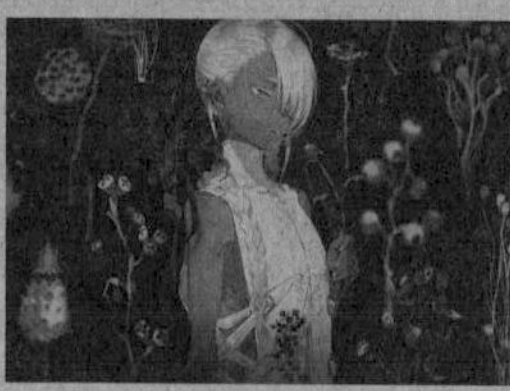

224
everlasting -plants-
2018

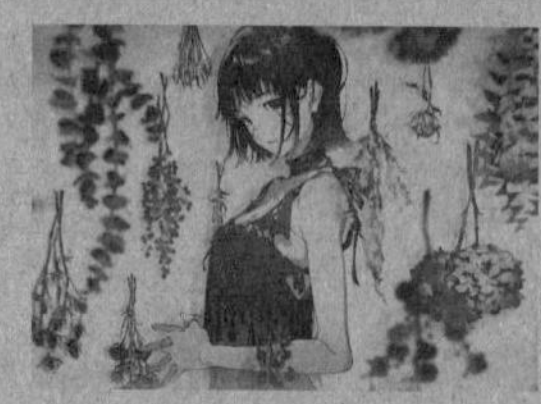

225
everlasting -flowers-
2018

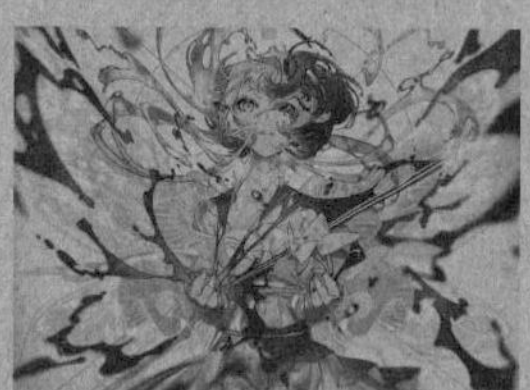

226-227
emergence
2020

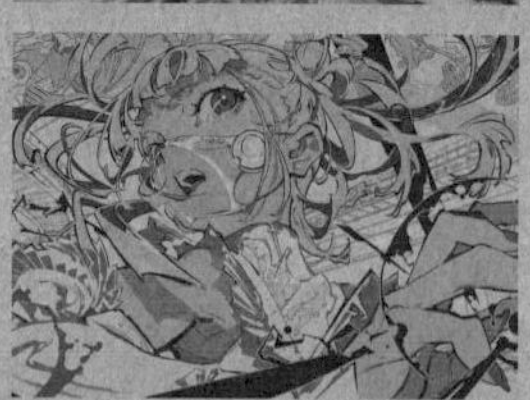

228-229
effect
2020

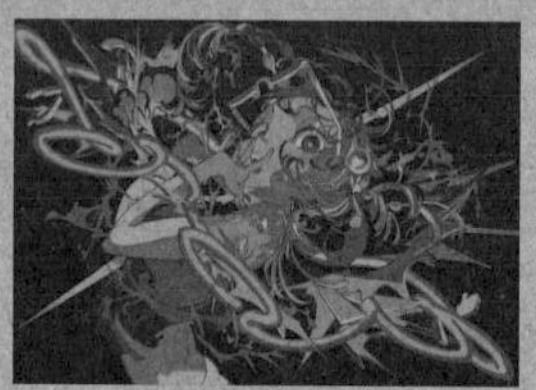

230-231
joy
2021

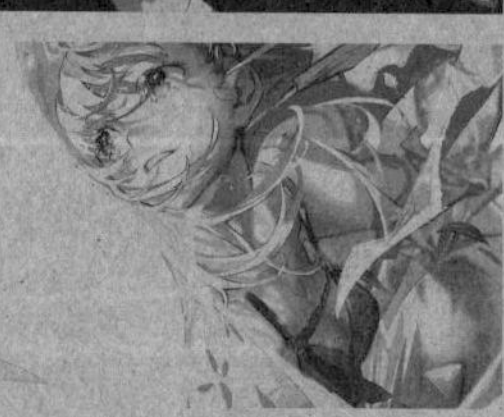

232
SEE YOU
2020

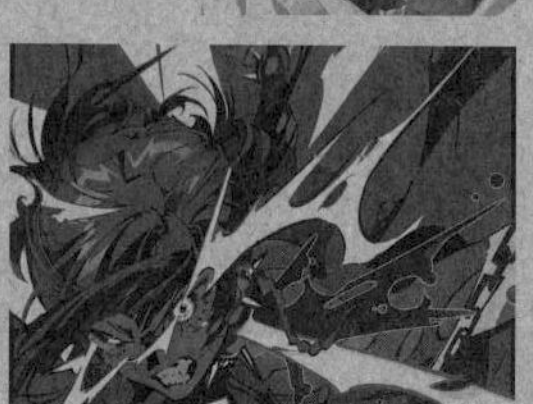

235
ÆFFECT - BLAZE

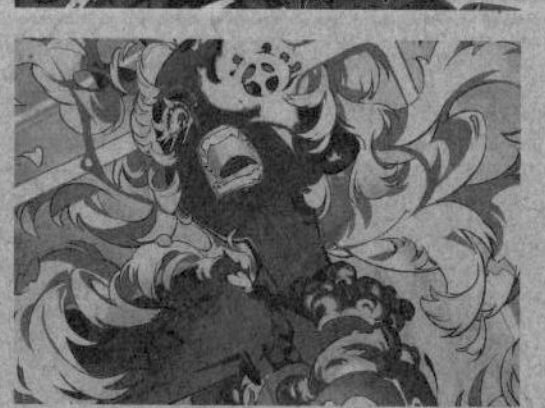

237
ÆFFECT - FLASH

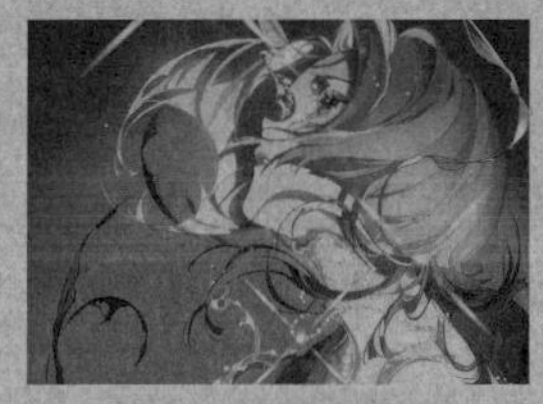

239
ÆFFECT - EMIT

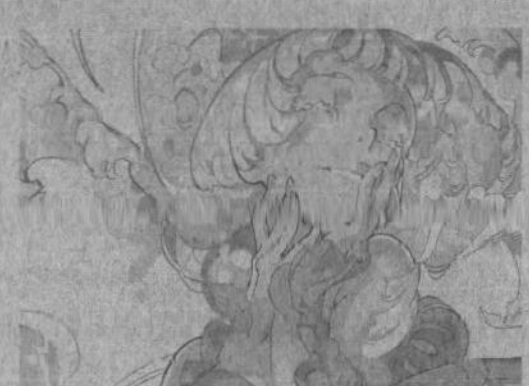

241
ÆFFECT - GLOW

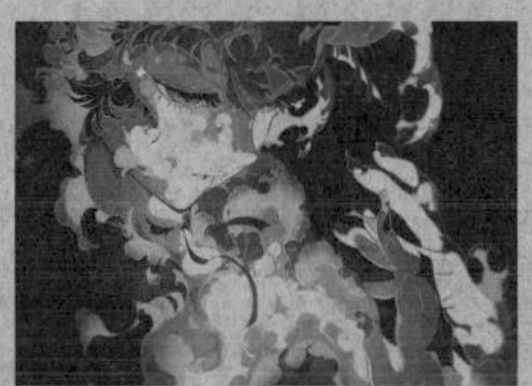

242-243
SKIN - MOLT
2023

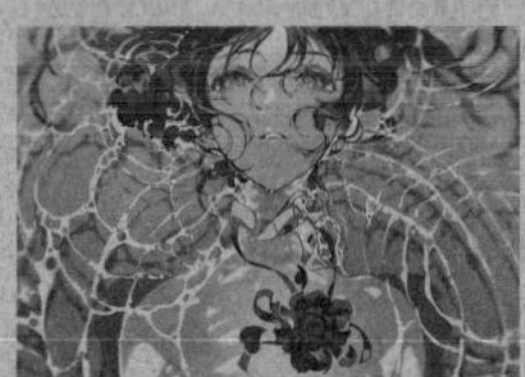

244-245
SKIN - WAVE
2023

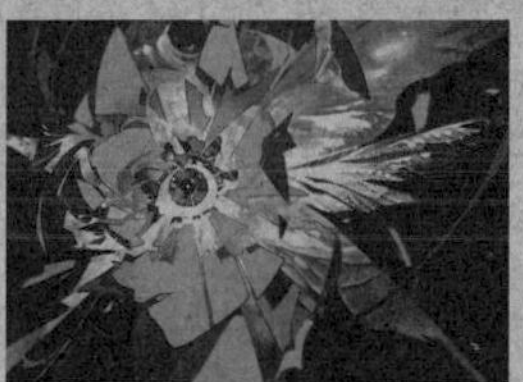

246-247
SKIN - FRACTURE
2023

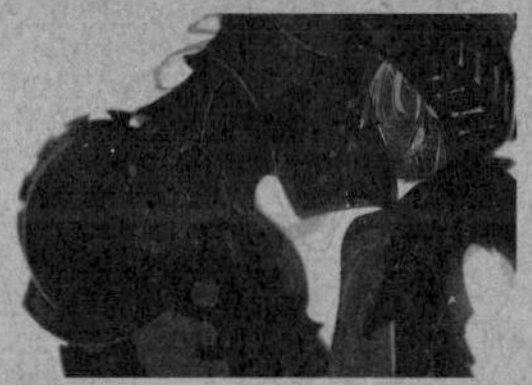

248-249
SKIN - HIDE
2023

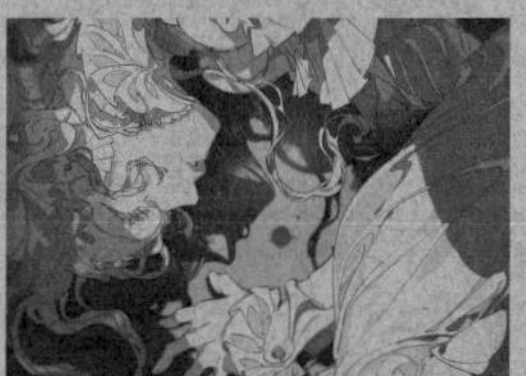

250-251
SKIN - BEHIND
2023

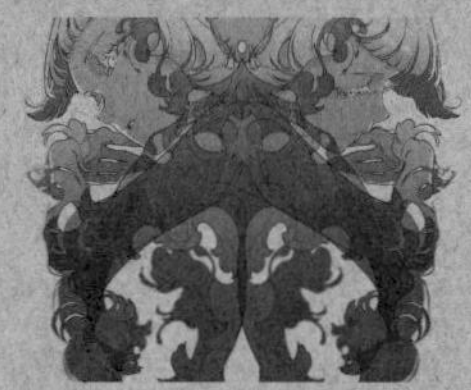

252-253
SKIN - DEPENDENT
2023

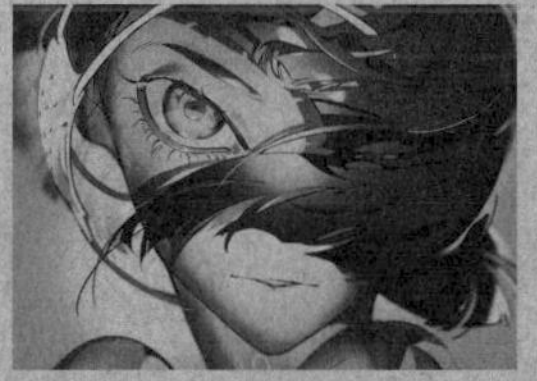

254-255
SKIN - VEIN
2023

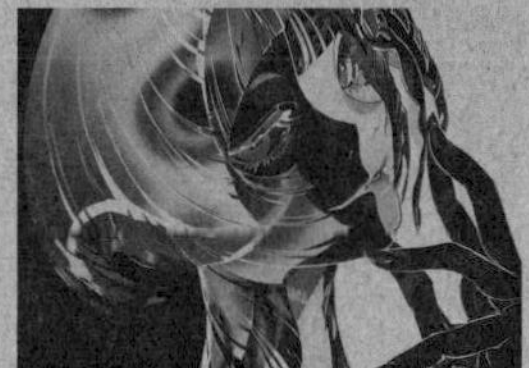

256-257
SKIN - REVERSE

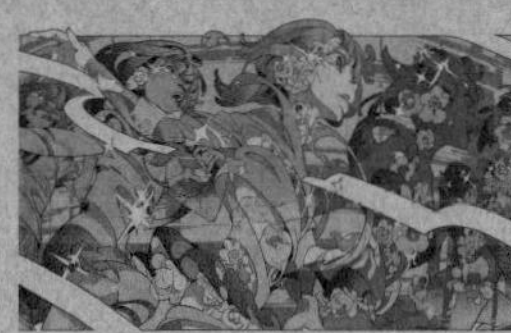

258-259
MORPH
2023

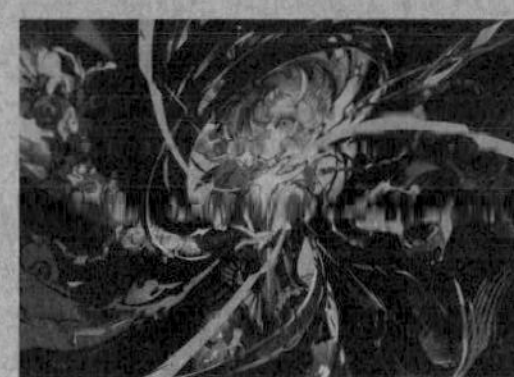

260
EYE

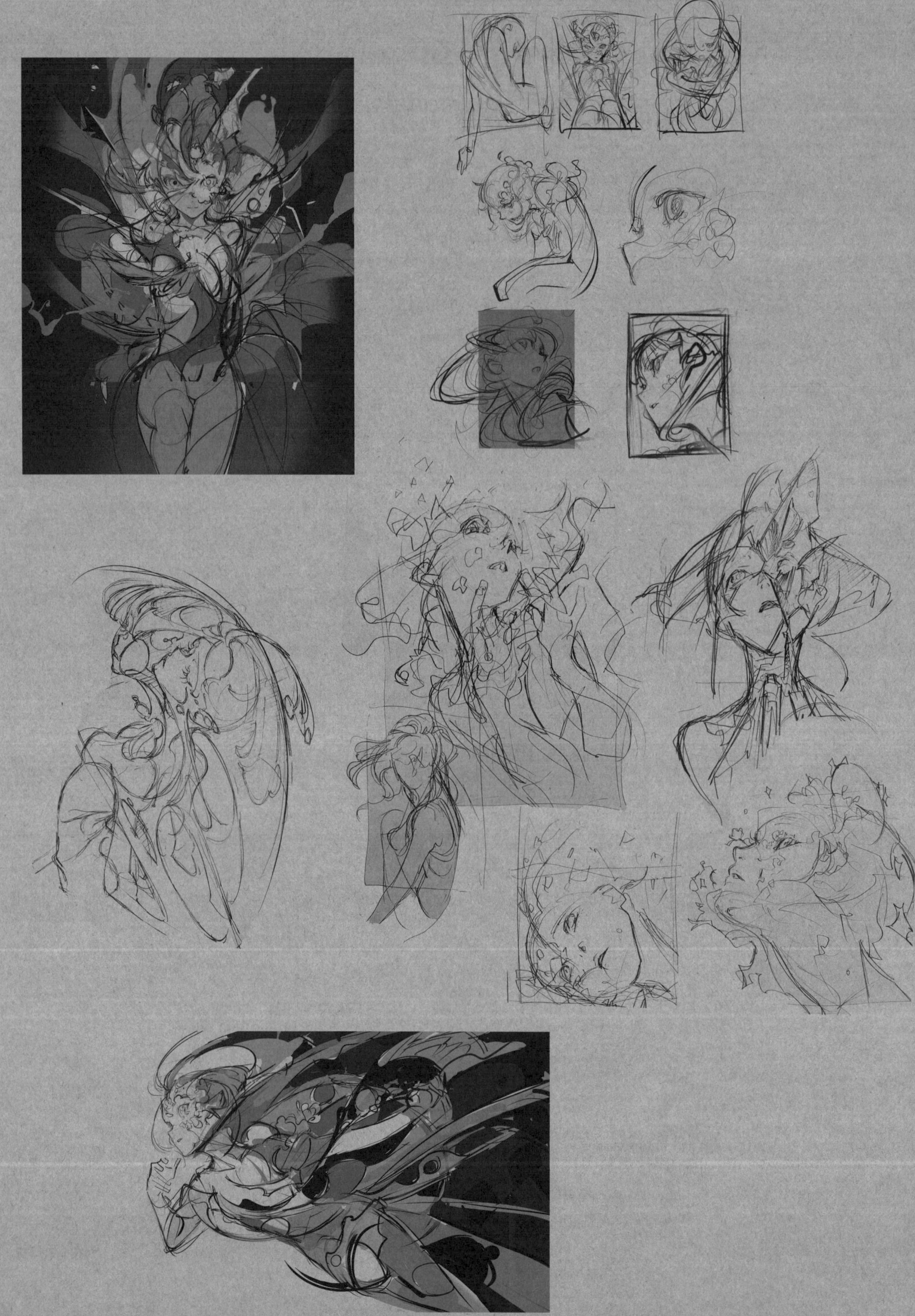

Final Thoughts

I'm the kind of person who likes to take on challenges and come up with ideas about the situation that I find myself in at any given time.
In recent years, I have been exploring and experimenting with the possibilities of the act of illustrating, and the illustrations themselves.

I was drawn to the communicative and technical capabilities of the animated works that I saw as a child, so I learned techniques from the people I respected, applied them to illustration, and even tried to reapply them to video.
Expressing the commonalities between these two and finding the shades of gray in between is what I find joy in. It's my desire, and it's what I want to do with animation, manga, illustration, and art, which have captivated me so much.
I'm grateful for the times when I can freely express these feelings, as well as the fact that there are people who enjoy them.

As a result of my experience with various styles and techniques, I've been gradually pushing the boundaries of what an illustration is and what I put out, and I think these transitions and changes can be seen in this book.
I hope I've been able to present my own kind of "gaze" in this book.
It's frustrating that my abilities and my mental preparedness are not yet at a level that allows me to execute most of the ideas I have in mind, but that's why I'm eager to continue taking on challenges.

In closing, I would like to express my deepest gratitude to Kusano-san for being so understanding of me when carrying out the design work for this book, to Oba-san for giving me this wonderful opportunity, to Shinano Publishing for accommodating even my most difficult requests, and to Koyama-san for always being there to give advice.
I feel grateful for my family and friends for their support, as well as to the artists who have shaped me, and at the same time, I feel the desire to continue transforming my gaze even further.

Mai Yoneyama
Illustrator / Animator

Born in Nagano

Assistant Chief Animation Director, Animation Director, and Original Artwork for KILL la KILL
Character Designer and Animation Director for Kiznaiver
Animation Director and Ending Director for DARLING in the FRANXX
Visual Developer for PROMARE
Ending Animation Director, Storyboard, Production, Original Artwork, Cinematography for Cyberpunk: Edgerunners
Advertising Visuals for RADIO EVA
Director, Storyboard, Character Design, and Animation for the Music Video for "YOKU" by Eve
Package Visuals for Kanebo Cosmetics' KATE

おわりに

自分はその時々の身を置いている状況に対して課題を持ったり、アイデアを巡らせるのが好きな性質なのだと思う。
近年は描くという行為、または絵自体に対しての可能性を模索したり実験したりしている。

幼い頃に見たアニメーションの伝達力や技術力に惹かれ、尊敬する方々から技術を学び、それをイラストレーションに持ち込み、更にそれを映像に戻したりしてみる。
お互いに通ずるものを表現したりその中間のグラデーションを作っていくことが自分が喜びを感じる部分であり、心躍らせてもらったアニメーション・漫画・イラストレーション・アートに対するやりたいことで、欲なのかなと思う。
そういった考えを自由に表現することができる時代と、楽しんでくれる方がいることを有り難く感じている。

さまざまな表現や技術との出会いにより、絵のあり方や出力に少しずつ挑戦をしているつもりで、この本にもその変遷や変化が見られるのかなと思う。
この本を通して自分なりの「まなざし」のようなものを提示できていたら良いなと思っている。
実力的にも精神的にもまだまだで、考えていることの大半も実行できていなくてもどかしいが、だからこそまた次に挑戦したくなっている。

さいごに、この本を作るにあたり深い理解でデザインをしてくださった草野さん、このような機会を頂いた大場さん、無茶な要望に応えてくださったシナノ印刷さん、いつも相談に乗ってくださるコヤマさんに深く御礼を申し上げます。
支えてくれる家族や仲間、自分を形成してくださった表現者の方々に感謝しつつ、更なる次のまなざしに変えていきたいと感じている。

米山舞
イラストレーター・アニメーター

長野県出身

「キルラキル -KILL la KILL-」総作画監督補佐・作画監督・原画
「キズナイーバー」キャラクターデザイン・作画監督
「ダーリン・イン・ザ・フランキス」作画監督・エンディング演出
「プロメア」ビジュアルデベロップメント
「サイバーパンク エッジランナーズ」
エンディングアニメ監督・絵コンテ・演出・原画・撮影
「RADIO EVA」広告ビジュアル
「Eve - YOKU」ミュージックビデオ
監督・絵コンテ・キャラクターデザイン・アニメーション
カネボウ化粧品「KATE」パッケージビジュアル

EYE YONEYAMA MAI

米山舞 作品集

2023年5月16日　初版第1刷発行

著者

米山 舞

デザイン

草野 剛（草野剛デザイン事務所）

編集

大場義行

発行人

三芳寛要

発行元

株式会社パイ インターナショナル
〒170-0005　東京都豊島区南大塚2-32-4

TEL 03-3944-3981

FAX 03-5395-4830

sales@pie.co.jp
印刷・製本

シナノ印刷株式会社

Printed in Japan

ISBN 978-4-7562-5387-3　　C0079